The Complete MBA For Dummies, 2nd Edition

W9-BRL-542

Cheat Sheet

Delegating Tasks the Right Way

Delegation is a very effective tool managers can utilize to get things done. Here are steps for delegating the right way:

1. **Communicate the task.** Describe to your employees exactly what you want done, when you want it done, and the end results you expect. Be clear and unambiguous and encourage your employees to ask questions.

2. **Furnish context for the task.** Explain to your employees why the task is important, how it fits into the overall scheme of things, and any possible complications that may arise during its performance. Encourage employees to ask questions, and don't get defensive if your employees push you for answers (someone always will).

3. **Determine standards.** Everyone needs to know when they cross the finish line. Agree on the standards that you'll use to measure the success of the task's completion. These standards should be realistic and attainable, and you should avoid changing them after performance has begun.

4. **Grant authority.** Empower your employees with the level of authority required to complete the task. They can do without constant roadblocks or standoffs with other employees.

5. **Provide support.** Determine the resources (money, training, manpower, advice, and so forth) your employees require to complete the task and then provide them.

6. **Get commitment.** Don't assume that your employees will automatically accept the assignment; you must make sure that they do. Reaffirm your expectations and confirm your employees' understanding of the commitment to completing the task.

Rewarding Your Employees

Employees perform better, remain happier, and tend to stick around longer when managers or executives recognize and reward them for doing a good job. Here are the four keys to making the rewards and recognition you give effective:

✔ **Specify the behavior you're rewarding.** When you reward an employee, be sure that you're clear about exactly what behavior merits recognition. Say, for example, "You did a great job yesterday afternoon when you helped that customer figure out which product was the best for her needs," or, "I really appreciate all the extra effort you put into the Scanlon project."

✔ **Give the reward sincerely.** People greatly appreciate sincere expressions of thanks, but they won't accept insincere or false praise — in fact, they may be insulted by it. Only offer your employees rewards and recognition when they've truly earned them.

✔ **Be positive.** When you give rewards and recognition, do so in a positive and uplifting way. Your goal is to inspire the employee — and, in turn, his or her colleagues — to continue exhibiting the behavior you're rewarding. And never immediately follow praise with a reprimand!

✔ **Give the reward as close to the event as possible.** To have maximum impact on employee behavior, give rewards as soon as possible. Waiting days, weeks, or months will greatly lessen the impact and perhaps extinguish it altogether.

The Complete MBA For Dummies, 2nd Edition

Designing Your Web Site's Home Page

When customers enter your company's Web address into their browsers, they arrive at your Web site's *home page* (also called the *jump page, landing page,* or *promotional page*). Your home page is where you want your customers to take action — preferably, doing something that *you* want them to do, such as registering at your site, answering a question, or buying a product or service. Here are some suggestions for how to design your company's home page:

- ✔ **Grab customers' attention.** For instance, you can create a specific headline that grabs readers' eyes. If your user is searching for gardening books and enters those words into your site's search engine, you want your site to pop up with a related headline. It should have the words "gardening books" in it rather than something completely general, like "Find any book you want here!"

- ✔ **Use pictures to convey your message.** Not only is a picture worth a thousand words, but it also takes up less space!

- ✔ **Motivate customers to act quickly.** Put a time limit on what they're looking for. For instance, offer a discount if they purchase an item today.

  There's no quicker way to get people to act than by giving away something for free. If you want your users to register for your site, for instance, consider giving them a free newsletter.

- ✔ **Offer customers payment options.** They should have a number of ways to pay for the products or services you're offering. For example, you can offer an online payment service such as Paypal, and you can accept credit cards either online or through an 800 number.

After you design your home page, test it with users and track the responses you get. We recommend that you create several versions of your home page. Practice makes perfect!

Creating a Concise Marketing Plan

An effective one-paragraph marketing plan has the following components:

- ✔ **Purpose:** What's the marketing plan supposed to accomplish?
- ✔ **Benefits:** How will your products and services satisfy the needs of the customer?
- ✔ **Customer:** Who's your primary customer, and what's your strategy for building long-term relationships with that customer?
- ✔ **Company image:** How will the customer see your company? Remember, customers will contribute to positioning your company in the marketplace.
- ✔ **Niche:** What's the niche in the market that your company has defined and will serve?
- ✔ **Tactics:** What specific marketing tools will you use to reach customers? You can utilize advertising, promotion, a Web site, publicity, and so on.
- ✔ **Budget:** How much of your budget will you allocate to this effort?

Check out Chapter 15 for more info on creating a marketing plan.

For Dummies: Bestselling Book Series for Beginners

Complete MBA FOR DUMMIES®
2ND EDITION

by Kathleen Allen, PhD,

USC Marshall Business School

and Peter Economy

Coauthor, *Managing For Dummies*, 2nd Edition, and
Building Your Own Home For Dummies

BICENTENNIAL
1807
WILEY
2007
BICENTENNIAL

Wiley Publishing, Inc.

Complete MBA For Dummies®, 2nd Edition
Published by
Wiley Publishing, Inc.
111 River St.
Hoboken, NJ 07030-5774
www.wiley.com

Copyright © 2008 by Wiley Publishing, Inc., Indianapolis, Indiana

Published by Wiley Publishing, Inc., Indianapolis, Indiana

Published simultaneously in Canada

For general information on our other products and services, please contact our Customer Care Department within the U.S. at 800-762-2974, outside the U.S. at 317-572-3993, or fax 317-572-4002.

For technical support, please visit www.wiley.com/techsupport.

Wiley also publishes its books in a variety of electronic formats. Some content that appears in print may not be available in electronic books.

Library of Congress Control Number: 2007941221

ISBN: 978-0-470-19429-4

Manufactured in the United States of America

10 9 8 7 6 5 4 3 2

WILEY

About the Authors

Kathleen R. Allen, PhD, is the author of *Entrepreneurship and Small Business Management,* 3rd Ed., *Launching New Ventures,* 5th Ed., *Bringing New Technology to Market,* and *Growing and Managing an Entrepreneurial Business,* as well as several other trade books. As a Professor of Entrepreneurship at the Lloyd Greif Center for Entrepreneurial Studies, based in the Marshall School of Business at the University of Southern California, Allen has helped hundreds of entrepreneurs start their ventures. At USC, she's also director of the Marshall Center for Technology Commercialization, where she works with scientists and engineers to help bring their inventions to market. As an entrepreneur herself, Allen has co-founded four companies and is presently the co-founder and president of N2TEC Institute, which is dedicated to technology-based economic development in rural areas of the United States (www.n2tec.org). Allen holds a PhD from USC, an MBA, and a master's degree in Romance Languages.

Peter Economy (La Jolla, CA) is Associate Editor for the Apex Award–winning magazine *Leader to Leader,* a member of the National Advisory Council of the Creativity Connection of the Arts and Business Council of Americans for the Arts, a member of the board of directors of SPORTS for Exceptional Athletes (www.s4ea.org), and bestselling co-author of *The SAIC Solution: How We Built an $8 Billion Employee-Owned Technology Company.* He has also worked on more than 30 other books, including *Managing For Dummies,* 2nd Ed., *The Management Bible, Enterprising Nonprofits: A Toolkit for Social Entrepreneurs,* and *Writing Children's Books For Dummies.* Peter invites you to visit him at his Web site: www.petereconomy.com.

Dedication

To the visionary business people who are infusing the entrepreneurial spirit into organizations — here, and around the world.

Authors' Acknowledgments

We would like to give our sincere thanks and appreciation to our talented publishing team at Wiley — particularly Joyce Pepple, Stacy Kennedy, Chad Sievers, and Josh Dials. Kathleen would like to thank her husband John and kids Rob, Jaime, and Greg, who have always been champs about putting up with an author in the house. Peter would like to thank his wife Jan and kids Peter, Sky, and Jackson, for being a constant source of wonder, love, and amusement, as well as his mother Betty Economy for helping to pay for his MBA courses. Will the circle be unbroken?

Publisher's Acknowledgments

We're proud of this book; please send us your comments through our Dummies online registration form located at www.dummies.com/register/.

Some of the people who helped bring this book to market include the following:

Acquisitions, Editorial, and Media Development

Project Editor: Chad R. Sievers

(Previous Edition: Tim Gallan)

Acquisitions Editor: Stacy Kennedy

Copy Editor: Josh Dials

(Previous Edition: Tina Sims)

Editorial Program Coordinator:
Erin Calligan Mooney

Technical Editor: Matthew Will, PhD, MBA

Editorial Manager: Michelle Hacker

Editorial Assistants: Joe Niesen,
LeeAnn Harney

Cartoons: Rich Tennant
(www.the5thwave.com)

Composition Services

Project Coordinator: Kristie Rees

Layout and Graphics: Reuben W. Davis,
Melissa K. Jester, Barbara Moore,
Christine Williams

Anniversary Logo Design: Richard Pacifico

Proofreader: Tricia Liebig

Indexer: Broccoli Information Management

Publishing and Editorial for Consumer Dummies

    Diane Graves Steele, Vice President and Publisher, Consumer Dummies

    Joyce Pepple, Acquisitions Director, Consumer Dummies

    Kristin A. Cocks, Product Development Director, Consumer Dummies

    Michael Spring, Vice President and Publisher, Travel

    Kelly Regan, Editorial Director, Travel

Publishing for Technology Dummies

    Andy Cummings, Vice President and Publisher, Dummies Technology/General User

Composition Services

    Gerry Fahey, Vice President of Production Services

    Debbie Stailey, Director of Composition Services

Contents at a Glance

Table of Contents

Introduction

*W*hether you work for a corporation, a nonprofit organization, or for the government, chances are you've considered getting — or have already obtained — a Masters of Business Administration degree, an MBA. Why? Because if you want to get ahead in your organization — or just to do a better job of managing or leading — obtaining an MBA is the best ticket in town. Studies show that MBA graduates — particularly those from the top business schools — are offered significantly higher starting salaries than their counterparts who don't have MBAs. And that effect carries on throughout the careers of these MBAs.

But is it the degree that makes the difference, or is something else at work here? Although that piece of paper with your name and the words "Masters of Business Administration" would mean a lot, what is even more important are the things you'd learn during the course of your MBA studies. *Complete MBA For Dummies,* 2nd Edition, presents and explains some of the same information that you'd encounter in a typical MBA program in any high-quality business school. Strategic planning, management, accounting, finance, marketing, negotiation — you'll find the key points here.

As you browse this book, keep one thing in mind: There isn't a monopoly of business skill and talent at the top levels of an organization. Indeed, employees at all levels can (and today are often expected to) play active roles in running their organizations. You can find engaged businesspeople in every part of today's dynamic organization.

The bottom line: This book provides you with the very best ideas, concepts, and tools taught in today's top business schools. If you apply them, we're sure that you'll see a noticeable difference in your everyday business dealings — a difference that will make you and your business partners even more successful in the future.

About This Book

Complete MBA For Dummies, 2nd Edition, is full of useful information, tips, and checklists that will help anyone who aspires to lead, manage, or participate in a business at a high level of competence. Your current level of leadership and management experience doesn't matter. For a fraction of the amount you'd pay to get your MBA, we provide you with an easily understandable roadmap to navigate today's most innovative and effective business techniques and strategies. And if you already have your MBA, you'll find that this book is a handy refresher and reference guide that you can carry with you wherever you go.

More good news is that the information you find within the covers of this book is firmly grounded in the real world. It isn't an abstract collection of theoretical mumbo-jumbo that sounds good but doesn't work when you put it to the test. No, we've culled the best information, the best strategies, and the best techniques — the same ones that professors teach in today's top business schools. In short, this book is a toolbox full of solutions to your every business question and problem.

And this book is fun (at least we think so!). Running a business doesn't have to be a bore. In fact, it can be a lot of fun. We help you to maintain a sense of humor in the face of the challenges that all businesspeople face from time to time. We're happy to say, though, that there will be many more days when the satisfaction of inspiring a team to develop an innovative new product or service, or hitting a new sales record, will bring you a greater sense of fulfillment than you ever imagined.

Finally, this book will inspire you with stories from some of today's most innovative and successful businesses — including Amazon.com, Whole Foods Market, MySpace, General Electric Medical Systems, and many more.

Conventions Used in This Book

When writing this book, we included some general conventions that all *For Dummies* books use. We use the following:

- ✓ **Italics:** We *italicize* any words you may not be familiar with and provide definitions.
- ✓ **Boldface type:** We **bold** all keywords in bulleted lists and the actual steps in numbered lists.
- ✓ **Monofont:** All Web sites and e-mail addresses appear in `monofont`.

What You're Not to Read

Ideally we want you to read every single word that we've written, but we're also realists. We know that you're very busy and only have time to read just what you need. In that case feel free to skip the sidebars — the shaded text boxes full of anecdotes and examples. Although they're interesting reads, if you do skip them you won't miss anything essential.

Foolish Assumptions

As we wrote this book, we made the following assumptions about you, our readers. We assumed that

- ✔ You're interested in taking a big step beyond merely going to work — that you really want to learn what business is all about.

- ✔ You're willing to change the way you interact with your coworkers and customers, and that you're ready to try some new techniques that will put you ahead of the competition.

- ✔ You're able to make a long-term commitment to becoming a better businessperson.

- ✔ You're considering whether an MBA program is right for you and you're looking at this book to help you make the decision.

How This Book Is Organized

Complete MBA For Dummies, 2nd Edition, is organized into six parts. Each part addresses a major area of the hows, whats, and whys of becoming a leader. Because of this organization, it's simple to find the topic that you're looking for. Whatever the topic, you can bet that we cover it someplace! Here's a quick overview of what you can find in each part.

Part 1: The New, Improved World of Business

Business today is changing at a record pace, and the best and most effective businesspeople are changing with it. In this part, we consider what business looks like today, and we take a very close look at the forces that have come together to flatten the world. Entrepreneurship seems to be on everyone's mind today and the tales of successful (and not so successful) entrepreneurs are in the daily news. We give you a good grounding in entrepreneurship concepts that can help you no matter what your career is. We also consider the global business environment and discuss the hows and whys of strategic planning.

Part II: Managing a Business in the New World

A working knowledge of the nuts and bolts of how to manage an organization and the people within it is still a very important part of business success. In this part, we outline the difference between managing and leading an organization, and we discuss the latest trends in leadership. We look at how to best motivate and reward employees and how to recruit and retain only the very best people. We also examine one of the most important tools in business today: employee teams.

Part III: Money: What You Don't Know Will Hurt You

As the saying goes, money makes the world go 'round. Nowhere is this saying more true than in business. Understanding where a business's money comes from — and where it goes — is important knowledge for any businessperson to possess. In this part, we present the basics of accounting and take a look at the most important and widely used financial statements. We decipher the mysteries of financial analysis and help you understand the ins and outs of stocks and bonds. Finally, we cover what it actually takes to make money.

Part IV: Marketing in the New World

A business with no customers is not a business. Customers are the focus of every successful business, so finding new ways to grab their attention and build long-term relationships is a topic of great importance. In this part, we explore how to understand your customers' needs and how to provide world-class customer service. We discuss the best approaches to developing a marketing plan, and we take an in-depth look at advertising and promotion — particularly the world of new media brought about by the Internet and the tools that let users become marketers.

Part V: Other Important Stuff

One of the most interesting things about leading, managing, or working in a business is that every day brings something new to learn or do. In this part, we take a look at a variety of important business topics. We discuss manufacturing, distribution, and service — and how the latest technology has had a major impact on each. We explore the most important concepts of risk management. We reveal the secrets of successful negotiation, and we review everyone's favorite business topic: economics.

Part VI: The Part of Tens

Here, in a concise and lively set of condensed chapters, you find tips that will help you to quickly become an effective participant in any organization. We show you how to avoid the most common mistakes that managers make, the best ways to market your products and services, how to improve your cash flow, and the best business resources out there so you can continue your binge learning.

Icons Used in This Book

We place little pictures, called icons, next to blocks of text throughout the book. Here's what they mean:

This text presents good ideas, tricks, or shortcuts that can save you time and trouble in the business world.

This information is important enough to remember, even if you forget everything else!

This information can help you avoid disasters that could cost you both time and money, not to mention your job.

Where to Go from Here

Although this book is overflowing with useful advice and information, it's presented in a fun, easy-to-access format. What good is all the information in the world if you can't get to it quickly and easily? Have no fear; we've designed this book with you, the reader, in mind. If you want to find out about a specific area — such as recognizing and rewarding your employees or understanding financial statements — you can check the table of contents and flip to the proper section to get your answers quickly.

If you're new to business — perhaps a new employee, supervisor, or manager — you may want to start at the beginning and work your way through to the end. A crash course in business! A wealth of information and practical advice awaits you. If you already have plenty of business experience under your belt and you're short on time (and what businessperson isn't?), you may want to turn to a particular topic to address a specific need or question.

Regardless of how you navigate this book, we're sure that you'll enjoy reading it. If you have any specific questions or comments, we would love to hear from you. Please contact us at `http://marshall.usc.edu/entrepreneur` (Kathleen) or `www.petereconomy.com` (Peter).

Part I
The New, Improved World of Business

The 5th Wave   By Rich Tennant

INTERVIEWS

"Well, apparently this is a company that doesn't value someone who can look at familiar things in a new and creative way."

In this part . . .

Today's increasingly global marketplace is in a constant state of change. Because of this, in this part — after a quick overview of the book's contents — we consider what business looks like today, and we take a very close look at the forces that have come together to flatten the world. We explore the role of entrepreneurship in the economy. Finally, we span the global business environment and discuss the hows and whys of strategic planning.

Chapter 1

The MBA in a Nutshell

*B*usiness owners and managers are faced with a perplexing array of management theories and practices and a variety of off-the-wall thoughts on how businesses should be run. Is it any wonder why they tend to resort to tried-and-true ways of running things? People find comfort in the familiar. Besides, it takes time to relearn old habits, and changing the culture of a business to deal with a fast-paced global environment is no walk in the park. If you conduct a search for the term "management" on Amazon.com, you'll come up with more than 600,000 books on the subject. Add to that the 600,000+ books on marketing and the 500,000+ books on finance, and you may be throwing up your hands and crying "uncle!"

Although all these books claim to offer the latest and greatest in management theory and tools, the reality is that most innovative, state-of-the-art tools are merely elaborate makeovers or the repackaging of fundamental management theory. A rose by any other name is still a rose. How many different ways can you talk about change management or empowered work teams, for instance? To be fair, however, the proponents of these "new" theories and practices do echo a shared truth: The world has changed dramatically, and the way managers run businesses hasn't always kept pace.

And if the business world has recognized the need for change, that change has been slow to echo in the hallowed halls of business schools, too. Even graduate business schools at the nation's leading universities are guilty of adhering to old traditions. In many MBA programs, the "big business/Fortune 500" mindset still reigns — the assumption that if you're plopped into an established business with plenty of cash flow and assets, all you have to do is manage them well. Most business models presuppose a stable and predictable environment, when the reality is that most business environments today are dynamic, fast moving, and anything but predictable.

This chapter provides you with a brief overview of the major areas of study in an MBA program — which just happen to be the same topics we cover in this book. As you read through this chapter, note any topics that you want to explore in more detail and then drop by the table of contents to find out where we locate the topics. Ready? Set? Go!

Do You Really Need an MBA?

For many years, people have gone back to school to get an MBA (Masters of Business Administration) because it's the "thing to do." Companies want to see the degree on your résumé, making the degree the fastest track to corporate executive positions and bigger paychecks. This has been the case for some time, and truth be told, this is still the case. Consider the statistics garnered from research with recruiters worldwide:

- ✔ Demand for MBAs is rising at about 20 percent per year.
- ✔ Demand for MBA/consultants is up about 35 percent.
- ✔ Salaries are on the rise, with the average new MBA graduate starting at $84,500; in some areas, the salary is well over $100,000.

But money is just one reason why you may want to seek an MBA. Here are some equally (if not more) important reasons:

- ✔ **To develop skills in business functions:** economics, finance, marketing, management, operations, and accounting.
- ✔ **To acquire valuable soft skills:** leadership, teamwork, ethics, and communication.
- ✔ **To develop an entrepreneurial mindset:** You want to become innovative and opportunistic to tackle the challenges of a dynamic, global world.

But what if you don't have the time, resources, or inclination to go back to school for two more years to get an MBA? If that describes your situation, this book is for you. An MBA isn't an end in itself; it's the means to achieving the goals you've set. The skills and attitudes you acquire by reading this book enable you to develop your career (and your company) to its fullest potential in less time and without all the resources school requires. Certainly, putting the techniques we describe to use is better than the trial-and-error method. In other words, the MBA lessons you take away from this book will give you a competitive advantage over peers or other companies.

Exploring the New World of Business

Due to the nature of competition — where only the fittest companies are destined to survive — businesses are always pushing the envelope of creativity, innovation, and technology. They're constantly testing new approaches, new procedures, new processes, and new ways of doing business — looking for a little (or large) advantage over their competitors. These are exciting times in business, as evidenced by the following:

- The Internet has leveled the playing field for small companies. They can now look and act as multinational corporations and reach millions of customers without the burden of physical assets such as plants and equipment.

- New business models, communication technologies, and distribution methods enable businesses to take their products and services anywhere they want.

- Successful entrepreneurs such as Bill Gates and Warren Buffet continue to demonstrate to the rest of the business world what it means to be philanthropic.

- A new generation of workers — the *New Millennials* — are changing management styles and corporate culture as they force baby-boomer bosses to consider a new definition of work ethic.

- The business world can watch in amazement as China grows at light speed. It will become the biggest economic power in the world in the not-too-distant future.

- Everyone with a computer and an Internet connection has access to the same information ("Just Google it!" has become a popular search engine phrase). Because of YouTube, for instance, everyone can have their 15 minutes of fame on the Internet.

Revolutionary changes, or *paradigm shifts,* aren't the exclusive property of the 21st-century business environment. They have, in fact, occurred many times over the centuries. Were it not for revolutionary change, societies would stagnate in their own traditional ways of doing things. The bottom line: Change is a good thing. Isn't it interesting that our grandparents and great-grandparents lived through a similar period of dynamic change when they faced the new century and a similar technology revolution 100 years ago? The following sections dig deeper into why change makes the business world go round. We also discuss why you should consider making the entrepreneurial mindset a part of the way you do business and why you should adopt a global and not just local perspective.

What's so great about change?

Have you ever ridden a rollercoaster? Or bungee jumped off a tower? These activities are exhilarating, terrifying, and glorious, all at the same time. What makes them so great is that you don't know what's coming next, but you do know that something is going to happen. So you try to prepare — perhaps you hang on tight and close your eyes or you go for it and throw your arms up and scream as loud as you can — before you plunge into the unknown. What a rush! Welcome to the real (business) world.

The world is about change — often unexpected change. Change is as unavoidable as death and taxes. You can't put your business into a vacuum and escape the changes — even though, as when it comes to death and taxes, you may try to avoid them as long as you can. Instead of seeking in vain to avoid change, though, welcome it. Savor it and use it to your advantage, because change is a fact of life.

Smart MBA programs, recognizing that change is a fact of life, are infusing an entrepreneurial mindset into their curricula, because their customers — people similar to you — demand it. In 1987, management guru Tom Peters predicted the dynamic market that we're experiencing today in his prophetic book *Thriving on Chaos* (Harper Paperbacks). He said, ". . . excellent firms of tomorrow will cherish impermanence — and thrive on chaos." The reason is that out of impermanence and chaos come opportunities that keep a business revitalized and growing. In other words, change = opportunity = growth. And he was right!

Making an entrepreneurial mindset part of your toolkit

Entrepreneurs are an important part of a healthy economy. They're the catalysts for change in the business environment, and because of their opportunistic and innovative nature, they know how to take advantage of change to bring about new business opportunities. The businesses they start are growth-oriented and *value-creating*, which means that entrepreneurs serve a need in the market that other businesses aren't currently serving.

In other words, entrepreneurs typically develop businesses that create new jobs (instead of stealing jobs from other companies) and have a distinct competitive advantage in the market. For example, when Craig Newmark launched his Web site Craigslist, he didn't create the first job-posting site on the Internet. He did, however, recognize an unmet need in the market — a simple, easy-to-use site where anyone could post anything. Enter his site, Craigslist, which is now in more than 50 countries and is the most efficient job-posting and help-wanted site on the Internet.

Here are some more of the specific things that entrepreneurs do (and that you can do with an entrepreneurial mindset, fostered by an MBA background):

- ✔ **They spot fundamental changes in the world.** They then create opportunities from these changes before they take hold in the general business population.

- ✔ **They create niches in the market that they can dominate.** Why go head-to-head with large, established companies in your market — unless you have a death wish? Instead, smart business owners create niches of customers who have needs that their larger competitors in the market aren't meeting.

- ✔ **They put customers at the center of everything they do.** Without customers, you have no business (see Chapter 15). So why don't more companies involve customers in their businesses? Businesses that involve customers in product design and development, quality issues, distribution — in fact, in every area of the business — are among the most successful companies in their industries. Exemplary companies include the following:

  - • 3M: a manufacturer of adhesive products

  - • Pelco: a manufacturer of CCTV/video surveillance systems

  - • Hewlett-Packard: a computer and electronics manufacturer

- ✔ **They implement flatter and more team-based structures.** In the business world, hierarchies are out; teams are in. A decision-making process that has to slug its way through layers of authority slows an organization down, and companies that can't respond quickly to changes in the marketplace are in a dangerous position.

- ✔ **They form strategic partnerships with other companies in their industries.** Companies headed by entrepreneurs with an eye toward opportunity are forming teams with other companies — including their competitors! Adversarial business relations have no place in a marketplace that's too complex for any one business to handle alone. Successful companies join forces with companies that have whatever expertise they need.

But what if you plan to work for a large company? Do you still need an entrepreneurial mindset? Absolutely! Remember, the times are changing for large companies, too. They have to find new ways to compete. Today, companies are looking for business people who can think like entrepreneurs, so if you're one of them, you'll stand out from the crowd. (Check out Chapter 3 for more info about entrepreneurship.)

. . . And a global perspective wouldn't hurt

In the first edition of this book, we said that going global was a choice left up to the business — particularly for smaller companies that may not have had the resources to do so. Well, guess what? Things have changed, and much faster than anyone expected. Today, going global is no longer a choice; it's practically a necessity for every company. Whether you have products you want to sell in the global market or you need to find a manufacturer in China or a software developer in Pakistan, in some way you'll likely be dealing with the global market in your everyday business affairs.

Dealing in a global marketplace means understanding global supply chains, intermediaries, local culture and ways of doing business, and currency, which can fluctuate dramatically and have a painful effect on your bottom line. Check out Chapter 4 for more info about a global business world.

Managing and Motivating an Engaged Workforce

Chances are, if you're reading this book, you're a manager or business owner — or you expect to be one someday. Knowing how to effectively manage and lead employees is a critical skill for men and women who are tasked with running a business. Although every manager must learn to plan, organize, lead, and exert control, a manager has plenty of other things to be concerned with, too, including

- ✔ Creating an environment that engages employees and encourages their involvement
- ✔ Tapping into the creativity of employees
- ✔ Setting an example for others

Good managers and business owners soon discover that they're only as good — and their businesses are only as good — as the men and women who work for them. This makes hiring and retaining great employees a particularly important task, as well as firing employees who don't work out. In addition to covering managerial techniques, in this book we consider how to identify and hire the best — and how to discipline and terminate the rest.

Today, more than ever, teams are having an enormous impact on organizations — particularly empowered, self-managing teams of employees. However, even with great teams out there doing great things for your company, a manager or owner still has to help set goals, track their progress, and lend a hand when necessary. (Check out the chapters of Part II for more info on managing and leading.)

Picking up the environment-scanning habit

Understanding what's going on in your industry and in the world is critical to your business's success and its ability to respond quickly to the innumerable changes it faces. The easiest place to start is the newspaper. If you regularly scan the pages of your local newspaper and one of the major national newspapers, such as *The Wall Street Journal* or *The New York Times,* you may start to see patterns in the kinds of stories being covered. These trends usually are the forerunners of legislation, laws, and regulations that could affect your business.

The Internet is another great source of information on what's going on in your industry and the world at large. Here are a few sites that you can bookmark and check regularly:

✔ **CNNMoney (money.cnn.com):** The online home of *Fortune, Money,* and *Business 2.0,* this site covers a broad range of business topics. You can get headlines, in-depth reports, and business information (such as Hoover's Online business profiles).

✔ **Department of Commerce (www.doc.gov):** This is a good source of links to many sites of interest to business owners.

✔ **IndustryLink (www.industrylink.com):** Offers links to sites about various industries.

✔ **OneSource (www.onesource.com):** The premier source for industry information, trends, current articles, and company information.

✔ **Wall Street Journal Interactive (www.wsj.com):** You must pay to use this site, but the charge may be worth it for the latest news from around the world. This site also offers good information about the economy and specific companies and industries.

✔ **SEC Edgar Database (www.sec.gov/edgar.shtml):** This is an excellent source for researching documents that publicly traded companies must submit to the SEC.

✔ **BusinessWeek Online (www.businessweek.com/smallbiz):** This is a great site for the latest in articles about business and industry.

✔ **Inc Online (www.inc.com):** If you're interested in business from an entrepreneurial perspective, be sure to check out the articles on this site. It also has a huge archive of useful materials.

If you're one of the millions of people who are incredibly busy with your everyday life in your corner of the world, make some time to become more aware of what's going on around you. Get out in your community and look around. Signs and signals everywhere can tell you what's important to people in your area, where the potential challenges are, and what's on the horizon. The goal is to develop a more opportunistic mindset. You'll be amazed at what you can discover after you make scanning your environment a habit.

One Part of Business Hasn't Changed: Money

Accounting isn't a sexy topic (although accountants may disagree), but it is a critical function of any business. You use accounting to keep track of your company's financial health. Budgets and bookkeeping make sure that the company doesn't spend more than it makes. If that excites you (and making more than you spend should), we encourage you to delve deeper into the subject. You can find many good texts out there that will satisfy your hunger for numbers (such as *Accounting For Dummies,* by John A. Tracy [Wiley]).

The outcomes of your company's accounting process are reflected in your financial statements — cash flow, income, balance sheet — which record the financial condition of your company at a particular point in time. Statements usually cover a quarterly or annual period. Financial statements are also used to secure loans and investment capital.

Analyzing business financials is both art and science. The scientific part comes in the formulas and ratios that you use to gauge the real health of your business. The art part comes when you attempt to forecast the future based on those financials. Get out your trusty crystal ball, because forecasting figures is difficult at best.

Finally, a thorough grounding in business finance wouldn't be complete without an excellent understanding of the financial markets, which include stocks, bonds, and debt and equity investment capital. A great business can and will tap many sources of financing, and in this book, you'll get a sense of what those sources are, when you should access them, and how you can access them. (Check out the chapters of Part III for the details on these various financial topics and for more on money issues.)

Reaching Out to Customers

Probably no area of business has changed more drastically in recent years than marketing. The Internet and easy, cheap access to production tools have made anyone a potential marketer. For proof of this assertion, just check out all the advertising and promotion utilized by users of YouTube, MySpace, Facebook, and Linked In. In addition, scores of bloggers have taken the media world by storm and now have the power to make or break a new product (or even a person). They reach millions of consumers who serve as their loyal followers.

It seems that everyone is fighting to get noticed in a very crowded space, so you have to be pretty creative to stand out. Even established corporate giants such as Nike have tapped into the power of YouTube to reach their target audiences in new ways.

And don't forget personal selling — still an important part of a company's marketing package. How do you sell more effectively in a world where everyone is bombarded with information? You can find all the answers in this book; after reading what we have to say, you'll come away with confidence that you can reach and satisfy your customers. Head to the chapters of Part IV for all your marketing needs.

The Rest of Your MBA Syllabus

Of course, running or managing a business involves more than just dealing with a changing world, managing employees, grappling with finances, and marketing your company's products or services. Every business owner and many executives and managers wear a variety of hats — taking care of whatever needs attention. We also cover the following topics in this book:

- **Manufacturing and production:** Some businesses (such as automobile manufacturers or computer builders) need to consider issues of manufacturing, distribution, and sourcing of materials and products. With the advent of advanced information systems technology, however, the inventory, purchasing, and distribution environment has gone through radical shifts — as have manufacturing processes themselves. If you work in manufacturing or distribution, you need to be on top of these changes. See Chapter 18 to begin your awakening.

- **Risk management:** Every business experiences risk; some businesses experience more than others, of course (lion taming school?). The question isn't whether your business has risks; the question is what you do about these risks. How can you minimize their potential impact on your operations? (Check out Chapter 19 for more info.)

- **Negotiations:** If you're in business (or a relationship), you know what it is to negotiate. Whether you're negotiating a pay raise or a multimillion-dollar deal, you can apply certain skills that will make you a more effective negotiator. Coincidentally, we discuss some of the most effective negotiation skills in Chapter 20.

- **Economics:** Although we don't promise you that it's the most exciting subject in the MBA canon, economics certainly is an important one — one that we give attention to in Chapter 21.

So, welcome to our world — a world filled with information, skills, and tips that can make you a much more effective businessperson. The information here applies no matter your position in an organization — from receptionist to chairman. We hope you enjoy the journey through the world of the MBA.

The best (free) business resources

Some things in life *are* free. Fortunately, anyone today can take advantage of plenty of free business resources and information, both on the Internet and off. The following list covers ten great free resources that can help your business. We also note where you can take advantage of premium resources at the sites for a small fee:

✔ **The Small Business Administration** (www. sba.gov) is the granddaddy of help for your business needs. Established by the U.S. government in 1953, the SBA provides financial, technical, and management assistance to people who want to start, grow, and run businesses.

✔ **MarketingProfs** (www.marketingprofs. com) is arguably the best marketing site on the Internet. Why? Because it isn't an aggregator of everyone else's marketing stuff; it generates new content from its network of marketing professors and professionals. Here you can find marketing articles, blogs, case studies, events, and online seminars. Much of the information on the site is accessible with no fee, but you may want to consider signing up for premium membership (about $49 a year) to gain access to in-depth articles and online seminars.

✔ **WSJ Entrepreneur** (www.wsj.com/ entrepreneur) provides a comprehensive set of online resources for businesses and the entrepreneur. You can discover and utilize great articles, business-plan tools, and maybe even your next business opportunity.

✔ **The Center for Business Planning** (www. businessplans.org) provides free business-planning guidelines, which include articles and templates for such things as a cash-flow statement, mission statement, and financial ratios. You can also find checklists for segmenting your market and looking at pricing, as well as a strategic marketing plan.

✔ **Kauffman Foundation eVenturing** (www. eventuring.org) is devoted to growing a business. We recommend that you check out the content under its Collections section, where you'll find groupings of information on finance and accounting, people and HR, sales and marketing, products and services, operations, and the entrepreneur. In addition to the topics you can explore on the site and its blog, it sponsors a monthly e-newsletter that you can sign up for.

✔ **Mind Tools** (www.mindtools.com) helps consumers learn 100 essential life, career, and management skills — free! Of course, the site also offers self-development courses and e-classes taught by experts — you'll pay for these courses, but the tuition is reasonable.

✔ **SCORE** (www.score.org), formerly known as the Service Corps of Retired Executives, bills itself as the "Counselors to America's Small Business." More than 10,500 volunteers — coming from the ranks of retired business owners, executives, and corporate leaders — answer questions, give advice, and share their wisdom and experience. SCORE has an online, 24/7 counseling service, and it has set up many offices nationwide for walk-in help.

✔ **U.S. Export Assistance Centers** are located in more than 100 cities around the United States. (You can find them through the U.S. Department of Commerce at www.doc. gov.) They provide assistance to businesses that want to export goods and services to foreign countries. If you've never done business with a foreign country, it can be a daunting task. The counselors at the assistance centers are trained to hold your hand through the process.

Chapter 2

Today's Hottest Business Trends

*B*usiness owners and managers live in a very exciting time. Every day brings new surprises, because no matter where you live and do business in the world, change is taking place — and not incrementally, so you can get comfortable with it. Change is happening radically — almost overnight — in ways that most businesses aren't prepared for.

What *is* going on? Less than a decade into a new century, change is happening faster than the business world can keep up with it. Adapting to change is a way of life in the business world, and one of the best ways for owners and managers to prepare for the changes that are bound to crop up in the future is to become more aware of the phenomenon of trends. Trends are patterns that we observe in the world around us, and which may signal that a major change is about to occur. In this chapter, we examine many of the key trends that affect how all businesses operate today.

The World Really Is Flat!

Thomas Friedman discusses trends and changes in his best-selling book, *The World Is Flat* (Picador), which is really an instructional manual for understanding what's going on in the business world today. By "flat," Friedman isn't referring to the physical nature of the planet (in Columbus's time, the world was physically flat — at least that's what they thought), but rather to the global marketplace. Technological advances and the Internet have leveled the competitive landscape so that anyone anywhere can compete — the good, the bad, and the ugly can all get into the game. This section delves deeper into why today's business world is flat and what that means to you, the business person.

From outsourcing to insourcing: Listing the flattening factors

According to Friedman, human history has seen three major periods of globalization:

1. The first period started with Columbus's trip to the New World and was characterized by demonstrations of power and imperialism.

2. The second period began in about 1800 and went to 2000. This period was exemplified by the growth of multinational companies and the decline in transportation and communication costs, which enabled goods to be traded globally more affordably than ever before.

3. The third period — going on now — is about shrinking the planet, flattening it, and giving individuals the power to compete and collaborate on a global level.

Friedman also named ten factors that have brought about this flattening of the world in the third period:

1. **The fall of the Berlin wall in 1989:** Tipped the balance of power toward democracies and free markets — that's good for business!

2. **Netscape's public offering in 1995:** Brought the Internet to the masses and made it possible for companies such as Amazon, Google, and eBay to start and grow to an enormous size.

3. **Workflow software:** Enabled communication and collaboration worldwide — that's why you can now work from home (called *telecommuting*).

4. **Open Source software:** Inspired self-organizing teams and community collaboration around a common objective.

5. **Outsourcing:** Enhanced the economies of developing countries by giving companies a way to reduce their cost of doing some business functions such as manufacturing.

6. **Moving offshore:** Increased the ability to compete globally as companies began putting offices and plants in other countries.

7. **Global supply chains:** Connected the world in a massive value chain.

8. **Insourcing:** Made it possible for small businesses to gain the competencies of much larger companies.

9. **Web search engines:** Brought information to anyone, anywhere, any time.

10. **Digital and wireless:** Enabled 24/7 connectivity and virtual collaboration.

Many of these flatteners have been around for a long time. Individually, each is powerful, but it's the convergence of these ten at this point in time that has created sufficient critical mass to flatten the world, making everything and everyone accessible to anyone.

And what does a flattened world look like? Friedman talks about visiting Bangalore, India, and being startled by Pizza Hut billboards; glass-and-steel buildings with familiar names such as Texas Instruments, IBM, and Microsoft; and people who speak English with a perfect California accent (if such a thing exists).

Hello, neighbor: When did China move in next door?

By taking advantage of technology and the Internet, China has moved from being a third-world country to growing faster than any other modern economy. In 2001, China joined the World Trade Organization (WTO) — a significant event because it signaled that China was willing to acknowledge and follow global rules of trade.

So, how did China begin growing so fast? It opened the floodgates for *off-shoring* — moving manufacturing plants from their home sites (for example, Europe or the United States) and plopping them down, lock, stock, and barrel, in China. Why? Because in China, you can (for now at least) produce products using cheaper labor, lower taxes, lower healthcare costs, lower energy costs, and far-less restrictive environmental regulations. Because China is such an attractive place to offshore, countries are clamoring to jump on the band-wagon and offer similar incentives — countries such as Malaysia, Thailand, Brazil, and Mexico.

If you're in business today, you have some important objectives: Figure out what you can outsource to China, what you can do in China via offshoring, and what you can buy from China in terms of low-cost goods and services. In a flat world, you can no longer afford to do business on your own, and you can't ignore your neighbors. (Check out Chapter 4 for more advice about doing business in China.)

Googlevision: Searching everywhere for Waldo

Thanks to Internet sensation Google (the 800-pound gorilla of search engines), anyone in the world with an Internet connection can find pretty much anything they want to find. Suppose you don't have time to go to the grocery store and you have to cook a meal with only the products you have on hand. Simply do a Google search using those items — milk, eggs, broccoli, tuna — in any one of a hundred languages and voila! You'll have a list of recipes containing those four items.

Today anyone can create their own sources of information, entertainment, and knowledge in the most obscure areas possible, and then they can distribute them to audiences of millions with equal ease.

The reason that Google surpasses everyone else when it comes to search capability is that it goes beyond mere keyword search. Google's founders Sergey Brin and Larry Page developed an *algorithm* (a fancy word for a mathematical formula that solves a specific problem) that ranks a Web page by the number of other Web pages that link to it. Using this algorithm, users always get the pages most relevant to their searches first. Then Brin and Page went one step further and linked users with advertisers that have products and services directly related to those searches.

Search engines aren't the only technology that enables users to find what they want more easily. With digital video recorders (DVR) such as TiVo, you can pause and replay live television, letting you decide what you want to watch and, more importantly, when.

The dark side of the search trend is the ability of anyone to find out information about you. Yes, that's right. Your reputation, words, and behaviors follow you wherever you go. In these days of Facebook, MySpace, and other social-networking Web sites — not to mention Google — this can be a problem for job seekers — especially job seekers who have lived, shall we say, *colorful* lives and choose to display them in public forums.

Turnabout: When little businesses get big businesses to work for them

Big businesses working for little businesses? That's right. Freidman calls this phenomenon *insourcing* and it has taken the traditional outsourcing model to a whole new level. Outsourcing is hiring someone else to do the business functions that you don't want to do or for which you don't have expertise. So you may outsource human resource activities such as payroll and hiring to a firm that specializes in these tasks. With insourcing, on the other hand, your outsourced partner becomes an integral part of your business.

Suppose your company produces unusual pieces of furniture that customers can't find anywhere else in the world. Your potential to sell worldwide, using the power of the Internet to get your message out, is huge. Logistics is the problem, and you have no idea how to begin. You can start by securing the help of an international shipping company, such as UPS Store, that can work with you to find the best packaging for your product and the best vendors to supply those packaging materials. Then UPS slaps smart labels on your packages so it can track them anywhere in its delivery area (which is likely to be worldwide in today's business environment). It also works with customs officials and makes sure your packages reach their destinations.

To achieve that level of collaboration with you, UPS gets inside your business to really understand how it operates. UPS may even help you redesign your production processes to make them more efficient. In fact, some companies never even touch their products; they just let third-party insourcing firms do all the work — sometimes even warranty repairs.

The basis for the successful collaborations that occur today (as with the previous example) is trust. To turn over a portion of your business to a supply-chain manager, you have to be sure that the company is reputable and reliable. Ask the company for customer references, check with the Better Business Bureau at www.bbb.org (it provides information on more than 2.5 million companies), and be sure to search online for any possible complaints that a disgruntled customer may have posted on a Web site somewhere.

Do It Yourself: User-Generated Everything

In today's flat world, people no longer depend on others to provide them with entertainment and information. Rather, when they want something, they create it themselves — everything from promotional videos and independent films to editorials and communities of interest on any topic imaginable. We don't know anyone who can pinpoint exactly when this phenomenon started, but we can identify a few technologies that converged to help make average Joes and Janes into household names — celebrities, first-class marketers, political pundits, and journalists. The possibilities are endless.

The technologies and related applications that converged to make this possible include the following:

- The Internet (no surprise here)
- Wireless technology (Apple's iPhone, global positioning systems [GPS], personal digital assistants [PDAs] — you get the picture)
- Low-priced, high-quality video and digital content production technology (Vegas Movie Studio and Adobe Creative)
- Advanced search engines (Google, Yahoo!, and MSN)
- eBay and PayPal (buy and sell products/services without the need to build retail stores or handle credit cards yourself)

✔ Social media networks (MySpace, Facebook, and YouTube)

✔ Web logs (blogs), podcasts, and vodcasts (technologies that make communication by text, voice, and video interactive)

In the following sections, we look at two key "user-generated" trends that are putting communication power into the hands of anyone with something to say.

Tapping the new opinion leaders

In the past, consumers looked to reputable sources with brand names to get opinions on everything from the best music and films to cars, electronics, and so forth — sources such as MTV for music, Ebert and Roeper for films, Edmunds for cars, and *PC Magazine* for electronics. Consumers still look to those sources today but in ever-declining numbers. Why? Because peer networks are becoming the trusted sources for critical reviews of products and services.

Customers who are unhappy with the service they receive can reach millions of people worldwide to make their cases against the offending companies, and companies really have no way to avoid this kind of bad press when they're doing a good job. In a connected, online world, every individual customer has power, and collectively customers can destroy a company or make it hugely successful.

Although big companies spend hundreds of millions of dollars on promotion and customer service, for almost every major consumer product company, you can find Web sites devoted to complaining about it. For example, if you Google "Microsoft hell," you come up with more than 2,550,000 pages of complaints about the company and its products. "Dell hell" and "Wal-Mart hell" produce the same number of pages.

What this tells you is that a company's brand image isn't really what it says it is, but what Google says it is. This means that today, the opinion leaders on any product are the customers who try it, buy it, and write about it. And a lot of those customers are out there.

What keeps all this consumer power from becoming a lot of noise? How do you filter the bad stuff and get to the good? That's the value of search engines such as Google — they can get to those specialized niche markets and you, the consumer, can get recommendations tailored to your specific needs. In other words, you can find out what the opinion leaders have to say about that rare book your grandmother recommended that's been out of print for decades.

Amateurs compete with experts online and over the airwaves

When Google entered the world of television with Google Video in January 2006, it changed the way that broadcast networks promote their shows, and it gave amateur TV producers a chance to get their 15 minutes of fame. Similar to the video marketplaces that followed — from Microsoft, Yahoo!, and AOL (and don't forget YouTube) — Google brought the amateurs and the experts together in a new way in a format that's a win-win for both. For example, broadcasters now have a global storefront to display trailers for upcoming shows and to sell their archived shows, and an independent movie producer can upload his video from his home in Kazakhstan and become an overnight success without ever tapping the traditional distribution channels.

Some of the top online-video shows are viewed by as many as 250,000 people, which rivals many cable TV shows. And when the shows become successful, they can actually sell 30-second advertising spots. These online shows have become so successful that network broadcasters such as NBC are now advertising and promoting on YouTube and associating their brands with popular bloggers.

Although television is in no danger of disappearing in favor of PC screens and Internet videos, the new generation (the New Millennials, which we discuss later in this chapter) is quite comfortable watching their favorite shows on their computers or iPods, and that's a trend that isn't going to stop.

Do It for Others: Becoming Socially Responsible

Making a profit isn't enough to announce success any more; businesses must also be socially responsible. *Social responsibility* is about operating your business in an ethical, legal, environmentally friendly, and community-conscious way. Today, businesses often have social missions as well as profit missions — in other words, serve as role models and change agents for the betterment of society. Those are lofty expectations, to be sure, but we're guessing that you'd rather figure out now how to be socially responsible before the watchdogs in the press conclude that you're not. This section takes a closer look at this trend of social responsibility in today's business world.

Doing good is good business

The fallout from the Enron and WorldCom scandals (among many others), and the revelation that "imperial" CEOs were serving short tenures and then walking away with hundreds of millions while their companies' stock struggled, was more than the public (not to mention shareholders and the government) could tolerate. Add in the fears about global warming, which have prompted environmental activists to point a finger at business's operational practices, and you have a new set of standards being applied to measure business success.

Finding ways to be socially responsible isn't too difficult. Here are a few ideas:

- You can donate products, services, or expertise to the community:

  - Many companies that produce products with a shelf life, such as bread and other food products, donate them to feed the homeless in their communities.

  - If your company has an expertise that may be valuable in the community, consider donating it for a day. Starving Students, a San Diego moving company, helps to relocate women and children from abusive homes, for instance.

- You can gather a group of local companies together to do something that has a bigger impact, such as adopting an elementary school.

  For example, Just Desserts, a San Francisco-based bakery, put together a group of 35 businesses to adopt an elementary school. They undertook renovation projects such as painting classrooms and planting trees.

- Give employees an opportunity to volunteer their time every month in charitable activities. You may even consider adopting a specific charity and focusing your efforts on it.

- Sponsor an event such as a food drive or highway cleanup.

- Sponsor a city league team for soccer, baseball, or another sport.

It's not easy being green

Being socially responsible is a worthy and attainable goal, but when businesses set goals that are extremely ambitious and rely on too many factors not under their control, they set themselves up for failure. Such was the case for Ben Cohen, co-founder of Ben & Jerry's, when he launched Community Products Inc. (CPI). He had the noble goal of saving the rainforest by donating 60 percent of the profits the company earned by importing nut products from the regions that encompassed the rainforest in South America.

Unfortunately, the nuts CPI received from the region often came with foreign objects in them (such as glass, rocks, coliform bacteria, cigarette butts, and insects). Cohen also ran into problems with working conditions and the workers themselves, so it was difficult to produce sufficient product of acceptable quality in a reliable way. Eventually, CPI was forced to declare bankruptcy.

The moral of the story is to set achievable social responsibility goals. Setting a very big goal will certainly capture the attention of the media, but remember: the media will also be there to report when you don't achieve it.

Take time to think about all the ways that your company can become more green. Some of them include using recycled office supplies, such as paper and printer cartridges, and hiring a consultant to check your business processes for ways to be more environmentally friendly. Don't forget even simple things can make a difference, such as using ceramic mugs for coffee instead of the usual paper cups.

The Changing Workforce: Harnessing the Power of the Millennials

You can classify the generations occupying today's workforce into four categories:

- The Mature Generation: veterans of WWII and the Korean War
- The Baby Boomers: born between 1945 and 1961
- Generation X-ers: born between 1962 and 1980
- The Millennials: born after 1981

If we asked how and where Kennedy died, the Mature Generation and the Baby Boomers would no doubt say, "In Dallas in a motorcade by Lee Harvey Oswald's gunshot." Generation X-ers might reply "In a plane crash off Martha's Vineyard." And the Millennials could possibly say, "Who's Kennedy?"

This simple question illustrates a critical trend in the workforce today: Four generations with very different attitudes are being forced to just get along. But with different styles of communication, different work ethics, and different value systems, this is no easy task.

Four different perspectives can wreak havoc when it comes to hiring, motivating, managing, and teaming — prominent topics throughout this book. If you look at the differences among the generations, you can see the problem clearly. Check out the groups in Table 2-1.

Table 2-1	Perspectives Across the Generations			
Characteristic	*Mature Generation*	*Baby Boomers*	*Gen X-ers*	*Millennials*
Value System	Discipline, respect for authority	Optimistic, active	Skeptical, informal	Realistic and confident, social
Communication Style	Phone, face-to-face conversations, letters and memos	Cell phone, e-mail	Cell phone, e-mail	Cell phone, iPhone, e-mail, iPod, text messaging
Money	Save, pay cash	Buy now, use credit	Cautious, savings	Spend what you earn
View of Work	Have to do it	Love to do it	Find it a challenge	Just a means to an end

As you can see, the communications styles of Baby Boomers and Gen X-ers are the same. Remember, Baby Boomers are workaholics, so technology has been a boon to them because it enables them to do even more work! Gen X-ers, on the other hand, seem to do a better job of separating work and pleasure. Of course, not everyone within each group is exactly the same, but on average, the characteristics ring true.

So, what's a manager or business owner to do? The only thing he or she can do is deal with the differences. Besides tailoring your work environment to satisfy the needs of the four generations, you can look at Chapter 7 for ideas for motivating employees in today's work environment. In the following sections, we focus on the generation coming up — the Millennials — because they're clearly the most unusual generation of the four.

The Millennials: Understanding the age of entitlement

To understand where business is going today, you have to appreciate the generation that was born after 1981 and hit the workforce at the start of the new millennium. Every couple decades or so, the younger generation is so different from previous generations that it actually precipitates a cultural shift. This is what's happening right now with the Millennials. Here are some characteristics of this generation:

- ✔ As employees, they've been called spoiled and entitled.

- ✔ Their baby-boomer parents raised them to never experience failure — the "everyone gets a trophy" attitude. Therefore, they're generally risk-averse.

- ✔ They're described as family-oriented, requiring clear and consistent expectations and living in the moment.

- ✔ Having grown up in a digital world, they're always connected.

This last point may be the key to understanding the Millennials. Most have been using computers almost from birth, so they've developed a set of attitudes that color the way they view the world. Here are some examples of these attitudes:

- ✔ Computers, cell phones, iPods, and so on are normal, required parts of life, not simply technologies or privileges. They want to feel connected 24/7.

- ✔ The Internet is more interesting than television.

- ✔ What you do is more important than what you know (the sense that information isn't permanent; it's constantly changing).

- ✔ It's better to solve problems by trial and error.

- ✔ Multitasking is a way of life, no matter the situation (which is why they're texting, surfing the Internet, and listening to music while in meetings with their bosses!).

- ✔ Delays are intolerable. The immediacy of the Internet and e-mail has made the Millennials impatient, with short attention spans.

- ✔ If something is digital, it belongs to everyone.

Why is this information important? Because employers today are having a difficult time adjusting to the very different work habits of this group. They're typically collaborative and don't like to be managed. They also see every job as a temporary stepping stone to the next opportunity. Businesses looking to tap this new market must try to understand what matters to the Millennials, because their motivation isn't always clear.

Motivating new Millennial employees

How do you, as an employer, inspire and motivate these young employees? Here are a few suggestions:

- ✔ Put your most people-friendly managers in charge of Millennials (and Gen X-ers for that matter) and make sure they are able to build trusting relationships.

- ✔ Reward them with time off rather than overtime. They will appreciate that!

✔ Avoid having them clock into an office — let them work from home — at least some of the time — if possible.

✔ Give them an opportunity for continuing education through conferences, night classes, and workshops you bring into the office — they love getting new information.

✔ Don't be concerned with titles but rather define jobs by responsibilities and make sure they know how they contribute to the success of the company.

✔ Ask for their input into how the company is run.

Chapter 3

Entrepreneurship for Everyone

● ●

● ●

*E*ntrepreneurship is one of the most popular words in the English language today. You see it everywhere. People are buzzing about entrepreneurs and entrepreneurial companies. In fact, if you watch and listen to enough forms of media to get your information, you may believe that just about anyone qualifies as an entrepreneur in some fashion — from lawyers and doctors to artists and teachers. And every type of business seems to qualify — shoe repair shops, accounting offices, home-based cosmetics sellers, and even General Electric. However, the term is so overused that most people aren't quite sure what it stands for.

We need to set the record straight with some definitions. An *entrepreneur* is an individual who recognizes opportunities, gathers the resources needed to act on those opportunities, and drives the opportunities to completion. Entrepreneurship is the study of entrepreneurs and their ventures. It's also a way of thinking, or mindset, that's opportunity-focused, innovative, and growth-oriented. Although entrepreneurship is most commonly associated with starting a business, it also exists within large corporations (called *corporate venturing*), where an individual identifies opportunities, gathers resources from inside and outside the corporation, and carries the opportunity through to completion; check out the last section in this chapter for more info. This chapter gives you the big picture of entrepreneurship and the world of the entrepreneur so you can think about whether becoming an entrepreneur is a business career path that makes sense for you.

Understanding the Importance of Entrepreneurship

Entrepreneurship provides a number of very important benefits to society — namely economic growth, new industries (and with them new opportunities), and new jobs. We examine these benefits in more detail in the following sections.

What's exciting about entrepreneurship is that it isn't limited to any specific country, gender, race, age, or socioeconomic sector. Anyone who has the passion to work for herself or himself can become an entrepreneur. You can learn and then apply the skills and behaviors required to be successful as an entrepreneur. What can't be taught or learned, however, is the passion and persistence that entrepreneurs must have to be the best at what they do. It's the same passion and persistence that great musicians, artists, writers, and scientists must have to excel in their fields.

Entrepreneurs contribute to economic growth

Economists have called entrepreneurship the catalyst for economic growth. When entrepreneurs identify new customer segments, new customer needs, existing customer needs that competitors haven't met, and new methods of manufacturing and distributing products and services, the result is economic growth. Today, companies can trade virtually any type of good or service over any distance — all because of entrepreneurs.

Entrepreneurs who have commercialized new technologies have played critical roles in the global economy. For example, Google's Internet search engine has made it possible to find almost anything anywhere in the world. Whenever an entrepreneur develops and markets a new technology to the marketplace, new jobs are created, suppliers of raw materials and other capabilities benefit from selling to the company, and wholesalers and retailers benefit from the revenues they receive for selling the technology. In short, entrepreneurship is good for the economy.

Entrepreneurship gives birth to new industries

Entrepreneurship results in new industries being formed that provide fresh landscapes for opportunities, businesses, and jobs, all which lead to economic growth. The mobile-device industry, for example, emerged out of the development of wireless technology. Today, everyone can carry their documents, music, and videos with them in handheld devices (your iPod and cell phone are with you 24/7, we assume). Because this is a relatively new industry, there are still plenty of opportunities to go around.

As the industry grows, however, the strongest and most successful entrepreneurial firms begin to acquire the weaker firms (or they fail, usually from poor management) and the industry consolidates. The large firms that remain become the opinion leaders in the industry and influence how the entire industry operates. Entrepreneurs who enter the industry at this stage usually introduce new innovations that will keep the industry growing. If entrepreneurs don't introduce new innovations to the industry or another industry emerges with innovations that make the old industry's technology obsolete, the industry can decline or even die out. You may have seen this happen with the decline of the typewriter industry when personal computers were adopted.

Entrepreneurs create new jobs

New opportunities result in job creation, and small entrepreneurial ventures are the major job creators in the economy. In 2003 (the most recent data we have from the Small Business Administration [SBA]), small businesses created 1,990,326 net new jobs, compared to 994,667 for large companies. That's not bad! In general, the SBA defines a small business as one with fewer than 500 employees that isn't dominant in its industry. Okay, that doesn't sound very small until you compare it with a company such as Microsoft, which has more than 60,000 employees, or Wal-Mart, which has more than 1.6 million employees worldwide!

Thinking as an Entrepreneur

One of the important things to know about entrepreneurship is that it's a personal journey. Entrepreneurship is about people — how you interact with them, make decisions, plan for the future, deal with conflict, and so on. All the decisions involved in starting, growing, and exiting a business affect not only the business and the people associated with it, but also the entrepreneur. This section helps you understand what entrepreneurial thinking is and identify if you're ready to think like an entrepreneur. And if you are, we give you several ideas to get you started.

Understanding entrepreneurial thinking

Perhaps you're reading this chapter front to back because you're completely sold on the idea of entrepreneurship. Before we go any further, however, we must agree on one thing: starting a business isn't for everyone. And thank goodness for that, because we do need some scientists, mathematicians, artists, and physicians to keep this world running. We're not trying to turn everyone into entrepreneurs, but we do think that there's value in learning how to think like an entrepreneur.

With that in mind, here are some characteristics of entrepreneurial thinking that are important to succeeding as an entrepreneur:

- **Entrepreneurs are comfortable with ambiguity and uncertainty.** They know that the best ideas come out of uncertainty. And they know that there will always be unanswered questions, so they attempt to find answers for as many critical questions as possible while moving forward, answering the rest as they go.

- **Entrepreneurs have self discipline and tenacity.** In other words, they know how to focus on a task and stick to it through completion. That's why they succeed more than they fail. And speaking of failure . . .

- **Entrepreneurs aren't afraid to fail.** They understand that if you never fail at anything, you haven't taken any risks. And taking risks is how you learn and grow a business.

- **Entrepreneurs believe that they alone control their destiny.** They know that if they screw up, they should look nowhere else but the mirror. But with this attitude, they also have the freedom to decide their future, regardless of what the government or a competitor does.

- **Entrepreneurs focus on opportunity and innovation.** They strive to identify all the great opportunities out there — not only for products and services, but also for new ways of doing business, new marketing strategies, and new distribution models. The more they network and take calculated risks, the more opportunity will come to them. This is nature's law, and entrepreneurs practice it daily.

No two entrepreneurs are exactly alike, but, in general, these characteristics can be found in people who launch new companies.

Testing your entrepreneurial mindset

If you've seen the list of ways that entrepreneurs think in the previous section, you may want to test whether you're ready to start thinking like an entrepreneur, too. If so, take our little test in Table 3-1. No one will see it but you, so be honest in your answers.

Table 3-1	Entrepreneur Preferences Quiz		
Question		**Yes**	**No**
Do you start projects on your own without waiting until someone asks you to start?			
Would you be able to work on growing your business for a year without pay?			
Do you always stick with a project until you finish it?			
Do you like working in teams?			
Do you like meeting new people?			
Are you comfortable asking for money?			
Are you comfortable with a lack of security?			
Do you have the time to devote to a new business start-up?			
Do you have the support of your family to start a business?			
Are you comfortable with debt?			

The more of these questions you can answer "yes" to, the more likely it is that you'll be comfortable with dealing with the issues related to being an entrepreneur.

Beginning to think like an entrepreneur

So, you think you have the entrepreneurial spirit burning within you. You can take a number of steps to help yourself begin to think like an entrepreneur — after which you can find an opportunity and do something great! The following sections present a few of these steps.

Find a mentor

A *mentor* is someone who's leading the kind of life you want to lead and who serves as a role model for you. Your mentor should be a sounding board for new ideas, a critic when you need to come back down to earth, and an advisor because he or she has been there. So, how do you find this superperson? By networking, of course (check out the next section for more on networking)! People who've been successful often enjoy helping others make the journey, so don't be afraid to ask any potential candidates.

Debunking myths about entrepreneurs

To understand how entrepreneurs think, you first need to drop a few myths or stereotypes you may be carrying around. Given the media's love affair with entrepreneurs, it shouldn't surprise you that these myths have grown up around them:

✔ **Myth #1: It takes a lot of money to start a business.**

Not true! In fact, every year, *Inc. Magazine* profiles businesses that have started on $1,000 or less. And among the mag's annual list of the 500 fastest-growing private companies, you see no relationship between the amount of start-up capital invested and business success (for more on start-up capital, see Chapter 14).

✔ **Myth #2: Entrepreneurs are in it for the money.**

Okay, some entrepreneurs think that way, but the number one reason that most entrepreneurs start businesses is independence — the ability to create something they can call their own instead of working for someone else. Entrepreneurs want to control their destiny.

✔ **Myth #3: Entrepreneurs are born, not made.**

This is the same as saying that you can't teach entrepreneurship. According to management guru Peter Drucker, entrepreneurship is a discipline, so it can be learned. Passion and persistence may be in your genes, but it takes work to develop the skills that entrepreneurs have.

✔ **Myth #4: You need a business plan to succeed.**

Yes, investors and lenders want to see a business plan before forking over cash, but if you don't need these resources at start-up, you may be able to launch your business based on the results of a feasibility analysis and then get some traction with customers (see the later section "Conduct a feasibility study"). Some Internet entrepreneurs, such as Richard Rosenblatt of Demand Media, know how to get a Web site up and make money within a couple weeks. These savvy entrepreneurs know that testing the market is more important than spending the time to write a business plan.

✔ **Myth #5: You have to be young and reckless to be an entrepreneur.**

This definitely isn't true. In fact, the Global Entrepreneurship Monitor Report (www. gemconsortium.org) found that men and women in the 45–64 age bracket start 35 percent of all the businesses in the United States and 22 percent globally. Entrepreneurship is for all ages!

Don't ask a prospective mentor to take the job on the first date! Take your prospective mentor to coffee and get to know him or her. A potential mentor needs to feel comfortable with you before he or she will even consider saying yes. If you've done your homework about this mentor, you'll be able to talk about things of interest to help build a rapport. After you establish a rapport, you can begin to talk about your needs as a budding entrepreneur.

Start shaking hands to network

One of the most important things you can do to start down the road to entrepreneurship is to build a network of people who can serve as resources for anything you may need. But not just any people — the right people. The right people are those who can open doors for you in communities of people you otherwise couldn't have tapped. For example, we've met key people who have introduced us to some really fascinating communities: physicists, astronauts, and the World Cup sailing community, to name a few. And these new communities have been the sources of a wealth of new business opportunities.

Read about and hang out with entrepreneurs

One of the best ways to discover whether entrepreneurship is right for you and to start thinking like an entrepreneur is to find out more about entrepreneurs by reading (you can't pick up a magazine today without seeing an entrepreneur on the cover). You also can go to events in your local community where entrepreneurs do their networking, such as the Chamber of Commerce, industry trade association meetings, and university networking events. Entrepreneurs love to talk, so after you get one started, watch out! You may learn more than you ever wanted to know about entrepreneurship.

Take charge of your life with entrepreneurial thinking

Hanging out with yourself may sound far less interesting than hanging out with entrepreneurs, but you must assess your personality and preferences so that if you decide to start a business or just want to take charge of your career, you'll be in a better position to do it. Research has identified six important barriers that prevent people from taking charge of their lives or becoming self employed. If you understand your feelings about these issues and deal with them, you'll be on your way to overcoming them and taking charge of your life. These six barriers include

- **Lack of confidence:** I've never done this before.
- **Financial needs:** Where will I get the money to do this (see Chapter 14)?
- **Knowing how to start:** What should I do first (see the following section)?
- **Personal or family issues:** I have a spouse, three kids, two dogs, and a mortgage.
- **Time constraints:** I don't even have time to sleep, let alone start a business.
- **Lack of skills:** What do I need to know to do this?

All these fears and barriers come from uncertainty. So, get up off the sofa and start learning. This book is a great start. You also can Google Entrepreneur, Start-up, or any other keyword related to the questions you want answered. The information is all out there waiting for you.

Finding an Opportunity

How do entrepreneurs find great opportunities? Do they have a special talent that others don't have? Not really. They're simply creative in their thinking.

Entrepreneurship is a creative process, not a scientific one. It's chaotic, not linear. In fact, if you're a highly organized person who wakes up every day knowing exactly how your day will go, your chances of discovering a new opportunity will be very low. On the other hand, if your life is a bit more chaotic — things change every day, and you're not stuck in any ruts — your chances of being more opportunistic are dramatically higher.

Fortunately, everyone has at least some creative juices flowing; you just need to know how to activate the creativity so you can make it work for you. This section focuses on uncovering the barriers to creativity and removing them so you can better identify opportunities and then act on them.

Identifying the barriers to creativity

People have plenty of excuses for not being creative, but maybe that's because they see creativity only as invention — coming up with a totally new product or service. Although invention certainly is exciting, it's probably the least common way that businesspeople express creativity. The following are a couple common barriers to creativity you may encounter:

✔ **I have no time to be creative!** Sure, entrepreneurs are busy people. In fact, today everybody is bombarded with info from conversations with other people, e-mail, the Internet, and their cellphones. And everybody wants answers, right now. No one wants to wait anymore because they assume that everyone is connected. It's also amazing how many people let others control their days by always being on call.

For 20 minutes every day, turn everything off and just listen to yourself. At first, you won't know what to do. Your mind will be racing about the things you think you should be doing, but eventually, with a little practice, your mind will settle down and open up. We promise! In time, you'll look forward to those 20 minutes — especially after the first great business idea pops into your uncluttered mind. Give it a try!

✔ **I have no confidence that I can do this!** It's much easier to take the path you already know than risk getting lost by trying the one less traveled. But it's the path you don't know that may hold the creative opportunity you've been looking for.

Often, people are afraid to be creative or offer creative ideas because they don't want to be criticized. But consider poor Thomas Edison, who tried and failed 6,000 times before inventing the light bulb. Don't you think he took some criticism along the way? Maybe a little ridicule, too? Did that stop him? Thank goodness it didn't, or we wouldn't be able to see this page we're writing on.

To build up your confidence, set some small goals and practice, practice, practice.

What's that? You don't have a creative bone in your body? We hate to tell you, but there's no such thing as a creative bone. Bones are just bones; they're either strong or weak, but never creative. However, your mind is an amazing thing, and it can be manipulated to cause you to believe whatever you want to believe. So, keep telling yourself that you're creative, and at least you won't be mentally blocking yourself from becoming creative.

Removing the barriers to creativity

Most entrepreneurs improve on a product/service/concept that already exists, or they find a way to solve a problem they see or have experienced. You probably show this type of creativity every day. When was the last time you didn't have a hammer handy and you had to find a way to pound a nail? Perhaps you took off your shoe or used a book or some other hard object. That's creative thinking at work!

However, sometimes barriers pop up and you may not know how to get rid of them. You need to be proactive about becoming more creative and opportunistic, so get out your sledgehammer and start removing the barriers to creativity. This section helps.

Find your most creative environment

Your chances of being creative increase when you're in the right environment. The environment in which you work can either stimulate or discourage creativity. For example, if your workplace has a rigid structure and military-like chain of command, it will be difficult to think "out of the box" you're currently in.

One study found that the place where people have the most creative ideas is the bathroom! Well, when you think about it, it makes sense. You're typically by yourself and probably aren't accessible — the perfect environment for contemplation (assuming you don't have a library of magazines with you). The basic idea here is to find a quiet place without a lot of distraction. Think about where you were when you had your last great idea. That may give you a clue as to the type of environment that encourages your creative juices.

Keep a journal

Writing in a journal can be a great way to overcome your creative barriers. How many times have you said, "I'll have to remember to write this idea down," but by the time you get a pen and paper, you've forgotten the idea? Keep a journal with you at all times so you can jot down those ideas so you don't forget them.

You really never know when you may get a great idea. Many people come up with exciting ideas in their dreams or when they're first waking up. Wouldn't it be wise to have a pen and paper near your bed so you don't lose those ideas?

Practice solving problems

As we stated earlier, most "new" ideas are based on something that already exists. And that something that already exists may be a problem that needs to be solved. Problems in the marketplace are great sources of business opportunities.

When was the last time you flew somewhere and spent some time in an airport? Airports are great sources of problems that need solving. To gain some experience, see how many airport problems you can identify and then practice finding ways to solve those problems. Granted, some of your solutions may be a bit off-the-wall, but, who knows, you may come up with an idea that could become a successful business.

Magazines, newspapers, and the Internet also are excellent sources of inspiration for businesses. And don't forget the government. It's always coming up with new laws and regulations that cause problems for people; however, these same problems can become opportunities for an entrepreneur. For example, all those recycling ordinances in cities have inspired many businesses, which have turned recyclable material into new products.

Network your way to opportunity

Business associates are the second most common source of new ideas after problems. Your network of business contacts is particularly useful when it includes people from a variety of different types of industries. For example, a technology or a method for producing a particular product may be familiar to you because you work in, say, the aerospace industry. You have a network contact in the automobile industry and through discussions with that person you discover that you may be able to take your aerospace technology or method into the automobile industry as a new venture.

We're not suggesting that you steal ideas from the people you know, but you *can* let the conversations you have with your associates open your mind to new ways of thinking about things. That's why it's so important *not* to hang around only with people like you. If you're a businessperson, go spend time with scientists or artists. These people look at the world differently and have different problems, and they may need someone like you (an entrepreneur) to solve them. (See the earlier section "Beginning to think like an entrepreneur" for more on networking.)

Testing a New Business Idea

From the moment you come up with a great business idea, the questions start. Does anybody else think this is a great idea? Is there a way to make money at this? Where do I start? The best place to start is testing the idea in stages to make sure you're not the only person in the world who thinks it's a great idea.

In this section, we give you a strategy for tackling your new business idea in manageable bites. Bon Appétit!

Develop a business concept

What's the difference between an idea and an opportunity? An *opportunity* is an idea that has commercial potential. One way that you can turn an idea into an opportunity is by developing a business concept. Think of the business concept as an elevator pitch on a very fast elevator. *Elevator pitch* refers to the 30 seconds that an entrepreneur has to impress a potential investor. If you have only 30 seconds to talk about your business, you want to capture the investor's attention and convey the essentials in a clear and concise manner.

An effective business concept identifies the following four components:

- ✔ The product or service you're offering
- ✔ The customer (the person or business that will be paying you)
- ✔ The benefit or value proposition (what's in it for the customer?)
- ✔ The distribution or how you plan to deliver the benefit to the customer

The following sections help you develop your business concept.

Define the product or service

You need to make sure you know specifically what you're offering to the customer. Today, the boundary between product and service business has all but disappeared as companies diversify their offerings, so you may decide to offer both a product and a service related to that product. Of course, that decision will depend on what your customer wants. The actual design of your product or service should come from a deep understanding of the customer's needs (see Chapter 15) and your team's capabilities.

It's also important to define your product or service's competitive advantage in the marketplace. In other words, how is your product or service different from what's already out there? Intellectual property such as a patent or trade secret can offer a substantial competitive advantage, but an innovative process or marketing strategy can also help you stand out from the crowd.

Define the customer and benefit

Many entrepreneurs get confused when they have to identify their customers and the potential benefits they'll provide those customers. That's because in many businesses, the customer isn't the end user or beneficiary of the product or service. For example, suppose you're manufacturing a new kind of golf club for women that better fits their grip and enables them to improve their swing. The end user for your club is a female golfer. But who pays you? Probably not the woman, unless you sell directly to the customer over the Internet. Most likely, you'll sell the clubs through a golf shop, so the golf shop pays you and is therefore your customer.

Identifying the customer is important because, in this example, the benefits that the golf shop wants (the ability to offer unique products with quick turnover and high margins) aren't the same as the benefits that the end user (consumer) wants (ease of use and improved performance).

The trick is that you must satisfy the needs of your primary customer *and* make sure that the end user's needs are satisfied as well. For more on customer identification, jump to Chapter 15.

Customers buy benefits, not features. The two are quite different. *Features* are the characteristics of the product or service; *benefits* are the intangible aspects that solve the customer's pain (such as convenience, health, and saving time). The female golfer benefits from a club that better fits her grip and enables a more accurate swing, not the color of the grip or the attractiveness of the club.

Define the distribution channel

You need to define your organization's distribution channel when developing your business concept. The *distribution channel* is the way you'll deliver your value proposition to the customer. You can distribute your product or service and its benefit in a couple ways (for more on distribution, head to Chapter 18):

- ✔ Directly to the customer, such as through the Internet or by providing a service.
- ✔ Indirectly through a distributor or retailer that sells your product. These companies are called *channel intermediaries;* they provide their service so that the entrepreneur can concentrate on what he or she does best.

Which route you take depends on your customers' expectations (how do your customers prefer to buy?) and the costs involved. Using intermediaries raises the price of the product to the end user but may make it possible for the entrepreneur's company to grow faster and reach more customers. Researching the industry to discover what similar businesses are doing is critical to making a decision between the direct and indirect channels.

Put your business concept together

After completing the steps in the previous sections, the only thing missing from the business concept is the compelling story. The compelling story conveys the pain or problem the customer has that your product or service will solve. Here's an example of a story:

> *Wildfire destruction is on the rise each year along with the amount of acres that are burned. More people are living in areas that are prone to wildfire. Over 38 percent of all homes being built are located in these urban/rural*

interface areas. The problem is that there are not enough fire personnel to protect homeowners against the wildfires that occur in these locations. Consumer Fire Products, Inc. (CFPI) has designed, developed, and will distribute directly to the customer the FOAMSAFE(tm) system, a new patent-pending exterior fire protection system that automatically activates whenever a property is threatened by fire. Homeowners in urban/rural interface areas will benefit from peace of mind, knowing that their homes are protected.

(Courtesy of Irene Rhodes, CEO, Consumer Fire Products)

Conduct a feasibility study

Putting together a concept statement (see the previous sections) means that you now have a business opportunity that you can test. One of the most important skills that an entrepreneur can acquire is the ability to conduct a *feasibility analysis*. Feasibility analysis tests the viability of a new business concept before you spend a lot of time and effort to prepare a business for launch. There's a lot of uncertainty in a start-up business; feasibility analys is gives you a way to reduce some of that uncertainty and the associated risk, which will help you and make potential investors happy!

The ultimate goal of the feasibility analysis is to assist the entrepreneur in thinking critically and answering fundamental questions about the business concept. You want to achieve a high level of confidence that the conditions are right to go forward and start your business. Table 3-2 summarizes the various tests and the key questions you need to answer for each, and the sections that follow go into more detail about the tests.

Table 3-2	Feasibility Analysis: Key Tests and Questions
Feasibility Test	*Key Questions*
Business Concept Analysis	Who is the customer?
	What's the benefit he or she is receiving?
	How can I deliver the benefit?
	What's my secret sauce (my unfair advantage)?
Industry and Market Analysis	What are the characteristics of the industry?
	Are there barriers to entry?
	Who are the opinion leaders?
	What are the demographics of my target market?
	Who's the first customer?

(continued)

Table 3-2 *(continued)*

Feasibility Test	Key Questions
	What does the competitive landscape look like?
	How much demand is there for my product/service?
Management Team Analysis	Who is my team? Co-founders, advisors, board of directors?
	What expertise and experience do we have?
	Where are the gaps and how will we fill them?
Product/Service Analysis	What products and services am I offering?
	How can I protect them?
	How will I prototype them, and how long will that take?
Cash Needs Assessment	How much money do I need to start the business and take it to a positive cash flow from the sales generated?
	What are the milestones I'll need to meet?
	What will cause changes in my predictions?

Conduct industry and market analysis

The feasibility process doesn't have to be linear, but it does help to start the analysis with the environment in which your business will operate. That environment is the industry, which is a group of businesses that will form the value chain for your new venture — manufacturers, suppliers, distributors, retailers, and so forth. These companies essentially represent your support network. Depending on the industry, it may also include government agencies, regulatory bodies, and trade associations, to name just a few possibilities.

You want to understand the industry's size and where it is in its life cycle. Yes, industries go through a life cycle just like humans do — birth, childhood, adolescence, adulthood, old age, and death. Your industry's stage in that cycle will affect your business strategy. For example, an emerging industry (early childhood) is like the Wild West — every company for itself. Companies are pushing and shoving, trying to grab their share of the industry and establish themselves as the industry standard. In this type of industry, tons of opportunities exist, which is a lot of fun. On the other hand, a very mature industry (old age) typically has major, established companies that dominate and don't really want to see anything change. Here, the only way for an entrepreneur to enter is by bringing something new to the industry. That's what happened when the Internet changed the way many mature industries operate. An industry in the growth stage of the life cycle means that a business will require a lot of capital and resources to sustain itself, and it may be a target for acquisition by a much larger company.

If industries are about value-chain players, markets are about customers. If you don't understand the market you're going to tap, the customers in it won't buy from you. You want to design a product or service that customers in the market will value. If you make a product or service that you *know* customers want, they'll have their credit cards ready when you are, which saves you money on marketing.

 The best way to research a market is to get out into it and start talking to people — particularly customers. Without a doubt, they'll help you figure out the best features and benefits for your product or service, and they'll help you calculate how much demand exists (one or two customers isn't enough!). Chapter 15 has the full scoop on getting to know the customer.

After you define your target customer and your market, you can start identifying potential competitors. Keep in mind that competitors aren't always obvious. Look for companies that have the same capabilities and expertise that your company has. Even if they're not serving your customers with your products right now, there's no reason they couldn't do so after they see how successful you are.

Configure the business team

Today it takes a team to start a new company. The business world is just too complex for any one person to have all the answers. Your team can consist of

- ✔ The founders of the company
- ✔ Professional advisors
- ✔ A board of directors
- ✔ Any strategic partners such as manufacturers and distributors (see Chapter 18)

You need to make sure your team has the expertise and experience needed to build your business (no, working at Goldman Sachs doesn't count as entrepreneurship). Sure, it helps to have someone on the team who has done it before (even if they failed), but absent that, get an experienced entrepreneur on your advisory board.

Plan for the product/service

You need to figure out what kinds of supplies and/or raw materials are required to produce your product/service. And, by the way, are you intending to manufacture in-house? Probably not. So now you have to find companies that can do your production work for you.

That leads to another choice: Do you manufacture domestically or follow the crowd to India and China (see Chapter 4)? Difficult decisions, but that's why you network, right? And that's why you study your industry — so you can learn what has worked for other businesses similar to yours.

Calculate how much money you need to start

How much money do you need to pull off your business concept? We hope as little as possible if you're thinking like an entrepreneur. What you want to find out during the feasibility analysis is how much cash you need to launch the business and operate it until the sales you generate produce a positive cash flow (you take in more than you spend, in other words). This isn't as easy as it sounds, because most entrepreneurs underestimate their expenses and overestimate their ability to generate sales — not a pretty picture.

Here are some steps for conducting this testing phase of your business:

1. **Make a list of everything you'll need to have in place to start your business and then attach dollar values to each item.**

   This is where having an experienced advisor (gained by networking in the industry) and searching on the Internet comes into play.

2. **Forecast sales for the first two years based on market research, on your understanding of how customers will pay, and from the experiences of similar businesses in your industry.**

   (You can read more about making forecasts in Chapter 12.)

3. **Forecast the expenses required to operate the business.**

   (Again, Chapter 12 will be a help here.)

4. **Create a cash-flow statement that shows all your projected cash inflows and outflows (just like your checkbook — if you still have one!), along with the net cash flow for each month.**

   Run a cumulative net cash flow line below the monthly net cash flow line so that you can calculate the highest amount of cumulative negative cash flow that you generate (this can be frightening). Negative cash flow means that you spent more cash than you took in from customers. It's pretty common to experience negative cash flow or loss in the first few months of a new business. If you then add that highest cumulative negative figure to the total of your start-up expenses, you'll get a reasonable estimate of how much money you need to get your business up and running.

Don't forget the old mantra "garbage in, garbage out (GIGO)". The numbers you use to make your forecasts have to be supported by research. Don't pull them out of thin air, or you'll be headed for some big surprises, and not the happy kind.

Drawing conclusions

Feasibility analysis is designed to help entrepreneurs make wise decisions and not reject a concept out of hand without giving it sufficient consideration. With all your research from the previous sections, review your plan and answer the following questions:

> ✔ **Do I really have a business?** A product or service alone isn't a business. The process of feasibility analysis helps you design a real business to deliver the benefits of your product or service to customers.

> ✔ **Does the business satisfy my personal needs and goals?** Starting a business is a full-time occupation. It requires that you have endurance, be in good physical and mental condition, and that you're passionate about what you'll do.

But how do you arrive at these decisions? As you go through all the tests in the feasibility analysis, at each stage along the way you'll be able to draw a conclusion about what you've discovered and how you feel about it. For example, if during the industry analysis you find out that Congress is about to pass legislation that will make it difficult for you to do business, that in itself should help you draw a pretty strong conclusion about the feasibility of your business. You'd probably stop your research at that point. The same is true about market research if you find that there aren't enough potential customers to make your concept financially feasible. Of course, during the analysis, you should be consulting with your advisors and people in the industry with whom you'll work. They can help you draw the appropriate conclusions.

If you want to dive deeper into the topic of feasibility analysis, you may want to consider the following book, which will walk you through feasibility analysis and the business plan: *Launching New Ventures,* 5th Edition, by Kathleen Allen (Houghton Mifflin).

Even with all the planning, sometimes businesses fail

You can't just close your eyes, make a wish, and will your business to succeed. Sometimes, despite the best efforts of the entrepreneur, a new business fails. The Small Business Administration reports that two-thirds of new businesses survive at least two years, so that's encouraging. At four years, however, the survival rate is 44 percent — not quite as encouraging, but not as disastrous as the often-reported "four out of five new businesses fail." Actually, research has found that the chances of survival increase with age (the age of the business, not the entrepreneur).

Corporate Venturing: An Oxymoron?

If you thought you had to quit your corporate job to become an entrepreneur, wait just a minute. You may not have to. In fact, for some types of ventures — particularly those that require significant resources to start and distribution networks to run — it makes sense to launch from inside a corporation. Today, big companies are finding that they have to be entrepreneurial to survive and grow in this global marketplace. But entrepreneurship is a whole new world for these giants, because they're not used to the high degree of uncertainty and risk of failure that accompany new ventures. Big companies have had to come up with some ways to cope. In the following sections, we talk about those ways, as well as how you can survive as an entrepreneur in the corporate world.

Learning from corporate entrepreneurship models

Before you decide to go to work for a large corporation, you may want to check to see if the company has a mechanism for encouraging entrepreneurship. There are a number of ways that big companies facilitate corporate venturing. Here are two of them:

- One of the first models for incorporating entrepreneurship into a big company was the "Skunk Works" model, conceived by the Lockheed-Martin team that developed the Stealth fighter jet. It describes a team that's left alone (hence the word "skunk," for obvious reasons) and not subjected to company bureaucracy so it can work on a secret project. Today, it represents a team that operates outside traditional lines of company authority and rules so it can benefit from flexibility, speed, and a more creative work environment. (For more on teams within an organization, see Chapter 9.)

- Another approach is to attempt to encourage entrepreneurship inside your current organizational structure. As you can imagine, this approach is difficult at best. A few companies, such as 3M and GE, have been successful with letting employees spend a portion of their time on individual projects that could lead to new ventures. This tactic has some specific requirements to succeed:

  - Commitment at the top to help expedite the venture

  - A champion (more than one is best) in the organization who can beat down doors at the top and shield the entrepreneur from attack

  - Access to the knowledge and resources of the entire company (why reinvent the wheel?)

- Clearly defined milestones and metrics so that go/no-go decisions can be made before getting in too deep (see Chapter 9 for more on metrics)

Surviving as an entrepreneur in a large company

So, you have your cozy corporate job, but you think you're really an entrepreneur at heart. Still, the thought of going out on your own doesn't excite you; you'd rather find a way to practice entrepreneurship in a nice, comfortable environment with plenty of resources at hand. That's all well and good, but you have to approach this challenge with a toolkit of tactics to survive. You may be the pioneer in your company, and the pioneers often are the ones with the arrows in their backs! (Just ask Apple's competitors, who often make it to market before the media giant.)

To help you succeed, here are some arrows to avoid and some tips for how to avoid them:

- In a large corporation, the plentiful resources are money, computing capability, and service providers. The scarce resources are time, talent, and management attention. Unfortunately, the last three are the most important. That's why you need to seek out people in the company who believe in what you're trying to do and who are willing to spend the time to help you. It doesn't take many people to get a project off the ground, but it does take a few dedicated people.

- Anything you do will take longer inside a large corporation, because you have to navigate through the bureaucracy and personal agendas — not an easy task. Make sure that you find a project champion — someone who's regarded highly in the company (in a higher status than you) — who can protect you from the slings and arrows of people trying to grab resources for their own projects.

- You get to trade on the reputation and legitimacy of your company (we hope it's a good one), but because your company has a reputation, it won't risk it on an entrepreneurial venture with a high risk of failure. Be careful about what you choose to develop. Here's where a feasibility analysis comes in handy. It will help you reduce the risk to a manageable level and increase your chances of getting the project approved.

- If you're a success, you'll get no equity, no wealth creation, and sometimes no credit. Most likely, your company will thank you and then take credit for your new venture. However, many corporate venturers with successful track records inside large companies have eventually left to start their own businesses on the outside, often with their former companies as customers.

 ✔ If you fail, you'll get all the credit, and it may ruin your career at the company — especially if it's a high-profile failure. That's why you need to do some homework on the company you plan to join.

Chapter 4

Global Business: Fun and Profit in Katmandu

*W*hether your company is a small retailer in a shopping center in Des Moines, Iowa, or a large plastics manufacturer in Pittsburgh, Pennsylvania, the global marketplace affects you. There's hardly a place left to hide from it anymore; but, then, why would you want to? In countries from Kenya to South Korea, people around the world may want your products and services. In years past, going global meant a huge outlay of capital to fund facilities and hire people, but today, going global can be as easy as turning on your computer and opening your Internet browser. This chapter explains how your organization can go global, including how to begin, what it takes, and how to get some help.

Going Global Is No Longer a Choice

In the past, companies may have struggled with the issue of whether or not to conduct business on an international scale. However, the decision is no longer a struggle because it has already been made for them. Even if you don't *want* to do business on a global level, international companies will do business with you, compete with you, or even put you out of business. Therefore, you need to think global. Want to know how easy it is? The minute you put your business on the Internet, you're a global entrepreneur, because anyone, anywhere can find you. And this is a good thing. This section shows you how by taking a closer look at conducting business in the global marketplace.

Understanding the appeal of being global

Increasing competition in domestic markets and saturated markets in some industries are prompting business owners to examine the international marketplace, where demand is great for U.S.-made products and where, in some parts of the world, money isn't an issue. In the international marketplace, many businesses have found new markets for their products, partners for their businesses, and complementary products that help increase their sales in their local markets.

The global market should be attractive to your business for several reasons:

- ✓ It enables you to build a broader customer base, which can minimize the impact of economic problems at home.

- ✓ You may be able to reduce the effects of seasonal market swings. Remember, countries south of the equator are in opposite seasons from the United States.

- ✓ If you have excess capacity in your manufacturing facility, you may be able to put it to use by finding more products to produce for global markets.

- ✓ You may find new life for a product that's losing ground in the U.S. market.

- ✓ You may be able to lower your production costs by manufacturing in a country with lower labor rates or reduce your supply costs by purchasing overseas.

Whether you're encouraged by one or all of these factors, you need to think about ways to go global.

There are also risks associated with going global. If finding customers and establishing a distribution network are challenging tasks in your domestic market, the tasks may be almost insurmountable in foreign markets. Even money can be a problem (and you thought money was simply a good thing!). Financing can be difficult in global markets, as one business owner found out when he shipped a $10,000 unit to a customer in France and later was billed $2,500 for value-added tax. He knew nothing about this tax, but he still had to take the loss. Just another example of why it's important to do your homework.

Determining whether your business has what it takes to go global

If you want to find new markets for your business, consider this: Not all businesses are suitable for global markets. For example, Uncle Bob's Shoe Repair or a local tax preparer service probably won't find eager markets in other countries. (Interestingly enough, many larger tax preparers *are* farming out the preparation part of their businesses to India and doing the advising and strategizing in-house.) But most types of businesses can find customers and partners in other parts of the world.

As in any marketplace, you must offer a high-quality product or service at a competitive price to go global. Beyond that, researchers have found that most successful global businesses have some common characteristics:

- **They have a strong global vision**. In other words, their strategic plans consider the influence of, effects of, and opportunities found in the international market.

- **Their management teams have some international experience.** Becoming familiar with the international market isn't as difficult as it sounds; in fact, gaining an understanding of other countries and how they do business is easier than ever. Today, some universities require their MBA candidates to spend some time in other countries to learn the way business is done abroad.

- **They've developed strong international networks of people and businesses that can help them.** One of the cardinal rules of going global is to find partners in the country in which you want to do business. These companies know how things really work and can save you a lot of time and effort, not to mention money.

- **They offer unique technology or know-how that another country doesn't have.** The United States used to ship all its outdated technology to other countries further down the technology ladder. With the Internet, television, and films, no matter where you live in the world, chances are you've seen what technology is available; find out where in the world your offerings would be most desirable.

Figuring out when to go global

There is no right or wrong time to make the decision to go global. However, some times *are* better than others. If your business is new and you foresee that about 25 percent or more of your sales will come from the international market, you may have a special type of business that's referred to as "born global." This business's competitive advantage lies in outsourcing and selling in several countries.

Whatever you plan to offer, it must be something that you can modify to meet the needs of the customers where you do business. For example, if you're introducing a new product that has never been in the market before, you may want to start domestically first to establish yourself. That way, your systems and controls can be in place for awhile, and you may have fewer problems when you expand to another country. Most U.S.-made products need adjustments and some redesign to be compatible with the electrical systems or to meet the regulations of other countries — not to mention the need to fit into other cultures. Hey, if you live in Rapid City, South Dakota, it will take a long time to get to Australia to solve a problem with your product! Of course, travel time is another good reason to have a partner in the country you select.

Spinning the Globe: Where to Begin?

With all the countries in the world, how do you know which one is best for your products or services? Actually, researching and choosing really aren't as difficult as you may think. When doing research on conducting business in a foreign country, you basically want to know four things:

- ✔ Who will use the product?
- ✔ How do the country's consumers define value?
- ✔ How will you know when a change in the market is about to occur?
- ✔ How can you increase your market share?

The following sections take you on a quick tour around the world so you can get an idea of what it's like to do business in China, India, the European Union, and Mexico. Are you ready to travel?

China: Possible, but not always easy

In December 2001, China became part of the World Trade Organization, which deals with governing trade rules between nations. This opened huge new markets and propelled the country to 9 percent average annual growth from that point forward.

U.S. companies, seeing dollar signs everywhere, could hardly wait to invest billions in China to see even more returned to them in the form of revenues. These multinationals presumed that they held the advantage in technology innovation and were more experienced in marketing and brand building than Chinese companies. They also figured that China had a long way to go before it would be competitive on the world stage. Boy, were they wrong!

The difficulties of doing business in China

Here are some of the problems these companies, and others that choose to do business in China, faced (or are facing):

- ✔ China's infrastructure is still in its early stages, so oftentimes global companies can't take advantage of their sophisticated marketing skills. For example, securing in-depth market research is very challenging because there are so few local market research firms that even know how to perform this function.

Using the Web to find the right country

A number of resources can make your seemingly daunting task of choosing a country much easier. For example, start with the United Nations Statistics Division, which is available online at `unstats.un.org/unsd/trade`. This site contains the SITC (Standard Industrial Trade Classification) codes established by the United Nations, which enable you to find information on demand for a specific product or service in the particular country in which you have an interest. You also should go to the site of the North American Industry Classification System (NAICS) at `www.census.gov/epcd/www/naics.html`. Its coding system has replaced the Standard Industrial Classification (SIC) system and provides business statistics about North American industries. (For other resources to help you find the right country for your products, see the section "Knowing Where to Go for Help" later in this chapter.)

NAICS and SITC codes are the keys to a wealth of information. You can calculate the demand for your product by looking at the following:

✔ The value of worldwide imports of the product measured in dollars.

✔ Import records over time, which show the amount of growth a particular product has experienced or the level of imports to a specific country over time. You're looking for countries where import demand is greater than worldwide averages. Such a statistic means that a country is probably more likely to purchase your product.

✔ The amount of U.S. imports to a country. You're looking for a country where U.S. imports exceed 5 percent of its total imports — the higher, the better. If the number is lower than 5 percent, it may signal that tariffs are affecting the country's ability to import from the United States.

✔ Logistics and distribution are relatively new ideas in China, so it can be difficult to find a national distributor or a competent supplier.

✔ Multinational companies must use international corporate standards that often place them in disadvantageous positions relative to local companies, which must follow only local customs.

✔ Any economies of scale that a company has in its domestic market often are lost in the face of local trade barriers across provinces and protectionism for local products.

✔ Companies often look at the Chinese market as a whole, but the reality is this: The sophisticated consumers they find in Beijing and Shanghai are only a relatively small portion of the more than one billion potential consumers who can afford only what they absolutely need to survive.

Making a mistake while doing business in China can be devastating to your company. News of a mistake travels like wildfire, and consumers can be unforgiving when the companies they admire let them down. Fast-food pioneer McDonald's, for example, made a colossal mistake when it produced a commercial showing a Chinese man on his knees begging a salesperson to give him a discount. The Chinese found this ad extremely offensive, and

Mickey Ds had to remove it. Although McDonald's was eventually forgiven its mistake, the Chinese are watching the business closely to make sure it doesn't make similar mistakes again.

Breaking through the business barriers

Several strategies seem to have worked for companies going into China. After five years of research, Peter Williamson and Ming Zeng — researchers at INSEAD in Singapore — now endorse some strategies that can improve your company's chances of succeeding in China:

- **Keep prices low.** Most unsuccessful companies entered the market at the high end of the price scale, which is a very small portion of the market, existent only in the major cities.

- **Work hard to get your costs down.** You want to be able to compete more effectively with local companies.

- **Get closer to the customer.** Using distribution channels with a lot of intermediaries just doesn't work well in China.

- **Do more of your research and development in China.** You want to be as close to your customers as possible so you can better meet their needs and get to market quicker.

In addition to Williamson and Zeng's suggestions, you may want to consider doing the following things:

- **Find a local partner.** Doing so makes it easier for your company to be accepted in the market, and you can figure out the local ways of doing business much more quickly. For example, Procter & Gamble sells its own brands of shampoo as well as the Chinese brand Jiejua through its Chinese partners, Hutchinson China Trade Company and the Guangzhous government's Construction Import & Export Corporation.

- **Sell direct to the customer.** One of the most successful U.S. companies to try this strategy is Avon, the cosmetics company. Avon executives understood that if they went through the normal Chinese distribution channels, the price of the company's products would skyrocket beyond the buying power of the target audience. So, the company decided to go where its customers were. They went to the factories where the women worked and sold directly to them. We should also mention that Avon, too, found a local partner to help it through the red tape.

- **Beat the Chinese to the market.** If you can get your product into China before the Chinese introduce a similar product, you have a great chance of success. Because the Chinese have an aversion to uncertainty, they generally seek out Chinese products first, which makes getting a foot in the door very difficult for foreign companies.

If you're truly interested in doing business in China, check out *Doing Business in China For Dummies,* by Robert Collins and Carson Block (Wiley).

India: Outsourcing heaven

India is home to one of the oldest civilizations in the world, dating back 5,000 years. It's also the world's largest democracy, with more than one billion people (and the world's second most populous country). It has become a popular choice for companies seeking outsourced skilled workers in telecommunications (call center support) and information systems (IT support). And the country is known for its expertise in hospitality, airlines, and retail.

Many multinational companies have benefited enormously from offshoring some of their processes to India (see Chapter 2 for more on offshoring). For example, GE saves about $350 million annually by sending around 900 processes to India. India's niche — and what differentiates it from China — is its focus on knowledge services that require skills, judgment, and discretion. Some of these knowledge services include

- Tax preparation
- Computer programming
- Market research
- Patent writing

India has moved up the value chain and left the low-paying, routine-type jobs to other countries. Is this bad news for U.S. companies? Not really. Most companies that utilize Indian resources are seeing huge productivity improvements, which enable them to do more business efficiently and effectively.

If you're interested in discovering more about what India has to offer your organization on a global level, check out *Doing Business in India For Dummies*, by Ranjini Manian (Wiley).

The European Union: Finding common selling ground

Europe is a difficult region to do business in, because there's no such thing as a European culture. Enormous differences exist among the countries in the European Union (EU). The simplistic approach to understanding these differences is recognizing what marketers often call the contrast between the "spaghetti culture" of the south and the "potato culture" of the north. These labels refer to the propensity of Italians to prefer pasta and northern European countries, such as Ireland, to prefer potatoes. But, of course, that contrast leaves out the middle. Where do you put France?

Marketers have found that where cultural variances are small, products move freely back and forth across borders. Such is the case in the Scandinavian countries. But where cultural differences are huge — between France and Germany, for instance — products that do well in one country may not do well in the other.

We bet you didn't know that countries have genders — at least when it comes to their advertising orientation. This is one way marketing people classify the variations in European markets. Some countries, such as Austria and Italy, are considered to be more masculine countries, because their people tend to be attracted to advertisements for products that are more assertive and achievement-oriented. Other countries, such as The Netherlands and Denmark, are considered more feminine in their orientation, because advertisements that show concern for the environment or that champion the underdog often do well.

One trick to successfully market your products in Europe is to find cross-cultural clusters, such as age. Children have commonalities across all cultures, so you can design and provide products that touch those commonalities. By the same token, however, don't assume that you can judge European children by looking at U.S. children. European children, for example, tend to play more with educational toys, whereas U.S. children prefer action toys. Young, European professionals, however, are more likely to adopt U.S. products along with the more traditional European products.

One problem you don't have to worry about as much anymore? Money. The introduction of the Euro makes the problem of currency exchange much easier for most businesses. You have a bit more control over prices and profits if one medium of exchange is common for most European countries.

Mexico: Doing business with a neighbor

The first thing to understand about Mexico is the distinction between the classes:

- ✔ Seventy percent of the Mexican population lives in poverty.
- ✔ One percent is very wealthy.
- ✔ Seven percent are middle class.
- ✔ Twelve percent are lower-middle class.

This economic situation presents a unique challenge to anyone trying to sell products in Mexico. In addition, Mexico is a large country with diverse consumer tastes, ranging from very traditionally Mexican to more U.S./Canadian. Here are a few examples:

- ✔ In the far south, home to the Mayan tribes, the culture is more like that of Central America, which is very tribal in nature and somewhat volatile in terms of its governments. This group is a very difficult nut to crack because it typically doesn't have a need for most U.S. products. It will take a significant amount of research to penetrate this group.

✔ In the central part of Mexico, the people hold their traditions dear, but there seems to be pent-up demand for more modern products. This is a good target for most U.S. products.

✔ The northern part of Mexico is heavily influenced by the United States and, therefore, is more accepting of U.S. products. This area is probably the best for entry into the Mexican market.

In general, the Mexican people are a very proud people who don't like talking about themselves. This cultural factor can make it difficult for companies to do market research. Moreover, linguistic barriers may be difficult to overcome. For example, many U.S. business phrases, such as "shelf space" or "mass customization," don't translate easily into Spanish, so you may want to work with a native speaker to find the appropriate phrases to describe what you're trying to say.

Mexicans often are very family oriented; consequently, when presenting the benefits of your product, you may want to show consumers how it will help their families. (Some say that this is a refreshing change from the "what's in it for me" attitude in the U.S. consumer market.)

Understanding the Role of Foreign Agents and Other International Types

You may think that foreign agents are found only in Tom Clancy novels, and that they work for the CIA or some foreign government. But in the business world, *foreign agents* aren't nearly so glamorous; they are, in fact, the workhorses who help make your life easier when you sell products/services in another country.

Every country in the world has a bevy of agents, trading companies, and sales representatives who specialize in importing U.S. goods. You need to be aware of the differences among the three:

✔ **Agents** purchase your company's products at a large discount off list price and then sell them in their countries and take responsibility for collections. This takes a huge load off your company's back, because any dealings with foreign countries tend to be costly and time-consuming.

You must realize, though, that when you sell to an agent, you lose control of what happens with your product after the sale. If an agent marks up the price too high to make some extra money, you may lose customers.

✔ **Export trading companies (ETCs)** typically specialize in a certain country or region and maintain a large force of sales representatives. Some ETCs even specialize in particular products. Here's how it works: The sales reps report back to the ETC that a country needs a specific product. The ETC then locates a manufacturer, buys the product, and sells it to the foreign country. Trading companies are the most common way that people export to Japan, for instance.

✔ **Sales representatives** work on commission and don't buy or warehouse your products. Typically, they find outlets for the sale of your products by operating as independent reps or as reps for export trading companies. The advantage of using reps is that they usually require little or no sales training. Moreover, because they know the country in which they deal, they aren't as likely to make cultural faux pas, which can be deadly to your business.

If your company is small and can't afford the services of a foreign agent (or if no agent is available in the area you're considering), you can place an ad in U.S. trade journals that showcase U.S. products internationally. Foreign companies may then contact you about distributing your product in their countries. Agents are one type of intermediary, but there are others and we discuss them in the next section.

Choosing your intermediary

We can't stress enough the importance of doing your homework before selecting an intermediary (an agent, rep, distributor, or export trading company) to represent your company in a foreign country. Remember, this person/organization is speaking for you and can affect the future of your company. Here are some good homework tips:

✔ **Find a good intermediary who is a referral from a satisfied customer.** Talk to business owners who are doing business in the countries you're interested in to see whom they're using. A name that comes up frequently may be a good lead. Asking your customers, on the other hand, may not be such a good idea because they probably don't want you to use an intermediary; it will cost them more!

✔ **Check with the Department of Commerce at 800-USA-TRADE.** Employees can't officially recommend individuals, but they can give you a list of qualified intermediaries in your industry.

✔ **Go to trade shows.** For some trade shows, the Department of Commerce sets up a booth for U.S. companies at a very low rate. You can gain access to top agents who exhibit there. You can also watch how the agents deal with potential customers.

Of course, you may want to draw up a contract with a seemingly qualified inter-mediary right away, but don't be eager to sign just yet. Here are a few more things you need to do before settling on a person who seems to check out:

- ✔ Ask for a current listing of the products that the intermediary carries to make sure your products are compatible and fit within the intermediary's expertise.

- ✔ Check to see whether the intermediary also handles your competitors' products. (Do you really want that situation?)

- ✔ Make sure that the intermediary has enough sales reps to cover the area in the country in which you want to do business.

- ✔ Check out the intermediary's sales volume to make certain that the number is showing a consistent level of growth over time.

- ✔ Find out whether the intermediary has enough warehouse space, as well as an up-to-date communication system.

- ✔ Look at his/her marketing plan to discover how the intermediary plans to promote your products.

- ✔ Check to see whether the intermediary has the ability to handle the servicing of your products. If not, you need to plan for another solution.

When working with an export trading company, try to find one that wants to partner with you — in other words, it will work with you to grow the international markets that you're interested in.

Putting your agreement in writing

We don't know how many times we've advised people to put agreements in writing. Taking this precaution doesn't mean that you're superstitious, nega-tive, or certain that things are going to go badly. It means that you recognize that things happen, and you want to have a mechanism in place to take care of them when they do. Your agreement with a foreign agent or intermediary needs to spell out the terms and conditions of the arrangement, and you need to consult with an attorney who specializes in overseas contracts, which are different from domestic agreements in many regards.

One of the most important clauses in a foreign agent agreement is the *perfor-mance clause*. Let us warn you that most intermediaries boldly ask for an exclusive five- to ten-year contract. You need to stand firm for a one- or two-year contract based on performance. After all, do you want to tie up your distribution capability in a foreign country if your intermediary there isn't selling enough products to make the arrangement worthwhile?

With the help of an attorney, here are some other recommended clauses you want in any foreign agent agreement to protect your business and to make sure that you're getting what you expect:

- **Aim for a nonexclusive contract that allows you to use other distributors as well.** This option gives you flexibility and more control over the situation.

- **Identify the specific products that the intermediary may handle.** Don't give a blanket agreement for all your products now and in the future! You may develop new products that you don't want this particular intermediary to handle. Protect your ability to withhold your property.

- **Define the territories for which the intermediary is responsible.** You want to eliminate confusion when you add other intermediaries.

- **Spell out the specific duties and responsibilities.** This should be done for both the intermediary and your company so you can manage expectations and avoid conflicts.

- **Include a statement of your agreed-upon sales quotas and performance expectations.** In other words, spell out what sales level the intermediary needs to reach by a certain date. Quotas and performance dates are negotiable; the more valuable your product is to the intermediary, the more clout you have in determining those figures.

- **Make sure that your home base is the jurisdiction in the agreement.** All agreements should have a statement regarding the jurisdiction for any disputes that may occur. You don't want to have to fly off to a foreign country to settle a dispute.

Avoid headaches: Using a freight forwarder

Although you can survive without a freight forwarder when doing business on a global stage, using one can definitely lessen your stress level. *Freight forwarders* are worth their weight in gold; their job is to handle all aspects of delivering your product to the customer. The following outlines exactly what a freight forwarder does:

- **Transportation:** Freight forwarders move product from the producer to the customer on land or over sea.

- **Documentation:** This task is the real headache. Shipping documents include a *bill of lading,* which is the contract between the shipper and the carrier, and an *exporter declaration form,* which details the contents of the shipment. These documents must be correct down to the last letter and point of punctuation; if not, your shipment may be delayed, or, worse, your order may be cancelled.

> ✔ **Collection:** The freight forwarder presents the shipping documents to your company's bank for collection. If you're shipping hazardous materials or certain food substances, for example, you're responsible for getting any licenses or certificates you may need and providing them to the freight forwarder.

The method you use to ship your product — land, air, sea — determines the product's cost in a foreign country. If you want to ship by container on ships, you should fill a container to reduce your costs. If you aren't shipping enough units to fill an entire container, you may be able to find someone else who's shipping to the same location who can share a container with you. Just make sure that your documentation is correct. Sometimes the freight forwarder can help you with this task. Otherwise, you'll need to find another company that is shipping to your destination so you can share a container.

Considering the Price of Global Growth

Many businesspeople mistakenly think that if you get a large order from a foreign source, banks will be clamoring to give you money so you can buy the raw materials you need to fill the order. Nothing could be further from the truth. Export lenders, just as with other lenders, want to know that you have the resources to fill the orders.

Now, if you secure a guarantee of payment from a governmental agency such as the Export-Import Bank of the United States, you limit the risk to the bank itself, and the bank's representatives are more likely to lend to you. Another alternative, if you can do it, is to ask the foreign buyer to pay an upfront deposit — enough to pay for the raw materials. Other strategies for financing global growth include obtaining private-investor capital, venture capital, and internal cash flow from your business.

The bottom line: To grow globally, you need the finances to back your business. This section looks at the most important document you need and what to do when you're ready to make a sale.

Getting a letter of credit

One of the most important documents in a global transaction is the *letter of credit (LC)*. This bank document is a guarantee that a customer's bank drafts (checks), up to a specified amount, are good for a specific period of time. The foreign buyer usually places the letter of credit in an escrow-type account, and the escrow company releases the money to your company at the same time the goods are released to the foreign buyer.

The letter of credit is another case where accuracy counts. Many things can invalidate a letter of credit, including the following:

- ✔ Your company fails to meet the ship date.

- ✔ Any typos, errors, or differences between the shipping documents (see the earlier section "Avoid headaches: Using a freight forwarder") and the letter of credit can invalidate the contract. Make sure that you have a clean airway bill or ocean bill of lading, in which the wording and spelling are exactly as they appear on the LC.

- ✔ Any variances in weight and size can invalidate the contract.

To prevent any LC disasters, create the details of the LC so that it protects you. If you control the wording of the LC, you can state that the goods become the customer's responsibility when the goods are in the customer's warehouse. But what happens if the ship hits a bad storm on the way and sinks or is raided by pirates (not too common, but not unheard of)? Then you become responsible for the loss. Or what if the customs official doesn't release the goods when they arrive without an under-the-table payment (otherwise known as a bribe)? Who takes care of that little problem if you let the customer determine where it will accept the shipment? The best way to protect your business is to make your shipment to the customer *FOB factory* (freight on board). That way, the customer is legally responsible for the goods from the moment they leave your factory.

Here are some additional tips to make financing your exporting life easier:

- ✔ Use your bank as the escrow holder and adviser to the transaction so that you can feel more confident that things will go smoothly.

- ✔ Put an *at-sight clause* in the LC. This clause ensures that when the documents listed in the LC are presented to the advising bank (your bank), you get paid within five days.

- ✔ Make absolutely certain that you can meet any shipping date you put on the LC. That means being sure that nothing can delay production. Give yourself some leeway. Remember Murphy's Law: If anything can go wrong, it will!

- ✔ Place the internal bank reference number on all documents to avoid having them rejected.

- ✔ Be sure that the expiration date for the LC is at least one month after the ship date. You want to give yourself enough time to get all the documents together and present them to the bank.

- ✔ Don't put minute details on the LC; doing so increases your chance of error. Details can go on packing lists, invoices, and purchase orders.

- ✔ Don't allow for *transshipments,* which means taking goods from one aircraft or vessel and placing them on another. For example, suppose that your customer's site is in the middle of the Moroccan desert. Don't take responsibility for having the cargo off-loaded and then placed on camels for the final journey to your customer's site. You run a huge risk of damage or loss.

✔ Allow for partial shipments — which means that you don't ship the entire order at one time — because this allowance can speed up payments and help your cash flow.

When it's time to make a sale

Picture this: You've just introduced a new product that you spent four long years developing, patenting, and manufacturing. It's now ready for introduction into the domestic market. You get your first units into the market and all of a sudden, people are offering to represent you in other countries, with big purchase orders in hand. It's very enticing to just grab them and run.

But before you start planning where you'll spend all your new-found money, you better find out a few things about your foreign buyer. For instance, you need to understand the country's payment patterns and whether it has any creditor protection laws. You also need to investigate your customer's credit history. Providing a big purchase order is easy; making good on that order is another thing entirely. If you extend credit to a company in another country, you are, for all intents and purposes, extending it to the country. Make sure that the country you pick is relatively stable and friendly to foreign companies. You can check out your potential foreign customer through your international bank, accounting firm, or most major credit reporting services.

Knowing Where to Go for Help

Taking your company into global markets can be an exhilarating time if you do your research first and build a global resource network that includes many resources for help:

✔ The U.S. Commerce Department and the U.S. Chambers of Commerce (if your company is a U.S. corporation)

✔ An international law firm

✔ A big four or equivalent accounting firm

✔ A large institutional investment bank

✔ An international representative

Smart businesspeople understand that you can't simply arrive in a country and immediately do business. It takes time to build the trusting relationships that eventually lead to sales.

Fortunately, for those of you in the United States, you're not alone in your efforts to begin dealing in the global market. You have many resources available to turn to in times of need. This section outlines a few of your other options.

For our readers in Canada, Mexico, Great Britain, France, Germany, Japan, China, and elsewhere, although you can't directly take advantage of the many international trade services sponsored by the U.S. government, your country has its own program that works in much the same way. Use the Internet, ask around, check with your government ministries, and find out what's available to you. You may be pleasantly surprised!

Hitting the road: Trade shows and trade missions

Trade shows often are mistakenly thought of as places to make sales. Although that does happen, it probably won't happen for a new company at a show. It's better to think of trade shows as places to get leads and to do research on the industry and your competitors. You also can find foreign agents there to represent you in another country (see the earlier section "Understanding the Role of Foreign Agents and Other International Types").

Attending a trade show in another country is a lot more complicated than attending one in the United States, however. Be sure to remember the following tips to make the experience go more smoothly:

- ✔ Make sure you bring copies of all the documents you received from the organizer of the trade show. That way, when your booth space isn't where you thought it was, you can prove you reserved and paid for it.

- ✔ You want to carry a detailed customs document, called a *carnet,* which lists all the valuables you take out of the United States. This document prevents you from running into problems with foreign customs agents who may think you purchased items in their country.

- ✔ Bring less of your product and more of your brochures because people in most other countries don't buy on impulse. They like to take a brochure and think about it for a while.

- ✔ Rent any presentation equipment you need instead of carting it all the way from the United States and enduring the customs inspections. Renting equipment also means that you don't have to worry about the different voltages and electrical plug configurations overseas.

Going on a trade mission has been a successful way for some companies to crack new markets. Trade missions, offered by the Department of Commerce and some private agencies, are designed to give businesses an opportunity to make contacts in foreign countries. A *trade mission* consists of an intense round of interviews and discussions in a number of cities during a period of about two to three weeks. Business owners get training prior to going and are matched with appropriate agents, distributors, or partners in the regions where they're going. To be selected for a trade mission, you need to produce a product that's on the "best prospect" list for a particular region. A trade mission costs between $500 and $4,000, depending on where you go.

You can find out more about trade missions by calling 800-USA-TRADE.

Calling on Uncle Sam

If you've never heard of the Overseas Private Investment Corporation (OPIC), you probably haven't been missing anything, because the OPIC is mostly known as the federal agency that provides political risk insurance for giant multinational companies investing in developing and emerging countries. But recently, the OPIC has recognized that disappearing global barriers are creating opportunities for smaller companies as well. Because small companies also are concerned about political risks and securing resources to go global, the OPIC has decided to reach out to businesses with annual revenues less than $250 million. It has done so by lowering its minimum loan guarantees to $100,000 and providing direct loans and loan guarantees up to $250 million.

The OPIC also has its own version of a micro-loan program for businesses with revenues less than $35 million, allowing them to borrow up to $10 million. You can find out more about the OPIC at www.opic.gov/smallbusiness.

Uncle Sam also offers the Commercial Service of the U.S. Department of Commerce, which is the trade-promotion unit of the International Trade Administration. With the help of this service, you can find trade specialists in 107 U.S. cities and more than 80 countries around the world, designed to help you secure sales in global markets. These specialists provide resources for market research, counseling, seminars, reports on foreign firms, and contact services. You can discover more about this service at www.ita.doc.gov/cs.

Chapter 5

Polish Your Crystal Ball for Some Strategic Planning

*F*or decades, executives of large companies have met in back rooms or in expensive resort retreats to strategize about the future of their companies. Although the strategies they devised often were very creative and visionary, the executives rarely considered the fact that the environments on which they based their strategies might change completely within a year or more. All it would take is for a company working in stealth mode to emerge with a new product — a product that made theirs obsolete, changing the whole ballgame instantly. Look at how Apple changed the digital music landscape overnight with the iPod, which overcame the mistakes made by industry pioneers Eiger Labs and Rio who didn't see this strategy coming.

So, what exactly does "strategy" mean for today's organization? A *strategy* is a plan of action that's mid- to long-term in duration and is designed to help your company achieve its broad mission. So, if your company's mission is to be number one in its market by 2010, the strategies you develop should form a plan of action for getting the company to that position.

However, the global business landscape isn't static; rather, it's in a constant state of change, so strategies must reflect the very real possibility that they'll need to be modified in the future.

Good strategic plans involve those individuals who are close to the market and deeply involved in the operations of the business. They include a cross-section of stakeholders in the organization — everyone from the customer to the worker on the factory floor. Strategic planners must be able to address long-term and short-term issues that face the organization. Although it may seem like a lot to think about, there is no need to worry. In this chapter, we look at the nature of strategic planning in a world that waits for no one and prepare you to do it effectively.

Comparing Strategy and Tactics

A *strategy* is a plan for achieving a major organizational objective. Objectives are important for a number of reasons:

- ✔ They give everyone a set of guidelines and a focus.
- ✔ They help motivate everyone to achieve.
- ✔ They provide a basis for measuring achievement.

Tactics, on the other hand, are the methods for carrying out the strategy. Marketing guru Seth Godin uses a skiing analogy to explain the difference. He says that negotiating turns on a ski slope requires great tactical skills that must be executed perfectly. But choosing the right place to ski is strategy. He claims that everyone skis better in Utah! Basically, the strategy sets you up so you can perform the tactics flawlessly, all conditions being perfect (which they never are).

The boundary between top management and middle management, and who does strategy and who does tactics, is quickly eroding in today's dynamic and complex marketplace. Today, strategy has seeped down into the lowest levels of management in the organization; at the same time, a CEO who doesn't understand tactics can't ensure that strategies are properly executed. The following sections take a more in-depth look at the various categories of organizational goals and the strategic planning process.

Strategic goals

Strategic goals generally are developed by top management and focus on broad issues that affect the company overall. Some examples of strategic goals are

- ✔ Growth
- ✔ Raising capital
- ✔ Reducing employee turnover
- ✔ New product development

But more and more, the responsibility for designing and implementing strategic goals is being shared with lower-level management and operations people — in other words, people closest to the market. In a time when global market conditions fluctuate rapidly (see Chapter 4), it's a very dangerous practice to rely on strategic plans and goals developed solely in the ivory towers of upper management, far removed from the street.

For example, product planners often have difficulty forecasting demand so that they can order the correct amount of raw material and schedule production efficiently (see Chapter 18). Some companies have formed departments of analysts to crank out copious volumes of numbers in an effort to correctly forecast needs. But the only thing you can ever be certain of is that the forecasts will always be off. Consequently, many companies are, for the most part, overstocked with costly inventory. Today, smart companies are approaching this problem not with forecasting tools, but with a strategy focused on more efficient and faster production times. They respond to actual market demand with rapid production. They order raw materials as needed and produce products as needed. So, strategic planning for production is now done on the factory floor rather than in the executive penthouse.

Tactical goals

Tactical goals generally are developed by middle managers or those directly responsible for executing a strategy. The purpose of tactical goals is to work out ways to make strategies happen. You can see some examples of tactical goals and their related strategies in Table 5-1.

Table 5-1	Strategies versus Tactics
Strategy	*Tactic*
25% year over year growth	Create a marketing campaign that targets a new customer segment.
Raising $5 million in investor capital	Attend a venture capital networking conference.
Reducing employee turnover	Develop an employee incentive program.

The metaphor most commonly used to describe tactics is that tactics are to the battle what strategy is to the war. Strategy is the big picture, and tactics are the steps taken to achieve the strategy. Where strategy generally is concerned with resources, market environment, and the mission of the company, tactics usually deal more with people and actions. In essence, tactics are about execution. To effectively execute a tactical plan requires that you take the following actions:

- ✔ Look at all the possible alternatives before proceeding.
- ✔ Give all those involved in executing the tactical plan the resources and the level of authority they need to do their part.
- ✔ Make sure that effective modes of communication are in place to minimize conflict or overlap of activities.
- ✔ Continuously monitor progress to ensure that you're on target.

Operational goals

Line managers — those who deal directly with the product — typically create *operational goals,* which are usually very narrow in focus and can be accomplished relatively quickly. Operational goals and plans come in many forms. Want to see them all at a glance? Look at Table 5-2 for an overview of common operational plans.

Table 5-2	Common Operational Plans
Type of Plan	*How It's Used*
One-time plans	Used to carry out an action that is not expected to be repeated.
Programs	Contains a large number of activities, such as a set of procedures for hiring and retaining technical employees.
Projects	Usually smaller and less complex than a program. For example, a project can be the development of an employee manual.
Standing plans	Used to manage activities that occur regularly during a longer period of time.
Policies	Guidelines for how the organization will respond in any particular situation, including any exceptions to typical responses. For example, a policy may state that technical employees must have a college education.

Type of Plan	How It's Used
Standard operating procedures (SOPs)	Describes the steps that employees must follow in a particular situation. For example, an HR manager may 1) check an applicant's résumé for the requisite college education; 2) call the college to verify the information; and 3) mark in the file that the candidate has met that requirement.
Rules and regulations	Takes the decision making out of the planning and execution process by stating emphatically what must be done. For example, a rule may state that the HR manager can override the requirement that applicants have a college education if the manager secures the signature of the Chief Operating Officer. There is no decision-making power in this directive.
Contingency plans	Takes into consideration what the company should do if the original plans can't be realized due to some unforeseen change in the environment. Contingency plans generally answer "what-if" questions.

Scanning the New Business Horizon

Don't make the mistake of thinking that strategic planning takes place only inside the organization — preferably behind closed doors, in rooms with plenty of coffee, bagels, charts, spirited banter, and brainstorming. That's only one way that strategic planning takes place, and it may not even be the most important way, as this chapter explains. A whole host of external environmental factors have a major impact on the planning you do for your business. This section takes a look at three of the most important factors: customers, dynamic markets, and competition.

Do you really know your customers?

One of the themes of this book is the importance of knowing your customers and involving them in your business. Today, customers are jaded by a selection of products and services that overwhelm them with choices. In some markets, customers no longer rush to buy things on sale, because a sale is always going on somewhere. Because customers have so many choices, they're more demanding. Levels of quality that were considered "above and beyond" only a short time ago are now considered minimum quality standards. You now have to go way beyond those old standards to grab your customers' attention.

Brand loyalty is declining, so businesses have to work much harder to keep their customers. Keeping customers is paramount, because a customer becomes more valuable over time from repeat purchases and referrals. Therefore, the solution to planning in this new, very complex marketplace lies in building long-term customer relationships built on trust. And you can't gain the trust of your customers if you don't interact with them. (For some important tips on building long-term customer relationships, check out Chapter 15.)

Riding the market rollercoaster

Market research has been the foundation of most strategic planning. Unfortunately, traditional market research has formed the basis for most of the market information that companies have used to do their planning (see Chapter 15). That kind of information typically is too general to be of much use in specific markets. The information you really need for planning purposes comes directly from the customer.

A classic case of the failure to listen to the voice of the customer is the introduction of New Coke, the beverage that taught Coca-Cola some important lessons. Coca-Cola, in an effort to break out of the Coke-Pepsi wars, decided to tweak its famous formula. It based the decision on faulty market research, in which they asked consumers if they would buy a product that tastes better than Pepsi but was still a Coke. Consumers, without ever having tasted the product, responded with a resounding "Yes!" However, Coca-Cola failed to ask the most important question: "Why?" The company went ahead and launched the product based on its feedback, and it was a disaster. At the end of 77 days, Coca-Cola reintroduced Classic Coke with great fanfare, telling its customers that it had made a mistake. Fortunately for Coca-Cola, their loyal customers became even more loyal.

Customers, however, sometimes don't readily reveal what they really want. Often they give the easiest, most expedient answer to a question such as "What do you think of this product?" No one wants to intentionally hurt someone's feelings, even if it is a big company like Coca-Cola. If you don't spend time out in the market listening to real people, you're taking a big chance that the information being used by your company doesn't reflect the real feelings of the customer. If the info doesn't match up, the strategies you devise won't hit the mark.

Keeping up with the changing competition

In the past, a business could create a sustainable competitive advantage — relatively easily — through such things as a unique market segment, lower costs, product/service differentiation, and superior execution. In today's fast-changing, global marketplace, staying ahead of the competition isn't that easy. Superiority in one or more of those areas can certainly get you started, but you won't be able to sustain an advantage with those factors alone.

Many businesses now say that you literally have to ignore the competition to gain a competitive advantage. (Look at the nearby sidebar to discover how Cirque du Soleil used this strategy to capture a competitive advantage and new value for its customers.) The strategy of imitating your competition or one-upping them doesn't work as successfully as it used to.

The blue ocean strategy

Take a moment to think back to your childhood. If we say the word "circus," what comes to mind? For most people, it's a vision of elephants, clowns, and acrobats; sawdust on the floor; and vendors hawking cotton candy and popcorn during the show. If you love the circus and want to create a company to compete in that space, Ringling Bros. is pretty stiff competition — it's the 800-pound gorilla in the market!

But what if you strategized that the competition isn't important — that there must be some space out there in which Ringling Bros. doesn't compete. In other words, you want to find customers it doesn't serve — a clear blue ocean of "uncontested market space."

That's exactly what the founders of Cirque du Soleil did when they invented a new art form that combines the best elements of the circus with an upscale theatrical experience. Guy Laliberté is the CEO and mastermind behind Cirque du Soleil, one of Canada's biggest successes. The company began in 1984 when a group of street performers decided that they could play on a bigger stage. As they scanned the landscape, it didn't seem like a very auspicious time to start a new circus act because the circus business was definitely in decline as other forms of entertainment took over. But Laliberté wasn't going to start a traditional circus; he strategized that he could capture not only those people who enjoy the circus in its traditional form, but also those that seek a more cultured and sophisticated experience.

According to Kim and Mauborgne, who wrote *Blue Ocean Strategy,* what the creator of Cirque du Soleil did was capture new customers and offer them new value in the form of more sophisticated entertainment. But that isn't all he did. He also determined that to achieve the company's big goal of becoming the circus for the 21st century, it needed a strategy that emphasized efficiency and speed. It also required tactics that would enable the company to streamline its costs, thereby producing bigger profits it could plow back into the company to facilitate rapid growth.

You may think that CEOs similar to Laliberté are the norm, because what he wanted to do makes perfect sense, but they're not. In fact, their way of strategically thinking about the market definitely is in the minority. Why? Because most CEOs focus on the competition — they're so concerned with beating the competition that they miss opportunities to actually render the competition irrelevant. Today's companies need to think in terms of blue ocean strategy and do five important things:

1. Look for uncontested market space.

2. Ignore the competition — concentrate on making them irrelevant.

3. Create new value for customers.

4. Shatter the value/cost tradeoff.

5. Define a strategy that focuses the company on differentiation *and* low cost.

Today, the key to standing out from the crowd seems to be in achieving operational excellence. In other words, you need to make sure that all your systems and operations are the best they can be, and that they're aligned to perfection with your business strategies. Reaching those goals will take some planning from the bottom-up, not the top-down.

Designing Your Strategy Right the First Time

No one wants to spend time designing a strategy that doesn't work or doesn't fit with the overall goals of the company. A well-designed strategic plan can do the following for your company:

- ✔ Provide information across the entire organization that may not otherwise be available.

- ✔ Force management to look at the big picture: Where are we going?

- ✔ Force people to communicate about goals and resources to achieve those goals.

- ✔ Create a sense of common focus and direction toward an agreed-upon goal.

You must turn your planning into behavior. It's all well and good to say that you want your company to increase sales by 50 percent in the coming year, but exactly how are you going to make that happen? What strategies and tactics will you set? Also, planners too often focus on structural changes and requirements, such as the plant and equipment, and never consider the human side of things — such as evaluation and reward systems and management development. What are you specifically going to do to provide incentives for your employees? (For more on incentives, see Chapter 7.)

Something New: Strategic Improvising

Face it: Doing business is a lot more difficult today than it used to be (don't tell that to the old timers). You certainly can't rest on your laurels, especially when someone is out there just waiting for the chance to puncture your happy balloon. That's where strategic improvising comes into play. *Strategic improvising* is a proactive approach to strategic planning where the entrepreneur is constantly scanning the business environment to look for trends — early patterns that signal a change is about to happen. It beats being smacked in the face with something you weren't expecting.

Getting surprised by something it wasn't expecting is exactly what happened to MP3. It had been the dominant player for digital music downloads until Apple Computer surprised the music world with the introduction of the iPod. Surprise was also in the cards for Sony's ACID, which dominated desktop music-editing software until Apple released GarageBand, its music-editing suite. In fact, through a process of strategic improvising, Apple was able to beat first-to-market technologies with the iPod, iTunes, iMovie, and GarageBand. Bravo! This section takes a closer look at strategic improvising and what you can do to help give your business an advantage.

Keep your head up

You can't see what's coming if your head is buried in the sand like the proverbial ostrich. And many business owners do just that. They become so caught up in the day-to-day activities of their businesses that they never stop to see what's coming down the road.

Strategic improvising must be a regular activity of your company, not something you do where there's nothing else to do (we find that business owners rarely have nothing else to do!). Regularly scanning the environment for changes that might affect your business will ensure that you have time to prepare to meet those changes. To make sure that your company is keeping its eyes on the business environment, we recommend doing the following:

- ✔ **Encourage everyone, from management employees to mailroom workers, to read trade journals for your industry.** You can't stay competitive and meet the needs of your customers if your focus is completely inside the business. You can now find many of these journals on the Internet.

- ✔ **Attend trade association meetings and business conferences.** Here you can network with others in your industry and get the latest information and hear the latest rumors on who's doing what.

- ✔ **Make sure that everyone stays close to the customer so that you're always up-to-date on their changing needs.** You can do that by talking to customers on the phone, by bringing them to your company for a visit or tour, or by giving them access to your company via a Web site (see Chapter 15).

The bottom line is that as you begin to think about strategic planning for your organization, you should think about it in terms of the changing environment in which your company is operating. Don't plan so rigidly that you forget to change your plans before the environment changes and it's too late. Here's a checklist of questions to ask yourself to make sure that you're planning for change in your organization:

1. What's the overriding mission for our company?

   _____

   _____

   _____

2. What goals do we have to reach to achieve our mission?

   _____

   _____

   _____

3. What's our company doing to encourage everyone to stay current on what's happening in the industry?

   _____

   _____

   _____

4. What are we doing to gather competitive intelligence so that we can find the blue-ocean markets (see the earlier sidebar "The blue ocean strategy")?

   _____

   _____

   _____

5. How are our employees, at all levels of the organization, participating in our strategic planning process?

   _____

   _____

   _____

6. In what ways are we staying close to our customers?

   _____

   _____

   _____

Power to the people

Today's employees want the ability to make a difference in their organizations. They want to have the opportunity to grow and develop their skills in a way that benefits their companies. In a word, today's employees want empowerment. Given that, the traditional top-down style of strategic planning and management just doesn't work anymore (see Chapter 6 for more on managing today). You need to give employees the opportunity to participate in the strategic planning for the future of the company. Their participation and drive will be important when you're ready to execute your plans and to make a big impact in your industry and your market.

Here's how you can get your employees involved in strategic planning and improvising:

- ✓ Have the various work groups in your organization meet individually to come up with at least one goal they'd like to achieve in the next six months. Also, ask them to think of one or more goals they want to achieve in the next year.

- ✓ Ask each work group to meet with management to discuss these goals and to formulate strategies and tactics to achieve them. These strategies and tactics should reflect a solid understanding of what's happening in the business environment (see the earlier section "Keep your head up").

- ✓ Management should then be prepared to discuss with each team how the stated goals will help the company meet its grand mission. In that way, all employees in the organization understand that they're contributing an important piece to the puzzle, and they'll be more likely to work harder to achieve their goals.

- ✓ Present the goals of each team to the entire organization. Doing this ensures that the goals of one team don't negatively affect the goals of another. This exercise is important for all employees because it enables them to clearly see that what they do affects everyone else and the company as a whole.

Employing a SWOT Analysis

One of the traditional jumping-off points in the development of strategies is a SWOT analysis (illustrated in Figure 5-1). *SWOT* is an acronym that stands for strengths, weaknesses, opportunities, and threats. The analysis is merely a guide for organizing your thinking about your company and the environment in which it operates. Strengths and weaknesses are part of the internal analysis of your organization. Opportunities and threats are part of the external analysis of the environment in which your company operates — in short, everything outside your organization that may affect it.

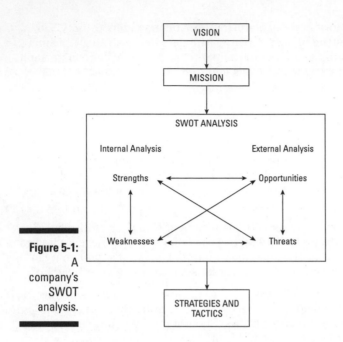

Figure 5-1:
A
company's
SWOT
analysis.

To conduct a SWOT analysis for your company, fill out the following brief form and see where your company stands. Then take a look at the sections that follow the form to get some ideas for how to look at your business and to see how the four components of a SWOT analysis interrelate:

1. What are my company's strengths?

   _____

   _____

   _____

2. What are my company's weaknesses?

   _____

   _____

   _____

3. What opportunities do I see for the future?

   _____

   _____

   _____

4. What are the threats that could prevent us from achieving our goals, and how will we deal with those threats?

_____

_____

_____

Examining your company's strengths

Your company's strengths are its skills, capabilities, and core competencies that work together to enable you to achieve your goals and objectives. Examples of strengths are an extraordinary team that works well together, a patented technology that you developed, or control of key distribution components.

Successful companies such as search-engine company Google capitalize on their strengths. One of Google's biggest strengths is its corporate culture. It's frequently labeled "one of the best companies to work for," and it takes pride in its creative and family oriented environment. Why is culture a strength? One of the biggest costs to any business is employees and employee turnover. If you keep employees happy, they won't want to leave, and they'll work harder to make sure your company succeeds. It's as simple as that; yet, most companies don't spend much time thinking about a strategy for improving their corporate cultures.

One or more of your strengths may become your competitive advantage in the marketplace. For example, suppose that your company is really good at coming up with innovative designs for new products. It's probably in your best interest to focus your efforts and resources on that strength to differentiate your company in the marketplace. Scattering scarce resources across too many diverse capabilities only weakens your competitive stance. You can outsource your weaknesses to other companies and focus on what you do best (see Chapter 18 for tips on outsourcing).

For example, many companies today outsource expensive manufacturing, distribution, and even payroll functions. Plenty of companies are leasing their employees back from PEOs (professional employer organizations), which take the tedious and time-consuming task of human-resource management from the companies so they can focus on their core competencies.

Evaluating your company's weaknesses

Your company's weaknesses (and every company has them) also play a role in your ability to achieve your goals. CEOs often can more easily describe their business' strengths than their weaknesses, generally because they don't like to admit that they have any weaknesses. Weaknesses are those skills, capabilities, and competencies that your company lacks and that prevent you from achieving your goals and objectives. If your company doesn't have a critical skill or capability that it needs to achieve a particular goal, you have three choices:

- ✔ Modify the goal to something achievable with the skill set you have.

- ✔ Raise the capital needed to acquire the skill or capability you need (see Chapter 14).

- ✔ Find another company that has the core competency you need and out-source that need or collaborate through a strategic partnership.

Suppose, for example, that you have a fast-food company that's known for its food and the ability to get it to the customer very quickly. Your weakness, however, is administering the business side of the business — accounting, payroll, and so forth. You should consider outsourcing those weaknesses to a company that specializes in providing these services to businesses.

Recognizing your company's opportunities and threats

Opportunities are those things that help your business grow to new levels. *Threats* are barriers to that growth. The classic books of Michael Porter on competitive strategy provide a framework for looking at the environmental factors that affect every business (*Competitive Strategy: Techniques for Analyzing Industries and Competitors,* and *Competitive Advantage: Creating and Sustaining Superior Performance* [Free Press]). These factors are worded as threats, but their corollary is really an opportunity. When you see a way around a barrier or threat, you're seeing an opportunity to move forward in the market.

Porter's basic assumption is that sustaining high performance levels requires a well-conceived strategy and a tactical plan based on how your industry works. He asserts that five forces affect the ultimate profit potential of a company. Here are Porter's five forces:

- ✔ **Threat of new entrants:** Barriers to entering an industry include economies of scale, brand loyalty, capital requirements, switching costs (the costs buyers incur in time and money to retrain staff and learn a new product or relationship), access to distribution channels, proprietary factors (for example, technology owned by someone else), and government regulations. If these barriers are very high, your company will need to be well funded (it takes a long time to tear down barriers) and find strategic partners to overcome them.

✔ **Threat from substitute products:** Substitute products may come from other industries, but they accomplish the same basic function as your product in a different way or at a different price. You need to know the likelihood that customers will use these substitutes and what it will cost them to switch to your product. If switching to your product is difficult or costly to the customer, you'll need to ensure that your marketing strategy educates the customer on the value of switching to your product (see Chapter 3 about the value proposition).

✔ **Threat from buyers' bargaining power:** Volume buyers in an industry can force down prices. In a world where a simple Internet search can provide buyers with an enormous amount of price information, buyers have a lot of bargaining power. Your ability to create complex products and services that can't easily be compared on price and that convey a strong benefit to the buyer will help you avoid competing solely on price.

✔ **Threat from suppliers' bargaining power:** Suppliers can exert pressure by threatening to raise prices or change quality or volume of supply. Here's where strategic improvising can really help. You should always have more than one supply source for anything you have to purchase to make your product. That way, if your main supplier hikes prices or runs low on materials, you can quickly switch to a backup supplier.

✔ **Threat from the rivalry among existing industry firms:** A highly competitive industry drives down profits and prices. Airline price wars are a good example of this situation. Competing on price is a no-win proposition. You need to compete on value, so making sure that buyers understand the benefit they receive from dealing with your company will be critical to your success. Again, a marketing strategy that's focused on a value message is important (see Chapter 15).

By looking at your industry from the five forces perspective, you can get a better sense of the opportunities and threats facing your business. Even when the environmental forces seem negative and threats appear to be more prevalent than opportunities, your business can still do well. For example, when steel companies were losing money in the 1980s and 1990s, an entrepreneurial upstart named Nucor Steel saw its stock prices skyrocket as the result of its lower overhead, mini-mill strategy.

Putting your company through a test

After you complete the SWOT analysis for your company and the environment in which it operates, you can ask four very important questions — sort of a final exam. Are you ready?

✔ **Do you have the resources and capabilities necessary to take advantage of opportunities in your environment and to neutralize the threats?** The answer you give today may not be the correct answer six months from now. The environment and its opportunities and threats are in a constant state of change, and that's why strategic improvising is a valuable skill to acquire.

✔ **How many competing firms already own the same valuable resources and competencies that your company has?** If several companies have the same resources and competencies you do, they probably won't be a source of competitive advantage for you. But they will be a barrier to entry for a new company trying to compete with you. Your mission is to find a competitive advantage that's unique to you.

✔ **If your company doesn't have a particular resource or capability, do you face a cost disadvantage in obtaining it?** If acquiring the resources and competencies you need will cost you a lot, catching up to your competitor's advantage in that area may be more difficult and take longer. However, if you can find a good substitute, you may be able to achieve competitive parity.

✔ **Is your company organized to take full advantage of its resources and capabilities?** To take full advantage of what you have, you need to create a good support structure that consists of control systems, a formal reporting structure, compensation policies, and technology. This way, when you start to grow, your strategies won't fall apart.

The bottom line: If you ensure that your company has strong resources and competencies, you can compete in nearly any environment — even if you appear to be facing few opportunities and many threats.

Planning for Success with Operational Innovation

One of the biggest trends in business during the past few years has been *process* or *operational innovation:* redesigning every aspect of a business in new ways to reduce costs, save time, or provide better service. What's the reasoning behind operational innovation? All systems — which include business organizations — are subject to *entropy,* a natural degradation that occurs over time. If your business strives to maintain its current status (never a good idea), ultimately you'll begin consuming your own resources just to survive and then you can't respond quickly when change occurs.

One of the best examples of the effects of entropy is what happened to IBM. IBM's managers believed that the company's enormous success would last indefinitely if they just kept the business in status quo. When the computer market suddenly changed, IBM was unprepared and dropped from its illustrious perch as the world's largest and most successful computer manufacturer. Microsoft, on the other hand, is an example of a large company that recognized — but almost too late — that the Internet was going to be a big thing. In a feat of re-engineering that should go down in the history books, Microsoft completely turned around its business and set its sights on this new frontier. It aligned its people and systems with strategies designed to establish a significant presence in the Internet market. This new strategy was critical to the company's continued growth.

And speaking of strategy, Google's auction methodology for ads that appear next to its search engine (Google AdWords) has been so successful, producing extraordinary revenues for the company, that Microsoft is now positioning itself to get into the ad revenue business. This proves once again that a spunky entrepreneurial company can push the 800-pound gorilla around a bit!

What operational innovation is all about

Be careful not to confuse the strategy of operational innovation with operational improvement, which really is just a way to achieve higher performance by using current methods. Operational innovation is about coming up with brand new ways of doing whatever processes are part of your business. The advantage of this strategy is that it's very difficult for a competitor to copy your operational plan. How many companies, for instance, have tried to achieve what Wal-Mart accomplished by using technology, such as RFID (radio frequency identification) to streamline how it purchases and distributes the products it sells? Because of process innovation, Wal-Mart was able to grow from $44 million in sales in 1972 to more than $44 billion in 1992.

Process innovations produce faster time-to-market and lower costs, which result in higher customer satisfaction and retention — a big payoff for any company that practices this strategy. Check out Chapter 18 for more info on the strategy.

Making process innovation work

Process innovation itself is quite simple. It has five components:

- ✔ Develops goals and a plan for fostering innovation in your company.
- ✔ Ensures that top management conveys its total commitment to the effort.
- ✔ Makes sure that everyone feels a sense of urgency.

Operational innovation usually has a better chance of working if it occurs under conditions of urgency. An urgent need is more easily felt by everyone in the organization, and the only way that innovation can be successful is if everyone commits to it.

- ✔ Starts the innovation effort by looking at your company as if you were starting from scratch. Anything goes.

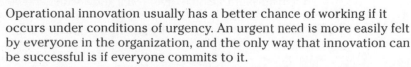

✔ Takes perspectives from the top of the organizational chart *and* the bottom. Meet in the middle with a new perspective that's comprised of the best of both positions.

Of course, any innovation strategy must begin with your customers. You need to ask your customers, "What are you trying to accomplish?" Then begin to find and put into place procedures and systems designed to meet those needs.

Measuring Strategic Planning Success

Unfortunately, the strategy-to-performance gap in most businesses is large because managers often fail to return to their plans to make sure they are on track to achieve their objectives. In fact, Michael Mankins and Richard Steel discovered some surprising results in their research of senior executives from 197 companies worldwide — companies that produced sales of more than $500 million. What they found was that less than 15 percent of these companies ever went back to their strategic plans to see if they actually had achieved their objectives! That apathy is astonishing when you consider how much time and effort went into creating and implementing those plans. Furthermore, the researchers learned that the strategies these companies executed delivered only 63 percent of potential performance. Putting those figures together, you can see why it's so important to put in place some metrics to measure your performance and then check your actual performance against the metrics on a regular basis.

This section takes a closer look at how you can set manageable benchmarks to measure your progress, how you can make adjustments, and how you can make accurate measurements.

Creating clear objectives

Suppose that one of your operational objectives is to increase productivity in the shipping department. Will you reach your objective when one more box a day goes out? Or will it take 500 boxes more a day to satisfy the objective? You need to state your objectives in measurable terms — for example, increase productivity in the shipping department by 50 percent per day, every day. With a clearly stated, measurable objective, you'll know when you've achieved it.

Try your hand at a little quiz. Look at the following list of objectives. Which ones are well-written?

✔ To reduce our inventory by 25 percent in six months.

✔ To increase sales this year.

> ✔ To reduce the employee turnover rate.
>
> ✔ To hire 20 new employees each month for the next six months.
>
> ✔ To beat our competitors.

Now, find out how you did. The well-written objectives are the first and the fourth bullets, because they display clearly measurable objectives. You'll know when you've achieved them. Now, how can you improve the other three objectives? Try rewriting them here:

To increase sales this year.

_____

To reduce the employee turnover rate.

_____

To beat our competitors.

_____

Now, check your responses against the following examples to see how you measure up:

To increase sales by 25 percent by December 31.

To reduce employee turnover by 30 percent in six months.

To sell 25 percent more product than our competitors by December 31.

As you can see, to produce effective objectives, you need to think about how you'll measure progress and performance.

Determining your metrics for success

When you turn goals into strategic action, you put them in a form that you can measure. In other words, you can now ask, "What's the benchmark point or metric for success?" Today, companies often have hundreds of metrics, old and new, competing for the attention of the decision makers. It's no wonder that so little is accomplished and that few people know what's important.

One large company in the video-surveillance industry, with about 1,800 employees, gears all its measures toward one overriding goal — fanatical customer satisfaction. So, the benchmark measures are simple: 100 percent on-time delivery, 100 percent quality, and 100 percent customer satisfaction. And, surprisingly enough, when the company doesn't reach its goals, it's off by only 0.03 percent! The financial goals for the company come second to its customer goals, but logically, when the company meets its customers' goals, it will also meet its financial goals.

Here are some tips for establishing meaningful metrics to measure progress toward your goals:

✔ Make your strategy statement simple and very tangible so that there's no confusion over how to achieve the objective.

✔ Ensure that your forecasts (the numbers you're attempting to achieve with your strategy) have underlying assumptions that align with market economics and the core competencies of your company.

✔ Make sure that the corporate management side of the business is speaking the same language as the functional side: marketing, finance, operations. That's the only way that both sides will know that the assumptions associated with the financial projections are reasonable and achievable.

✔ Talk about what resources you'll need to deploy — and when — early in the process. You don't want resources to become a stumbling block to executing your strategy.

✔ Identify and agree on your priorities. Every strategy is implemented through a series of tactics, but not all strategies and tactics are created equal. Depending on the availability of resources — human, operational, and financial — you may end up having to choose among several strategies, and then you have to choose among the tactics available to execute the most important strategy.

✔ Plan to monitor the specific drivers of performance on a regular basis. These are the activities that affect your bottom line, such as sales, occupancy rate, and turnover. If you stay on top of the drivers that are important to your business, when something deviates from your plan, you can respond and make corrections before things get too far off track.

✔ Reward execution. The people charged with implementing the strategic plan carry a very significant responsibility — arguably more important than the team that created the plan in the first place. If the "doers" don't have an incentive to drive the plan toward the objective, the plan will never be achieved. It's as simple as that.

Measuring during and after operations

Measuring and monitoring performance is the only way to ensure that your strategic plans meet your objectives. Measuring needs to occur during and after operations. Monitoring is an ongoing process to check the results of your measurements and keep you on track.

You can use four basic sets of measures to gauge progress toward your goals:

✔ **Leading measures** look at the immediate results of an operation and measure such things as defects, cycle time, time-to-customer, and break-even time. These measures give you a sense of the efficiency and effectiveness of the process.

✔ **Lagging measures** depict the results of completed operations over a period of time, and include such things as earnings, cash flow, revenue, customer satisfaction, market share, and so forth. These measures give you a sense of the effectiveness of the product/process as a whole.

✔ **Internal measures** gauge the effectiveness of the organization itself, and include such things as backlog, design costs, material costs, distribution costs, and end-product costs. But they also include non-cost-based measures such as percent of on-time delivery, number of new products, and design cycle time.

✔ **External measures** assess how the business performs in its environment, and include such things as the business's performance relative to its competitors, suppliers, and the marketplace in general. They also include cost-based measures, such as relative R&D expenditures and labor costs, and non-cost-based measures, such as number of repeat buyers and number of customer complaints.

Figuring out how to juggle

You want to measure many aspects of your business, but remember that you can't measure them in a vacuum. Anything that happens in one area of your business has a measurable impact on at least one other area. You need to know how to adjust for those effects.

One team of management strategists uses the example of a company whose objective was to maintain only one day's supply of inventory on hand. This objective improved cash flow considerably, but it also required the company to make some very fundamental (and potentially expensive) changes in the way it did business. Here's what that company needed to do to accomplish its objective:

✔ Reduce its manufacturing lead time.

✔ Put its parts on a just-in-time system (see Chapter 18).

✔ Design right the first time to avoid costly redesign.

✔ Invest in highly capable machine tools.

✔ Speed up machine setup.

✔ Schedule machine usage more effectively.

✔ Purchase high-quality components.

✔ Reduce the number of parts.

✔ Design products that are easy to manufacture.

Each of the tasks in the preceding list has its own measure of success. Suddenly, this seemingly simple objective has become quite complex for the company. It must weigh the gains from reducing inventory against the costs of setting up the process and equipment that will allow the reduction to occur. In short, the company must perform a juggling act. Now, throw another ball into the mix. The objective in this example is to maintain a one-day's supply of inventory on hand. We sugges ted some ways the company could make that happen if it plans to manufacture in-house. But what if the company outsourced its manufacturing to a company that's already on a just-in-time system? It could achieve the same goal with a different strategy. Isn't juggling fun?

Part of setting objectives, and ultimately measuring them, is weighing alternatives and judging the cost/benefit of each.

Part II

Managing a Business in the New World

The 5th Wave   By Rich Tennant

Remember Robin — lead, follow, or get out of the forest.

In this part . . .

Today, successfully managing a business is no easy task. For your benefit, in this part we consider the difference between managing and leading an organization, as well as the latest trends in leadership. We look at how to recruit and retain the best employees and then motivate and reward them so you can keep them for the long haul. We also examine one of the most important and effective tools in business today: employee teams.

Chapter 6

Managing Is Hard; Leading Is Even Harder

*T*he focus of management used to be a fairly simple proposition. According to most any traditional management textbook, all you had to do was master the four classic roles of management to achieve success: planning, organizing, leading, and controlling.

Today, however, the organizations that managers run and the environment in which those organizations operate are more complex. As a result, the profession of management is undergoing tremendous change. Leadership as a field of study also is undergoing change, brought about by the influence of entrepreneurship on leadership style (see Chapter 3). This chapter takes a closer look at what a manager is and does, as well as the differences between managers and leaders.

Understanding What Managers Do

The very definition of *management* — getting work done through others — is deceivingly simple. As every manager now knows, management can be a very complicated, stressful, traumatic, and exhausting job. Whereas many employees — software engineers, human resources coordinators, sales representatives, and the like — are specialists and can focus their efforts on a fairly narrow range of responsibilities, companies expect managers to be generalists.

Instead of knowing a lot about only a few topics, managers need to know a little bit about most everything that falls within the boundaries of their organizations.

For example, an accounts payable clerk may spend all day paying invoices and dealing with vendors to clear up problems in their billings. However, the manager of the accounting department has to understand not only what that particular employee is doing, and why he or she is doing it, but also the jobs of the employees in charge of accounts receivable, payroll, management information systems, budget, audit, and more. And having technical knowledge and expertise in these many different areas isn't enough for the manager; he or she also needs to understand how to enable and encourage the employees to give their best efforts day in and day out (see Chapter 7 for more on motivating employees). This section takes a closer look at who managers are and exactly what they do.

The different levels of management

Management, in most organizations that have enough employees to merit it, is split into three levels — each with its own unique set of responsibilities and functions:

- **Top management:** The chairman of the board, president, chief executive officer (CEO), chief operating officer (COO), chief information officer (CIO), chief financial officer (CFO), vice presidents, and other executives comprise an organization's highest-ranking management team. Top management usually creates an organization's vision and key goals, communicates them to other managers and workers, and monitors the organization's progress toward meeting them (refer to Chapter 5).

- **Middle management:** Department managers, deputy project managers, brand managers, assistant plant managers, and many other kinds of managers who report to top management make up the middle management level. Middle management must create the plans, systems, and organizations to achieve the company's vision and key goals. Middle managers generally report to top managers.

- **Supervisors:** Going by an amazing array of titles, supervisors are the employees closest to the frontline workers — and, therefore, often closest to the organization's customers and clients. Supervisors execute the plans developed by middle managers and monitor worker performance on a day-to-day basis. Supervisors generally report to middle managers.

As every MBA student learns during the course of his or her studies, four traditional functions of management exist. In today's fast and furious world of global business, however, these traditional roles are undergoing significant change. To be successful, managers must learn to adapt to this new world of work. Today's workers are taking on roles that were once reserved for managers. This shift in the traditional roles of managers and workers has led to incredible productivity gains in progressive companies.

Planning

Organizations need goals. Goals reflect what's most important to an organization, and they make it easy for managers to prioritize work and the allocation of resources (such as people, money, and capital equipment; see the following section). Management's key jobs include developing organizational goals and then *planning* the strategies and tactics that the organization will use to reach these goals (see Chapter 5).

An example of the planning function of management is when a company's management team flies to Palm Beach, Florida, to attend a week-long, offsite meeting. The goal of the gathering: to create the organization's five-year (long-range) plan. Of course, if the meeting is like most management offsite meetings, little actual work occurs until the last day, after everyone is too tired to golf or too sunburned to hang out at the pool!

Research has found that in most growing companies, regular planning falls by the wayside. Managers in these companies end up spending most of their time putting out daily fires. What, unfortunately, results from this lack of planning is a ship without a rudder. Even worse, individual members of a management team could actually have completely different goals for the same organization!

Organizing

Organizing is the allocation of resources (such as people, money, and capital equipment) to achieve an organization's goals (see the previous section). Managers allocate through organizational charts, staffing plans, and budgets. As many of you have probably noticed, managers spend endless hours developing new and exciting staffing and organizational configurations, only to change them again in six months. Why? Because doing so is part of the job!

Today's organizations must be faster and more flexible than ever before. The days of the old-fashioned, rigid organizational chart — with its built-in bureaucracy and hierarchy — are fast disappearing. In its place are self-managing work teams (see Chapter 9), cross-trained workers, virtual employees, flexible work schedules, hot groups, and more.

This makes organizing more challenging for managers, of course. One key to success in an increasingly competitive global marketplace is the ability to adapt to rapidly changing business conditions — and to do so quickly and completely. Putting new organizational plans into place as you strive to adapt is the job of managers.

Leading

Leading employees means inspiring them, motivating them to higher levels of performance, and directing their efforts. Managers have a wide variety of positive motivational tools at their disposal, including the following:

- ✔ Communicating a vision
- ✔ Rewarding and recognizing
- ✔ Encouraging
- ✔ Personally thanking employees

They also have negative motivational tools such as

- ✔ Disciplining
- ✔ Threatening
- ✔ Coercing

Today, simply being a manager isn't enough. Organizations need their managers to also be leaders — to inspire employees and to encourage them to give their very best every day of the week. For more on motivating your employees, head to Chapter 7.

Controlling

Control is the process of monitoring and evaluating activities to ensure that a company's goals are being achieved. To plan, organize, and lead isn't enough. For managers to be effective, they must also review the organization's progress toward achieving its goals. This review indicates whether plans and goals need to be updated, modified, or scrapped altogether; whether the organization as designed is up to the task; and whether the manager's efforts at leading employees are having the desired impact (see Chapter 5 for more on reviewing strategic plans).

Picture this all-too-common scenario: As managers review weekly departmental finance reports, they quickly realize that the reorganization they so painstakingly designed isn't having its desired effect. Sales are down, costs are up, and employee morale is heading south. Something has to be done — and soon! The time to plan another management offsite meeting has arrived!

Highlighting the Differences between Managers and Leaders

Although each of the four roles of managers (see the previous section) is important to a manager's overall success, leading employees is the one role that seemingly generates the most interest in organizations. What about leadership makes it different from management? Why is leadership so important to organizations today? Can managers learn to become better leaders? This section and the rest of this chapter answer these questions.

Managers are responsible for making organizations work, and one of their key functions is leading the employees within the organizations. Good leadership is a skill that can turn an okay manager into a superstar. Employees want to work for strong leaders, and they consistently give their best efforts when they do.

What makes a leader? What subtle mix of tangible and intangible qualities sets someone apart from the pack and brings out the follower in others? In general terms, leaders are

- ✔ **Charismatic:** They attract people's interest.
- ✔ **Convincing:** They have the ability to sway people's opinions toward their own.
- ✔ **Credible:** They're honest and have integrity; people trust them.
- ✔ **Capable:** They're very good at what they do, and they inspire others to meet their high standards.
- ✔ **Visionary:** They can see a clear vision of the future and communicate it to others in compelling detail.
- ✔ **Focused:** They're supremely focused on attaining their vision.

When it comes to the workplace, managers are more effective when they're also good leaders. The best managers are equally adept at both management skills and leadership skills. Perhaps U.S. Navy Admiral Grace Murray Hopper was right when she said, "You manage things; you lead people."

Management focuses on things: systems, processes, procedures, paperwork, and the rest of the matters that make businesses run. Leadership focuses on people: inspiring, leading, convincing, and motivating. Leaders perform duties that keep employees motivated and engaged in their jobs.

Leaders are in demand in organizations today — not just within the ranks of management, but throughout an organization. If you're good at managing things but not so good at leading people, focus on developing your leadership skills. Read books on the topic of leadership. Observe how leaders whom you respect and admire lead others, and model yourself after them. Above all, keep striving to improve your leadership skills. Your employees will thank you.

Getting Work Done through Others

As we say earlier in this chapter, management consists of getting work done through others. That's all well and good, but exactly how do managers make that happen? A number of different ways exist — each with its own advantages, disadvantages, and limitations. This section points them out.

Power and influence

Five key sources of power exist in an organization. Every employee wields one or more of these sources of power within his or her own job, and the sources can change from situation to situation. Power gives managers the ability to influence others to do what they ask of them.

Which of the following sources of power do you use to get things done at work?

- **Personal power** comes from within you. This power springs from your personality, your charisma, the strength of your beliefs and convictions, and your ability to express them. For example, a hard-working, front-line employee who inspires her coworkers to work harder by her example has personal power.

- **Relationship power** comes from the strength of your network of friends, contacts, and business associates. Have you ever heard the phrase, "I've got friends in high places?" You get the idea! An example of relationship power in an organization is the incredible power that assistants to CEOs and other top managers wield. They often have as much (or perhaps even more) real power as the executives to whom they report.

- **Position power** comes from your place within a company's hierarchy. A company's president has high position power. The mailroom clerk has low position power.

- **Knowledge power** comes from your experience, training, schooling, and expertise — in your particular job, within your organizational unit, and in the organization as a whole. This power includes technical prowess, as well as your ability to manage the personalities of those you work with. Because computer networks — and their care and maintenance —

have become extremely important in most organizations, information technology professionals have very high knowledge power.

✔ **Task power** comes from the job itself. For example, in an advertising agency, account reps who sell new clients on the agency and who have a direct impact on bringing in revenues have higher task power than employees in the accounting department whose job it is to send out invoices and collect payments.

Responsibility, authority, and accountability

Responsibility, authority, and accountability are extremely powerful forces in an organization, because they're the key ways that managers get work done through others:

✔ **Responsibility** signifies who in the organization must complete a specific task or job. When you assign a task to an employee (or delegate it; see the following section), you should also assign responsibility for its successful completion. Employees who are given responsibility for tasks are more likely to do them well and feel like they're significant parts of the organization.

✔ **Authority** means that your organization has formally granted you the power you need to do a specific job. When you delegate this power along with an assigned task, you're delegating authority to the employee to complete the task.

✔ **Accountability** means answering for the results you accomplish — or don't accomplish — when you take on a task. When you assign a task to an employee, you should also assign accountability for whether the task is done correctly or not.

Delegation

No manager can do everything alone. Managers leverage themselves — multiplying the work they can accomplish many times — by delegating work, responsibility, and authority to employees. Delegation is a great tool for managers to increase the amount of work they can get done, and it often achieves better results.

So why do so many managers have such a hard time delegating work to their employees? Fear causes part of the reluctance — fear that employees can't or won't do the work as well as the managers can. Some managers also feel that they're too busy to take the time to train employees to do the tasks well;

therefore, simply tackling the jobs themselves seems easier. And perhaps the desire to bask in the spotlight alone for completing important tasks contributes to some managers' reluctance to delegate.

In any case, delegation is the first choice for managers to get work done through others. It can be an incredibly effective tool when done right — and a remarkably destructive tool when done wrong. Here are six steps for delegating the right way:

1. **Communicate the task.**

   Describe exactly what you want done, when you want it done, and the end results you expect. Be clear and invite your employee to ask a lot of questions until you're convinced he or she understands what you want done.

2. **Furnish context for the task.**

   Most people want to know the reasons why they should do something. Explain to your employee why the task needs to be done, its importance in the overall scheme of things, and any possible complications that may arise during its performance. Again, invite questions and don't get defensive if your employee pushes you for answers.

3. **Determine standards.**

   We all need to know when we cross the finish line. Agree on the standards that you'll use to measure the success of a task's completion. These standards should be realistic and attainable, and you should avoid changing them after performance has begun.

4. **Grant authority.**

   You must grant the employee the authority necessary to complete the task without constant roadblocks or standoffs with other employees.

5. **Provide support.**

   Determine the resources necessary for your employee to complete the task and then provide them. Successfully completing a task may require money, training, advice, and other resources.

6. **Get commitment.**

   Make sure that your employee has accepted the assignment. Confirm your expectations and your employee's understanding of the commitment to complete the task.

One of the biggest problems with delegation occurs when a manager delegates responsibility for a task but not the authority and resources necessary to carry it out effectively. Inevitably, the task becomes much more difficult to carry out than it needs to be — perhaps impossible — and the employee becomes frustrated and even angry. Don't forget that we all want happy employees. Happy employees lead to happy customers and clients. Be sure that when you delegate a task to an employee, you also give the employee the authority that must go along with it.

Goals

Goals do two things: They show you where you've been and where you're going. Managers and employees should work together to develop personal goals to help the employees attain the overall goals of the organization. The acronym SMART signifies five traits that will ensure your goals are well-designed, because well-designed goals are much more likely to have the outcomes you and your organization desire:

- ✔ **S**pecific: All goals should be clear and unambiguous. Fuzzy goals lead to fuzzy outcomes.

- ✔ **M**easurable: Goals are useless if you can't measure them. If you can't measure an outcome, you'll never know whether it was achieved.

- ✔ **A**ttainable: Nothing is more demoralizing than being assigned goals that are impossible to attain. Be sure that you work with employees to develop realistic and attainable goals.

- ✔ **R**elevant: Don't waste your employees' time (or yours) by asking them to pursue goals that will take your business somewhere it shouldn't be! Every goal should take your employees closer to meeting the overall goals of the organization.

- ✔ **T**ime-bound: Be sure that your goals have beginnings and endings. The endpoints of goals should never be so far out that employees have no hope of attaining them. Developing plenty of milestones along the way is better than creating only one or two end-all, be-all mega-goals (for more on this topic, head to Chapter 5).

Designing a Better Organization

One of the four traditional roles of managers is organizing (see the first section in this chapter for more info). A manager must continuously improve systems and processes to make them more efficient, more effective, and less costly. Because the environment of business is always changing — new employees, new technology, new sources of supply, new competitors (see Chapter 4) — managers have to be aware of the need to restructure their organizations to keep them competitive in the marketplace. As you work to design a better organization, be sure to consider the factors in the following sections.

Division of labor

The very first step in organizational design is assigning specific employees to specific jobs. This is commonly called *division of labor*.

In a one-person organization — say, a home-based public-relations agency — only one person completes all the jobs that need to be done. The business owner types the letters, answers the phone, places advertisements, designs promotional materials for clients, writes press releases, schedules clients for media interviews and radio and television appearances, does the accounting, pays the bills, and even takes out the trash!

As soon as the sole owner and worker hires an employee, however, he or she can make the operation more efficient through effective division of labor. The new hire can take on tasks that the owner isn't so good at or that require a lot of work but don't generate revenues — perhaps typing letters and answering phones. This way, the owner can concentrate his or her efforts on the tasks that he or she is best at (such as landing new customers and designing publicity campaigns) and that have a better cash return on the investment of his or her time.

When you assign a specific job to an employee, ensure that

- ✔ The duties of the job are clear and that the boundaries are well-defined.

- ✔ The job isn't too complex or too simple for the particular employee.

- ✔ You give the employee the authority to execute the job without undue management interference.

- ✔ The job is kept interesting by varying tasks, goals, and approaches.

- ✔ The employee is well-trained to do the job.

Although division of labor has a time-honored place in modern business, today's most successful organizations are going a step further — they're cross-training employees in the jobs of their coworkers. Employees who know one another's jobs are more flexible, and the organizations they work for can be much more responsive to changing market conditions or to the challenges of competitors. At the very least, a flexible employee can fill in for an absent worker! Also, cross-trained employees often have higher morale because the varied tasks make their jobs more interesting.

Departmentalization and cellular manufacturing

In traditional organizations, after managers hand out individual jobs to employees, the managers then determine whether they can group any jobs into logical divisions (called *departmentalization*). For example, the managers group every employee assigned a sales-oriented task with other sales-oriented employees to form a sales department. Employees who have an accounting function — payroll, accounts receivable, or accounts payable — come together to form an accounting department. And so it goes throughout the organization.

This method, however, is the old way of doing business. It put up organizational walls that led to massive production inefficiencies. A newer method of structuring manufacturing concerns using manufacturing cells. *Cellular manufacturing* consists of closely linking work steps in a specific process. For example, if 20 work steps are involved in completing a piece of work (work, in this case, means making a product in a plant or processing paper in an office), cellular manufacturing places the people and the machines they use next to each other in a work cell. In a traditional manufacturing organization, these 20 work steps would've been accomplished in different functional departments spread throughout the business — perhaps in different buildings, cities, states, or even countries. Thankfully, this cellular approach also works for other types of businesses.

Flexible work teams now comprise many functions within organizations, and some entrepreneurial-type businesses aren't based on departments at all (see Chapter 3 for more on entrepreneurial businesses). Chapter 9 covers these new team-based organizations in detail.

Span of control

Span of control refers to the number of employees reporting to a particular supervisor or manager. A narrow span of control consists of only a few employees; a wide span of control includes many employees. One of your authors, Peter, once indirectly managed a staff of more than 200 employees, working at some 45 locations nationwide, for instance. If each employee had reported directly to Peter, his task would've been almost impossible — he would've spent almost every working hour on the phone answering questions, walking workers through problems, and discussing customer requests.

Narrowing the span of control made Peter's job feasible. Only four employees reported directly to Peter — three project managers and an administrative assistant. And each of the project managers managed a group of ten or more site supervisors. This arrangement freed up Peter to focus on the big picture — marketing to new customers (see Part III), keeping current customers happy, and ensuring that the company effectively utilized staff throughout.

The tendency these days is to flatten organizations by widening the span of control and decreasing the layers of management (the hierarchy). Organizations also rely more on employee teams to take on many of the roles formerly performed by managers (see Chapter 9). Why flatten an organization?

- ✔ The flatter an organization, the fewer layers of management, and less management leads to less bureaucracy and quicker decision making.

- ✔ The fewer layers of management, the more money available to spend on more productive activities (such as the company picnic — yum!).

Creating a Culture of Innovation

Corporations today are spending millions of dollars hiring consultants and enrolling in workshops, all to create a culture of innovation within their organizations. Innovation depends on the creative efforts of an organization's employees. In today's fast-changing, technology-driven global marketplace, innovation isn't just something nice to have — it's *essential*. However, too many years of corporate conformity have made creativity a rare and valued commodity; smart managers are constantly on the lookout for new ways to release the hidden creativity in their existing employees. Hence the consultants and workshops. In this section, we further discuss why having a culture of innovation is important for your organization, and we explain what you can do to make your culture more creative.

Recognizing why innovation is important

For a business owner or manager, asking if innovation really matters is sort of like asking if it matters whether Earth's atmosphere has oxygen — only if you want to survive! Without innovation, organizations (and people) stagnate, they fall behind the competition, and they eventually become irrelevant. Ever wonder why you see all those advertisements for "new and improved" products that have actually been around for a million years? Innovation. The people who produce Tide detergent, Coca-Cola soda, or Campbell's soup, for example, know that they can't rest on yesterday's successes. To thrive and to grow in the future, companies must constantly innovate.

According to Austrian economist Joseph Schumpeter (the hero of entrepreneurs everywhere), there are five specific types of economic innovation:

✔ **The introduction of a new good (product):** A company can introduce a completely new product, unfamiliar to consumers, or add new qualities to an already existing product. Think about all the advertisements for "New and Improved!" laundry detergents or cheeseburgers that "Taste better!"

✔ **The introduction of a new method of production:** Innovation can come about through the adoption of a new way to manufacture a product, which may or may not be based on new technology or scientific discoveries. For example, automobiles used to be mostly assembled by hand. Today, robots have taken on many duties formerly assigned to humans.

✔ **A new market in a country where the market hasn't previously existed:** This includes the opening of a new market into which the particular branch of manufacture of the country in question hasn't previously entered — whether or not this market has existed before. For example, a few decades ago, there wasn't a market for the production of Japanese beer in the United States. Companies fulfilled whatever demand existed for Japanese beer by importing the beer directly from Japan. However, a surge in U.S. demand for Japanese beer has led to the current market situation — a vast majority of the Japanese beer sold in the United States today is actually brewed in the United States and Canada.

- ✔ **The conquest of a new source of supply of raw materials, or half-manufactured goods:** This type is irrespective of whether the source already exists or must be created. An example is the discovery of petroleum-rich tar sands in Canada. New ways of extracting the material from the ground required the introduction of innovative new approaches to oil production.

- ✔ **The carrying out of the new organization of any industry:** For example, a company can create a monopoly position or break up a monopoly position. Both AT&T and Microsoft, at various times in their respective histories, had to innovate new ways of doing business as a result of government and court-mandated curbs on their monopoly power.

If you were to spend any time in an MBA program, you'd probably find out that the academics who specialize in innovation have gone well beyond Schumpeter's five basic types of innovation. The following list presents some of the more specific types of business innovation you're likely to encounter:

- ✔ **Business model innovation:** Innovation in the way business is done, usually resulting in the creation of new value. Dell's model of building personal computers to order rather than stockpiling them in a warehouse is a business model innovation that revolutionized the personal-computer market and gave customers their computers quicker and at a lower price. And, at least until recently, it brought the company great success. (Remember, business environments change and businesses must too.)

- ✔ **Marketing innovation:** Innovation in marketing methods — specifically in the areas of product, price, place, promotion, and customers (see Chapter 15). Google's innovation of Adwords, the pay-per-click online advertising program, has generated billions of dollars in revenue while filling a vital need for advertisers to access online customers in niche markets.

- ✔ **Organizational innovation:** Innovation in the design and execution of business structures, practices, and models, which may involve innovation in other business areas as well. The Internet, for instance, enables people to do business anyplace, anytime, which results in entirely new organizational practices and structures that are independent of traditional, fixed office space and hierarchies.

- ✔ **Process innovation:** Innovation in production or delivery methods (see Chapter 18). Henry Ford's widespread application of the assembly line to automobile production revolutionized the industry, and it made automobiles affordable to most anyone.

✔ **Product innovation:** Innovation in products — specifically, a product or service that's new or significantly improved over whatever is in current use. Product innovation may touch on the following areas, among others:

- Functional characteristics (works two times faster!)

- Smell (new fresh scent!)

- Performance (works better than the other brand!)

- Technical abilities (now cleans grass stains, too!)

- Ease of use (look how easy it can be!)

✔ **Service innovation:** This is the same as product innovation but is specific to services.

✔ **Supply chain innovation:** Innovation in the sourcing of input products from suppliers and the delivery of output products to customers. Wal-Mart revolutionized its supply chain, creating efficiencies that put it far ahead of the competition and vaulting it into the position of the world's largest retailer.

Four keys to a more creative (and innovative) workplace

So you've decided that having a more creative and innovative workplace wouldn't be such a bad thing. (Either that, or you read that having one is necessary.) Now what? Here are four sure ways you can up the creativity (and innovation) quotient in your organization:

✔ **Institute fluid and situational hierarchies.** Fluid, situational hierarchies quickly adapt to fast-changing environments. You want to be able to morph to fit tomorrow's needs instead of constantly playing catch up with structures based on yesterday's needs. You can do this by being flexible, non-bureaucratic, attentive to shifts in markets, and ready to respond to changes in the environment quickly and decisively.

For example, at executive search firm Egon Zehnder (which has annual billings of more than $300 million), the rigid hierarchy typical of a large, international firm has been supplanted by a fluid organization that empha-sizes high levels of cooperation, communication, and teamwork, which unleashes creativity and innovation. Egon Zehnder has become the most profitable search firm per capita in the world, with productivity that's 60 percent higher than the industry average.

✔ **Value and foster communication skills throughout the organization.** Communication is the lifeblood of any organization. When channels of communication are open and unfettered throughout an organization, information can travel quickly across operational boundaries, from front-line employees to management and back again.

✔ **Solve problems by letting "1,000 flowers blossom."** This phrase is attributed to former Chinese leader Mao Tse-Tung. Smart leaders empower people throughout their organizations to come up with ways to meet core organizational objectives. They let the chaotic environment determine the winners through the process of natural selection. They monitor workers very carefully, have rigorous criteria to evaluate them, and kill off the failures fast — making it perfectly clear that they're killing off the failures and not the people who worked to create a solution.

For instance, the original IBM personal computer was developed by a team of 12 employees who were given carte blanche to develop a revolutionary new product as quickly as possible. They were even given express authority to ignore standard company policies when necessary to get the job done.

✔ **Value and make use of improvisation.** Just as musicians open up the gates to their personal creativity when they improvise the playing of their instruments, employees can channel their personal creativity — and strengthen their capacity to think on their feet — by improvising as they seek solutions to solve problems. This means looking beyond the tried-and-true and considering alternatives that may not have been tested before.

In general, innovation can be *incremental* — it occurs steadily, on a step-by-step basis (think gradual improvements in automobile fuel efficiency) — or *radical* — involving a large and sudden leap (such as when the Manhattan Project scientists harnessed the power of the atomic bomb or, more recently, when the Internet changed the way business is conducted). Whether incremental or radical, innovation can have a significant and positive impact on the fortunes of the businesses that foster it.

Ethics: Following Your Business Compass

In today's business world, it seems that not a day goes by without news of a business scandal. A CEO backdated his stock options, a board member secretly taped confidential meetings and then used the information to blackmail other board members, an employee embezzled $100,000 from the company's owners, and so on. With a seemingly endless parade of business scandals, you may begin to wonder whether anyone in business knows the difference between right and wrong. This section points out what ethics are and what you can do to make ethical decisions.

Understanding what's right and wrong

Ethics are the standards, or beliefs and values, that guide conduct, behavior, and activities — in other words, a way of thinking that provides boundaries for your actions. In its most common usage, ethics is simply doing the right thing. And not just *talking* or *thinking* about doing the right thing, but really doing it!

When you have high ethical standards on the job, you generally exhibit some or all of the following qualities and behaviors:

✔ Honesty

✔ Integrity

✔ Impartiality

✔ Fairness

✔ Loyalty

✔ Dedication

✔ Responsibility

✔ Accountability

Ethical behavior starts with each person. Just because someone else is doing something that's unethical (morally wrong) — or illegal (legally wrong) — doesn't mean that you should do it, too. When you behave ethically — whatever your position within an organization — others will follow your example and behave ethically, too. And, if you practice ethical conduct, it will reinforce and perhaps improve your own ethical standards.

Setting an example for others to follow

As a leader, it's up to you to set a good example of ethical and honest behavior for your employees to follow. This means working within the rules of your organization, not breaking the law, and treating people fairly and honestly. People make ethical choices on the job every day — how do you make yours? Here are six keys to making better ethical choices:

✔ **Evaluate circumstances through the appropriate filters.** Filters include such things as culture, laws, policies, circumstances, relationships, politics, perception, emotions, values, bias, and religion.

✔ **Treat people and issues fairly within the established boundaries.** Fair doesn't always mean equal.

✔ **Hesitate before making critical decisions.**

✔ **Inform those affected by the standard/decision that has been set/made.**

✔ **Create an environment of consistency for yourself and your working group.**

✔ **Seek counsel when any doubt is present** (from those who are honest and who you respect).

It's one thing to have a code of ethics; it's another thing altogether to behave ethically in all your day-to-day business transactions and relationships. Each individual comes into a workplace with a unique sense of ethical values, based on upbringing and life experiences. In addition to the ethics that people bring with them, organizations and their leaders are responsible for setting an example of high ethical standards.

Examining Management Trends in Business Today

Who says that you can't teach an old dog new tricks? The past decade has been a revolutionary one for managers in every industry, all around the world. Although the classic definition of management — plan, organize, lead, and control — still reflects the basics of what managers do, there's now much more to the job. It seems as though every month you hear about a hot, new management trend or fad, based on some best-selling business book. Do the phrases "total quality management," "business process re-engineering," or perhaps "the learning organization" ring a bell?

All those trends were hot at one time but today have cooled off significantly. After all, management consultants and the press are constantly in the hunt for the next big idea — or the next old idea that gets repackaged with new buzz words to grab attention in a very jaded world. The following sections describe some of the most prominent management trends at work today — the ones that are built to last (at least until the next edition of this book!).

Corporate transparency

The idea of corporate transparency is taking hold in the world of business. *Corporate transparency* means disclosing more information on the inner workings of a business, in a quicker fashion and to a wider audience than before. This movement is partly driven by the following factors:

- The string of high-profile corporate ethical implosions during the past decade
- New laws such as Sarbanes-Oxley (see Chapter 10)
- The power of the Internet to instantly transmit anyone's deepest, darkest secrets around the world (in the form of e-mail messages, blog postings, specific Web sites, and more)

Although some information — for example, personnel information — must by law remain confidential, the idea of corporate transparency is for businesses to be more open and forthcoming with stakeholders and with the public.

Public companies are required to make significant disclosures under the rules of Sarbanes-Oxley, but private companies should consider some common disclosures as well (you can check out *Sarbanes-Oxley For Dummies,* by Jill Gilbert Welytok [Wiley], for more info). Some of the more common approaches companies take to become more transparent include:

- ✔ Disclosure of senior executive pay and benefits packages
- ✔ Instituting codes of conduct and related training programs
- ✔ Prohibiting firms from providing both management consulting and audit services
- ✔ Establishing an independent board to ensure compliance with laws (such as Sarbanes-Oxley), codes of conduct, and ethical standards
- ✔ Punishing employees who submit misleading reports

Although some companies and managers welcome transparency — convinced that their customers will respond favorably to their efforts — others aren't yet persuaded. They're worried that too much transparency will damage their competitive advantages in the marketplace. Whatever the case, only time will tell if transparency is a trend that will stick around.

Entrepreneurial leadership

There's a new kind of leader in town: the entrepreneurial leader. An *entrepreneurial leader* creates new opportunities in his or her business and assembles the resources necessary — money, people, and organization — to successfully exploit these opportunities. Entrepreneurial leaders think like entrepreneurs; that is, they

- ✔ Are comfortable with ambiguity and uncertainty.
- ✔ Have self-discipline and tenacity.
- ✔ Are not afraid to fail.
- ✔ Believe that they alone control their destiny.
- ✔ Are opportunity-focused and innovative.

Plain-old, vanilla leaders can no longer keep up in fast-changing business markets. Entrepreneurial leadership brings new perspectives and opportunities to businesses that thought they had already exhausted every chance to move ahead of the pack. The risks may be higher — loss of resources and competitive advantage — but so are the rewards. For more on entrepreneurship, see Chapter 3.

Work–life balance

If you're a reader who works in the United States, do you feel as though you're working harder than ever? There's a good chance that this is more than just a feeling. Truth be told, U.S. workers put in more time on the job than employees in most other industrialized countries — an average of 1,978 hours a year. By contrast, Australian, Canadian, Japanese, and Mexican employees work about 100 hours — or 2.5 weeks — less each year. British workers manage to make do with 200 hours less a year, and German workers log 500 fewer hours a year. With busier family lives and increased demands on their time outside of work, it's no surprise that more and more American workers are clamoring for a better work–life balance.

Many employers are responding by instituting programs and policies specifically designed to bring about a better work–life balance. Such programs include flexible work schedules, telecommuting, job sharing, compressed workweeks, and much more. According to fans of improved work–life balance, companies that institute these policies can expect the following benefits:

- Increased employee loyalty and commitment to their jobs
- More motivated, efficient, and effective employees
- Improved relationships between workers and managers
- Improved worker self-esteem, happiness, and health
- Decreased absenteeism
- Decreased disability and worker's compensation claims
- Increased employee engagement and retention

With such high-profile recognition, such as *Fortune* magazine's "100 Best Companies to Work For" — which rewards companies that provide their employees with greater opportunities for work–life balance — at stake, it appears that this is a trend that's here to stay. How is your organization's work–life balance, and what can you as a manager do to make it better?

Chapter 7

Carrots and Sticks: The ABCs of Motivating Employees

In This Chapter

▶ Reviewing the content and process theories of motivation

▶ Recognizing and rewarding employees

▶ Building long-term employee/employer relationships

*G*o ahead, ask a manager what his or her toughest job is. What answer do you think you'll get? Working out a new operating budget for the upcoming fiscal year? No, probably not. Designing an assembly line for a new manufacturing plant in Yakutsk? No, not that either. Negotiating a new wage contract with the machinist's union? No, not even that (although that job is definitely no piece of cake). The toughest — and, in many ways, the most important — job for most managers is keeping their employees motivated, engaged in their work, and productive.

What's so hard about that? Well, if you've been in business for some time, you know that everyone is different. Some employees seem to be naturally motivated, bouncing from task to task as though the world may end tomorrow. These employees get things done and make things happen without any prodding from a manager. Other employees don't seem to be motivated at all; they barely do the minimum required by their jobs — if they even do that.

Of course, every manager's dream is to have a team filled with high achievers. Unfortunately, this is rarely the case. A few under-motivated employees are bound to be in the mix — especially as your team continues to grow. Motivating these seemingly unmotivated men and women is the real key to success. How do you motivate employees who aren't motivated to begin with, and how do you keep employees who are driven motivated? The answers to those questions are the very essence of carrots and sticks. This chapter can help you answer them.

Grasping the Theories of Motivation

Why do people do what they do? Understanding personal motivation on the job has been a source of endless speculation on the part of legions of business theorists, academics, and social psychologists. And as any good MBA knows, you can point out about as many theories of motivation as you can stars in the sky.

Regardless of which particular theories of motivation they ascribe to, experts generally agree that there are two primary sources of motivation on the job:

- ✔ **Intrinsic motivation,** which comes from forces within an individual. Examples include the pride that comes from doing a job well, the satisfaction felt when beating a deadline, and the excitement derived from being part of a high-performing team.

- ✔ **Extrinsic motivation,** which comes from forces outside an individual. Positive examples (*carrots*) include receiving a cash bonus for doing a particularly good job on a project and being publicly recognized by the boss in a staff meeting. Negative examples (*sticks*) include receiving a reprimand from the boss or getting fired.

Of these two sources of motivation, most experts in the art and science of motivation consider intrinsic motivation to be the strongest. If, for example, you absolutely love your job and feel great satisfaction when doing it (intrinsic motivation), a cash bonus or a pat on the back (extrinsic motivation) will have little or no impact on your job performance — certainly not in the long run. You'll still be motivated to do your job anyway. Similarly, if you absolutely hate your job, no amount of money or words of encouragement will make you like it more or improve your performance over the long haul. Well, a million dollars may help just a bit — but not for long!

Therefore, matching the right employees to the right jobs and setting realistic, attainable goals are absolutely critical tasks for managers. By completing them, you leverage the power of intrinsic motivation within each and every employee and rely less and less on extrinsic motivation — the carrots and sticks — to keep them engaged in their work. Every professional has a deep well of intrinsic motivation. It's your job to help your employees find and tap into the well. In the immortal words of management theorist Frederick Herzberg, "If you want someone to do a good job, give them a good job to do."

In the following sections, we take a close look at a variety of different theories of motivation and consider how your employees may respond to your motivational efforts.

You can find no single right answer here when it comes to motivation. Each of the theories that follow has something to offer supervisors and managers. The best approach is to try a variety of different approaches; experiment until you find the approach that works best in your particular situation. Every employee is different. You may find that one approach works best with Susan, but another approach works best with Tom. And an entirely different approach works with Chuck. The key is to keep trying until you hit upon an approach that works best for each one of your employees.

Eyeing content theories of motivation

Content theories of motivation focus on the specific factors that stimulate, direct, sustain, and stop behavior in individuals. In essence, content theories of motivation answer the following question: "What specific employee needs cause motivation?" The following sections break down different content theories of motivation from noted smart people.

Maslow's hierarchy of needs

In the 1940s, Abraham Maslow organized all human needs into five different levels — one on top of another — in the form of a pyramid (see Figure 7-1). According to Maslow, humans strive to fulfill their lowest-order (physiological) needs first. After we fulfill the lowest-order needs, we move up the pyramid to achieve the next level (safety). The process keeps going until we reach the top. Maslow's hierarchy of needs — from lowest to highest — is as follows:

- **Physiological:** The very essentials of life: food, water, shelter, and sex. These needs are of the highest priority, because if they're left unfulfilled, the very survival of the individual — and of the species — is in immediate jeopardy. Not only that, but life would be quite boring with these needs left unfulfilled!

- **Safety:** Security, protection from danger, a safe work environment, job security, and a stable paycheck. (Funny, does anyone have a job that provides any one of these anymore?)

- **Social:** The need to have social interactions with others, to be a part of a group or team of individuals, and to experience friendship and love. Of course, some people spend a lot more time at the coffeemaker than others!

- **Esteem:** The need to feel good about yourself and the work that you do. You want your contributions to be worthwhile and to have the respect of others. If you're a manager, here's a question for you: What have you done to build an employee's self-esteem lately?

- **Self-actualization:** The human desire for a sense of purpose. As the highest-order need in Maslow's hierarchy, it's achieved only after all other needs are satisfied. Based on our experience, this need can be a challenging level to attain, indeed.

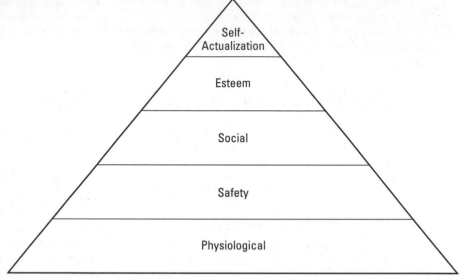

Figure 7-1:
Maslow's
hierarchy of
needs looks
a lot like a
pyramid.

Unfortunately, even though Maslow's hierarchy sounds good on paper (and the pyramid looks really cool), it hasn't been borne out in the real world of business. Do employees really work their way up the pyramid systematically, step by step? No. And sometimes they fall back or skip a level or two. In addition, research shows that although lower-order needs become less important as people satisfy them, higher-order needs don't decline in importance as people satisfy them — in fact, the importance of higher-order needs may actually increase after initial satisfaction.

Despite all that, the application of Maslow's work to business has had a very positive influence on management practice. The theory helps managers realize that workers aren't simply machines that they can turn on and off (we're not talking about the copy machine); employees are living, breathing people with needs and aspirations of their own. And this is something that managers, even today, sometimes forget.

Herzberg's two-factor theory

Management theorist Frederick Herzberg proposed a unique approach to the theory of motivation, based on an extensive study of engineers and accountants in the 1950s. Herzberg determined that you can classify the factors that influence employee behavior on the job into one of two categories:

✔ **Hygiene factors:** These factors don't relate to brushing your teeth or taking a shower; they relate to the environment external to the job itself. They include salary, work environment, job security, company policies and administration, relationships with peers, and relationships with supervisors. These factors directly influence the level of an employee's dissatisfaction with his or her job. The absence of sufficient hygiene factors can lead to employee turnover, absenteeism, burnout, and even outright sabotage. However, when hygiene factors are available in sufficient amounts, increasing their presence has little or no positive impact on employee motivation.

✔ **Motivators:** These items relate to the job itself. They include personal responsibility, achievement, challenges, advancement, professional growth, recognition, and the interest level of the work itself. These factors directly influence the level of an employee's satisfaction with his or her job. When motivators are insufficient, employees become less motivated; as the amount of motivators increases, employees become more motivated.

Herzberg showed that job satisfaction and job dissatisfaction are rooted in two completely separate sets of factors. Before Herzberg, management theorists assumed that employees were, above all, motivated by money. (Gee, more than 50 years later, most managers still think that's the case. Wrong!) A lack of money leads to dissatisfaction with one's job, but giving an employee professional growth opportunities, recognition for a job well done, responsibility, and challenge — all motivators — leads to a satisfied and, therefore, motivated employee who's fully engaged in his or her job.

As a result of Herzberg's work, managers know that they can increase employee motivation by increasing motivators. Primarily, they should focus on the structure of employee jobs — how work is arranged and the amount of control employees have over their work.

And *you* can increase motivation, too. Take a close look at the hygiene and motivational factors in your workplace. Are they sufficient to keep your employees motivated and satisfied? If not, what can you do to improve them? If you're not sure, you can use one tried-and-true way to find out: Ask your employees. Most workers will be happy to tell you what kinds of things motivate them and what kinds of things don't. In fact, your employees will probably be pleased that you took the time to ask about their feelings and desires.

McGregor's Theory X and Theory Y

During the 1960s, psychologist Douglas McGregor's Theory X and Theory Y were very popular theories of motivation. Even today, hearing a manager referred to as either a Theory X- or Theory Y-type is a commonplace event. In essence, *Theory X* and *Theory Y* describe two basic sets of assumptions that managers make about their workers:

✔ **Theory X managers** assume that workers inherently dislike work — that they must be coerced, directed, and closely controlled to meet the organization's goals. The manager believes the average worker has little ambition, avoids responsibility, and seeks security above all else. You've never thought that about any of your employees, have you? Come on, you can be honest with us!

> ✔ **Theory Y managers** assume that workers inherently like work — that they exercise self-direction and self-control to achieve an organization's goals. The manager believes that under the right conditions, the average worker not only accepts responsibility, but also seeks it out.

As you may imagine, if you're a Theory X manager, you'll treat your employees far differently than someone who's a Theory Y manager. A Theory X manager operates in a task-oriented style, focused on directing employees and coercing them to complete assigned tasks. A Theory Y manager operates in a people-oriented style, focused on building trust, empowerment, and autonomy.

Is one style better than the other? The answer depends on different factors:

> When you have a new employee — one who's just learning the ropes of a new job — the Theory X, directive style of motivation, is better.

> As an employee matures and is able to do the job without day-to-day supervision, the Theory Y, supportive style, is better.

The best managers are able to adjust their styles to match the needs of their employees. As a manager, what kinds of assumptions do you make about your employees? How do those assumptions color your approach to managing them? How do your employees react to the way you treat them — are they more or less motivated? The answers to these questions and others like them will help you understand whether you lean toward Theory X or Theory Y.

Ouchi's Theory Z

During the 1980s, business professor William Ouchi developed a motivation theory based on his study of the characteristics of Japanese business managers. *Ouchi's Theory Z* takes Theory Y's assertion that employees desire responsibility (see the previous section) one step further. Theory Z determines that organizations should empower employees to participate in the kinds of decision making formerly reserved solely for managers.

For some reason (we can't imagine why), many managers at first weren't very excited about giving up power to their employees. In fact, some had to be dragged kicking and screaming to get with the program. But, indeed, it seems that Ouchi had it right. Self-managing work teams — which give employees authority to manage themselves and their work without executive interference — are a given in many businesses today, and they're making organizations much faster and much more flexible — essential in a business world that's running on Internet time. Today, the Theory Z workplace is rapidly becoming the norm rather than the exception. (For more on teamwork and employee empowerment, check out Chapter 9.)

Identifying process theories of motivation

Process theories of motivation are different from content theories (big surprise there, eh?). Instead of focusing on employee needs, as content theories do (see the previous sections), *process theories* of motivation focus on *how* behavior is stimulated, directed, sustained, and stopped. In other words, process theories explain how motivation occurs — or at least they *try* to explain how motivation occurs. The following sections break down the different process theories of motivation.

Equity theory

According to social psychologist J. Stacy Adams, employees constantly compare the fairness of their work outcomes to the work outcomes of others in similar positions. If you've ever talked to an employee who didn't get a raise when a coworker did, you know exactly what we're talking about here! In general, employees are concerned not only about the absolute amount of an outcome — say, the amount of a pay raise given concurrently with the annual performance appraisal — but also about the amount relative to coworkers and peers in the geographic area or across an entire industry. This, in a nutshell, is the equity theory.

The following model illustrates this relationship:

Employee's rewards   Others' rewards

compared to

Employee's efforts   Others' efforts

As long as the ratio of the employee's rewards to effort expended is close to the ratio of other people's rewards to effort expended, the employee perceives equity and is most likely to be satisfied. And that's what every manager wants: happy employees!

However, if the employee's ratio of rewards to effort expended is significantly less than other people's, the employee perceives a negative inequity and takes steps to restore equity. This isn't a good thing. Why? Because the steps taken to restore equity can conflict with and even damage the overall goals of the business. Some of these steps may include the following:

- ✔ Decreasing the quality and quantity of his or her work
- ✔ Asking for a transfer to another supervisor or department
- ✔ Quitting

Similarly, if the employee's ratio of rewards to effort expended is significantly greater than what he or she sees in other people, he or she perceives a positive inequity and will take steps to restore equity. This time, however, the steps taken are likely to be consistent with and supportive of the employee's efforts to achieve company goals. Employees often take the following steps to restore equity in this situation:

✔ Increase the quality and quantity of work

✔ Request more work

✔ Ask for more responsibility

In any case, wise managers are sensitive to their employees and their perceptions of equity — and inequity — on the job. If your employees are disgruntled, you can bet that they have good reason. Your job as a student of the mysterious art and science of motivation is to figure out why. To get to the root of the problem, talk to your employees about it and then see what you can do to remove the sources of perceptions of inequity. Communication is key — just do it!

Expectancy theory

During the 1960s, Yale professor Victor Vroom was the first to apply E.C. Tolman's *expectancy theory of motivation* (developed in the 1930s) to the workplace. According to Vroom's application of the expectancy theory, the probability of an employee taking a specific action depends on

✔ The strength of the expectation that the action will lead to a given outcome

✔ The attractiveness of that outcome to the employee

Under this expectancy theory, the motivational force (MF) within an employee is represented as

$$MF = Expectancy \times Instrumentality \times Valence$$

In the preceding formula, *Expectancy* is the belief that an employee's effort will result in the attainment of desired performance goals. *Instrumentality* is the belief that if the employee gains desired performance goals, he or she will be rewarded for doing so. *Valence* is the value that he or she personally places on the expected reward.

The expectancy theory has been used to explain a variety of employee behaviors, including leadership effectiveness, turnover, absenteeism, career choice, and more. It can be a very effective tool to help managers understand why employees behave the way they do. For instance, for employees to be motivated, they must believe that not only can they achieve a desired level of performance, but also that doing so will lead to a desired reward. If either of those pieces is missing in your organization, your employees won't be motivated to perform at the high level that you expect of them.

Take a close look at your organization and ask yourself these three questions:

✔ Are your goals realistic and achievable, or are they placed too high above your employees' ability to achieve them?

✔ Do you make rewards available for employees who achieve these goals?

✔ Do the employees find the rewards desirable?

Do your research, and if you say no to any of these questions, you can't expect your employees to be motivated until you fix the broken links. Roll up your sleeves and get busy! (For more on rewards, check out the later sections of this chapter.)

If you've read all the theories so far, stick with us — we're getting close to the end of our list! Go grab a cup of coffee and stretch your legs for a minute. There, that's better. If you just picked out this one, you should be well rested. Check out the others!

Behavior modification

Okay, for this section, we have to get all scientific on you, so fasten your seatbelts and return your tray tables to their upright and locked position. Ready? *Behavior modification* states that external consequences determine an employee's behavior. This process theory is rooted in psychologist B.F. Skinner's pioneering work in operant conditioning (unless you were asleep during the video, all you psychology majors will remember the famous Skinner Box, with its food pellets and electrified floor used to modify the behavior of laboratory rats and wayward workers). The business application of Skinner's theory uses various methods of reinforcement to modify behavior through that behavior's consequences. *Reinforcement* means any stimulus that makes a behavior more likely to occur.

Types of behavior modification reinforcement

Under behavior modification, four different kinds of reinforcement exist — each with a different outcome:

✔ **Positive reinforcement:** Strengthening a behavior by applying a pleasant consequence. When an employee gets a word of congratulations from her boss for meeting a sales goal, she's receiving positive reinforcement from her boss. As a result, the employee is more likely to meet sales goals in the future, which is a good thing.

✔ **Negative reinforcement:** Strengthening a behavior by removing an unpleasant consequence — also known as *avoidance learning*. When employees show up on time for a staff meeting to avoid a reprimand from their supervisor, negative reinforcement has entered the picture.

✔ **Punishment:** Weakening a behavior by applying an unpleasant consequence. When an employee receives a reprimand for breaking a company
policy, he or she receives punishment. A reprimanded employee is less
likely to break company policy in the future.

Most managers tend to focus more on these sticks of motivation rather
than the carrots of positive reinforcement. Doing so is a mistake, because
positive reinforcement works and doesn't come with the negative consequences that often result from the application of punishment (resentment,
anger, and so forth).

✔ **Extinction:** Weakening a behavior with the application of a neutral consequence, or not following the behavior with a pleasant consequence. For
example, suppose that an employee puts in several weekends of extra
work to meet a customer deadline. If that employee's boss fails to reward
or even acknowledge the behavior, the employee will be less likely to
devote weekends to meeting customer deadlines in the future. Eventually,
absent some other motivator, the behavior will die away altogether.

Partial reinforcement versus continuous reinforcement

The frequency with which you reinforce behavior influences the effectiveness
of behavior modification. *Continuous reinforcement* occurs when you reinforce
behavior after every correct response. When you reinforce a behavior after
some responses but not after others, *partial reinforcement* develops.

When applying a partial-reinforcement schedule, you have two major
options:

✔ Vary the frequency of the reward according to the rate of response, which
is called a *ratio schedule*. The timing of the reinforcement is irrelevant.

✔ Vary the frequency of the reward strictly according to time intervals,
which is called an *interval schedule*. The number of responses that occur
after the first correct response in an interval is irrelevant.

You can choose between four basic partial-reinforcement schedules —
all others are combinations or variations of these basic four:

✔ **Fixed ratio (FR):** Reinforcement occurs after a fixed number of
responses. For example, an employee receives a reward from his boss
every third time he completes his work on time.

✔ **Variable ratio (VR):** Reinforcement occurs after a variable number of
responses. For example, an employee receives a reward from her boss
once every five times, on average, that she gets a letter of thanks from a
customer. Sometimes it may be one in five, sometimes one in four, and
sometimes one in six.

Vary the awards you give

By introducing an element of surprise and novelty into the reward process, partial-reinforcement schedules help rewards maintain their potency for long periods of time. The best managers constantly vary the rewards that they give their employees, as well as the circumstances under which they give them. For example, at Seattle-based law firm Perkins Coie, an employee-run happiness committee keeps the firm's employees on their toes by varying the rewards given, as well as their frequency. Some of the committee's employee-recognition events have included the following:

✓ A sack-lunch field trip across Puget Sound on a ferry. The trip required employees to bring permission slips signed by coworkers allowing them to attend.

✓ An Earth Day celebration. Department employees received plants, bags of dirt, and fertilizer; a prize was awarded to the person who could do the best job growing the plant. (One unexpected benefit: Employees asked one another about the plants. Said one employee, "I don't know if I'd ever have talked to some of these people before. These kinds of things really break down the barriers.")

✓ An end-of-summer barbecue, in Seattle's famous liquid sunshine (rain), on the 48th-floor deck of the building (which also happened to be under construction at the time).

✓ A Veterans Day celebration, at which 35 coworkers honored their department's five veterans with a potluck lunch, cake, and festive red, white, and blue balloons.

✓ **Fixed interval (FI):** Reinforcement occurs on the first response after a fixed time interval has passed. For example, a boss rewards an employee exactly 15 minutes after he or she arrives to work on time.

✓ **Variable interval (VI):** Reinforcement occurs on the first response after a variable time interval has passed. For example, a boss rewards an employee one week, on average, after the employee submits her expense report on time — sometimes five days, sometimes nine days, and so on.

Over time, partial-reinforcement schedules are much more effective at causing desired behavior than continuous schedules, which reward employees every time they perform the behavior. They're also much more resistant to change or extinction. Why? When you give rewards on a continuous schedule, employees will begin to take them for granted. In the words of behavioral scientists, they *habituate* to the stimulus, meaning the stimulus has progressively less impact on their behavior. The rewards, in other words, have a diminishing effect on behavior. (Check out the nearby sidebar, "Vary the awards you give" for some examples.)

A boring rewards and recognition program is a recognition program that isn't working; shake it up! The following section dives much deeper into rewards.

You Get What You Reward

We'll let you in on a little business secret — a secret that can make your life as a supervisor or manager much easier and the results of your employees much better. If you were enrolled in an MBA program right now, you'd have to pay thousands to learn this secret. But because you decided to plunk down your hard-earned cash for this book instead, we give it to you for free:

You get what you reward.

Bob Nelson, co-author with Peter on both *Managing For Dummies* and *Consulting For Dummies* (Wiley), coined this phrase more than a decade ago. And it's true — if you dangle rewards so people strive to achieve their goals, they very likely will do just that. Conversely, if you don't reward people when they achieve their goals, they're less likely to do so. In fact, they may not even bother to try to achieve them.

This section gives you the lowdown on rewarding your employees, including when and how to do so.

In a perfect world, perhaps rewarding and recognizing employee effort wouldn't be necessary. If all employees were 100 percent intrinsically motivated in their jobs (wouldn't that be nice!), you wouldn't need to dangle the carrots of rewards and recognition. However, the world isn't perfect. Most managers will see immediate and positive results when they initiate a program of regular and systematic rewards and recognition.

The good and bad news about rewards

The good news is that the most effective employee rewards cost little or no money. A study of 1,500 employees — conducted by Dr. Gerald Graham, management professor at Wichita State University — reported the following top five employee motivators:

1. Personal (oral) thanks from one's manager

2. Written thanks from one's manager

3. Promotion for performance

4. Public praise

5. Morale-building meetings

The bad news is that few managers reward their employees often, and many don't bother at all. When Dr. Graham asked the study group of 1,500 employees to report how often they received the top five employee motivators listed previously, the results were shocking:

✔ 58 percent seldom, if ever, received personal thanks from their managers.

✔ 76 percent seldom, if ever, received written thanks from their managers.

✔ 78 percent seldom, if ever, received promotions based on performance.

✔ 81 percent seldom, if ever, received public praise in the workplace.

✔ 92 percent seldom, if ever, participated in morale-building meetings.

Here's a quote from Mac Anderson, founder and former CEO of Successories, Inc. — a leader in the employee motivation and self-improvement industry, located in Lombard, Illinois:

> "A recognition culture literally has to start at the top. The guy at the top has to believe in it, has to bring the managers together to create a recognition culture. The key is the manager of each department, who has to do things that make employees feel important. It's a basic human need. Most managers don't recognize that."

Starting up an employee recognition program doesn't have to be difficult, and it doesn't require a big budget. In fact, it can be quite simple and inexpensive (can you say, *free?*). Oh, and you can start today!

The four keys to effective rewards and recognition programs

Interestingly enough, many managers think that they reward and recognize their employees plenty — perhaps even too much — when, in reality, they don't even come close to being adequate. In some cases, managers don't bother to reward and recognize their employees' good efforts. In other cases, managers do try to give rewards and recognition, but they do it in the wrong manner. When a manager doesn't give a reward in an effective manner, the message is lost on the employee to whom it was directed. And if the message is lost, as far as the employee is concerned, he or she hasn't been rewarded for his or her good work.

You can do your part to make your employee rewards and recognition program effective — regardless of what kinds of rewards and recognition you decide to apply in specific situations. Follow these four keys:

✔ **When you reward an employee for a certain behavior, be sure that the reward is clearly linked to that behavior.** For example, make a big deal about an employee landing a new account by presenting him or her a bonus check in your weekly staff meeting. As a part of the presentation, be sure to explain that the employee is receiving the bonus for bringing in the new account, and remind the others that similar behavior on their parts will bring a similar reward. By doing so, you reinforce the behavior of not only the employee who gets the reward, but also the other employees at the meeting. And think about the impact you'll have if you print a story about the presentation along with a photograph in your company employee newsletter!

✔ **Give the reward sincerely.** Employees know when you're giving sincere thanks and when you're faking it. If they sense that you aren't being sincere in your thanks, they'll discount what you say or do or — even worse — will be insulted by it. Give rewards and recognition only when you feel that your employees deserve it, but don't hesitate to do so when the situation merits. There's no such thing as too much praise — unless the praise is insincere.

✔ **Give the reward in a positive tone.** Good rewards and positive recognition given in an encouraging manner is what you're shooting for. Rewards should be positive and uplifting. They should highlight the behavior that you want more of and inspire employees to strive to become even better in the future.

Don't ever, ever immediately follow praise with a reprimand. You know, the old hug and slap in the face. For instance, "Thanks, Sherry, you handled that irate customer perfectly, but I'm really upset that you made five spelling errors in this report." The employee will immediately discount your praise, and your long-term relationship with the employee will be diminished. If you keep repeating this approach with the employee, he or she will soon be looking for a new place to work.

✔ **Give the reward as close to the event as possible.** To have maximum impact, give rewards and recognition immediately after the behavior you want to reinforce. However, because that isn't always possible, be sure that whatever the reward is — praise, cash, a gift certificate, a trip to Hawaii — you give it out no more than a few days to a couple weeks after the event.

At all costs, avoid relying only on an annual awards ceremony to hand out all employee rewards and recognition. Unfortunately, for all the excitement, glitz, and glamour of an annual awards banquet or ceremony, much of the impact is lost when you give out rewards months after the behaviors you want to reinforce actually occur.

Informal rewards and recognition

Rewards fit into two categories: informal and formal. The best employee rewards and recognition programs offer a mix of both.

Informal rewards and recognition are just that — spontaneous, requiring little or no planning and generally costing little or nothing. Company policies and procedures often choke formal rewards and recognition efforts (see the following section), but they don't constrain informal rewards, which can be given spontaneously as the behaviors occur. They can be incredibly effective because they demonstrate that managers (or the employee's peers, if one employee gives the reward to another) really care about them — enough to take the time and effort to recognize the employee's good work.

The following list presents a few terrific examples of informal rewards and recognition in organizational settings:

- Managers at Seattle, Washington-based Nordstrom department stores shared letters submitted by customers about exemplary employee service. They read them over the store intercom systems before the stores opened in the morning. The managers then posted the letters on the employee bulletin boards for all to read.

- At Apple Computer in Cupertino, California, all employees who worked on the design and development of the original Macintosh computer had their signatures engraved on the inside of the production model's case.

- A group of employees at the Milne & Craighead division of CF Canada — an international transportation logistics firm located in Calgary, Alberta — sponsored an impromptu two-day golf tournament. Held inside the company's headquarters building, the event rewarded employees for their long-term hard work. The 18-hole course, which wound its way throughout the building, was complete with real grass greens, water hazards, refreshment stops for thirsty players, and a variety of prizes and trophies.

- At Tennant Company — a manufacturer of industrial and commercial floor maintenance equipment and floor coatings in Minneapolis, Minnesota — employees awarded other employees with a "koala-tee bear" award for showing commitment to quality. The award was a stuffed toy koala bear wearing a hard hat emblazoned with the Tennant logo. Recipients proudly displayed the bears in their work areas as visible demonstrations of their personal commitment to quality.

- When an engineer at Palo Alto, California-based electronics giant Hewlett-Packard announced to his manager that he'd just found the solution to a particularly tough problem, the manager fumbled for some item to acknowledge the accomplishment. The result? He handed over a banana from his lunch bag. This simple gesture soon became immortalized as the Golden Banana Award — a highly sought after, informal award given to employees by their peers.

Only your imagination limits informal rewards and recognition. As Hewlett-Packard's example shows, it isn't so much the award itself that has meaning — it's the thought behind it.

Formal rewards and recognition

Formal rewards and recognition programs are the norm in most organizations — even those that have a strong culture of informal recognition.

The programs are regular (weekly, monthly, or annual), subject to very specific criteria or rules, and often involve tangible rewards or things of value. You've no doubt seen formal recognition at work in your organization. Here are a few examples:

- ✔ Employee-of-the-month awards
- ✔ Certificates of achievement
- ✔ Cash awards for cost savings
- ✔ Years-of-service pins
- ✔ Stock options

A two-year study of formal rewards programs in 15 federal agencies, conducted by the Office of Personnel Management, found mixed employee opinions about the programs. However, the study did find agreement on what employees like, and the lessons learned from this study can help you create a highly effective program of formal rewards and recognition in your organization.

The study reported that employees prefer the following:

- ✔ Peer involvement in designing and evaluating rewards programs, nominating individuals for awards, reviewing nominations, and recommending reward amounts
- ✔ On-the-spot rewards because they're timelier and are not based on appraisal ratings that have low credibility
- ✔ Group/team rewards, where the predominant mode of getting the work done is through formal and informal teams (see Chapter 9)
- ✔ Standard formulas for determining rewards budgets and individual reward amounts
- ✔ Prestigious honorary rewards to recognize extraordinary professional or personal efforts that best represent the organization's values and that reflect nicely on the organization, its mission, and its workforce
- ✔ Public recognition to demonstrate management's support and confidence in the validity of the rewards decisions and to reassure everyone that deserving employees will be rewarded for high performance in the future

The study also recommended a variety of strategies for improving formal rewards programs:

- ✔ Link performance recognition programs and decisions to strategic plans, goals, and results.
- ✔ Establish balanced, flexible recognition programs that feature a variety of group and individual rewards instead of focusing on one or two types of rewards.

✔ Consider making more use of competitive and prestigious non-monetary (honorary) rewards, with provisions for peer nomination and peer involvement.

✔ Improve publicity about individual reward recipients and rewards program activity.

✔ Publish and disseminate to all organizational levels annual rewards policies, expectations, and funding guidance for the year as soon as possible at the beginning of each fiscal year.

✔ Consider employee concerns — including inconsistency in distribution, non-credible basis for awards, and awards given unfairly — when developing reward policies.

✔ Establish accountability systems to monitor adherence to rewards policies and expectations, to spot problem trends, and to identify opportunities for program improvement.

Be careful what you reward

You have to be very careful to reward the behavior you actually want in your organization. Think, for example, about a common reward given in manufacturing plants or warehouses: the famous "Days without an Accident" award. Although you may think you're rewarding employees for not having accidents — and decreasing the frequency of accidents in the process — you may actually be rewarding employees for hiding accidents and not reporting them when they occur. This behavior ends up resulting in even more accidents, because the conditions that caused the accidents in the first place aren't addressed and fixed.

Consider these alternative ideas when establishing your rewards system:

✔ If you want teamwork, reward collaboration rather than internal competition.

✔ If you want high performance, reward results rather than seniority.

✔ If you want problem solving, reward problems found and solved rather than problems hiding.

✔ If you want creativity, reward creative ideas rather than conformity.

✔ If you want customer service, reward customer loyalty rather than a lack of complaints.

Be aware of exactly what behaviors you want your employees to engage in and what behaviors you're actually rewarding. Are they one in the same? If not, you need to correct your rewards and recognition program immediately!

Chapter 8

Hiring and Firing: How to Get Good Employees and Keep Them

In This Chapter

▶ Recruiting and selecting the best employees

▶ Disciplining and terminating employees when necessary

▶ Understanding employment law issues

*E*very business in the world depends on employees to make it run and flourish. Businesses need more than buildings and inventory stacked to the rafters, in countless warehouses in endless cities. And they certainly require more than computers humming away as they direct the flow of bits and bytes over worldwide telecommunications networks. Without people to oversee the buildings, manage the inventory, and operate the computers, businesses can't exist.

In this chapter, we focus on people — your people. We explain how to find and hire the best people for your company, how to monitor and correct performance, how to lay off employees when times get tough, and how to fire them if they just don't work out. Finally, we briefly cover some of the most important legal issues related to dealing with employees.

Hiring and Keeping the Very Best Employees

Creating the very best products and services requires having the very best employees to produce them. And the most effective way to have the best employees on staff is to recruit and hire only the best. Instead of hiring average employees and hoping that they develop into exceptional employees, why not take the time and effort to hire only the finest employees from the start? This section shows you how.

Defining the available job

Before you place an advertisement in the newspaper, post a job notice on the bulletin board at work, and submit a job opening on an Internet career-search site, you must create a detailed job description. A *job description* explains the duties and responsibilities of a particular position and defines the special requirements or skills that the ideal candidate needs.

Here are some specific elements that every job description should contain, regardless of the position:

- **Job title:** The name of a position — for example, "mailroom clerk," "programmer/analyst," or "vice president and chief bottle washer."

- **Department/division:** Specifies the department or division in which the specific position is located — for example, in the accounting department or the operations division.

- **Responsibilities:** The list of responsibilities isn't just a one- or two-sentence summary of a job's most important duties; it should include every task included in the position.

Writing a complete description of a position's responsibilities isn't a simple job. If you want to create a thorough job description, follow these simple steps:

1. Ask your employees exactly what they do — every single thing.

2. Compare your employees' lists against what you think they should be doing.

3. Compile your final list of responsibilities within this section in a narrative/paragraph format or as a bulleted list.

- **Required skills/expertise:** Does a person need specific skills to do this job — perhaps experience with spreadsheet programs or the ability to build wooden forms for pouring concrete building foundations, for instance? This part of the job description should include the skills, expertise, and number of years of experience required.

- **Required licenses/certifications:** Some jobs require the acquisition of specific licenses or certifications. Messengers most likely need to have valid driver's licenses. Certain kinds of accounting positions may require a CPA (Certified Public Accountant). Stockbrokers may need to provide a series 7 or 63 license (or both).

Don't put a requirement in this section unless it's truly essential to doing the job. Otherwise, you may be exposing yourself (and your company) to a nasty lawsuit. Also, job descriptions that are too exact may prompt lawsuits. Be sure that your explanations contain wording or clauses that allow you to expand tasks as necessary. The most famous of these clauses — " . . . and other duties as assigned" — works for many companies, but be sure to get advice from your legal counsel before including this terminology.

If you've never prepared job descriptions before or if you just want an easy way to deal with them, we suggest automating the process. Take a look at the Descriptions Now! software program (www.hrtools.com; click the Products tab) or at the online job descriptions available on the Job Results Management Institute's Web site (www.jrmi.com). If you're a manager who dreads writing performance appraisals, you'll think you've died and gone to heaven after you give either of these tools a test drive.

Paying employees what they're worth

All people, from managers down to the entry-level workers, believe that they deserve to be paid what they're worth. But how do you know if each person in your organization is being paid what he or she is worth? One way you can determine worth is by looking at the salaries of employees in similar positions in your geographic area or by determining the relative value of your employees' contributions to your organization.

Paying employees what they're worth is particularly important when the job market is tight and unemployment is low. If you aren't offering competitive pay rates and salaries, you'll have a tough time attracting the best employees to your firm — and keeping them. Other elements of an overall compensation package — such as health benefits, retirement plans, and stock options — also are important and can enter into a candidate's decision about whether to accept a job offer, so you can't forget to include them.

So how do you figure out how much to pay your employees? First, you want to develop an overall compensation philosophy for your organization. This philosophy will become the guide for compensation decisions for all your employees. In his book *Human Resources Kit For Dummies,* 2nd Edition (Wiley), Harold "Max" Messmer, Jr., lists the following five considerations that you must take into account when developing your organization's compensation philosophy:

✔ Are you going to make your basic salaries simply competitive with the going rate for employers in your area or higher?

✔ Are you going to establish a structured pay scale for specific jobs in your company, or are you going to set salaries on an individual basis, based on the qualities and potential of the person filling the job?

✔ To what extent are the monetary rewards you offer your employees going to take the form of salary, performance bonuses, or benefits?

 ✔ Are salaries based on how well people perform or on other factors, such as how long they stay with you or what credentials they bring to the job?

 ✔ Are you going to award bonuses on the basis of individual performance, tie bonuses to company results, or use a combination of the two?

After you've developed an overall compensation philosophy, you can decide how much to pay your employees. For example, if you want to base salaries on the going rates within your geographical area, your first step is to do a wage survey to determine exactly what those going rates are for each position within your organization. Wage information is available from a variety of sources, including the Internet, state employment offices, chambers of commerce, local business newspapers and magazines, and employment consulting firms.

Understanding the hiring process

It would be nice if you could simply snap your fingers and automatically hire the best and brightest employees whenever you wanted them, but the process isn't quite that simple. In fact, if you're serious about hiring the best employees to work in your firm, the hiring process is a lot of work. But the good news is that the rewards of making a good hire are tremendous and long-lasting. These rewards include

 ✔ Increased productivity

 ✔ Improved morale

 ✔ Better customer satisfaction

 ✔ Increased revenues

 ✔ Increased profit

In the following sections, we explain the key steps in the hiring process and offer advice on how to conduct the process the right way, every time.

Finding the best of the best

Where do you go to find the very best employees? To some extent, the answer depends on the kind of position you have to fill and the kind of candidates you're seeking. To increase the chances of getting your message in front of the right people, first decide what kind of person you want to hire and then choose the most effective method for communicating your opportunity to that person.

You can choose from a variety of ways to advertise a job opportunity to a targeted set of candidates. Here are some of the most commonly used methods:

 ✔ **The Internet:** The Internet has exploded as a resource for those seeking work and for those doing the hiring. Hundreds of Web sites cater to people seeking and offering jobs. Many such Web sites are specific to different kinds of opportunities — for example, information technology, purchasing, or sales. Here are some of the most well-established job-hunting sites:

- Monster (www.monster.com)
- Jobs.com (www.jobs.com)
- CareerBuilder (www.careerbuilder.com)
- Jobs.net (www.jobs.net)
- Craigslist (www.craigslist.org)
- Indeed (www.indeed.com)
- Guru.com (www.guru.com)

✔ **Newspaper advertisement (want ads):** The newspaper is traditionally the first place where employers think of looking for new employees, and it's often the first place that job seekers go to look for new employers. But is placing an advertisement in your local newspaper the optimum way to find the people you're looking for? Maybe yes, maybe no. Perhaps the best candidate for the job will see your advertisement, but you may miss many other terrific candidates, both locally and outside of your immediate geographic area.

✔ **Business and personal networks:** You have networks of contacts, both in your business and in your personal life. Your friends and professional contacts can be excellent sources of job candidates. People in your networks know about your business and the kind of people you want, so they're unlikely to send you candidates who would reflect badly on them.

✔ **Associations:** You can find all kinds of industry and professional associations out there — from the Association for Computing Machinery (ACM), to the Society for Human Resource Management (SHRM), to the American Bar Association (ABA). Each one has its own specialized membership population. Most associations have their own job referral services, which they offer to their members as a free benefit of membership. Many associations also post job listings on their Web sites, which may be available only to association members as a benefit of membership.

✔ **Employment agencies:** Although you may be required to pay to use their services, employment agencies (including temporary agencies, executive search firms, and so-called "headhunting firms") can be terrific sources of job candidates. Many companies use temporary agencies to try out new employees on a short-term, risk-free basis. If a temporary employee doesn't work out, your organization can simply send the employee back to the agency and ask for another person. If a temporary employee does work out, you can hire the person directly from the agency, sometimes for no fee.

Be careful when using employment agencies. Some agencies prohibit a company from hiring a temporary employee for a specified period of time after his or her temporary employment stint, or if they do permit it, they may charge an exorbitant fee to do so.

✔ **Inside your organization:** One of the best sources of top-quality job candidates is looking within your own organization. The beauty of internal candidates is that you usually can get very candid references on their job performance from their coworkers and past and present supervisors. Another plus is that internal candidates are familiar with company policies and procedures. As a result, they can transition into their new positions quickly. Don't overlook this rich resource of job candidates.

Recruiting is very much a numbers game. The larger your pool of candidates, the greater your chance of finding the employee who's just right for your organization. Unless you're specifically targeting only one candidate or a small group of candidates, cast your recruiting net as widely as you possibly can. The time, money, and effort you put into finding the best candidates up front will pay off after you make the hire.

Interviewing candidates

The interview is one of the most critical — and often the most dreaded — parts of the hiring process. For job candidates, the interview presents an opportunity to answer detailed questions about their experience and to give their potential employer a glimpse of what kind of employees they will be. For employers, the interview presents a unique opportunity to ask questions that go beyond the one-sided marketing pitch of most résumés and gets a feel for how candidates would fit into the organization.

From the employer perspective, here are the three main reasons for interviewing job candidates:

✔ To get further in-depth information about a candidate's work skills and experience — straight from the job seeker's mouth. This process gives you the opportunity to see whether what the candidate tells you is consistent with his or her résumé.

✔ To assess the candidate's personality and determine how that personality will fit into your existing work team.

✔ To test on a real-time basis a candidate's enthusiasm, intelligence, poise, and ability to think quickly.

You can't guarantee that someone who shines during an interview will work out as a new hire. Every manager has tales of stellar interviewees who got the jobs but didn't last long. However, a well-done interview will greatly increase your chances of landing the best candidate for the job.

Here are some tips on conducting an effective interview:

✓ **Welcome the applicant and put him or her at ease.** Most job applicants are more than a little nervous when interviewing for a job, and it's no wonder — job interviews often make or break candidates. Conduct the interview in a quiet office or conference room that's free of interruption from phones, computers, and other employees. Greet the candidate warmly; offer coffee, water, or a soft drink; and direct him or her to a seat. Instead of launching right into the interview, spend a couple minutes breaking the ice to take the edge off the interviewee's nervousness.

✓ **Summarize the position.** Take a minute or two to give the candidate a brief summary of the position. Include details of job responsibilities; how the job fits into the organization, reporting relationships, and expected customer interactions (see the earlier section "Defining the available job").

✓ **Ask a variety of questions.** In his book *What Color Is Your Parachute?* (Ten Speed Press), author Richard Nelson Bolles suggests asking questions that fall into any one of four categories:

- Why are you here?

- What can you do for us?

- What kind of person are you?

- Can we afford you?

Take plenty of notes during your interviews. Better yet, prepare an interview form in advance to guide you through your questions and to enable you to jot down notes on your candidates' responses. This advice is especially important if you have a lot of candidates to interview or if you won't have a chance to review the candidates' performances immediately after the interviews.

✓ **Probe the candidate's strengths and weaknesses.** Chances are, you picked up on some of the candidate's strengths and weaknesses when you reviewed his or her résumé before the interview. Now's the time to probe the candidate further about those strengths and weaknesses, as well as any others that become apparent during the interview.

✓ **Conclude the interview on an "up" note.** Ask your candidate whether he or she has any other information that you should consider in your decision process. Give the candidate a chance to explain that information. Thank the candidate for his or her interest in the job (no matter how well or how poorly the interview went) and give the person some idea of when you'll be making a decision or whether you'll be conducting an additional round of interviews.

Don't make any sort of promises, such as, "You're definitely the best candidate — we'll be making you an offer for sure." Not only are you setting yourself up for a potential lawsuit if you don't follow through on your promise, but also the next candidate you interview may be even better than the last.

Never ask these questions in an interview

You can choose from plenty of good questions to ask potential employees, but there are some questions that you should never, ever ask. Why? Primarily because in some cases, it may be against the law to do so. In addition, certain questions have little or no relevance to a candidate's potential ability to do a job.

So here's a word to the wise: Avoid at all costs questions that have anything to do with the following topics.

✔ Race or skin color

✔ Country of origin

✔ Gender or sexual orientation

✔ Marital status

✔ Religious beliefs

✔ Arrest and conviction record

✔ Height and weight

✔ Debts

✔ Disability

Make sure that questions on these topics are not a part of your company's job application either. Possible exceptions include questions related to height and weight for firefighters, and similar work-related physical requirements for other jobs.

For a terrific, in-depth discussion of how to interview candidates (much more in-depth than we have the space to present here) — as well as sample questions, interview forms, interview evaluation forms, and much, much more — be sure to check out Harold "Max" Messmer, Jr.'s book, *Human Resources Kit For Dummies,* 2nd Edition (Wiley).

Checking references

Although many employers are wary about providing reference information about former employees (and understandably so; some employers have been sued for giving bad references), it's still very much worth your time to check out all available references. You just never know what kind of information will turn up in your investigation; you may uncover info that will have great bearing on whether you extend a job offer to a candidate.

Reference checks most often occur after the initial round of interviews, when the employer narrows the list of candidates to just a few people. When you make a reference call, don't forget that the person you're calling is doing you a big favor by telling you anything at all about the candidate. Be patient, polite, and thankful when someone provides the information you need.

Here are some of the best places to dig deeper to find out how your candidate may fit in the job and in your company:

✔ Current and former supervisors

✔ Current and former customers/clients

✔ Colleges, universities, and other schools

> ✔ Networks of common acquaintances, such as industry associations or professional groups
>
> ✔ Public sources, such as the Internet or local newspapers

Increasingly popular are companies that verify a candidate's résumé or references for a fee. If you decide to go this route, be sure that you pick an experienced, reputable firm and that you notify all candidates in advance that you'll be using such a service (if required to do so by your state or locality; check with your state employment office to be sure).

Using the Internet to research candidates

Wouldn't it be nice to get more information about your job candidates than the 400 or 500 carefully crafted words on their résumés? Well, with the power of the Internet at your fingertips, you may be able to do just that! The latest generation of job seekers lives much of their lives online, so they leave online crumbs for recruiters to track down and read. Now, you can hire investigators to check out a job candidate's background, but that isn't what we're talking about here. We're talking about a quick-and-easy background investigation that you can do yourself for no cost — beyond the short amount of time it takes you to do it.

Some sites that you can check out for personal information about potential candidates include the following:

> ✔ www.google.com
>
> ✔ www.facebook.com
>
> ✔ www.myspace.com
>
> ✔ www.orkut.com
>
> ✔ www.linkedin.com

For example, say you have a job candidate named Nancy Tufnel who graduated from Brown University and worked for *USA Today*. At least that's what she claims on her résumé. By doing a quick search on Google, using keywords "Nancy Tufnel" and "Brown," you may find a number of matches related to your job candidate — including a MySpace page, mentions on the Brown Web site, plenty of photos and related text at a campus sorority Web site, and perhaps even a byline on *USA Today*. Or you may find nothing at all (which brings up its own set of questions).

Ranking your candidates

After you've completed your interviews and conducted your reference and research checks, you must rank each of your candidates against the others. The easiest way to rank is to put the name of each candidate along the left side of a piece of paper and list your hiring criteria along the top of the page. You can create a grid similar to the one in Figure 8-1 for a hypothetical group of three candidates.

	Customer Service Skills (A)	Help Desk Experience (B)	References (C)	Total Points (A+B+C)
Maria	1	2	1	4
Tom	3	1	2	6
Sally	2	3	3	8

Figure 8-1: A sample candidate ranking sheet you use to make hiring decisions.

Rank each employee on each of the hiring criteria. In our example, Maria ranks number one for customer service skills, while Sally ranks second and Tom third. Go through each of your hiring criteria (you may have many more items than our simple example does) and assign rankings in this manner. After you've ranked all the candidates, add the total for each employee and note it on the worksheet. The candidate with the lowest score is the one you should consider hiring. In this case, it's Maria.

Making the hire

Congratulations! Now you can make your job offer to your top candidate. However, before you do, be sure to check your organization's policies on hiring new employees. Some companies allow managers to make a verbal offer — on the phone or in person — and others insist that any job offers be in writing. Still others insist not only that job offers be in writing, but also that they undergo review by the human resources department or legal counsel before going out to candidates.

Our advice is to always use written job offers. After the written job offer is signed and on the way to the candidate, however, we also encourage you to call him or her with the good news. The candidate may be weighing more than one offer, so you want to be sure your offer gets to the candidate before any others.

Here are the key elements to include in a written offer letter:

✔ Job title

✔ The candidate's name

✔ Date employment will start

✔ Terms on which employment is offered (salary, full-time versus part-time, probationary period, and so on)

✔ Any conditions that must be met before hire can be made (pre-employment physical, drug test, evidence of U.S. citizenship, and so on)

✔ Any action required by the candidate (make appointment with company drug-testing lab, sign and return offer letter, and so on)

If, for some reason, your top candidate declines the offer, you have three main choices:

✔ You can revise your offer to answer the objections of your top candidate.

✔ You can go to the next-ranked candidate on your worksheet.

✔ You can initiate the entire hiring process all over again.

You need to weigh the pluses and minuses of each avenue. For instance, if you have just one strong candidate and your positions aren't too far apart, revising the offer may make more sense than offering the job to a weaker candidate or starting the hiring process all over again.

Don't allow desperation to rule your hiring decisions. Leaving a position unfilled usually is better than hiring an inferior candidate. If your first round of recruiting and interviews doesn't uncover the right candidate for the job, by all means try it again. It's far less painful to interview more candidates than to terminate someone who doesn't work out the way you hoped.

Structuring your new employee's first day at work

The first few days and weeks of work for your new employee can be both exciting and disorienting. No matter how much experience a new hire may have under his or her belt, starting a new job, to some extent, means starting from scratch. And when you add in a new office, new coworkers, and entirely new relationships, policies, and procedures to sort out, you have a recipe for instant confusion.

You can help make your new hire's transition into your organization relatively painless and quick. Here are some tips on how to make your new employee's first day at work productive and easy:

✔ **Make your new hire feel welcome.** Set plenty of time aside for your new employee. Be sure that others who will supervise or be supervised by the new employee also allot some time for interaction. Nothing is worse for a new employee than to be shoved aside for hours (or days or weeks) because no one can spare a few hours of time to help welcome a new member of the team.

✔ **Provide a sense of place and belonging.** Be sure that the new hire's office or workstation is ready to move into right away. Stock it with a full complement of office essentials (paper clips, pens, pencils, paper, stapler, and so on), and make sure that the phone and computer are properly hooked up and immediately available.

✔ **Introduce your new employee to the team.** Take the time to introduce your new hire to his or her coworkers. You can escort the person around your offices to meet people on an informal basis, or you can schedule an informal get-together early in the day or over lunch so that your work unit or department can get to know the new employee.

✔ **Take care of only the essentials on the first day.** Don't drown your new employee in forms and paperwork. Although new-hire paperwork is a necessary evil, you can avoid it on the first day. Give the new employee a week to complete the forms and turn them in.

✔ **Make the first day a fun day.** Above all, make sure that your new employee's first day is a fun day — one that starts off on the right foot with your organization. You have plenty of time down the road for the job to get serious, so you don't need to rush it now.

You only have one chance to make a first impression. Take the time to ensure that the first impression of your organization is that you truly care about the new hire's well-being. And don't let that impression end after the first day of work; renew it every day with all your employees through your own thoughts and actions.

Disciplining (and Perhaps Terminating) Deserving Employees

At times, no matter what you do to try to work with an employee or to help him or her achieve an acceptable standard, an employee may fall short of your expectations. You may need to discipline him, and if the discipline doesn't work, you may be left with no choice but to remove the employee from his or her job. Firing an employee certainly is the toughest job by far for any manager or supervisor. The pain of terminating an employee is felt by not only the employee, but also by the entire organization — especially his or her coworkers and the employee's supervisor or manager.

In the sections that follow, we take a close look at how to properly discipline and terminate employees when the need arises.

The first resort: Discipline

The term *discipline* applies to a wide range of actions meant to provide feedback to employees about deficiencies in their conduct or performance. Employers generally provide disciplinary feedback in the hope that employees will change their behavior or performance trends so that supervisors or managers don't need to take further action. The following sections break down the disciplinary process in case you need it.

Identifying why you may need to discipline

Why should you discipline employees? Wouldn't everyone be much happier if you simply left well enough alone? Not exactly — well enough often isn't good enough. If an employee isn't performing up to the standards you mutually agreed to, you must take action, not ignore the problem.

Here are two key reasons for disciplining employees:

- **Misconduct:** Every organization has policies and procedures that employees are supposed to follow. Breaking certain rules (for example, taking two reams of paper from the supply cabinet when you're supposed to take only one ream at a time) may have only a minor impact on the organization. But other infractions — including stealing from coworkers, lying to the boss, and making fraudulent travel expense claims — are quite serious and require serious discipline.

- **Performance:** Every employee is expected to achieve a certain level of performance — whether it's producing 50 widgets an hour, selling $50,000 worth of products a month, or answering the telephone before the third ring 90 percent of the time. These may be the minimum levels of performance; falling below these minimum standards repeatedly or for a prolonged period of time usually triggers the disciplinary process.

Progressing through the different stages of discipline

When an employee's behavior or performance requires discipline, reviewing the discipline process is important to ensure that the employee understands the importance of making a change. As a supervisor or manager, you generally have some discretion as to which level of discipline to apply, and you may or may not use each one of the levels.

You need to keep in mind, however, that the level of discipline should be appropriate for the level of employee transgression, and that the discipline chosen should be consistently applied to all employees in similar situations.

The most commonly accepted discipline in use today is called *progressive discipline*. With this method, the feedback becomes progressively more serious for repeated or major performance lapses or cases of misconduct. The following represent a common model of progressive discipline. Discipline generally starts at the least-severe consequence and works up to the most severe — depending on how the employee responds or on the severity of the original offense. Fraud, for example, is grounds for immediate termination; you don't have to go through all the other steps for such a serious offense. Here are the steps, from least to most serious:

- **Verbal counseling:** This is informal, verbal feedback given by an employee's immediate supervisor for very minor transgressions or first offenses. In many cases, this is the only discipline an employee needs to get back on track.

- **Verbal warning:** A verbal warning is a bit more serious than verbal counseling. An employee's immediate supervisor gives a verbal warning for more serious transgressions or when an employee ignores his or her verbal counseling. In a verbal warning, you explicitly state that you're giving the employee a verbal warning. You also let the employee know that repeated transgressions will result in a written warning or a higher level of discipline.

- **Written warning:** This form of discipline is much more serious than verbal counseling or warnings. The written warning — created and delivered by the employee's immediate supervisor — generally becomes a part of the employee's personnel file and may be a factor in future promotional opportunities or job references.

- **Reprimand:** A reprimand is similar to a written warning, but it serves as a final notice for the employee to correct his or her performance or behavior immediately. A manager one level or more above the employee's immediate supervisor usually delivers the reprimand.

- **Suspension:** Suspension puts an employee on mandatory leave without pay for a period depending on the seriousness of the transgression. The purpose of a suspension is to give the employee time away from the company to think about the problems that led to this disciplinary outcome. The time also gives the employee a chance to consider ways to correct his or her behavior or performance shortcomings.

- **Demotion:** Demoting an employee may be appropriate if doing so will make him or her better able to meet performance goals at a lower level of expectation. Demotions aren't appropriate in cases of serious misconduct.

- **Termination:** When employees are guilty of extremely serious or repeated transgressions or when they don't correct their repeated performance shortfalls after some or all the preceding steps, termination is called for. The following section goes into detail on this topic.

When disciplining employees — especially as the discipline escalates beyond verbal counseling or warning — be sure to notify your supervisor and the human resources department about the problem and the actions you're taking to solve it. These people not only want and need to know what's going on, but also can offer you their support and assistance during the process. To protect your company against a lawsuit, they also consult with the company's attorneys who will make sure that you proceed in the appropriate manner (see the final section of this chapter for more on the legal issues of hiring and firing).

The last resort: Termination

Termination should always be the last resort in an organization. Terminate an employee only after the employee has been given ample opportunity to improve his or her performance or behavior — and has failed to do so — or when a transgression is so serious that it merits immediate dismissal. Here are some examples of transgressions that merit immediate dismissal:

- ✔ Using or selling illegal drugs at work
- ✔ Stealing from coworkers or from the organization
- ✔ Fraud
- ✔ Violating confidentiality agreements
- ✔ Gross insubordination
- ✔ Extreme violation of safety rules
- ✔ Misrepresentation on employment application

Before you ever get to the point of termination, do whatever you can to help the employee get back on track and become a productive member of your team. In some cases, discipline will be all the wake-up call that the employee needs. In other cases, you may have to transfer the employee to another job or to another department. In fact, you should always explore the possibility of a transfer if the employee shows the potential to become a productive member of the organization.

But if the situation eventually warrants a termination, the following sections will take you through the process.

Taking steps before you terminate

Firing an employee is bound to unleash all kinds of hurt and resentment and can even land you in court. For these reasons, be sure that you follow all the proper procedures before you terminate an employee. The following list presents the criteria you need to satisfy:

✔ **Documentation:** If you're planning to fire an employee for performance shortcomings, be sure that you have written proof of those shortcomings and that you have the support of evidence. Documentation can be anything from a supervisor's written notes in a daily planner, time cards showing that an employee is habitually late, or falsified expense reports or other documents.

When you make the decision as to what kind of documentation will be most appropriate for a particular situation, first ask yourself this question: Would the documentation convince a court jury that terminating your employee was justified?

✔ **Fair warning:** Fair play says that employees with performance problems should be given fair warning of the consequences of continued problems. If you plan to terminate an employee for performance shortcomings, be sure that you give him or her fair warning. However, serious misconduct can be grounds for immediate dismissal and doesn't necessarily require advance warning.

✔ **Response time:** If an employee's job is in jeopardy if improvement isn't soon forthcoming, you must give the employee sufficient time to improve. You can reasonably expect an employee's performance to improve after a couple weeks to a month.

✔ **Reasonableness:** The ultimate punishment of termination should be reasonable and appropriate for the offense that led up to it. Firing an employee for being five minutes late to work once isn't reasonable. Firing an employee for consistently being two hours late for several weeks — with no change in behavior after repeated oral and written warnings — is reasonable.

✔ **Avenues for appeal:** Your firm should offer employees the ability to appeal termination to higher management. You never know when a lower-level manager or supervisor may have acted rashly or outside the bounds of your company's termination policy. A review by higher management will help protect good employees from being unjustly terminated.

Terminating an employee

After you've gone through all the criteria and have determined that you've complied, the time has come to terminate your employee. Letting an employee go is one of the most unpleasant aspects of being an employer. Regardless, terminating employees is a key duty that you can do well or not so well.

Here's a five-step guide that will help you through this process; by following these steps, you can minimize the pain to the employee and the pain to coworkers and the organization as a whole:

1. **Meet with the employee in a private location.**

   Find a private office away from other employees to conduct the termination meeting. Most HR professionals now believe that you should terminate employees late in the day (to spare them the embarrassment of clearing out their desks in front of their coworkers). Also, try to schedule the termination early in the week (to allow employees sufficient time to apply for unemployment and to mount a search for a new job).

Some companies suggest that an HR professional be present when you terminate the employee. It's always wise to have a witness, which is part of documentation (see the previous section).

2. **Tell the employee that he or she is being terminated.**

   Be straightforward and direct. This isn't the time to beat around the bush. Let the employee know that the action is final and that there's no recourse.

3. **Explain exactly why the employee is being terminated.**

   Give the reasons in concise terms. Avoid going into too much detail or getting drawn into an argument about the merits of the action.

4. **Announce the effective date of the termination and provide details on the termination process.**

   Most firings are effective immediately, and, in the majority of cases, this is the best approach to take. Discuss the pay and benefits the employee will receive, including severance pay, pending commissions, vacation pay, and health-care benefits covered by COBRA — the Consolidated Omnibus Budget Reconciliation Act of 1985, which requires an employer to allow the employee to continue his or her identical group health coverage for a period of 18 months or more at the same price that his or her coworkers pay for comparable coverage. Also, explain the next step in the process of obtaining the benefits.

5. **If the firing is effective immediately, escort the employee to his or her office or workstation and then off the premises.**

   At the end of the termination meeting, walk the employee out and go through your termination checklist, collecting any keys, passes, and company property in the employee's possession. Give the employee any termination pay and personnel forms resulting from the firing. After the employee packs up his or her personal possessions, escort the worker off the premises.

   If the firing is to take effect sometime in the future, the employee may need a day or two to recover from the shock of the situation, so consider offering this time off during the termination meeting.

   Be careful not to say during the termination anything encouraging such as "We'll give you a recommendation" or "It was a pleasure having you here." The employee could use such statements against you if he or she takes you to court.

As you can see, you need to plan for a termination so that you have the necessary forms and materials — including a termination checklist — ready for the final meeting.

1 Fought the Law (and the Law Won)

If you discover one thing from running a business — often from the school of hard knocks — it will be that federal, state, and local governments have enacted many laws to protect employees from abuse by their employers. Whether it's a minimum-wage law, a law prohibiting discrimination, or any number of others, a law or regulation exists for just about every occasion.

Be sure that you're intimately familiar with the key employment laws that will affect the way you run your business. If you run afoul of these laws and you get sued by an employee or by the government, you can literally be put out of business. And although you may depend on your human resources manager or administrator to be an expert on labor laws, every manager should have a working understanding of the laws, as well. Check out the Department of Labor Web site (www.dol.gov) and the U.S. Equal Employment Opportunity Commission (EEOC) Web site (www.eeoc.gov) to research many of these employment laws or to find links to places that have them readily available for you to browse at your leisure.

With apologies to readers who live outside the United States (you'll just have to stand back and marvel at the wonders of the American legal system), here's a list of 11 American laws (all enacted by the federal government) that you need to be very familiar with. Most have been amended one or more times since they were first enacted:

✔ **Age Discrimination in Employment Act:** Prohibits all employers with 20 or more employees from discriminating against employees aged 40 or older. Also eliminates company policies that mandate retirement at age 70 (with the exception of certain executives who may be required to retire at age 65).

✔ **Americans with Disabilities Act:** Requires employers with 15 or more employees to make reasonable accommodations for applicants and employees with disabilities.

✔ **Employee Retirement Income Security Act of 1974 (ERISA):** Requires employers to meet minimum standards for most voluntarily established pension and health plans in private industries. Companies must also follow rules on the federal income tax effects of transactions associated with employee benefit plans.

✔ **Equal Pay Act:** Requires employers with two or more employees and that produce goods for interstate commerce to pay men and women equally for the same job. In other words, you must offer "equal pay for equal work."

✔ **Fair Labor Standards Act:** Requires all employers that sell their products across state lines to pay legislated minimum wages and overtime, among other salary-related standards.

✔ **Family and Medical Leave Act:** Requires employers with 15 or more employees to grant a qualified employee unpaid leave for serious illness, birth, adoption, or a variety of health-related issues that the employee or his or her immediate family members may experience. In other words, employers must keep the employee's job open until he or she returns.

✔ **Immigration Reform and Control Act:** Requires all employers to determine whether their employees are legally able to work in the United States.

✔ **Older Workers Benefit Protection Act:** Prohibits employers with 20 or more employees from discriminating against employees aged 40 or older with regard to early retirement and other benefit plans.

✔ **Pregnancy Discrimination Act:** Requires employers with 15 or more employees to class pregnancy as a medical condition. This ensures that pregnant employees receive the same benefits and medical leave as employees who aren't pregnant.

✔ **Rehabilitation Act:** Prohibits employers holding federal government contracts and subcontracts totaling more than $2,500 in value from discriminating against handicapped people. If an employer holds federal government contracts and subcontracts worth more than $50,000, it has to develop and implement a written affirmative action program for handicapped people.

✔ **Title VII of the Civil Rights Act:** Prohibits employers with 15 or more employees from discriminating against employees on the basis of race, gender, color, religion, or national origin.

This list is by no means a complete and in-depth guide to employment law. It's simply meant to give you an idea of what you're dealing with. For much more detail on these laws and on employment law in general, please seek competent legal counsel. (In other words, get a good lawyer!)

Chapter 9

One for All and All for One: Building Teams That Really Work

*T*eams have taken the world of business by storm, and for good reason — they really work! No one person can be an expert at everything or be expected to get everything done in an organization. Teams combine the talents of employees with a variety of skills and experience to find and implement solutions that would be impossible for one person alone to do. In other words, team members leverage their talents to create an outcome much greater than the sum of the team's parts.

Teamwork can make a tremendous difference in the way employees work together — a difference that can positively affect the quality of products, services, and customer satisfaction. When employees work *with* rather than *against* one another, the result is a much more effective and efficient organization — one with quicker decision making, less wasted time, and a reduction in expenses.

In this chapter, we take a close look at the many different kinds of teams and how companies use teams to improve products and services — which will surely make customers happy. You also find out about empowering your employees — a very important part of successful team processes — and about how to set and monitor goals. Finally, we explore business meetings, and you discover how to make them better.

The Construction and Evolution of the Team

Although there will always be a place for individual effort and personal initiative on the job, teamwork is the lever for growth and effectiveness in most businesses today. An employee who practices teamwork skills will be a more valuable asset to her organization — and to customers and coworkers.

To create the best products and services, you need to have the best employees available to produce them. And the best way to have the most-qualified employees on staff is to recruit and hire them to begin with. Don't settle for hiring average employees in the hopes that you can develop them into exceptional employees. Instead, take the time to hire the best employees you can from the very start. To find out how to do just that, head to Chapter 8. This section runs down the different forms teams can take and how teams can develop over time.

Eyeing the different kinds of teams

Would it surprise you if we told you that many kinds of teams are at work in many kinds of organizations today? Although a company's managers often assemble formal teams of employees to tackle specific issues, informal teams of employees form and disband all the time, of their own accord. The following sections discuss the most common types of teams that form in a business.

Formal teams

Formal teams are teams organized by managers — or sometimes by self-managing groups of employees — to accomplish specific tasks. They generally are the most visible teams within an organization, and they are often launched with great fanfare and pomp. Formal teams hold great promise in getting useful things done for an organization, but they do their best work with a minimum amount of interference by management.

The three kinds of formal teams include

- **Command teams:** Teams comprised of a manager or supervisor and all his or her employees. Sales teams, management teams, and executive teams are examples of command teams.

- **Committees:** Teams of employees pulled together to solve an ongoing or long-term organizational problem, or to achieve a specific organizational goal. Committees can exist for years, with membership changing as employees come and go. Safety committees, employee-morale committees, and investment committees are examples of committees.

✔ **Task forces:** Teams of employees pulled together to *quickly* solve organizational problems or to respond to specific business opportunities. Task forces usually have very specific goals and strict deadlines.

IBM's Hispanic Executive Task Force, for example, is focused on tapping into the $653-billion Hispanic business market. Within this market, two million businesses have grown at three times the U.S. average. Task force members are working with the Hispanic Chamber of Commerce, other selected organizations, and Latino business partners to increase IBM's marketing to the increasingly populous Hispanic demographic.

Informal teams

Informal teams are the most common teams in business. By nature, they aren't sanctioned by an organization's management, but they can hold a power that far exceeds their apparent authority.

Although informal teams aren't, by definition, a part of a company's formal structure, they're important parts of the organization nonetheless. In fact, they're often an organization's backbone, its continuity, and its long-term memory — factors that contribute to their power. Successful managers know the importance of informal teams in swaying employee opinion, and they're mindful of their power when making decisions that affect the organization. Managers can't run an organization by themselves — they have to win the hearts and minds of the people they lead to get things done. This means securing the cooperation of informal employee teams.

Specifically, informal teams have a couple of important benefits:

✔ Informal teams provide employees with channels of communication outside of the organization's sanctioned, formal channels.

✔ Informal teams allow employees to let off steam about issues of concern with others in their peer groups.

Examples of informal teams include the groups of employees who sit at the same table together during lunch; the lunch shifts of fast-food workers who are pulled together by the common bond of working in a particularly hectic environment day after day; the accounting clerks who chat with each other as they rubber-stamp invoices to be paid; and so on.

Self-managing teams

Perhaps the most revolutionary of teams are self-managing teams, which are teams of workers who have replaced traditional managers in many organizations. *Self-managing teams* are, as the title suggests, teams of workers who are granted the authority to manage themselves. Instead of a supervisor or manager calling the shots, a self-managing team decides what needs to be done and then figures out the best way to do it.

In most organizations, self-managing teams are an everyday occurrence. Managers enable them because their companies can no longer afford to have managers make all the decisions. For an organization to be competitive in today's fast and furious global marketplace, the responsibility and authority for decision making has to be pushed as far down into the organization as possible, where it's closest to the customers and their needs.

Self-managing teams can be formed to take on most any business task or to consider any issue and either make recommendations or institute solutions themselves. To work properly, self-managing teams have to truly be free of the interference of supervisors and/or managers. Although supervisors and managers can set overall goals for teams, self-managing teams should be granted the authority to make decisions that will determine how they'll achieve these goals.

Successful self-managing teams display several characteristics:

- ✔ They make the most of their own decisions — especially the most important ones.
- ✔ They select their own leaders.
- ✔ They add and remove members of the teams.
- ✔ They often create their own goals and schedules.
- ✔ They create and execute their own training programs.
- ✔ They get rewarded as a team.

Any organization — from small two- or three-person operations to the largest Fortune 500 multinationals — can employ self-managing teams. It isn't the kind of organization or its size that matters; it's the willingness of managers to give up some of their decision-making authority to workers. The workers also must accept the responsibilities that go along with authority.

Do self-managing teams work? The evidence seems to indicate that they do. Here are some self-managing team success stories from the business world:

- ✔ Self-managing teams at the San Diego Zoo successfully design and operate popular attractions, such as the zoo's Tiger River exhibit. Employees from these teams submitted 30 percent fewer workers' compensation claims than their coworkers.
- ✔ Self-managing teams at the Boeing Company — the Seattle, Washington-based aircraft manufacturer — designed and built the 777-model passenger jet — with less than half the problems experienced in any previous jet program.
- ✔ The *Star Tribune* newspaper in Minneapolis, Minnesota, cut billing mistakes in half when it implemented self-managing work teams.

Spanning the stages of team growth

Business teams don't just happen. As with a primordial organism, the teams evolve, becoming stronger and more effective over time. If you've spent any amount of time on a team, you've probably experienced the different stages of team growth. In the beginning, team members are tentative, and little real work gets done. As time passes, however, the team becomes extremely cohesive and productive. At least that's what this model predicts. The following sections run down the four stages of team growth. Do you recognize which stage your team is in?

Stage 1: Forming

During the first stage of team growth, known as *forming,* team members get to know one another while cautiously testing the boundaries of the team and its leadership by interacting and noting reactions — or lack thereof. Participants generally are energized and excited by the prospect of getting their task accomplished, but they're a bit nervous about how the team will go forward. In this stage, the team actually accomplishes very little.

Stage 2: Storming

The second stage of team growth, *storming,* is marked by a panic among team members as they begin to realize the difficulty of the tasks the organization expects them to accomplish. Participants become impatient about the lack of progress in the first stage. They react by arguing with one another, questioning the team's leadership, and choosing sides. In this stage, progress toward accomplishing the team's goals is minimal. However, team members are learning more about — and becoming more comfortable with — one another.

Stage 3: Norming

During the third stage of team growth, called *norming,* team members finally begin to accept the makeup of the team and follow the team's ground rules. Members establish roles and start supporting each other in their efforts. The fear encountered in the storming stage disappears and is replaced by the belief that the team will accomplish its goals.

Stage 4: Performing

In the fourth, or *performing,* stage of team growth, team members feel fully comfortable in their relationships with one another. They begin to have insights into the behavior and thought processes of their teammates. Team members are happy with the team's progress; they should be making substantial strides toward goals and working at peak efficiency. The team is truly performing as a team: Every member supports every other member, and the team is pulling together to create an entity that can achieve more than any one person can do alone.

Teaming up at the Mayo Clinic

When Dr. William Mayo and Dr. Charles Mayo founded the Mayo Clinic in Rochester, Minnesota, in the early 1900s, they touched off a revolution that reverberated throughout the worldwide medical community. The revolution was all about one thing: teamwork.

"It (has become) necessary to develop medicine as a cooperative science; the clinician, the specialist, and the laboratory workers uniting for the good of the patient," explained Dr. William Mayo. "Individualism in medicine can no longer exist." As Harry Harwick, who worked alongside the Mayo brothers for 31 years, wrote: "The first and perhaps greatest lesson I learned from the Mayos was that of teamwork. For 'my brother and I' was no mere convenient term of reference, but rather the expression of a basic, indivisible philosophy of life."

Here are the five key principles that guide teamwork at the Mayo Clinic:

✔ **No one is big enough to be independent of others.** According to Dr. William Mayo, doctors should freely draw on the expertise of others — including other doctors, social workers, and religious advisers — to create a team that best serves the needs of the patient.

✔ **Teamwork is part of the culture.** At the Mayo Clinic, teamwork isn't an option — it's a way of life. Teamwork starts at the top, within the clinic's management team and governing boards, and it flows down throughout the entire structure of the organization, permeating and unifying it.

✔ **Language matters.** Doctors at the Mayo Clinic call one another "consultants." Why? Because doctors at the Mayo Clinic are expected to consult with one another about patients and cases. Instead of becoming islands, doctors create networks and teams for the benefit of clinic patients.

✔ **Money talks.** Every doctor at the Mayo Clinic is on salary. Doctors have no incentives for ordering expensive tests for patients or for denying them. The Mayo Clinic is unlike an HMO (health maintenance organization), where doctors often complain about being under pressure to reduce costs, at the risk of good patient care.

✔ **The customer is part of the team.** Patients at the Mayo Clinic can be as involved in their diagnoses and treatments as they want. They're just as important as the doctors, nurses, and others assigned to their cases. Imagine what teams would be like in your organization if your customers could join and become part of them!

More than 500,000 people are treated at the Mayo Clinic each year. It encompasses sites in three states, employing more than 50,000 physicians, scientists, nurses, administrators, and allied health workers. Through all its growth and change, the Mayo Clinic remains committed to its guiding principle, as articulated by Dr. William Mayo: "The best interest of the patient is the only interest to be considered."

Of course, the scenario we paint of these stages is a bit idealized. Not every team that performs is an effective team, and not every team that's dysfunctional is broken. Indeed, many dysfunctional teams achieve great things. The key for a team is to do the best with what it has. Try to keep all members focused on the task at hand and working toward common goals. Management (or team leaders) should reward good performance and shine the spotlight on team members when they earn it.

Empowering Employees

Employee empowerment was the business buzz phrase of the 1990s. Although everyone was talking about the power of empowerment, few companies actually put their words into action. For those that did, though, the result was an unleashing of employee energy unmatched in the history of business. And in the new millennium, empowerment is just as hot a concept. But empowerment is much more than a management buzzword; in business today, it's a concept that will separate the firms that thrive from those that fail. Empowering employees allows an organization to tap into the almost boundless energy and talents contained within every employee. The power is there — don't let it go to waste!

Exactly how do you empower your employees? Is it good enough to simply declare your employees "empowered?" No, it's not. You have to take several steps to give your employees the authority to make decisions that will have an impact on their work lives. The following list presents five easy tips for empowering your employees:

- Clearly define your employees' responsibilities, and be sure that they understand them — as well as your expectations of performance.

- Be sure that your employees have the training necessary to successfully undertake their responsibilities.

- Give your employees the complete authority to successfully undertake all their responsibilities.

- Treat your employees with respect at all times and trust them implicitly.

- Err on the side of giving your employees too much information rather than not enough.

Many companies in today's business environment embrace these actions of empowerment. The following list presents some examples of empowered employees in action, illustrating the authority and trust given by their companies:

- A janitor in a central distribution center for Domino's Pizza became a hero when he fielded an after-hours call from a busy store that had run out of pepperoni. The empowered employee threw a box of pepperoni in the back of a company-owned truck and drove several hundred miles to make the delivery to a grateful store manager.

✔ When items are missing price tags at Target retail stores, the cashiers are empowered to ask customers whether they know the prices. If a stated price seems reasonable, the clerk can enter it into the register without first getting management approval.

✔ At Florida's Walt Disney World, employees at all levels are given the authority to replace lost tickets, spilled food, and damaged souvenirs, regardless of the cause.

Setting Goals and Monitoring Progress

Everyone needs goals in their lives to provide direction. Without goals, you may not be motivated to do anything in particular with your life — both at the office and away. With goals, however, you give your life direction and focus as you strive to achieve milestones.

But although all employees need goals — and companies need systems to monitor their progress — setting and monitoring goals is particularly important in team situations, where team dynamics can cause loss of focus and confusion when clear goals are absent. The best business goals direct employee effort (which includes teams) toward the tasks and behaviors that are most important to an organization's long-term success. Goals also should clearly indicate when an employee has achieved them. In this section, we consider how you can set effective goals with employees and how you can monitor employee progress toward achieving those goals.

Setting goals

Establishing goals is a necessary part of doing business. From strategic, to tactical, to operational measures, goals are central to an organization's planning process. Basically, setting goals is the way that work gets done.

There are a number of steps involved in actually setting goals:

1. **Imagine the future desired state of your organization and determine what exactly you want to accomplish.**

   Do you want better customer service? Development of a new product? Faster deliveries?

2. **Write a concise, measurable, and achievable statement (your goal) that can mobilize employees to work toward the desired future.**

   For example, "Improve customer satisfaction ratings by 20 percent during the next six months," or "Develop a new low-voltage memory chip within one year," or "Shorten the time it takes to deliver packages from three days to two days."

3. **If necessary, break the goal into subgoals that can be assigned to the appropriate people or departments.**

Setting goals with your employees doesn't have to be a complicated process. In fact, the best goals often are short, concise, and to the point. Employees are more likely to accomplish goals if they can easily understand them and if they have no more than two or three goals to work toward at a time. (For an in-depth look at planning and the role of strategic, tactical, and operational goals, be sure to check out Chapter 5.)

Tapping the power of employee involvement

Andy Grove — former chairman of chip maker Intel Corporation of Santa Clara, California — is a big believer in the power of employee involvement and initiative. This belief is all a part of his policy of "organized common sense." He has nine tips for encouraging employee involvement and initiative on the job:

✔ Motivation comes from within. The most you can do as a manager is create an environment in which motivated people can flourish.

✔ Good coaches take no personal credit for the success of the team. They've played the game and understand it completely, and are tough enough to get the very best performance that the team can give.

✔ Think about what you have to do today to solve and avoid tomorrow's problems.

✔ Do everything within your power to provide coworkers with the best possible service.

✔ Time is your one finite resource. Remember that when you say yes to one thing, you have to say no to something else.

✔ Schedule one hour every day to deal with inevitable interruptions in a planned, organized manner.

✔ Performance reviews are absolutely necessary.

✔ To gather information about a corporate division or department, go on an unannounced visit and observe what's going on.

✔ If an employee isn't doing his or her job, there are only two possible explanations: The employee either can't do it or won't do it. To determine which reason is applicable, apply the following test: If the person's life depended on doing the work, could the employee do it? If the answer is yes, the problem is motivational. If the answer is no, the problem is a lack of ability.

Unfortunately, many managers shy away from setting goals with their employees, because they may consider themselves to be too busy or they may not be sure how to do it. They do so only when forced to by company planning or performance-review processes. And when managers set goals by this schedule, the goals set are often flawed or are dictated to employees without employee involvement in crafting them.

Monitoring progress toward goals

Setting goals is an important step in the process of getting things done at work, but it's only the beginning. To ensure that your organization's goals are met, you have to monitor and track specific task performances during the course of completion. Monitoring and tracking is important because you need to know if there are problems that are interfering with goal accomplishment. The sooner you identify such problems, the sooner you can take action — and avoid major problems down the road. Fortunately, you have several ways to monitor your progress toward goals; the following sections outline a few of the most common ways to keep track of employee performance.

Milestones

To monitor progress toward a goal, you can break a project into a series of individual tasks, the completion of which will comprise the achievement of the intended project goals. *Milestones* are scheduled events that indicate delivery or completion of some part of a task or goal. By breaking down a project into its individual tasks, you can easily track employee performance to ensure that the project stays on schedule. Close monitoring of the project milestones helps prevent any unfortunate surprises along the way.

Here, for example, are sample milestones for the production process of a company newsletter:

- ✔ Interview five employees from several different divisions: February 1.

- ✔ Write articles and submit to editor: February 15.

- ✔ Type up newsletter and check for typographical errors: March 1.

- ✔ Drop newsletter off at printer: March 15.

- ✔ Pick up newsletter from printer and distribute to all employees: April 1.

Although employees may be responsible for achieving an organization's goals, managers are responsible for monitoring employees' progress. Managers typically decide who and how many employees to assign to a task, balancing quick completion with the need to attend to other company needs.

Charts and graphs

As your projects become more complex, using a graphical format to chart milestones can be extremely useful. Charts and graphs make project monitoring much easier than eyeballing pages of text. With just a glance, you can quickly assess project progress and pick out problem areas that may require more management attention.

When monitoring project performance, a picture really does tell a thousand words. A variety of graphing options are available to you and your teams, including the following:

- ✔ **Gantt charts:** Also known as *bar charts,* Gantt charts are the most commonly used method for monitoring project completion graphically.

- ✔ **Flowcharts:** Some projects — especially complex ones — require more than simple Gantt charts to keep track of performance. In these cases, flowcharts are just what the doctor ordered. By following the longest path in terms of operations (activities or tasks), you can determine the critical path of the project, which determines the overall duration of your project plan. The *critical path* generally represents the shortest time in which you can complete a project.

Software

If you manage projects as a key part of your job, be sure to take a look at project management software. Several software programs are available that are devoted to tracking projects; they provide all kinds of tools to those who need it, including, but not limited to, the following:

- ✔ Project planning and scheduling

- ✔ Task assignment

- ✔ Graphical reporting

- ✔ Task grouping

- ✔ Web publication

Indeed, the business world has recently seen a veritable explosion of project management software solutions — both standalone software programs and Web-based solutions.

Rather than try to list the most popular or most effective software solutions available — which are changing all the time — we suggest you do some research before settling on the best package for your organization's or team's needs. You can start with the Project Management Software Directory (www. infogoal.com/pmc/pmcswr.htm), which lists all the available software according to the kind of project management you want to do. Each package has its own unique qualities. Pick a package that does all the following:

✔ Enables you to track multiple projects simultaneously

✔ Enables you to break projects into tasks and subtasks

✔ Enables you to create a variety of graphs and charts

✔ Enables you to view the project from a number of different angles

Conducting Better Business Meetings

Almost every business, whether it has only two employees or more than 200,000, holds meetings as a regular part of getting business done. Although your employees can communicate with one another in many different ways, meetings can be incredibly effective — if you conduct them the right way.

Meetings allow not only individual employees to communicate within organizations, but also the teams they work on. Although individual team members work on their tasks outside of meetings, team meetings give members the opportunity to come together to determine the team's goals, its plans for achieving its goals, who will do what — and when — and so on. In this section, we take a close look at what makes meetings tick and give you tips for conducting better business meetings.

The good (and bad) news about meetings

You've probably experienced more than your fair share of both good and bad business meetings. (We know we have.) What makes some meetings terrific and others the pits?

The following list presents the positive side of business meetings:

✔ **Meetings can be empowering.** Meetings provide a forum for employees to have their voices heard — no matter their positions in the hierarchy or their seniority or experience. Employees in a well-run organization can even call their own meetings if they like. They don't need to wait around for someone else to do it.

✔ **Meetings can be a great way to communicate.** When a message needs to reach a large number of people at once, a meeting is a great way to accomplish that task. Have you ever been to a company meeting where the CEO sketched out his or her vision of the future? Such meetings can be extremely inspirational and can galvanize an entire group of people to take action to achieve the vision. Smaller meetings can be just as effective when you want to solicit employee ideas and focus employee efforts on developing solutions to problems.

✔ **Meetings can develop work skills and leadership.** Becoming full and active participants in meetings requires employees to develop their work skills and to become leaders. When they're assigned tasks in meetings, complete them, and then report their progress and results in follow-up meetings, employees learn to work with others on teams and under deadline stress. Meetings also give employees a chance to present their results in front of others, thus boosting their self-confidence.

✔ **Meetings can be morale boosting.** Good employees want to know what's going on in their organization, and they want to feel like they're important parts of the organization's present and future. Effective managers lay out their plans for the future in meetings and engage employees in the organizational changes that will be necessary to move from the present to the future state.

Unfortunately, we also have some bad news to present about many poorly run meetings. Here's the negative side of meetings (along with tips to make meetings better):

✔ **Meetings may not have focus.** If you've been to a meeting that wandered all over the place — from topic to topic, with little or no focus — you know exactly what we're talking about. Meetings without focus rarely achieve the goals that required the meetings in the first place. The solution? Keep focused on the topics at hand!

✔ **Companies can have too many meetings.** One of the biggest complaints about meetings is that companies have too many of them. When meetings aren't working well in an organization, it probably holds too many of them. The key is to have fewer meetings and to make those meetings more efficient and more effective. The solution? Fewer (and better) meetings.

✔ **Attendees may come unprepared.** Unprepared attendees are unproductive attendees. And unproductive attendees do little to help you accomplish the goals you've set for your organization or team. The solution? Require employees to come prepared.

✔ **Most meeting time is wasted.** Research shows that, on average, 53 percent of all meeting time is wasted. For most organizations, this percentage amounts to thousands of hours of wasted time a year. The larger the organization, the more time it wastes. The solution? Check out the eight surefire ways to make your meetings better in the next section.

Eight surefire ways to make your meetings better

You can make your team's meetings better. The power is within you — whether you're a meeting leader or a low-level participant. You don't have to tolerate meetings that accomplish little or nothing. Here are some surefire ways to ensure that you'll hold or participate in better business meetings:

- ✔ **Be prepared.** Meetings are work; so, just as with any other work activity, the better prepared you are for them, the better the results you can expect. For example, suppose that the topic is the next fiscal year's budget. Before the meeting, dig up your budget for this fiscal year and become totally familiar with it. Review any budget reports that you may have received along the way.

- ✔ **Have an agenda.** An *agenda* — a list of the topics to be covered during the course of the meeting — can play a critical role in the success of any meeting. It shows participants where they're going but leaves it up to them to figure out how to get there. Be sure to distribute the agenda and any prework in advance so participants can prepare and you can avoid wasting time.

- ✔ **Start and end on time.** Sitting through a meeting that goes way beyond the scheduled ending time would be fine if the participants had nothing else to do at work. But in these days of faster and more flexible organizations, everyone always has plenty of work on the to-do list. If you announce the length of a meeting and then stick to it, fewer participants will stare at their watches, and more participants will take an active role.

- ✔ **Have fewer (but better) meetings.** Call a meeting only when it's absolutely necessary. Before you call a meeting, ask whether you can achieve your goal in some other way — perhaps through a one-on-one discussion, a telephone conference call, or a simple exchange of e-mail.

- ✔ **Include rather than exclude.** Meetings are only as good as the ideas the participants bring forward. Great ideas can come from anyone in an organization, not just its managers. Roy Disney, former vice chairman of the Walt Disney Company, tells a great story that illustrates this point perfectly. Says Disney, "There's an old story about Walt from the early days when we were making short subjects — really just a collection of gags. Every week, Walt had a gag contest, and everybody was free to enter — the winner got $5, which was a lot of money during the Depression. And who kept winning, week after week? The janitor. You see, it's not about who's the boss. It's about who's got the best ideas."

Morphing chatter into effective discourse

Holding constructive and effective discussions is an important part of having successful meetings. And successful meetings are critical to the smooth functioning of teams within an organization. In their book, *The Team Handbook,* Peter Scholtes and coauthors Brian Joiner and Barbara Streibel present the following list of tips for improving discussion skills in your meetings:

✔ **Ask for clarification.** If you're unclear about the topic being discussed or the logic in another person's arguments, ask someone to define the purpose, focus, or limits of the discussion. Ask members to repeat ideas in different ways. Ask for examples, pictures, diagrams, data, and so on.

✔ **Act as gatekeepers.** Encourage equal participation among group members. "Throttle" dominators (ask them to allow others to participate) and make openings for less-aggressive members by directly asking their opinions or making a general request for input.

✔ **Listen.** Actively explore each other's ideas instead of debating or defending each idea that comes up.

✔ **Summarize.** Occasionally compile what's been said and restate it to the group in summary form. Follow the summary with a question to check for agreement.

✔ **Contain digression.** Don't permit overlong examples or irrelevant discussion.

✔ **Manage time.** If portions of the agenda take longer than expected, remind the team of your deadlines and time allotments so that work can be either accelerated or postponed, or so you can rebudget time appropriately.

✔ **End the discussion.** Learn to tell when nothing can be gained from further discussion. Help the team close a discussion and decide the issue.

✔ **Test for consensus.** Summarize the group's position on an issue, state the decision that you've made, and check to see whether the team agrees with the summary.

✔ **Constantly evaluate the meeting process.** Throughout a meeting, assess the quality of the discussion. Ask the following: "Are we getting what we want from this discussion? If not, what can we do differently in the remaining time?"

✔ **Maintain the focus.** Meetings that get off track and stay off track don't achieve their goals. Meeting leaders and participants must actively work to keep meetings focused on the agenda items. Topics shouldn't include the results of the latest football game, who had lunch with whom, or who's driving that shiny new Porsche. When you notice the meeting drifting off track, speak up and push the other attendees to get it back in focus.

✔ **Capture and assign action items.** Unless meetings are held purely to communicate information or for other special purposes, most meetings result in action items, tasks, or other assignments for participants. Don't assume that all participants will take their assignments to heart and remember all the details. Instead, have someone record every action item on a sheet of paper (flip charts are great for this, or you can use regular notebook paper). If some action items haven't been assigned to specific individuals for completion, do so before the meeting adjourns.

Immediately after the meeting, summarize the outcome of the meeting, as well as assignments and timelines, and then e-mail a copy of the summary to all attendees.

✔ **Get feedback.** No meeting is perfect. Be sure to solicit feedback from meeting attendees on how the meeting went right for them — and on how it went wrong. Was the meeting too long? Did one person dominate the discussion? Were attendees unprepared? Were the items on the agenda unclear? Whatever the problems, you can't fix them if you don't know about them. You can use a simple form to solicit feedback, or you can speak informally with attendees after the meeting.

Part III

Money: What You Don't Know Will Hurt You

The 5th Wave

By Rich Tennant

"Our goal is to maximize your upside and minimize your downside while we protect our own backside."

In this part . . .

Money is a critical aspect of any business — securing it, managing it, spending it, and so on. In this part, we present the basics of accounting and take a look at the most important and widely used financial statements. We decipher the mysteries of financial analysis, and we help you understand the ins and outs of stocks and bonds. Finally, we cover what it takes in the business world to make money — namely, money itself.

Chapter 10

All You Ever Wanted to Know about Accounting

In This Chapter

▶ Scrolling through the basics of accounting

▶ Creating and utilizing different types of budgets

▶ Monitoring financial results

▶ Examining the effect of Sarbanes-Oxley

1 f you've ever played in or watched a competitive sporting match — football, cricket, baseball, tennis, badminton, hockey, rock/paper/scissors — you know the importance of keeping score. Every competitive game has a winner and a loser (except in the relatively rare event of a tie score), and the outcome of many games is determined by the total number of points scored. An individual or team score instantly tells you two things:

✔ During the course of competition, you know who is ahead or behind, and by how much.

✔ At the end of competition, you know who won and by how much.

Business works in much the same way. However, instead of tracking the number of points or runs, business tracks money, using accounting practices. *Accounting* is simply the science of tracking money in a company. This chapter gives you the lowdown on accounting and explains what you need to know to determine budgets and keep an eye on your organization's finances.

Grasping the Basics of Accounting

In business, as in sports, there are winners and losers. Although some businesses make a lot of money and thrive, others lose tons of money and die. So, how do you keep track of how your business is doing so you can react and take appropriate measures? You use an accounting system. An *accounting system,* in simple terms, tracks how much money comes into a company and how much goes out (preferably your company has more coming in than going out!). It has many responsibilities when tracking your money:

- ✔ It monitors how much cash you have in your bank account.
- ✔ It shows how much money you owe to other companies and individuals and how much money others owe you.
- ✔ It tracks the value of the products you keep on hand to sell to customers.
- ✔ It tracks the money that you pay to employees in the form of salary and benefits.
- ✔ It reports the money that's left over at the end of each month — your company's profit. Unfortunately, it sometimes indicates how much money your business has lost in a particular period of time.

For the most part, winning and losing in the world of business is determined on the basis of financial measures. The most important financial measures are sales (revenue) and profit. *Sales* represent the total amount of money that flows into a company as a result of selling goods and services. *Profit* represents the money that's left over after a company subtracts its expenses (payroll, benefits, cost of goods sold, rent, telephones, and so on) from its revenues. However, before we get too far ahead of ourselves, this section discusses the basics of accounting, including the accounting cycle and the all-important accounting equation.

A small business may process relatively few transactions a day, making its accounting system relatively simple. An accounting system for a very large business — one that does millions of dollars of business a day — is quite complex. In either case, accounting systems — along with the computers that run them and the people who run the computers — are always important.

The accounting cycle

The entire accounting process — from beginning to end — is called the *accounting cycle.* The accounting cycle has three parts:

- ✔ **Transaction:** A *transaction* is something your business does that generates a financial impact, which is then recorded in the accounting system (a journal). For example, if a member of your sales staff sells a three-year subscription of your magazine to an anxious customer and the check for $110 arrives and is deposited into your company's bank account, that's a transaction. Similarly, when your company makes a payment to Joe's House of Cheese for supplying food for your company's annual picnic, that creates a transaction.

✔ **Journal:** As each transaction occurs, it gets posted to a journal. A *journal* is nothing more than a general file to temporarily hold transactions until you can classify them by transaction type.

✔ **Ledger:** On a regular basis — daily, weekly, monthly, or other frequency — you classify transactions in the journal by type and move them into individual accounts called *ledgers*. Individual ledgers include such accounts as payroll, travel, and sales. The collection of all ledgers for a company is called its *general ledger.*

After all transactions have been posted to their ledgers, managers have access to a wide variety of reports that summarize the organization's transactions and their effect on the business. We detail these reports, which include the income statement, balance sheet, and so on, in Chapter 11.

The accounting equation

The *accounting equation* is the foundation of the science of accounting. A day without the accounting equation is like a day without sunshine — at least it is in our Certified Public Accountant's (CPA's) office! According to the accounting equation:

Assets = Liabilities + Owners' Equity

The following sections break down each part of the accounting equation and how it affects your organization's finances.

Assets

An *asset* generally is anything in a business that has some sort of financial value and can be converted to cash. The products you have stocked in your warehouse are assets (they're converted into cash as you sell them) — along with the cash in your register (which could also be converted into cash if you sold it on eBay!) and the microwave oven in the employee breakroom.

Assets come in two different flavors; these categories represent how quickly assets can be converted into cash:

✔ **Current assets** are assets that can be converted into cash within one year. Think checks that arrived in the mail today, invoices for a month's worth of consulting services, or the computers for sale on your showroom floor. Assets that you can quickly convert into cash also are known as *liquid assets;* and the speed by which you can convert assets into cash is called *liquidity.*

✔ **Fixed assets** are assets that take more than a year to be converted into cash. Think that custom-built industrial milling machine that only three companies in the world have any use for, the building that houses your headquarters, and that finicky, old copier down the hall that may now make a better boat anchor than reproduction machine.

Here's a list of the most common kinds of business assets:

✔ **Cash:** Cash includes good old-fashioned money and money equivalents such as checks, money orders, marketable securities, bank deposits, and, if you live on Pago Pago, coconuts.

✔ **Accounts receivable:** Accounts receivable represent the money that your clients and customers owe you for purchasing your products or services. When you allow a customer to buy your goods today and pay later, you're creating a receivable. If you work strictly on a cash basis (hot dog stand, ticket scalper, e-commerce site), you don't have any receivables, and this item will be zero.

✔ **Inventory:** Inventory comprises the finished products that you purchase or manufacture to sell to customers, as well as raw materials, work in process, and supplies used in operations. If you run a grocery store, your inventory consists of every item on display for sale in your store — the carrots, the tubs of margarine, the boxes of donuts, and so on. (For more on inventory, see the section of the same name later in this chapter.)

✔ **Prepaid expenses:** When you pay for a product or service in advance, you create an asset known as a prepaid expense. Examples include a prepaid maintenance contract on a typewriter, an insurance policy with a one-year term paid in advance, and an agreement for security-alarm monitoring paid in advance on a quarterly basis.

✔ **Equipment:** Equipment is the wide variety of property that your organization purchases to carry out its operations. Examples include desks, chairs, computers, electronic testing gear, forklifts, and lie detectors.

✔ **Real estate:** Real estate includes assets such as the land, buildings, and facilities that your company owns, occupies, and utilizes. Some companies have little or no real estate assets, and others have sizable ones. For years, Dole owned 98 percent of the 141-square-mile Hawaiian island of Lanai and used it as a huge pineapple plantation. When the world pineapple market collapsed a decade or so ago, Dole transferred ownership of the island to Castle & Cooke Properties, Honolulu. Now that's a fixed asset!

Liabilities

Liabilities are money owed to others outside your organization. They may include the money you owe to the company that delivers your office supplies, the payments you owe on the construction loan that financed your warehouse expansion, or the mortgage on your corporate headquarters building.

As with assets, liabilities come in two flavors, each representing the amount of time it should take to repay the obligations:

- ✔ **Current liabilities** are to be repaid within one year. Think the money for next week's employee paychecks, the payment your company owes to your office-supply business, and payment on a short-term loan from the bank.

- ✔ **Long-term liabilities** are to be repaid in a period longer than one year. Think the payments on the company delivery van, the mortgage on the company's distribution facility, or the money owed to holders of corporate bonds.

Here's a list of the most common business liabilities, from both the current and long-term categories:

- ✔ **Accounts payable:** Accounts payable are the obligations owed to the many individuals and organizations that have provided goods and services to your company. Examples include money owed to your computer network consultant, your local utility company, and an out-of-house advertising agency that your marketing department uses for ad campaigns.

- ✔ **Notes payable:** Notes payable represent loans made to your company by individuals or organizations such as banks and savings and loans. The notes could be anything from an IOU promised to an individual for a small amount of cash to a multimillion-dollar loan secured from a large bank.

- ✔ **Accrued expenses:** Sometimes a company incurs an expense but has no immediate plans to reimburse the individual or organization that's owed the money. Examples include future wages to be paid to employees, interest due on loans, and utility bills.

- ✔ **Bonds payable:** When companies issue bonds to raise money to finance large projects, they incur obligations to pay back the individuals and organizations that purchase them. (Bonds are described in more detail in Chapter 13.)

- ✔ **Mortgages payable:** When companies purchase property, they often do so by taking out mortgages — long-term real estate loans, just like the one you may have on your home, secured by the property itself. Mortgages payable represents the mortgages that an organization has on all its properties.

Owners' equity

Owners' equity is the money that remains when you take all your company's assets and subtract all your liabilities. Owners' equity represents the owners' direct investment in the firm or the owners' claims on the company's assets. Another way of expressing a company's owners' equity is its net worth. *Net worth* is simply a snapshot of your company's financial health for a particular period of time.

Here are the two types of owners' equity:

- **Paid-in capital:** The money that people invest in a company. When companies such as IBM, Ford Motor Company, or PepsiCo offer to sell shares of stock to investors in a *secondary offering* (new stock), or when companies do an *initial public offering* (go public for the first time), investors provide paid-in capital to the companies when they pay money to buy the stock.

- **Retained earnings:** A company's earnings that are held within the company. The money gets reinvested, not paid out to shareholders as dividends.

Although owners' equity generally is a positive number, it can go negative when a company takes on large amounts of debt — for example, to acquire another company.

Double-entry bookkeeping

The accounting equation — Assets = Liabilities + Owners' Equity — is similar to any other equation: A change to one side of the equation causes a change in the other. Therefore, every financial transaction you make results in not one, but two entries to your accounting records — noted as *double-entry bookkeeping*. This nifty observation was made many years ago (actually, more than five centuries ago, in 1494) by Luca Pacioli, an Italian mathematician and Franciscan monk.

For you trivia buffs, Pacioli's book containing this and other topics of mathematical interest — *Everything about Arithmetic, Geometry, and Proportions* — was one of the first books printed on Gutenberg's famous printing press. Unfortunately, much to the disappointment of accounting fans around the world, it still isn't a bestseller on Amazon.com.

So, for example, when Susie's Sushi (best sushi in the tri-state area!) buys a big yellowfin tuna to slice up for customers, it affects her accounting equation. For this example, assume that Susie's Sushi starts with assets (inventory) of $1,000, liabilities (accounts payable) of $500, and owners' equity of $500:

Assets = Liabilities + Owners' Equity

$1,000 = $500 + $500

When Susie purchases that yellowfin tuna from the local fish market for $100, and the fish market agrees to bill her for it, she acquires an asset (inventory — literally, raw material). She also takes on a liability of $100 — the money owed to the fish market (accounts payable). After this transaction, the accounting equation now looks like this:

Assets = Liabilities + Owners' Equity

$1,100 = $600 + $500

As you can see, Susie added $100 of inventory to her assets, but she simultaneously added a payable of $100 to her liabilities. The owners' equity doesn't change. As this example shows, every transaction on one side of the accounting equation results in a transaction on the other side of the accounting equation.

Inventory

Inventory includes the finished products that you purchase or manufacture to sell to customers, as well as raw materials, work in process, and supplies used in operations. Although the nature of inventory may seem simple on the surface, the way your accounting system handles its value is actually quite complex.

You have two major ways of accounting for the value of your inventory:

- **FIFO (first in, first out):** Under this method of inventory accounting, the inventory that a company purchases first is the inventory that it sells first to customers. When prices are rising (and when, exactly, aren't they rising?), the FIFO method results in a higher income figure as inventory is sold off to customers.

- **LIFO (last in, first out):** Under this method of inventory accounting, the inventory that a company purchases last is the inventory that it sells first to customers. When prices are rising, the LIFO method results in a lower income figure as inventory is sold off to customers.

Okay, that's all nice and well, but which method should you choose? In the United States, the Internal Revenue Service and GAAP (Generally Accepted Accounting Principles) allow for the use of either FIFO or LIFO — it's completely up to your organization to decide. However, after you pick a method, you have to stick with it. Of course, as with anything else in life, each method has its pluses and minuses.

Business owners who want to show higher earnings to their investors, bankers, and other sources of financing have a strong incentive to go with FIFO. However, this higher income comes with a tax burden, which may create a stronger incentive to go with LIFO. LIFO reports a lower net income but results in a lower tax burden. The method you choose depends on what you consider more important: raising investment funds or avoiding taxes. Every company is different, and the choice depends on your unique circumstances. However, you should definitely consult an accountant about the best choice for your business!

Depreciation

Just as with people, fixed assets have finite lifetimes. No asset lasts forever (especially if it has anything to do with technology), and each asset is different. A computer may have a useful lifetime of only 4 or 5 years, whereas a steel mill may have a lifetime of 50 or 60 years. As you use assets during the course of their lifetimes, they gradually wear out or become functionally obsolete. In the case of the steel mill with a 60-year lifetime, the mill doesn't retain 100 percent of its value through year 59 and then suddenly lose all its value on the first day of its 60th year. Instead, this fixed asset gradually loses value as it experiences normal wear and tear over a long period of time. In other words, it depreciates.

Depreciation represents the loss of value of a fixed asset and is a method of allocating the cost of the asset over its useful lifetime. Depreciation is a non-cash expense that reduces the value of an asset due to deterioration, obsolescence, or age. There are many different accounting methods to calculate depreciation (methods that aren't necessarily IRS requirements). The following sections take a look at some of the most common traditional methods, as well as one that is currently required by the IRS.

Straight-line

Straight-line depreciation is the simplest method of depreciating an asset. In the straight-line method, you divide the cost of the asset by its expected lifetime in years. Table 10-1 shows the straight-line depreciation of a $2,500 computer that has an expected lifetime of five years. In this example, the total cost of the asset, $2,500, is divided by 5, resulting in an annual depreciation expense of $500.

Table 10-1	Straight-Line Depreciation	
Year	*Depreciation Expense*	*Cumulative Depreciation*
1	$500	$500
2	$500	$1,000
3	$500	$1,500
4	$500	$2,000
5	$500	$2,500

As you can see, the amount of the asset depreciated each year is exactly the same: $500, or 20 percent each year. At the end of the five-year life of the computer, the asset's original cost of $2,500 has been fully depreciated. Nothing could be easier or more straightforward than that!

Double-declining balance

The double-declining balance method of depreciation is what's known as an *accelerated method of depreciation,* because it pushes the majority of the total depreciation amount into the early years of ownership. You calculate the *double-declining balance* by multiplying the book value of an asset (the original cost of the fixed asset, less cumulative depreciation) by double its straight-line rate. So, if a computer is valued at $2,500 with a straight-line rate of 20 percent per year, the double-declining balance method allows a depreciation rate of 40 percent per year of the asset's book value.

Table 10-2 shows the application of the double-declining balance method to a computer valued at $2,500.

Table 10-2	Double-Declining Balance Depreciation		
Year	**Book Value**	**Depreciation Expense**	**Cumulative Depreciation**
1	$2,500	$1,000	$1,000
2	$1,500	$600	$1,600
3	$900	$360	$1,960
4	$540	$216	$2,176
5	$324	$130	$2,306

Why would anyone want to accelerate the depreciation of an asset? The main reason concerns the payment of taxes. Under the straight-line method, all other things being equal, the tax deduction for the asset will be the same each year for the duration of the asset's life. However, by accelerating the depreciation, you can maximize your tax deduction in the early years of the asset's life. This is a good thing.

As Table 10-2 shows, more than 60 percent of the computer's depreciation occurs in the first two years of its useful life. In general, it's best to defer the payment of taxes as long as possible. Accelerated depreciation enables companies to do just that.

Sum of the years' digits

The *sum of the years' digits* method of depreciation is another way to accelerate depreciation. For this method, you follow these simple (yeah, right) steps:

1. **Determine how many years of life an asset will have.**

2. **Add the digits together to create the denominator of a fraction, with the year of depreciation as the numerator, in reverse order (year 1 is year 5, year 5 is year 1 and so on; lost yet?).**

3. **Multiply the fraction by the asset's original cost to determine the depreciated value.**

In the example of a computer with an effective life of five years, first find the sum of the digits: 1 + 2 + 3 + 4 + 5 = 15. This is your denominator. Table 10-3 shows the rest of the calculation involved to determine depreciation of the computer during its useful life.

Table 10-3		Sum of the Years' Digits Depreciation		
Year	**Original Cost**	**Fraction**	**Depreciation Expense**	**Cumulative Depreciation**
1	$2,500	$\frac{5}{15}$	$833	$833
2	$2,500	$\frac{4}{15}$	$667	$1,500
3	$2,500	$\frac{3}{15}$	$500	$2,000
4	$2,500	$\frac{2}{15}$	$333	$2,333
5	$2,500	$\frac{1}{15}$	$167	$2,500

As with the double-declining balance method, the sum of the years' digits pushes depreciation into the early years of an asset's life. This maximizes tax deductions sooner rather than later, resulting in a better financial outcome for your company. And what's good for your company is good for you!

Modified Accelerated Cost Recovery System (MACRS)

For IRS purposes, you must use the Modified Accelerated Cost Recovery System (MACRS) — an accelerated form of depreciation — to depreciate assets. Under this system, most business assets will use the GDS (general depreciation system) as defined in Publication 946 (2006). In simple terms, this means that you can choose from three depreciation methods with recovery periods defined by the IRS. The three methods are

- ✔ The 200-percent declining balance method during a GDS recovery period
- ✔ The 150-percent declining balance method during a GDS recovery period
- ✔ The straight-line method during a GDS recovery period

So, for example, say you own computer equipment. The IRS says that you can depreciate this equipment across five years, using any one of the three methods in the previous bulleted list.

The IRS warns that you can only depreciate property that you hold for business purposes and that has a useful life greater than one year. You start depreciating the asset when you put it into service and stop depreciating it when you've recovered your cost.

Understanding Budgets and Estimates

One of the keys to running a successful business is its owners' and managers' ability to predict how the business will perform financially. If you can accurately predict your firm's performance, you can be certain that you can deploy resources such as money, people, equipment, manufacturing plants, and the like appropriately and in the most effective way. A *budget* is nothing more than a written estimate of how an organization — or a particular project, department, or business unit — will perform financially.

The real value in budgets comes when you compare estimates of expected performance to actual performance. When the numbers match, you know that your organization or project is performing just as it should. When the numbers differ markedly, you know that you need to ask the question, "Why?" and take a very close look at what's going on. The process of comparing expected financial results with actual financial results is called *variance analysis* (see the section "Keeping Your Eye on the Numbers" later in this chapter for more discussion).

With the speed of business increasing all the time, why bother doing budgets at all? Aren't things changing too fast for budgets to be of any value? In most cases, the answer is a resounding "No!" Budgets offer the following benefits to organizations that use them:

- **Budgets are milestones on the road to your goals.** Every organization has (or at least should have) goals. Budgets are quick and easy ways to see whether your organization is on track to meet its financial goals. If, for example, you've already spent half your travel budget but you're only one quarter of the way through the year, you know that you potentially have an overspending problem.

- **Budgets make decisions easier.** When you budget a project, initiative, or business activity, you'll quickly have a picture of what it will cost. Armed with that information, you can decide whether the costs you'll incur make good business sense or not. Will you make money or lose money as a result? How much money? For how long? The answers are important elements in the decision-making process, and they come from the budgeting process.

- **Budgets can be fast.** A budget can be as quick and simple as a few figures scribbled onto the back of an envelope over lunch. (Ever heard of doing a "back-of-the-envelope" projection?) A budget also can be a simple, one-page computer spreadsheet. Not every budget has to weigh ten pounds and result in mass deforestation. With simple budgets, you can make changes quickly, in near-real time, and print them out or e-mail them immediately.

✔ **Budgets can be flexible.** Need to hire a few new employees to take care of an unexpected order? No problem. A budget can accommodate the change and create an up-to-date picture of how your organization is performing. Or you can simply freeze your budget to see the variance between what your budget predicted and what really happened. Regardless of how fast your markets are moving, you can always keep up, no matter where you are.

✔ **Budgets are fun.** Okay, maybe we're stretching things just a bit here. But, honestly, creating a budget in which the actual results match your expectations is a real thrill. The only bigger thrill is when your results are even better than you expected!

Whereas extensive, long-range *(strategic)* planning seems increasingly less valuable to most organizations today, near-term *(tactical)* planning is becoming incredibly valuable. Budgets are a very necessary part of the tactical planning process. Now that we've sold you on the value of doing budgets (you are sold, right?), this section looks at some of the most common kinds, as well as how to create and use a budget.

Perusing different kinds of budgets

When it comes right down to it, you can budget any activity that has a financial impact on your organization. Want to budget a self-managing work team? No problem. A research and development project? Piece of cake. The new headquarters construction job? All in a day's work. The following list presents some of the most common budgets used in business today:

✔ **Cash budget:** An estimate of a company's cash position for a particular period of time. By using your current cash position as a baseline, you can estimate all cash inflows (sales) and outflows (expenses) during the time period you specify — say, a month — to determine a projected cash position at the end of the period.

✔ **Operating budget:** Shows a business's forecasted revenues along with forecasted expenses — usually for a period of one year or less. The operating budget is a top-level budget; the budgets that follow on this list are line items in the operating budget:

• **Labor budget:** Takes every person in an organization, department, or project and multiplies the number of hours they're expected to work by their wage rates. The result is the total labor cost to be expended for a set period of time.

• **Sales budget:** An estimate of the quantity of goods and services that you'll sell during a specific period of time. In the case of products, you estimate total revenue by multiplying the total number of units projected to be sold by the price per unit.

- **Production budget:** Starts with the sales budget and its estimates of the total number of units projected to be sold. The production budget then translates this information into estimates of the cost of labor, material, and other expenses required to produce the units.

- **Expense budget:** Every business — from a one-person home business to a huge multinational corporation — incurs a variety of expenses during the course of normal operations. You prepare expense budgets for travel, utilities, office supplies, telephone, and many other common and not-so-common expenses.

- **Capital budget:** If you plan to buy fixed assets with long, useful life spans (many organizations consider this to mean a year or more), the capital budget is the place to budget for them. Items in your capital budget may include buildings, production machinery, computers, copiers, furniture, and anything else that will still be in your office long after you're gone.

Some type of budget is available to you for almost any occasion. To see what a real operating budget looks like, check out the sample in the sidebar "A sample operating budget."

Creating a budget

What's the best kind of budget? The one that works! There are many different types of budgets and three key approaches to developing a budget: bottom up, top down, and zero based. Each approach has its advantages and disadvantages, and each approach can work well — although the pendulum is clearly swinging in favor of the bottom-up approach:

- ✔ **Bottom up:** In bottom-up budgeting, supervisors and middle managers prepare the budgets and then forward them up the chain of command for review and approval. Middle managers have the benefit of a close working knowledge of the organization and its financial performance. As a result, bottom-up budgets tend to be more accurate than top-down budgets. In addition, bottom-up budgets can have a positive impact on employee morale, because employees assume an active role in providing financial input to the budgeting process.

- ✔ **Top down:** In this approach, top management prepares the budgets and imposes them on the lower layers of the organization — generally without any consultation or involvement on the part of those outside of top management. Top-down budgets clearly express the performance goals and expectations of top management. These budgets, however, can be unrealistic, because they don't incorporate the input of the very people who will implement them.

✔ **Zero-based budgeting:** The process in which each manager prepares estimates of his or her proposed expenses for a specific period of time, as though they were being performed for the first time. In other words, each budgeted activity starts from a budget base of zero. By starting from scratch at each budget cycle, managers must take a close look at all their expenses and justify them to top management, thereby (at least in theory) minimizing waste.

A sample operating budget

What's the saying? A picture is worth a thousand words. Or is it ten thousand words? Whatever it is, here's a picture of what a real monthly operating budget looks like for a typical company with annual revenues of about $1 million:

Spacely Sprocket Company

Revenue Source	Monthly Budget
Product sales	$81,250
Royalties	$1,000
Web site ads	$8,500
Other income	$100
Total revenue	**$90,850**

Expenses	
Rent	$1,403
Wages	$10,000
Taxes	$1,325
Licenses and permit	$100
Insurance (health and welfare)	$1,000
Insurance (other)	$500
Advertising and promotions	$5,000

Dues and subscriptions	$300
Training	$400
Miscellaneous	$100
Office supplies	$2,000
Outside services	$2,000
Postage and delivery	$2,500
Printing and reproduction	$2,500
Telephone	$1,000
Entertainment	$50
Gifts	$50
Meals	$500
Travel	$5,000
Commission	$2,000
Cost of goods sold	$5,000
Interest	$100
Total expenses	**$42,828**
Profit (Loss)	*$48,022*

Companies prepare budgets for small operating units or departments. These budgets roll up into larger budgets — for divisions or groups — which then combine into an organization's overall budget. In this way, managers at all levels can play a role in an organization's financial health and well-being.

Utilizing budget tricks of the trade

Budgets provide a kind of early warning system that, when compared to actual results, can inform you when something is going wrong and needs your immediate attention.

When your expenditures exceed your budget, you can do several things to get back on track:

- **Review your budget.** Sometimes, it's the budget — not the spending — that's out of line. Before you do anything else, take a close look at your budget to make sure that the assumptions on which it's based are accurate and make sense in your changing market. If your market is growing quickly, you may need to adjust your estimates.

- **Freeze spending.** One of the quickest and most effective ways to bring spending back in line with a budget is to freeze spending. For example, you can freeze expenses such as pay raises, new staff, and bonuses.

- **Postpone new projects.** New projects — including new product development, acquisition of new facilities, and research and development — can eat up a lot of money. If spending is over budget, a common solution is to postpone new projects until you have enough revenue to support them.

Be sure to carefully balance your desire to bring spending back in line against the need to develop new products and services. If you're too zealous in this area, the result can be disastrous for the future growth and prosperity of your company.

- **Ask your employees for help.** Here's an old but very wise saying: None of us is as smart as all of us. If your expenditures are exceeding your budget and you can't sort it out on your own, ask your employees to suggest ideas for getting back into the black. Chances are, someone in your organization has some ideas you hadn't considered, and these ideas may make the difference between sinking and swimming.

- **Lay off employees and close facilities.** When you're trying to cut expenses, the last resort is to lay off employee and close facilities. Although these actions will result in an immediate and lasting decrease in expenses, you'll also face an immediate and lasting decrease in the talent available to your organization. In addition, the morale of employees who survive the budget ax can (and likely will) suffer — at least for a while.

Keeping Your Eye on the Numbers

One of the manager's classic roles is to control. And one aspect of the controlling function of managers is the review and analysis of accounting reports; managers carry out this function to determine the financial health of the organization. By regularly reviewing accounting reports and analyzing the information they present, managers can make better, more informed decisions. In this section, we look at some ways that managers keep their eyes on the numbers in an organization.

Accounting provides a kind of scoreboard for an organization. As such, understanding how accounting works and how to get the most out of accounting reports is an important skill for any manager (or aspiring MBA). For a much more complete discussion on accounting information and reports (about 408 pages worth!), check out *Accounting For Dummies,* 3rd Edition, by John A. Tracy (Wiley). You'll be glad you did.

Variance analysis

A simple way to use a budget to keep your eye on the numbers is through variance analysis. In simple terms, *variance analysis* is a comparison of the financial estimates that you budget for a particular period with your firm's actual financial results. The variance is the difference between budget and actual, which can be a positive or negative number or zero. This method gives you an immediate picture of financial issues that may require a closer look on your part.

In the monthly expense report in Table 10-4, look at the variance between the budget and the actual figures (***Note:*** The parentheses around a number mean that it's negative).

Table 10-4	Variance Analysis		
Expenses	*Budget*	*Actual*	*Variance*
Rent	$1,403	$1,403	$0
Wages	$10,000	$12,500	$2,500
Taxes	$1,325	$1,500	$175
Internet access	$60	$0	($60)

Expenses	Budget	Actual	Variance
Licenses and permits	$50	$50	$0
UPS service charge	$25	$100	$75
Telephone system	$200	$200	0
Insurance (health and welfare)	$1,000	$1,500	$500
Insurance (other)	$500	$500	$0
Total expenses	**$14,563**	**$17,753**	**$3,190**

In this example, fixed expenses were originally budgeted at $14,563 for the month. However, when the month ended, the accounting system reflected actual fixed expenses of $17,753. This resulted in a total variance — or overspending — of $3,190.

After you determine that you have a budget variance for the period in question, the next step is to decide whether it's significant and, if so, to figure out why it occurred. A variance of $3,190, which is 22 percent of the original budget of $14,563, is definitely significant and warrants a very close look by the responsible manager.

If you were that manager, what would you identify as the most significant variance in Table 10-4? A quick look indicates that wages are the main source of the variance, with spending for the period totaling $2,500 more than the plan. This may mean that employees are charging excessive overtime, someone got a raise that you hadn't anticipated, or any number of other possibilities. As the manager, it's your job to determine the reason behind the numbers and then decide if corrections need to be made.

Audits

The accuracy of accounting records and reports is incredibly important — especially to two particular groups of people. The people within the organization rely on accounting information to make informed business decisions, and the investors and lenders outside the organization rely on accounting information to make informed decisions on the use of their funds.

For these reasons, organizations conduct regular audits of their accounting systems to ensure that all results are accurate and that the system treats all financial information fairly and honestly.

There are two key kinds of audits:

- **Internal audits:** Conducted by employees of an organization, internal audits serve as an internal check to ensure the integrity of accounting information and the reports that are generated from this information. Many large companies have entire departments devoted to this task and make audits an annual event. And with the emphasis on financial transparency resulting from legislation such as Sarbanes-Oxley (described in detail in the next section), internal auditors are more important than ever before in public companies.

- **External audits:** Examination of a company's accounting system by an unbiased, outside individual or organization — most often a Certified Public Accounting (CPA) firm or chartered accountant. External audits typically are conducted on an annual basis, after the end of a company's fiscal year. Companies use these audits to ensure the integrity of the numbers that go into annual reports and financial statements and to guard against fraud.

The Lowdown on Sarbanes-Oxley

No matter how honest or how principled the vast majority of businesspeople may be, a few bad apples are always out to spoil things for the rest. Such was the case in the late 1990s and early 2000s, when a parade of bad apples such as Enron, Tyco International, WorldCom, and others became entangled in a variety of embarrassing corporate and financial scandals. These scandals undermined the public's trust in the reliability of public corporation accounting and financial reporting, and they also devastated many investors. When Enron collapsed, for instance, $60 billion in market value evaporated into thin air, and investors were left with worthless stock certificates.

In response to these scandals, Congress passed a new law: the Public Company Accounting Reform and Investor Protection Act of 2002 — more commonly known as *Sarbanes-Oxley,* or simply SOX for short. This section looks a bit closer at the good news and bad news the law brings and what it may mean to you and your business. (You can also check out *Sarbanes-Oxley For Dummies* by Jill Gilbert Welytok, JD, CPA [Wiley].)

The good news

Sarbanes-Oxley (SOX) has indeed succeeded in strengthening corporate accounting and financial reporting practices. In the wake of the passage of SOX, confidence in public companies has rebounded, which is a good thing indeed for businesses — and for the American public as a whole. And although many executives aren't too happy about all the extra paperwork and oversight that SOX requires them to take on, investors are quite pleased with SOX. There's now more transparency in corporate financial dealings, and the risk in their investments is reduced.

When Congress passed SOX and the legislation was signed by President George W. Bush, the government implemented the following boards or specific requirements:

- ✔ It required companies listed on stock exchanges to have fully independent internal audit committees, and external auditors are required to be truly independent.

- ✔ It banned most personal loans to executive officers or directors, closing loopholes in compensation, stock trading, and blackout rules that were widely abused at Enron, Tyco, and other corporations.

- ✔ It prohibited insider trades by executive officers and directors during pension fund blackout periods, leveling the field with other employees who were already prohibited from such trades.

- ✔ It required accelerated reporting of insider trading.

- ✔ It created the Public Company Accounting Oversight Board (PCAOB), which helps protect the interests of investors and further the public interest in the preparation of informative, fair, and independent audit reports.

- ✔ It required public companies to evaluate and disclose information about the effectiveness of their internal controls as they relate to financial reporting. Not only that, but it required the company's independent auditors to attest to this disclosure.

- ✔ It required certification of financial reports by chief executive officers and chief financial officers.

- ✔ It put new protections in place for corporate fraud whistleblowers.

- ✔ It increased criminal and civil penalties for violations of securities law.

- ✔ It increased jail sentences and fines for corporate executives who knowingly and willfully misstate financial statements.

The bad news

When Congress drafted SOX, it decided that *all* public companies — no matter how large or small — must comply with the law. As it turns out, complying with SOX can be an expensive proposition. One study shows that it costs large companies around $10 million to make the changes necessary organization-wide. Although smaller public companies may not have to shell out *that* much money, implementing SOX can be quite a burden for small businesses that don't have extensive financial resources to draw on (compared to larger companies).

In addition, some executives have quit their jobs rather than put up with the tough restrictions that SOX put into place — and face the possible consequences. You probably can't find a CEO or CFO alive who hasn't given serious consideration to the potential ramifications of certifying company financial reports that may turn out to be incorrect — or, worse, fraudulent. Indeed, when Jim Clark, co-founder of Web pioneer Netscape Communications, resigned from his position as chairman of online photo service Shutterfly in early 2007, he specifically cited the negative impact of SOX as a reason. According to Clark, SOX has gone too far and is stifling innovation in the United States because companies are spending money on fulfilling these legislative mandates that they could be using to create new products and services.

What does the future hold for Sarbanes-Oxley?

As of this writing, members of Congress are rushing to try to relieve businesses — particularly small public companies — of the added burdens brought about by Sarbanes-Oxley. In addition to relief, Congress hopes to retain at least some of the provisions that it hopes will prevent the next Enron or WorldCom corporate disaster. So, given its problems, is there a future for Sarbanes-Oxley?

According to Governance Metrics International Inc. — a business that rates 4,000 public companies around the world on more than 400 variables, from training to directors to financial restatements — companies that behave ethically perform better than those that do not. Although the Standard & Poors 500 showed investment returns of 11.32 percent, Governance Metrics found that companies with below-average ethics returned less — 10.53 percent — and companies with above-average ethics returned more — 13.46 percent.

Whether or not there's a future for SOX, you can clearly see a future for companies that behave ethically and that are good corporate citizens. Sure, bad apples will always try to beat the system, no matter what laws Congress decides to put into place. But the vast majority of businesses — and the people who run them — will continue to behave ethically and with integrity. And they'll prosper as a result.

Whether or not you agree with Clark's assessment, you can't ignore the fact that a lot of money is being diverted from productive uses (and from shareholder returns) to pay for the accounting firms that are helping most large American corporations comply with SOX. In a *Wall Street Journal* editorial, Kenneth Wilcox — president and CEO of SVB Financial Group — cites the example of his own firm. Not only are audits taking significantly longer to complete, but they're also involving more employees in the process, diverting them from their regular jobs. In 2006, SVB Financial Group paid more than $20 million to Big Four accounting firms — an average of $17,000 per employee. This represents an amount five times higher than it paid just three years ago, before the full impact of SOX was felt.

Negative experiences with money and incorrect information are leading many businesspeople — and the lobbyists who work for them — to push Congress for legislative relief. But will this push show results? That remains to be seen. (Check out the nearby sidebar "What does the future hold for Sarbanes-Oxley?" for more info.)

Chapter 11

Working Your Way through Financial Statements

. . . .

In This Chapter

▶ Understanding how to track your money

▶ Keeping an eye on a point in time with the balance sheet

▶ Using an income statement to count your wins (or losses)

▶ Putting a cash-flow statement to work for you

. . . .

*E*very studious, hard-working business student — and even some of the slackers — knows that management encompasses four traditional functions: planning, organizing, leading, and controlling. Each of these management functions has its own unique charm, and each is important in the running of an organization, but they won't get equal treatment here. Controlling is the one we focus on in this chapter — controlling in the form of keeping an eye on financial transactions and using that information to inform your decision making.

Many experienced businesspeople believe that they can get a fairly accurate, intuitive sense for the success of their operations, of a project, or of a product by simply asking the right people the right questions. Such questions may take the form of, "So, do you think we'll get the product out on time?" or "What do our customers think about the changes we're making to our services?" Although the answers to these questions may provide some important insight, they don't provide all the information necessary to run an effective organization. Truth be told, focusing on subjective assessments can be inherently risky, because by nature they overlook important quantitative metrics that are critical to the understanding of what's going on in a business. You can gain insight into the workings of your business only by closely reviewing and analyzing hard, objective data. In most organizations, hard, objective data takes the form of accounting reports and financial statements.

This chapter takes a close look at the most commonly used financial statements to help you understand when and how to use them to better gauge the progress of a business. (Feel free to also check out *Reading Financial Reports For Dummies,* by Lita Epstein, MBA [Wiley], if you want more in-depth info.)

Reviewing financial statements is a great way to start analyzing a company's financial health and its long-term outlook. However, to get the most mileage out of these reports, you need to undertake a deeper level of analysis. You must apply financial ratios to the numbers contained in the balance sheet and income statement and do financial forecasting. We address these topics and more in Chapter 12.

Financial Statements Are Your Friends

When it comes to assessing the overall financial health of an organization, businesspeople worldwide use three key financial reports. These reports — known more precisely as *financial statements* — are

- ✔ The balance sheet
- ✔ The income statement
- ✔ The statement of cash flows

Managers often receive a variety of financial and project reports tailored to their exact needs. For instance, a software-engineer manager may receive a weekly labor report that shows her exactly who worked on the team's software projects, how many hours each employee worked, the cost of those hours, and a variance above or below budget. An accounts-receivable manager may get an "aging list" of receivables that outlines who owes money to the company, how much is owed, and for how long. And a production manager may receive regular reports on the cost of returned products customers didn't approve of because of quality problems.

Each of these reports offers a unique perspective for looking at a company's financial health — and no one financial report can tell you the full story. A doctor who's faced with a patient who has an undetermined illness doesn't order only a blood test; he also orders a chest X-ray and a complete physical examination. The doctor doesn't know which test will reveal the source of the problem, so she orders several different tests. Likewise, you come to understand the complete picture of your organization's status only by reviewing all the financial statements and sometimes by digging even deeper for more information. This section (and chapter) helps you get started.

Who reads financial statements?

If you're a manager or business owner, you're probably very familiar with the three major financial statements. A manger or owner's job description is to keep close tabs on his organization's performance and to make changes in the allocation of company resources to maintain a high level of financial return.

If you're part of a self-managing work team, or if you work for an *open-book organization* — one that shares financial and other performance data with all employees — you, too, are probably familiar with the financial statements and the information they provide. If you're in one of these positions and you aren't familiar with financial statements, then read on.

People in the following lines of work also pay close attention to financial statements:

✔ Banks need financial statements to make judgments on whether to extend loans or lines of credit.

✔ Accountants require financial information to assess the health of an organization.

✔ Investors and financial analysts need financial statements to determine the attractiveness of a particular organization when compared with a wide range of other investment opportunities.

What do financial statements tell you?

Each different type of financial statement exists for a specific purpose, and it provides information that other statements don't. In general, financial statements offer their readers the following important status information:

✔ **Liquidity:** The company's ability to quickly convert assets into cash to pay expenses such as payroll, vendor invoices, creditors, and so on

✔ **General financial condition:** The long-term balance between debt and equity (the assets left after you deduct liabilities)

✔ **Owners' equity:** The periodic increases and decreases in the company's net worth

✔ **Profitability:** The ability of the company to earn profits (revenue that exceeds costs) consistently during an extended period of time

✔ **Performance:** The organization's performance against the financial plans developed by its management team or employees

As you review financial statements for your organization, keep in mind that there's no such thing as a good number or a bad number (unless you made an entry error). A high profit number may or may not be good news, depending on the situation. Similarly, a low revenue number may not be bad news, again depending on the situation. If a particular figure isn't what you expect it to be (too high or too low), research why the number is different from what you expect. In other words, take the time to look beyond the errant number itself before you suffer a heart attack or fire your sales staff!

For example, if profit declined from one period to the next, you may view this as a bad thing. In fact, your boss may say that it's a very bad thing! However, after researching the subject, you may find the decline to be a result of your CFO's decision to *draw down* profits (reduce profits by expenditures elsewhere in the company) to minimize the impact of income taxes on your company — definitely a good thing.

Taking a Snapshot: The Balance Sheet

The *balance sheet* gives you a snapshot of your organization's financial health at an exact point in time — not over a period of time. You use this snapshot to determine the book value of a company's assets and liabilities (including equity) at a particular date. The famous tagline on the heading of any good balance sheet is some form of "As of December 31, 2009, . . ." or "At December 31, 2009, . . .". Your company's financial picture could be vastly different on January 1, 2010 (after your CFO electronically transfers $15 million out of the company's cash account and into his numbered Swiss bank account before flying out of the country to start his early retirement!).

Before we move forward, we have a question for you: Do you know what the accounting equation is? If not, check out Chapter 10. For those of you who don't feel like turning the page right now, here's the accounting equation without any context:

Assets = Liabilities + Owners' Equity

The accounting equation is the basis for creating the balance sheet (see Figure 11-1 for an illustration):

- ✔ **Assets** include cash and things that you can convert to cash.

- ✔ **Liabilities** are obligations — debt, loans, mortgages, and the like — owed to other organizations or people.

- ✔ **Owners' equity** is the net worth of your company after you subtract all liabilities from the organization's assets.

In the balance sheet, assets are listed in order from the *most liquid* (readily convertible to cash) to the *least liquid*. Liabilities and owners' equity are listed in the order in which your company plans to pay them. ***Note:*** You can convert current assets to cash within a year; current liabilities are scheduled to be paid within a year.

As you can see in Figure 11-1, the value of Acme Dog Food's assets is balanced by its liabilities and owners' equity. The balance sheet demonstrates the fact that a company's liabilities and owners' equity pay for its assets. Conversely, the company uses its assets to generate cash to pay off its liabilities. Any excess cash (gains) is added to owners' equity.

Acme Dog Food
Consolidated Balance Sheet - As of December 31, 2005
(In millions)

ASSETS
Current Assets

Cash and cash equivalents	$25
Accounts receivable	150
Inventory	50
Total Current Assets	225

Fixed Assets

Equipment	200
Furniture, fixtures, and improvements	150
Allowance for depreciation and amortization	(20)
Total Fixed Assets	330
Total Assets	**$555**

LIABILITIES AND OWNERS' EQUITY
LIABILITIES
Current Liabilities

Notes payable to bank	10
Accounts payable	50
Accrued compensation and benefits	75
Income taxes payable	20
Deferred income taxes	10
Current portion of long-term debt	5
Total Current Liabilities	170
Long-Term Debt	100
Deferred Rent Expense	50
Deferred Income Taxes	50
Total Liabilities	**370**

OWNERS' EQUITY

Common stock	100
Additional paid-in capital	60
Retained earnings	25
Total Owners' Equity	**185**
Total Liabilities and Owners' Equity	**$555**

Figure 11-1:
A balance sheet for a fictional online company.

By reviewing changes in your balance sheets over time, managers, bankers, investors, and so on can pick up on trends that may affect the long-term viability of the firm and that may positively or negatively impact the value of its stock. In Chapter 12, you find out how to use financial ratios and forecasting tools to make sense of the numbers in the balance sheet and spot changes and trends.

Making Money: The Income Statement

Why does a business exist? To leave a lasting legacy in the world? Maybe in some cases. To employ thousands of people and pull a city or region out of an economic slump that threatens the fabric of the community? That's happened on more than one occasion. To save the world? Perhaps. The number one reason that businesses exist is to make money — to make a profit for their owners. Because making money is such an incredibly important part of the day-to-day focus of a business, companies need a quick and easily understood way to figure out how much money they're making. Such a tool exists: the income statement.

An *income statement* (see Figure 11-2 for an illustration) — also known as a *profit and loss statement,* a *P&L,* a *report of earnings,* or a *statement of income and losses* — gives its readers three key pieces of information:

- ✔ The business's sales volume during the period of the report
- ✔ The business's expenses during the period of the report
- ✔ The difference between the business's sales and its expenses (its profit or loss) during the period of the report

The income statement in Figure 11-2 indicates that Acme Dog Food had $49,000 in net sales revenue and a cost of goods sold of $10,000, leaving a gross profit of $39,000. However, the gross profit saw further reduction from the expenses of selling products, running the company (advertising, printing, rent, salaries, bonuses, and so forth), and income taxes. The result was a net income of $9,000. Divided by 250,000 shares of stock in the hands of investors and the company, the $9,000 works out to an earnings per share of $0.036. At about 18 percent of net sales revenues, a net income of $9,000 is a very good result indeed.

```
                         Acme Dog Food
       Income Statement - Twelve Months Ended December 31, 2005
                         (In thousands)
         REVENUES
            Gross sales                              50
            Less: Returns                            (1)
                  Net Sales                          49
         COST OF GOODS SOLD
            Beginning inventory                      50
            Purchases                                10
            Less: Purchase discounts                 (2)
            Net purchases                             8
            Cost of goods available for sale         58
            Less: Ending inventory                   48
                  Cost of Goods Sold                 10
         GROSS PROFIT                                39
         OPERATING EXPENSES
            Total selling expenses                    5
            Total general expenses                   10
                  Total operating expenses           15
                  Operating income                   24
            Other income and expenses
            Interest expense (income)                 5
                  Total Other Income and Expense      5
            Income before taxes                      19
            Less: Income taxes                       (10)
                  Net Income                          9
                  Average Number of Shares      250,000
                  Earnings Per Share             $0.036
```

Figure 11-2:
A sample
income
statement.

Pat Boyce on the value of financial statements

Pat Boyce — former president and COO of Horizons Technology, Inc., of San Diego, California, and vice president and corporate controller for SAIC, Inc., of La Jolla, California — is an independent consultant who specializes in setting up financial and accounting systems for technology start-ups. In his many years of financial experience, Boyce has seen just about everything — and maybe even a little bit more. We asked him for his perspective on the importance of financial statements:

The *Complete MBA For Dummies:* Of the three key financial statements, which do you consider to be the most valuable for a business, and why?

Pat Boyce: That definitely depends on the state of affairs of the business, and the type of a business that it is. For example, in a small start-up company, the only one that matters is the cash-flow statement. Assuming that you've got limited resources, managing your cash flow is your top priority.

(continued)

(continued)

Complete MBA: Why is that?

Boyce: If you don't have enough cash or resources to afford to meet your payroll and other liabilities, then you've got a big problem.

Complete MBA: How often should a company run a cash-flow report?

Boyce: First, there's a difference between a cash-flow report that you might see as a financial statement and a cash-flow report that you use to operate a business. The internal, operating cash-flow report is done differently than the one that is seen by the public. Most companies that I know do operating cash-flow reports on a very frequent basis. Certainly, they try to do it at least once a week, and it's not uncommon for businesses to run a daily cash-flow report. The cash-flow report that goes with your financial statements is different, however, and it is defined by what your CPA and the accounting standards require. If you look at the classic one used as a financial statement, first of all, you can only do that on an irregular basis, and second, it doesn't really lend itself to decision making. It's more analytic. It doesn't help you on a day-to-day basis.

Complete MBA: Does keeping close tabs on cash flow become less important as you grow out of the start-up phase?

Boyce: Definitely, assuming you've got your financing positions well established. You've still got to keep an eye on your cash flow, but you can delegate the task to your accounting people with some general ground rules as to where it should be. As long as your cash flow stays within these ground rules, then it doesn't get management attention. Once you've generated some working capital that you can rely on, the sense of urgency on a day-to-day basis drops. It doesn't mean the urgency goes away; your cash flow just doesn't require the same level of attention.

Complete MBA: How about the balance sheet? What's the point?

Boyce: The relevance of the balance sheet varies dramatically from business to business. Say that at one extreme, you've got a consulting business, and at the other extreme, you've got a bank or other financial institution. In the case of the consulting business, the balance sheet is important in the sense of managing certain assets like accounts receivable or payments to vendors, or whatever, and seeing that your overall financial position is acceptable in a broad sense. When it comes to the financial institution, the balance sheet really represents the working assets and liabilities of your business — which generates your income — so its purposes are much broader.

Complete MBA: When you look at a balance sheet, what makes you feel good?

Boyce: Balance sheets are impacted very much by the type of business and the industry that they're in. Using our example of a consulting business and a bank, their balance sheets would never look at all alike, either in the description or in the relative magnitudes of types of assets and liabilities. If you look at a balance sheet in the context of an industry, and you know what that balance sheet should look like in that industry, then you can make a judgment about it. If you don't know that, then it's pretty hard to judge whether an individual balance sheet is really good or really bad. If you tie the income statement together with the balance sheet, you can start doing more classic financial analysis than you would get in a textbook about how that business operates. But you still want to have that reference point back to the ndustry. The other reference point would be to the point in time. Just a snapshot of a balance sheet at any point in time isn't nearly as valuable as a comparison over time. Ideally, to make a judgment, you'll want to look at a comparison of that balance sheet over time and be able to compare it to the industry.

Complete MBA: How about the income statement?

Boyce: It's the one that everyone relies on the most, and the techniques for presenting the income statement are continually being refined by accountants. It's a test to give you the real economic earnings of the company during the period of time portrayed in the statement. Depending on the business, some of the things that affect the income and expenses may be so theoretically obtuse that the average person may not understand them.

Complete MBA: What's the use of an income statement for a working manager or employee?

Boyce: Ideally, what you do is break the company's published income statement down into pieces that are your internal responsibility accounting reporting system. Then you take each aspect of your income statement — and for that matter, some or all of your balance sheet — and assign it to responsible parties on the basis of the areas that they can control. The things that they can't control themselves by their actions as a manager are best left to someone who can control them. Eventually, there will be a few items that are not subject to control — for example, depreciation expense based on prior acquisition of capital equipment — and that don't make sense to be assigned to someone to control. Then each responsible person has his or her own mini-income statement to manage.

Complete MBA: Why is it more valuable to look at a comparison over time versus just a snapshot?

Boyce: If you're really trying to assess what's going on within the company, looking at what's changing will give you a feeling about where the company has been going over that past period of time, which can give you an indication of where the company will go in the future.

Complete MBA: Is there a general rule for how many periods you need to see to get a fairly accurate trend?

Boyce: The theoretical answer that a professor might give you is that you would want to see it for two or three business periods, depending on whether the business has a seasonality. Just as with any mathematical analysis, if you can get two points, you can draw a line, but if you can get three points, you can start getting some information about trends. So, typically, you would like to see three periods. For example, if you took software developer Intuit's financial statement, it has a very, very seasonal business because of the sales of its Quicken tax return software in the early part of the year. Then revenues drop off substantially, changing the balance sheet dramatically. To really get a good sense of Intuit's business, you would have to look at it at the same point in time for three years. Other companies may not have much seasonality at all, in which case you can go with shorter periods of time. Followers of *open-book management,* on the other hand, believe that all workers should have access to a company's financial statements. They also believe that employees should receive training in what these statements mean and in how the work they do impacts both the company and them as employees. However, financial statements aren't exactly exciting topics for most employees. So, if you want to use the philosophy of open-book management, you have to think carefully about how you develop financial literacy in your company. Here are some pointers to follow:

- **Get the people in your company to speak a common language.** You don't want to use the language of accounting (debits and credits); use the numbers and ratios (see Chapter 12) that relate directly to the company. And be sure to train your employees in how to translate and understand this new language! For example, many companies offer their employees classes on how to read financial statements.

(continued)

(continued)

✔ **Make your employees understand how their work contributes to the profits of the business.** Making that link gives employees a vested interest in doing quality work. For example, you can explain to your electronics assemblers how whenever a product is returned due to poor quality, company costs increase, profits decrease, and the amount of money available to pay bonuses also decreases.

✔ **Demonstrate what you're talking about in terms that can be easily understood.** Don't assume that employees will understand terms that you take for granted, such as profit and loss. Spell them out in terms that they will understand as clearly as you do. For example, at one manufacturing company, the plant supervisor wanted to reduce the amount of scrap material in its production process, but his employees didn't seem to understand his goal. He decided to try a demonstration to get their attention. He asked them to join him in the break room, where he had placed an old sofa. Pulling out a huge chainsaw, he cut off a third of the sofa. Afterward he said to the shocked employees, "That's how much it costs for the materials that go into our product." He then lopped off another third of the couch and proclaimed, "That part represents labor." Finally, he pointed to the remaining piece of sofa and announced," That's how much money we're wasting in scrap." His demonstration got their attention, and he had made his point. From then on, employees in the plant were determined to reduce scrap — it became their mantra.

The point is if you want to use open-book management, you need to make financials interesting and relevant to your employees. When Southwest Airlines introduced its employees to its financials, it created a colorful, fun-to-read document that captured the attention of the company's employees.

Keeping Your Business Afloat: The Cash-Flow Statement

Have you ever heard the phrase, "Cash is king"? No, not queen or prince — *king*. For any business, cash truly is what matters. It takes cash to pay employees, to purchase supplies, to pay bills, and to execute many more business functions. A *cash-flow statement* — also known as a *statement of cash flows* by some — is a specialized report that tracks the sources of cash in a company, as well as its *inflows* (money coming into the business) and *outflows* (money going out of the business). The statement is an extremely valuable tool for ensuring that your company has the cash it needs to meet its obligations when you need it. This can mean the difference between keeping your business afloat and watching it sink.

Going for financial literacy to get better performance

Many years ago, the open-book management revolution swept through the world of business, led by Jack Stack of Springfield ReManufacturing Corporation in Springfield, Missouri. (Jack turned his philosophy of business into a popular book, *The Great Game of Business* [Currency].) His revolution sparked a brand-new way of doing business in the United States, and that method has gained a foothold in many businesses today. Traditionally, the production and analysis of financial statements was a closely held duty of management. Not only did nonmanagement employees have no need to see these statements (as far as most managers were concerned), but it also was assumed that these employees wouldn't understand the statements anyway.

The business world features a number of different kinds of cash-flow statements — each one suited to a particular business need. Some work best strictly inside a business, and some work best outside a business (for investors, creditors, and other interested parties). Here are a few of the most common types of cash-flow statements:

- ✔ **Simple cash-flow statement (or cash budget):** Arranges all items into one or two categories — most often cash inflows and cash outflows.

- ✔ **Operating cash-flow statement:** Limits analysis of cash flows to only items dealing with the operations of a business — not its financing.

- ✔ **Financing cash-flow statement:** Includes cash raised by issuing new debt or equity capital, as well as expenses incurred for repaying debt or paying dividends on stock.

- ✔ **Statement of cash flows:** Often an external statement that depicts the period-to-period changes in balance sheet items and the actual dollar amount for the period in question for income statement items. This statement shows the following categories:

  - Operating cash inflows

  - Operating cash outflows

  - Priority outflows (such as interest expense and current debt payments)

  - Discretionary outflows (such as equipment expense)

  - Financial flows (things you borrow or changes in equity)

Although you can find plenty of different cash-flow statements to meet your every mood, whatever you do, don't forget the first and perhaps the most important rule of cash management: Happiness is a positive cash flow. Having a positive cash flow — more coming in than going out — means that you're in a better position to meet your current and future financial obligations. Figure 11-3 shows an example of a simple cash-flow statement meant for internal use.

Cash flows (4th Qtr.)	October	November	December
Cash inflow	$5,000,000	$7,500,000	$6,500,000
Cash outflow	$4,500,000	$8,000,000	$7,000,000
Cash surplus (need) this month	$500,000	($500,000)	($500,000)
Cash surplus (need) last month	$0	$500,000	$0
Cumulative cash flow	$500,000	$0	($500,000)

Figure 11-3: A simple cash-flow statement.

The top line of the example indicates the three months of the company's fourth quarter: October, November, December. By working down the column for each month, you can quickly and easily determine the cash flow. For example, in October, cash in was $5 million, and cash out was $4.5 million, resulting in a net cash surplus of $500,000. When combined with the last month's cash surplus (need) of $0, the cumulative cash flow in October was $500,000. In November, cash in was $7.5 million, but cash out was $8 million, resulting in a negative cash flow for the month of ($500,000). Combining November's negative cash flow of ($500,000) with October's cumulative cash flow of $500,000 results in a cumulative cash flow of $0 for November.

Chapter 12

Deciphering the Mysteries of Financial Planning and Analysis

*A*lthough cash takes up only one line on a company's balance sheet, it plays an incredibly important role in the day-to-day health of the organization. Cash pays employee salaries and benefits. It pays vendors for the raw materials, services, and supplies needed to operate the business and manufacture its products. Cash keeps the lights on. It pays for the inventory of products that are stockpiled for customers to buy. Bottom line: Without a constant and reliable supply of good old-fashioned money, most businesses would go kaput before too long.

It shouldn't surprise you to learn, therefore, that managing, planning, forecasting, and analyzing financial situations is high on the list of priorities for the people who own, manage, and run organizations. As Harold Geneen, the famous former chairman of ITT, put it,

> *"To be good at your business, you have to know the numbers — cold."*

So, what's involved in managing a company's finances? We believe that, with the proper tools, most people can become proficient in managing the finances of a company, division, or department. And, in this chapter, we provide you with the tools to do just that. We cover everything from forecasting and budgeting to financial ratios and investment analysis tools you need to understand. We also take you through the process of reading an annual report.

Manage Your Finances (Before They Manage You!)

You have a choice: You can either manage your business and the systems and processes within it or you can let it manage you. We have many years of experience in business and have interviewed a variety of people who own and run businesses. Based on information from those sources, we know that the best route to success is to be proactive and manage your business instead of letting it manage you.

Although every business has many systems and processes that can benefit from proactive management, your company's financial situation is among the most important areas to manage. Every business — from the smallest start-up to the largest Fortune 500 multinational — needs a financial plan. Financial plans serve as blueprints for the financial needs of your company. As such, they enable your decision makers to determine when and where funds will be necessary in the organization, and how much to allot. Financial plans also let managers know whether it's prudent to promise new projects or ventures or whether it's necessary to terminate old, underperforming ones.

The financial planning process has three parts: preparing forecasts, developing budgets, and establishing financial controls. The following sections take a closer look at each part.

The old acronym GIGO (garbage in, garbage out) definitely applies when it comes to making forecasts. Financial forecasts of *any* sort are only as good as the data on which they're based. As the horizon for your forecasts extends further into the future, their reliability naturally declines, and they become less dependable. Many companies in fast-moving industries are happy to forecast a year into the future with *any* degree of accuracy. Companies in more stable industries, however, can safely forecast up to five years out.

Preparing accurate forecasts

Have you ever tried to guess what will happen tomorrow — or next week or next year — in your business? If you can count on one thing in business, it's that nothing will stay the same for very long. In business today, change is a constant.

Therefore, savvy businesspeople try to anticipate, forecast, and predict change before it occurs. And because financial considerations can mean the difference between life and death to a company, financial forecasts and projections are keystones of proactive business management practice.

Ask questions similar to the following if you want to prepare accurate financial forecasts for your business:

- How many employees will we have on board this year, and will we have the money to pay them when we need to?

- Will we have sufficient funds to invest in new manufacturing equipment that will improve the productivity of our workers while increasing output and lowering rejects?

- How much money will we need to stock up our inventory in time for the holiday season? Will the money be available when we need it?

- By what amount can we expect revenues and profit to grow (or, heaven forbid, shrink) over the next year?

- What is the timing of payments from our major customers, and how will they affect our cash flow?

These questions, and others like them, should constantly be on the minds of financial managers — chief financial officers (CFOs), controllers, presidents, vice presidents — and others who are responsible for ensuring that a business meets all its financial obligations. For this reason, managers conduct regular financial planning and forecasting sessions.

There are two key kinds of financial forecasts and projections: short-term and long-term. In addition, many businesses regularly produce cash forecasts to keep close tabs on the cash going in and out of the company. In the sections that follow, we cover all three.

Short-term financial forecasts

If a financial forecast is for a period of one year or less, it's considered a *short-term forecast*. Many firms use a variety of short-term financial forecasts and *pro forma* (informal) financial statements to manage day-to-day operations. These types of forecasts and financial statements include

- Cash
- Sales or revenue
- Profit and loss (income statement)
- Balance sheet
- Receivables

Each of these short-term forecasts — and others that an organization may select — is important to the people in charge of monitoring a company's near-term financial position.

Long-term financial forecasts

If you need to plan for a period that extends more than a year into the future, *long-term financial forecasts* are just what the doctor ordered. But given how fast the business environment is changing, why would you want to make plans for more than a year into the future? Won't things change at least five or ten times before then? Of course they will. But part of financial planning is planning for change.

Done right, long-term plans can provide your business with a definite competitive advantage. How? By giving your business focus and direction. Business owners typically have a vision for where they want their companies to be in, say, ten years; so, it makes sense to think about the financial milestones you should cross along the way.

In short, long-range plans require long-term financial forecasts to support them. Although they can never be as accurate as short-term forecasts, they're often better than nothing. Just as with short-term financial forecasts, you can forecast all kinds of financial data well into the future. Here are some of the most popular kinds of financial data subject to a long-term look:

- Cash
- Sales or revenue
- Profit and loss (income statement)
- Assets, liabilities, and net worth (balance sheet)

Although long-range forecasting can help you support your long-range plans, the further out you forecast, the more likely your figures will be inaccurate. That's why it's important to base your forecasts on sound numbers and an understanding of business trends.

Long-term financial forecasts are comprised of much the same information as short-term forecasts, just with much longer horizons. These longer horizons require careful attention to long-range trends in markets and technology, and they assume the possibility of greater swings. Here are some tips for putting together accurate, long-term financial forecasts:

- **Look for long-term trends in revenues and expenses.** Are your revenues and expenses gradually trending up or down over a period of five years or longer? Chart these trends as graphs and make an educated guess as to where the trends will lead in the future.

- **Determine whether there are any business cycles.** A *business cycle* is a periodic variation in the economic activity of your business resulting from such things as consumer demand, which may rise in anticipation of the holidays and decline immediately thereafter. Many businesses and markets go through regular business cycles. By looking at the big picture, you should be able to pick out the cycles and factor them into your long-term financial forecasts.

✔ **Figure out what kinds of random events are most likely to disturb the long-term trends in revenues and expenses.** What would happen if your company bought out a key competitor? How would that affect revenues and expenses? What if a competitor develops a new process that cuts its costs of production in half? Random events are just that — random. By nature, they're hard to predict, but the more you factor them into your long-term financial forecasts, the more accurate your forecasts will be.

Cash forecasts

By far the most important forecast for most companies is the cash forecast (as you can see, this type of forecast shows up in both short- and long-term predictions). In business, cash makes the world go 'round. Especially for young start-up companies, cash, or the lack thereof, can mean the difference between success and failure.

Figure 12-1 is an example of the kind of simplified cash forecast a typical firm may use on a regular basis. The frequency of reporting depends on the needs of the business and the importance of keeping close tabs on its cash position. For some companies, "regular" means daily or weekly. For others, it means monthly, quarterly, or even longer. The cash forecast in Figure 12-1 is for a business that provides software engineers directly to a Fortune 500 company at a variety of locations nationwide. Software engineers are the company's main product, as well as its major expense. In this example, the company pays employees weekly but receives payment from its client only once each month.

As you can see, in each of the first three weeks of the month, the company incurs a negative cash flow of $20,000, accumulating to $60,000 by the end of the third week. However, when the client makes a $150,000 payment in week four, the cash flow goes positive in a big way — to the tune of $70,000. Now, just imagine what the company's cash forecast looks like when it adds all 14 of its clients to the mix!

Using similar cash forecasts, companies can determine when they'll be taking in more money than they pay out to meet their obligations. They can use this knowledge to guide many decisions, such as

✔ When and how much to pay vendors

✔ What levels of inventory they can comfortably keep in stock

✔ Timing investments in capital equipment

Forecasted cash flows	Week 1	Week 2	Week 3	Week 4
Cash inflow (client payment)	$0	$0	$0	$150,000
Cash outflow (payroll)	$20,000	$20,000	$20,000	$20,000
Cash surplus (need) this week	($20,000)	($20,000)	($20,000)	$130,000
Cash surplus (need) last week	$0	($20,000)	($40,000)	($60,000)
Cumulative cash flow	($20,000)	($40,000)	($60,000)	$70,000

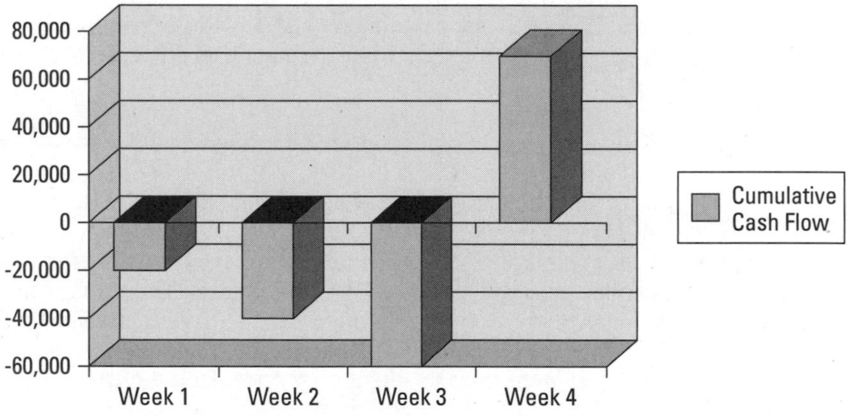

Figure 12-1:
A simplified cash forecast for a typical company.

Developing and executing budgets

The second part of the financial management process is the development and execution of budgets. Budgets are similar to financial forecasts, but much more detailed. For example, a sales forecast may simply reflect a total revenue estimate of $500,000 for the upcoming fiscal quarter; a *sales budget* for the same period, on the other hand, is a breakdown of each of the various individual components of the sales forecast. Take a look at the following table, which shows an example sales budget for a hypothetical computer components retailer's 3rd quarter:

Item/Service	Projected Sales
Monitors	$75,000
Keyboards	$30,000
Hard drives	$100,000
CPUs	$150,000
Motherboards	$25,000
CD-ROM drives	$25,000
Installation	$50,000
Service contracts	$45,000
Total Sales Budget	$500,000

This budget shows how much the company is predicting it will sell of each product or service during a specific period of time — in this case, a fiscal quarter. The neat thing about budgets is that they not only provide a detailed picture of what the future may bring, but also create a baseline against which you can measure your actual performance. In the preceding budget, the amount of estimated total sales is $500,000. After the third quarter is over, the company's accounting system will provide the actual results — for each line of the sales budget, as well as an overall total.

By comparing the budgeted totals versus the actual results, you can quickly grasp exactly where company performance is better or worse than antici-pated and redirect your resources accordingly. For a much more detailed dis-cussion on the budgeting process, including all the whys and how-tos you need, be sure to drop by Chapter 10.

Establishing financial controls

Accounting systems and financial statements and reports are wonderful things, but they aren't worth the software they're built from, nor the paper they're printed on, if no one analyzes and interprets them. Numbers by themselves mean nothing. Numbers with context and justification mean everything.

The whole point of preparing financial forecasts and budgets is to attempt to predict future performance while creating baselines by which you can compare actual results. If results you experience are as predicted, terrific — you're right on track toward your goals. If the actual results are significantly less or significantly more than predicted, however, it's time to look for the sources of these variances.

Here are some ways that you can analyze your company's performance against expectations:

- ✔ **Variance analysis:** By comparing your organization's actual results versus its budgeted results (for example, your actual revenues versus budgeted revenues), you get a quick picture of whether your company is on or off track and by how much. (We discuss variance analysis in detail in Chapter 10.)

- ✔ **Ratio analysis:** By comparing certain financial results within your company's financial statements (particularly the income statement and balance sheet), you can determine whether your company is operating within the normal limits for your industry. For example, dividing your company's current assets by its current liabilities results in a ratio (the *quick ratio*) that tells you whether your company is solvent and can meet its financial obligations to your lenders.

- ✔ **Cost/volume/profit analysis:** By determining what products/services are the most — and the least — profitable for your company, you can make decisions about where to invest your company's time and resources. There are a couple key approaches to cost/volume/profit analysis:

  - • **Break-even analysis:** A *break-even analysis (BE)* allows you to determine at what sales volume you can earn a profit after paying all the expenses of producing your product/service. BE is the point at which the cost of the product/service equals the sales volume. Everything above that point is *gross profit.* Using electronic spreadsheets, you can run all sorts of what-if scenarios with a variety of different cost and price assumptions.

  - • **Contribution margin analysis:** *Contribution margin analysis* compares the profitability of each of your company's products or services, as well as the product's/service's relative contribution to your company's bottom line. This analysis quickly points out underperforming products and services that your company should either restructure or terminate.

If your company is underperforming, you can redirect resources to boost performance, or you can change plans to bring your expectations in line with reality. If your company is overperforming, you can identify the reasons why and do more of the same. At the same time, you can modify your budgets upward to accommodate the improved performance.

You can use many tricks of the trade to determine how your business is performing based on all sorts of financial data. In the next section, we explore some of our personal favorites.

Identifying Financial Tricks of the Trade

In life and in business, people seek rules or shortcuts that will put complicated processes or data into simple, easily understood terms. In that spirit, when looking at a company's financial situation — certainly about as complicated a task as anyone could imagine — businesspeople like to use a variety of financial tools to derive powerful but simple ratios to measure performance. We take a look at these tools in this section.

As you read through the financial ratios in this section, keep in mind that they can vary considerably for companies in different industries. Manufacturing companies, as a group, have different ratios than consulting firms or utilities. Be sure that when you compare one company's numbers with the numbers for another, you're comparing apples with apples and oranges with oranges. However, some ratios — many of which we explain here — are common to all businesses.

Liquidity ratios: Measuring solvency

Liquidity ratios are ratios that measure the *solvency* of a business — its ability to generate the cash necessary to pay its bills and meet other short-term financial obligations.

Current ratio

The *current ratio* is the ability of a business to pay its current liabilities out of its current assets. Here's how the current ratio works (along with an example):

Current ratio = Current assets ÷ Current liabilities

= $250 million ÷ $100 million

= 2.5

In this example, the 2.5 ratio says that the company has $2.50 dollars in assets for every $1.00 in liabilities. In general, a ratio of 2.0 or better is good; in fact, many banks require that their borrowers maintain a current ratio of 2.0 or higher as a condition of their loans.

Quick ratio (acid test)

The *quick ratio* — also known as the *acid test* — is a measure of a business's ability to pay its current liabilities out of its current assets. However, the quick ratio subtracts inventory out of the current assets, providing an even more rigorous test of a firm's ability to pay its current liabilities quickly.

Inventory often is difficult to convert to cash because it may be obsolete (or, in the case of some fraudulent practices, nonexistent). Here's how the quick ratio works:

Quick ratio = (Current assets − Inventory) ÷ Current liabilities

= ($250 million − $20 million) ÷ $100 million

= 2.3

A ratio of 1.1 or higher is considered to be acceptable.

Activity ratios: Can you raise the cash?

Activity ratios are indications of how efficient your company is at using its resources to generate revenue. The faster and more efficiently your firm can generate cash, the stronger it is financially and the more attractive it is to investors and lenders. And the less likely it is that managers will be laid off!

Receivables turnover ratio

The *receivables turnover ratio* indicates the average amount of time that your company takes to convert its receivables into cash. The ratio is a function of how quickly your company's customers and clients pay their bills; basically, it points out problems that your company may be having in the collections process. Here's how it works:

Receivables turnover ratio = Net sales ÷ Accounts receivable

= $100 million ÷ $15 million

= 6.67

The higher the ratio, the better (and the bigger your bonus — congratulations!).

Average collection period

You can discover a very interesting piece of information by using your receivables turnover ratio (see the previous section). By dividing 365 days by your receivables turnover ratio, you find out the average number of days that your company takes to turn over its accounts receivable. This result is known as the *average collection period*. Here's the breakdown:

Average collection period = 365 days ÷ Receivables turnover ratio

= 365 days ÷ 6.67

= 54.7 days

In this case, the lower the number, the better; a low number indicates that your customers are paying their bills quickly, which gives you more cash to work with.

Inventory turnover ratio

The *inventory turnover ratio* provides an idea of how quickly your company turns over inventory (sells it off and replaces it with new inventory) during a specific period of time. This information represents the ability of your firm to convert inventory into cash. The higher the number, the more often you turn over inventory — a good thing. Figure 12-2 shows an example.

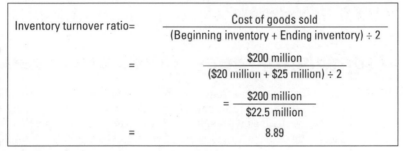

Figure 12-2: A sample inventory turnover ratio.

$$\text{Inventory turnover ratio} = \frac{\text{Cost of goods sold}}{(\text{Beginning inventory} + \text{Ending inventory}) \div 2}$$

$$= \frac{\$200 \text{ million}}{(\$20 \text{ million} + \$25 \text{ million}) \div 2}$$

$$= \frac{\$200 \text{ million}}{\$22.5 \text{ million}}$$

$$= 8.89$$

Debt (or leverage) ratios: Avoiding the borrowing blues

For most organizations, going into debt is a normal part of doing business. Debt can plug holes when cash flows can't cover all your necessary operating expenses for short periods of time. Debt also allows companies that are growing quickly to finance their expansion. However, you *can* have too much of a good thing; too much debt, for instance, can be a financial drag on any organization. For your measuring pleasure, *debt ratios* are measures of how much debt a company is carrying and who's financing the debt.

Debt-to-equity ratio

The *debt-to-equity ratio* measures the extent to which a company is financed by outside creditors versus shareholders and owners. Here's how it works:

Debt-to-equity ratio = Total liabilities ÷ Owners' equity

= $100 million ÷ $150 million

= 0.66

A high ratio (anything more than 1.0) is considered bad because it indicates that your company may have difficulty paying back its creditors.

Debt-to-assets ratio

The *debt-to-assets ratio* measures how much of a company's assets are financed by outside creditors versus the percentage that the owners cover. In other words, you divide the long-term liabilities you have by your total assets:

$$\text{Debt-to-assets ratio} = \text{Long-term liabilities} \div \text{Total assets}$$

$$= \$50 \text{ million} \div \$500 \text{ million}$$

$$= 0.10$$

Ratios of up to 0.50 are considered acceptable; anything more may be a sign of trouble. (Note, however, that most manufacturing firms have debt-to-asset ratios between 0.30 and 0.70.)

Profitability ratios: The return of return

Except for new start-up companies — which aren't expected to make money right out of the gate — all companies are expected to generate profit from their operations. And, as with sales and revenue, the more profit you generate, the merrier your owners and shareholders/investors will be. *Profitability ratios* indicate the effectiveness of management in controlling expenses and earning a reasonable return for shareholders and owners.

Profit ratio

The *profit ratio* is a measure of how much profit your company generates for each dollar of revenue after you account for all costs of normal operations. The inverse of this percentage (100 percent-profit ratio) equals the *expense ratio,* or the portion of each sales dollar that's accounted for by expenses from normal operations. The higher the ratio, the better. Here's how to calculate a company's profit ratio:

$$\text{Profit ratio} = \text{Net income} \div \text{Net sales}$$

$$= \$50 \text{ million} \div \$100 \text{ million}$$

$$= 0.5$$

The expected ratio can vary considerably from industry to industry. For example, although grocery stores — which make money by turning over high volumes of inventory quickly — generally are satisfied with profit ratios of just a couple percent, many software developers have profit ratios of 30 to 40 percent or more.

Gross margin

The *gross margin* is an indication of the profitability of a firm. To determine gross margin, you use your sales revenues and gross profit, which is what's left over after you subtract the cost of goods sold (COGS; the direct costs of making a product) from revenues. Gross profit tells you how much you have left to pay overhead costs and make a net profit. Here's how to calculate gross margin:

Gross margin ratio = Gross profit ÷ Sales revenues

= $75 million ÷ $100 million

= 0.75

In this example, the company's COGS is $25 million, which leaves $75 million (extraordinarily high) to pay overhead. The gross margin is 75 percent, which is typical for software companies. The gross margin also tells you how much room you have to make mistakes. An independent grocer with margins of 2 or 3 percent must sell in large volume to compensate for low margins.

Return on investment ratio

Return on investment — better known as *ROI* — is one of the stars of the world of financial tools. *Return on investment* measures the ability of a company to create profits for its owners. The percentage it spits out represents the number of dollars of net income earned per dollar of invested capital. As such, ROI is of great interest to investors, shareholders, and other people with a financial stake in your company. These folks want to make as much money as they possibly can on their investment dollars, so the higher the return on investment, the better! Here's the calculation breakdown:

Return on investment ratio = Net income ÷ Owners' equity

= $50 million ÷ $150 million

= 0.33

In this example, a company invests $150 million, resulting in net income of $50 million and an ROI of 33 percent. This is a very healthy return on the investment, especially compared to other investments such as putting the money into a money market fund, which might yield an ROI of only 5 or 6 percent.

Return on assets ratio

The *return on assets ratio* — also known as *ROA* — takes the EBIT (earnings before interest and income tax) that a company earns from the total capital used to create the profit. In this sense, ROA indicates the effectiveness of a company's utilization of capital. Here's the way to calculate return on assets:

Return on assets ratio = EBIT ÷ Net operating assets

= $75 million ÷ $300 million

= 0.25

Acceptable ROA ratios vary depending on the industry. For example, ratios below 5 percent are generally indicative of asset-heavy businesses such as manufacturing and railroads, while ratios of more than 20 percent are indicative or asset-light companies such as software and advertising firms.

Analyzing Investment Risk

Because nothing in this world is certain but death and taxes (a collective tip of the hat to Benjamin Franklin), any investment — no matter how conservative — has some element of risk. Of course, some investments — say, investing in an unproven new technology — are riskier than others. But investors are constantly making decisions about how much risk they're willing to bear when they invest their money, and they weigh this risk against the anticipated reward.

As every manager and business owner knows, a company has limited resources to fund *capital investments* — long-term investments in assets such as manufacturing equipment, office equipment, buildings, and so on. Therefore, a company must analyze capital investments by using a set of simple mathematical equations — equations that are part of the basic toolbox given to MBA students around the world. Managers and executives regularly use these equations to help guide their investment decisions.

In the sections that follow, we present the investment analyst toolbox, equipped with equations, that all MBAers should carry. Proper application of the tools shows which investment options offer the best returns to your organization and to its investors.

Net present value (NPV)

Net present value (NPV) is the anticipated profitability of a particular investment, considering projected cash flows discounted by a risk factor that takes into account inflation, level of risk, and returns required. In simpler terms, you compare a dollar invested today to projected dollars generated from the investment at some point in the future — the time value of the money. By calculating NPV, you can determine whether your company should pursue a particular investment — in capital equipment or other assets.

Following is the official formula for calculating net present value. However, we suggest that you bypass much of the heavy lifting here by using tables readily available on the Net or in financial reference books to obtain your discount rates. Then you can simply multiply the discount rates from the tables times your annual cash flows to calculate NPV.

t is the time of the cash flow.

n is the total time of the project.

r is the discount rate.

C_t is the net cash flow (the amount of cash) at time t.

C_0 is the capital outlay at the beginning of the investment time ($t = 0$).

$$NPV - \sum_{t=1}^{n} \frac{C_t}{(1+r)^t} - C_0$$

For example, say that you're thinking about acquiring a building for $1 million for your business. Also assume for a moment that your financial projections suggest that the building generates the following cash flows during the course of five years:

Year 1: –$1 million (acquisition cost)

Year 2: $300,000

Year 3: $400,000

Year 4: $400,000

Year 5: $350,000

Net total: $450,000

On the surface, it appears that this investment is a sure winner. It's projected to generate a profit during five years of $450,000, on top of the initial acquisition cost of $1 million. But, not so fast! The time value of money will reduce this outcome. Why? Because money in your hands today — right now — is worth more than money in the future. Assuming a cost of capital (risk factor, in other words) of 9 percent, the actual NPV works out as follows:

Year	Cash Flow	×	Discount Rate	=	Present Value
Year 1	($1,000,000)	×	1.000000	=	($1,000,000)
Year 2	$300,000	×	0.917431	=	$275,229
Year 3	$400,000	×	0.841680	=	$336,672
Year 4	$400,000	×	0.772183	=	$308,873
Year 5	$350,000	×	0.708425	=	$247,949
Net present value					$168,723

Although the investment won't produce the $450,000 of profit that you thought it would, $168,723 isn't exactly bad news. At least NPV gives you a more realistic picture on which to compare this particular investment against others you may make, along with a reasonable basis to make a decision.

When working with NPV, you need to keep the following points in mind:

- When NPV is greater than 0, the investment is adding value to your firm. If it offers more value than competing investments, you should pursue it.

- When NPV is less than 0, the investment is taking value away from your business and you should reject it.

- When NPV equals 0, there's usually no advantage to pursuing the investment, unless you're investing for other factors — such as positioning in your industry or securing important customers.

Internal rate of return (IRR)

Internal rate of return (IRR) is another approach to determining whether the return of a particular investment makes it worthwhile to pursue. IRR is simply the rate of return that the investment produces or the reward for making the investment. IRR is related to the NPV in that it represents the discount rate in which the NPV of a cash flow stream (inflows and outflows) equals zero. In fact, IRR and NPV are two sides of the same coin. With NPV, you discount a future stream of cash flows by your minimum desired rate of return. With IRR, you actually compute your break-even rate of return. Therefore, you use a discount rate above which you'd have a negative NPV (and a poor investment) and below which you'd have a positive NPV (and a great investment, all things being equal). IRR often is used to compare a potential investment against current rates of return in the securities market.

When calculating IRR, you make the present value of an investment's cash flow equal to the cost of the project. The result is an interest rate — say, 5 percent — that you can then compare to the interest rates of other investments. In equation form, IRR looks like

$$\text{NPV} = 0 = \frac{\text{initial}}{\text{investment}} + \frac{\text{Cash flow Year 1}}{(1 + \text{IRR})^1} + \frac{\text{Cash flow Year n}}{(1 + \text{IRR})^n}$$

Assume for example, the following series of net cash flows:

Initial = $I(0) = -\$1,000,000$

Year 1 = $I(1) = \$1,750,000$

Year 2 = $I(2) = \$1,750,000$

Year 3 = $I(3) = \$1,750,000$

To solve this equation, plug in the initial investment of \$1,000,000 and net cash flows of \$1,750,000 for each of the three years. Next, using an iterative process, insert a number into the IRR variable. Does the NPV equal zero?

Probably not. So increase or decrease the IRR a bit, and keep doing so until the NPV equals zero. Eventually, you'll get your answer. Or you could simply use a calculator with a built-in IRR function. In this example, the IRR that results in an NPV of zero is 166 percent.

Payback period

The *payback period* equation gives you a way to calculate how long it will take to earn back the money from a particular investment. You calculate payback period by using the following formula:

> Payback period = Investment ÷ Annual cash inflow

For example, if you have a project that requires an initial investment of $1 million, and the investment generates annual revenues of $250,000, you calculate the payback period as follows:

> Payback period = 1,000,000 ÷ 250,000
>
> = 4 years

The lower the number — indicating a faster payback period — the better because the investment will become profitable sooner.

Profitability index

Profitability index — also known as the *benefit-cost ratio* — gives you a way to evaluate different investment proposals that have determined net present values. You calculate profitability index by using the following formula:

> Profitability index = Present value of future cash flows (NPV)
> ÷ Initial investment

For example, say that your initial investment in a capital item is $1 million. The present value of future cash flows for the item is $1,450,000. You calculate the profitability index for this item as follows:

> Profitability index = 1,450,000 ÷ 1,000,000
>
> = 1.45

The higher the profitability index moves above 1.0, the better the investment is for your firm.

Reading an Annual Report: A How-To

Without a doubt, annual reports — more formally known as *annual reports to shareholders,* and distinctly different from the 10-K annual reports that the Securities and Exchange Commission (SEC) requires of public companies — are at the pinnacle of corporate communication. With their glowing words, evocative photographs, and lovely, full-color graphs, annual reports can be very compelling reading. The point of the annual report is to provide a summary of exactly how a company has performed in the preceding year, as well as to provide a glimpse of the future. The report is the best source of information for most people to determine the financial health of a company and to learn of any potential problems or opportunities.

Building a compelling annual report is a real art and science affair, and more than a few consulting firms are doing very well, thank you, by hiring themselves out to create reports for all kinds of companies.

The nine parts of the annual report

Reading an annual report can be a daunting prospect if you don't know exactly what you're looking for and where to find it. The good news, however, is that most reports are now standardized around a common model of nine key parts; this organization makes it easy to review any company's annual report after you get the hang of it. Here are the nine parts, generally presented in the following order:

- ✔ **Letter from the chairman:** The letter from the chairman of the board is the traditional place for a company's top management team to explain what a great job it did during the preceding year and to lay out the company's goals and strategies for the future. The letter also is a great place to find apologies for problems that occurred during the year, which may or may not have been solved. Oops!

- ✔ **Sales and marketing:** This section contains complete information about a company's products and services, as well as descriptions of its major divisions and groups and what they do. When reading this section, you should be able to figure out which products are most important to a company and which divisions or groups are most critical to the company's success.

- ✔ **Ten-year summary of financial results:** If the company is at least ten years old, its annual report contains a presentation of financial results during that period of time. This section is a terrific place to look for trends in growth (or nongrowth) of revenues and profit and other leading indicators of a company's financial success.

✔ **Management discussion and analysis:** This section is the place where a company's management team has the opportunity to present a candid discussion of significant financial trends within the company during the past couple years.

✔ **Letter of CPA opinion:** To be considered reliable, a company's financial statements have to be reviewed and audited for accuracy by a Certified Public Accountant (CPA). In this letter, a CPA firm states any qualifications that it has with the company's financial statements. These statements can have great bearing on the reliability of the data or of management's assessment of it.

✔ **Financial statements:** Financial statements are the bread and butter of the annual report. This section is where a company presents its financial performance data. At a minimum, expect to see an income statement, a balance sheet, and a cash-flow statement.

Be sure to watch for footnotes to the financial statements and read them carefully. You often find valuable information about an organization's structure and financial status that hasn't been publicized elsewhere in the report. For example, you may notice information on a management reorganization or details on a bad debt that was written off by the company.

✔ **Subsidiaries, brands, and addresses:** Here you find listings of company locations — domestic and foreign — as well as contact information, brand names, and product lines.

✔ **List of directors and officers:** Corporations typically have boards of directors — senior businesspeople from both inside and outside the organizations — to help guide them and to provide a broader view of markets and business environments than what's seen by internal managers. Officers include the president, chief executive officer (CEO), vice presidents, chief financial officer (CFO), and so forth.

✔ **Stock price history:** This section gives a brief history of the company's stock prices and dividends, showing upward and downward trends over time. Included is information on a company's stock symbol and the listing stock exchange — for example, the New York Stock Exchange (NYSE) or NASDAQ.

If you want to read a company's annual report but can't find it, you can go online. With the help of online search engines, finding a company's annual report is easier than ever. Many companies also have Investor Relations pages on their Web sites where you can find copies of annual reports and quarterly filings with the Securities and Exchange Commission. For example, in 2006, General Electric created an interactive annual report on its site. You can check it out at www.ge.com/ar2006. The site even features a video of the Chairman of the Board and the CEO talking about how they're going to build a better company.

Analyzing the annual report

An annual report is the best tool that the public has to review the performance of a company. Most annual reports contain plenty of useful information. But now that you have all this terrific info, what should you do with it? We thought you'd never ask! You can analyze the information in a report to get a sense of the near- and long-term health of a firm.

Here are some definite musts when it comes to reading and analyzing an annual report:

- **Review the company's financial statements and look for trends in profitability, growth, stability, and dividends.** Refer to the section "Identifying Financial Tricks of the Trade," earlier in this chapter, to check the most common financial ratios.

- **Read the report thoroughly to pick out hints that the company is poised for explosive growth — or on the brink of disaster.** Places to look for such hints include the letter from the chairman, the sales and marketing section, and the management discussion and analysis. Of course, it also pays to keep an eye on the company through the business press and analyst reports. (For some tips on recognizing an impending disaster, see the upcoming sidebar.)

- **Carefully read the letter of CPA opinion.** Be sure that the firm agrees that the company's financial statements are an accurate portrayal of its financial reality.

- **Carefully read any footnotes to the financial statements.** These footnotes often contain information about company assumptions that can be critical to a full understanding of the financial statements.

Seven deadly sins: Annual report edition

Annual reports consist of equal parts marketing glitz, feel-good platitudes, and hard financial data. After you get past all the hype, plenty of interesting data is just waiting to be viewed and analyzed. As you review the data in an annual report, stay on the lookout for the following seven deadly warning signs:

- **Revenues stagnant or falling:** By comparing a company's revenues across two or more years, you can get a sense of how fast its revenues are growing. You also can see whether revenues are likely to continue to trend upward in the future. When revenues stop growing — or, worse, begin to fall — this is a major warning sign of trouble within the organization. Stagnant or falling revenues can be the result of all kinds of problems: poor product quality, increased market competition, or internal management problems, to name a few. You have to decide whether this change is a one-time aberration or a trend that's going to get worse before it gets better. To find out more, search for articles in the financial press that discuss the company and its prospects, as well as prospects for the industry as a whole.

✔ **Earnings per share inconsistent with the company's profit:** The value of a company's stock is to some extent based on the firm's profitability and the number of shares in the hands of investors. So, if profit increases 15 percent from one year to the next, you may expect the earnings per share of stock to also increase by 15 percent. This won't be the case if the company dilutes (reduces) the value of the stock by issuing more shares during the course of the year. If earnings per share are lagging behind the company's profitability, raise the red flag because this requires further investigation.

Be aware, however, that stock price frequently is affected by things that have nothing to do with the business itself. For example, institutional investors, concerned about a recent announcement from the federal government, may pull their investments out of the sector, driving the price down.

✔ **Indications of financial distress:** A company can have phenomenal growth in sales and profit but still go out of business. Have you ever heard someone who went out of business lament that he or she was a victim of his or her own success? As odd as it sounds, it can happen. If a company isn't solvent — in other words, it doesn't have enough cash in the bank to cover its current liabilities — it's in trouble. Run some numbers on companies of interest — specifically, a quick ratio and an acid-test ratio — to see whether they're solvent. If the results are marginal and the trend is downward, the ratio doesn't bode well for the future.

✔ **Unusual gains or losses:** Although every company goes through natural and regular business cycles during the course of

months or years, unusual gains or losses can be red flags deserving of your attention. Unusual gains or losses are to be expected from time to time, but they should be just that — unusual. Ongoing unusual gains or losses are cause for concern because they indicate a fundamental problem in the company's ability to manage its operations and finances.

✔ **Profit ratios falling:** Because profit is the best measure of success for many companies, growing — or, at minimum, maintaining — profit ratios is an important goal of management. If a company's profit ratios are falling from year to year, the financial health of the firm is in clear jeopardy. Something in the company is broken and needs to be fixed.

✔ **Adverse auditor opinion:** For the most part, the letter of CPA opinion is a perfunctory exercise that confirms that a company's financial statements are accurate. Occasionally (today it happens more often because of Sarbanes-Oxley; see Chapter 10), however, a CPA firm takes exception to a company's financial results and issues an adverse opinion. Pay close attention to the letter of CPA opinion. Watch for words such as "fairly present" (good) or "adverse opinion" or "reservations" (bad).

✔ **Disconnect between narrative and financials:** If an annual report's narrative doesn't match up with the realities of the company's financial position, you can bet that the company's spin doctors are in high gear. The chairman may go on and on about what a great job the company did in a tough business environment, and about the tremendous prospects for the company in the future. But if the leading financial indicators are pointing in a different direction, there's more to the report than meets the eye.

Chapter 13

Understanding Stocks and Bonds

*I*t seems you can't watch a news broadcast today without hearing about the ups and downs of the financial markets. Sometimes the slightest news event in the farthest reaches of the world can send investors into a spiral of selling or buying. The volatility of the financial markets is something that should interest all businesspeople as well as those seeking to diversify their portfolios of investments. The reason is that when the market is on a roller-coaster ride, business owners, who often have stock portfolios as a cushion for down times, start conserving their expenditures, which then affects the revenues of other companies, such as advertising firms, that provide products and services to the business.

In this chapter, you get the full picture on *securities markets* — the stock market and the bond market, and you uncover some effective investing techniques. We don't cover many other types of investments in this chapter in depth — options, metals, collectibles, and so on — because stocks and bonds are the staple of the investment community and certainly a good place to start.

Lessons from the investment master

Benjamin Graham was arguably the most famous and successful investment advisor of the 20th century. He's been called the "father of value investing," and Warren Buffet — one of the most successful investors of all time — claims that he learned his investment principles from Graham. Graham's book, *The Intelligent Investor* (HarperBusiness Essentials), is still the investor's bible decades after his death. During his life, Graham developed a set of fundamental, common-sense principles, outlined in his classic book, that are still valuable today:

✔ A stock is an ownership interest in a business whose underlying value is independent of its share price.

✔ The stock market constantly sways from "unsustainable optimism" to "unjustified pessimism." An intelligent investor will sell to optimists and buy from pessimists.

✔ The future value of any investment is dependent on the price you paid for it today. The higher the price, the lower the return.

✔ If you never overpay for an investment, you reduce the downside of being wrong, something you can never avoid.

✔ Strive to be a disciplined, not an emotional, investor. Invest patiently, but with confidence that you've done your homework.

The last principle is particularly important. We've seen too many investors being swayed by the mood of the market — a follow-the-herd-over-the-cliff mentality. For instance, we saw it in 1999 when technology and Internet stocks were rocketing into the stratosphere. At that time, fund managers claimed that the only stocks worth owning were Internet stocks. Alberto Vilar of Amerindo Technology Fund was one of those people. After seeing his fund increase by 248.9 percent in 1999, he suffered one of the most devastating financial disasters in the history of mutual funds because he was heavily invested in Internet stocks. Had you invested $10,000 in his fund in December of 1999, by 2002 you would have been left with only $1,195.

Had Graham been alive, would he have weathered the storm? Probably. We say that because he survived the stock market crashes of 1929–1932, and until he retired in 1956, his fund beat the stock market by a significant amount every year.

Grasping the Secondary Market

The financial market, in which securities are traded (such as stocks and bonds), is divided into two segments:

> ✔ A *secondary market,* which consists of existing securities
>
> ✔ A *primary market,* which consists of new securities created when companies seek investment capital in exchange for equity in their companies (check out Chapter 14 for more info)

Within the secondary market, you find the major stock exchanges that you often hear about in the news: the New York Stock Exchange (NYSE), the American Stock Exchange (AMEX), the NASDAQ Stock Market, the Tokyo

Stock Exchange (TSE), and the Australian Securities Exchange (ASX), to name just a few. You also find dealer or *over-the-counter market* (OTC) where securities are not listed on an exchange but are traded through a network of middlemen, and numerous Futures Exchanges for trading commodities (such as crude oil, soybeans, and gold). This section gives you a brief overview of the secondary market. The rest of this chapter delves into specific aspects of the secondary market.

Stock exchanges

Most people think of the New York Stock Exchange (NYSE) when they think of the stock market. The NYSE is the largest exchange in the world, and only companies that meet specific minimum requirements on earning power, total value of outstanding stock, and number of shareholders can join. What exactly do we mean by a stock exchange? A *stock exchange* is simply a voluntary organization that's formed to provide a way to trade securities and facilitate the payments of dividends and income. The members of the stock exchange own "seats" on the exchange, and they're the only people who can trade on the floor of the exchange. The memberships in the exchange also are traded, and their prices vary with the stock market ups and downs. Orders to buy and sell always go through members of the exchange.

In exchanges that have trading floors, such as the NYSE, you see a form of controlled chaos. The floor of a stock exchange is an actual place, and it's a hotbed of activity. If you visit the floor of the NYSE, you'll see that it contains an enormous amount of communications equipment and computers, because the members must have access to information from the outside as well as the capability to handle stock transactions from investors. You'll also see a variety of people on the floor, from actual investors to wire services people, exchange employees, and brokers who take orders from the public. At times, it looks as though they're all shouting at each other, but bona fide trading is actually going on.

Over-the-counter markets

Another type of secondary market is the *over-the-counter market (OTC)*. In this market, no trading floor exists and securities don't need to be registered with the SEC. Traders are scattered around the country and their buyers deal directly with them. The traders are much like retail stores that keep an inventory of stocks, bonds, commodities, or derivatives for sale. A *derivative* is basically a security, such as an *option* (right to buy) or *futures contract* (contract to buy or sell at a specific date), whose value depends on how its underlying asset performs. Derivatives can be contracted for stocks, bonds, currencies, and commodities, among other things.

The NASDAQ market

A third type of secondary market is the *NASDAQ,* or National Association of Securities Dealers Automated Quotation market. You may know it as the home of most high-technology companies such as Electronic Arts and, of course, most of the big Internet companies such as Yahoo! and Google. NASDAQ is a derivative of the OTC market (see the previous section), but unlike the OTC, NASDAQ securities must be registered with the Securities and Exchange Commission (SEC). The NASDAQ is the largest U.S. electronic stock market and trading takes place via computer and mostly without telephone assistance.

Today, many people trade on the NASDAQ via their computers through discount brokers, or at locations set up by companies with access to the exchange. The PC and the Internet have opened up a whole new category of stock investor: the *day trader,* an individual who buys and sells multiple times in a single day to make quick profits. However, day traders typically work on borrowed money, which can be very risky if their bets don't pay off. Day trading is like gambling. If you have the stomach for it and the enormous amount of time it takes to monitor the market, day trading might be for you. Just make sure that you're trading with money you can afford to lose, or you may be in trouble very quickly.

Understanding Stocks

A *stock* is essentially an ownership interest in a company that may be private or public and listed on one of the stock exchanges. For purposes of this chapter, we talk about stock in a publicly traded company. Owning stock is a way to participate in the economic growth of the nation as well as the global economy. Purchasing stocks traditionally is a great way to hedge inflation and achieve good returns on investments over the long term.

The general rule is that you'll make money in stocks if you hold them at least five years. The following sections provide more advice about the types of stocks available, as well as other business issues to consider.

Types of stock

Two basic types of stock exist: preferred and common. Each is quite different from the other, so it's important that you understand these differences before you purchase.

Preferred stock

In general, *preferred stock* doesn't carry voting rights in a company, but it does have a guaranteed dividend or payout (usually quarterly) that's a percentage of its par value. That guaranteed dividend is what you receive for giving up voting rights. (*Par value* is simply the face value of the stock at purchase or at the date at which dividends are declared.)

Common stock

Common stock is the basic form of ownership in a corporation — no corporation can exist without it. Common stock has what's known as a residual claim on the assets of a company. *Residual claim* means that common stockholders get paid after all other claimants are paid. Consequently, common stock is more risky than preferred stock, but the shareholder's liability is limited to the amount of the shareholder's investment in the company.

Common stockholders enjoy cash dividend rights *and* voting rights, and they may also benefit from stock dividends and stock splits:

- ✔ With a *stock dividend,* the company issues stock rather than cash — usually as a percentage of the shareholder's existing shares. For example, a company may issue 0.08 shares for each share an investor owns.

- ✔ In a *stock split,* the percentage increase in the number of shares you hold goes up by more than 25 percent. Suppose that you hold 100 shares of stock in XYZ Corporation, trading at $60 a share — making the total value of your holdings $6,000. Now, suppose that the company declares a two-for-one stock split. This means that you now hold 200 shares, but they're valued at $30 each at the time of the split.

One reason companies choose to do stock splits is to keep their per-share values at a level most investors can tolerate. It's conceivable that if a company didn't split its stock, the price could go beyond the affordability of most investors.

Stock quotes

A *stock quote* is simply a listing of prices for a stock at a specific point during the trading day. It provides the basic information you need to check on the status of any stock in your portfolio. Look to Figure 13-1 to see an example of an online stock quote from *The Wall Street Journal* for Wells Fargo & Co. (WFC).

Wells Fargo & Co. (WFC)

08/03/07   12:26 p.m. EDT   NYSE

Last	Change	% Change
34.17	−0.25	−0.73%

Open	High	Low
34.11	34.49	33.84

Volume	Prior Day's Volume	Prior Day's Close
12,030,651	19,725,506	34.42

52-Week High	52-Week Low
36.99 (10/20/2006)	33.01 (03/14/2007)

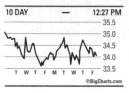

Stock Data
115,727.30 Market Cap (Mil)
13.20 P/E Ratio
3.6% Dividend Yield
$0.31 Latest Dividend
09/01/07 Pay Date of Latest Dividend
100% stock div. Last Stock Split
08/14/06 Date of Last Split
3,362.21 Shares Outstanding (Mil) 3,354.60
Public Float (Mil)

Figure 13-1: Sample stock quotation from *The Wall Street Journal.*

Here's a summary of the information that the stock quote provides:

✔ The stock closed at $34.17 (Last) — a decline of $0.25 from its price at the closing of the market the previous day ($34.42).

✔ The stock opened at $34.11; during the trading day, it was traded as high as $34.49 and as low as $33.84.

✔ The total number of Wells Fargo shares traded during the day was 12,030,651; the volume for previous day was higher, at 19,725,506.

✔ For the previous 52 weeks, the stock had traded at a high of $36.99 and a low of $33.01.

Note: The quote also displays a graph of the previous ten days of stock value; the graph indicates a lot of movement in the stock price on a daily basis.

Observe that investors received a dividend of $0.31 per share on September 1, 2007, which amounted to a 3.6-percent *dividend yield* (the amount of dividends paid per share over a year divided by the stock price). Also note that on August 14, 2006, investors received a 100-percent stock dividend (one for one). Wells

Fargo has more than 3 billion shares outstanding (held by investors) and more than $3 billion in *public float,* which is the amount held by investors who aren't company officers, directors, or controlling-interest investors (10 percent or more of the outstanding stock).

Moving to the stock data, you can see that the *market cap* for the company is $115 billion. This is how much money you'd need to purchase all the shares of the company at its current price per share.

The *P/E ratio* (price/earnings) — which is the market value per share divided by the earnings per share — typically reflects the company's last four quarters of earnings. A high P/E ratio normally forecasts higher earnings growth in the future, making it a good way to compare one company with another within the same industry. Sometimes called a *multiple,* the ratio tells you how much investors will pay per dollar of earnings. In the case of Wells Fargo, a P/E of 13.20 suggests that investors are willing to pay $13.00 for every $1.00 of earnings the company generates.

When investing, don't ever make a decision to invest based solely on P/E ratio, because the figure is only as good as the basis on which the earnings were determined. You need to go back to the financial statements to check how earnings were calculated. The P/E ratio is just one metric to consider before making a decision. We discuss other metrics in the section on "Investing in Stocks."

Investing in Stocks

Everyone has an opinion on the best way to pick a winning stock. This section explains in detail three popular strategies for picking stocks: value investing, going for dividend growth, and picking businesses you like.

Bargain hunter: Value investing

If you're the kind of person who never buys a new car so you can avoid the immediate depreciation in value as you drive it off the lot, or if you're the kind of person who spends hours looking for the best bargain, *value investing* may be for you. Value investors in the stock market look for cheap stocks that don't make the news because either everyone has left them for dead or they're just not sexy enough. Well, some cheap stocks may make the news if they're particularly bad, but for the most part, you'll find these stocks by looking for ugly, boring securities with low price/earnings ratios (less than ten times earnings during the past year). You also can discover them by looking for stocks that the analysts aren't crowding around.

Deciding when to buy is more art than science, but if you determine that a stock is a great buy at 10, you can deduce that it's an even better buy at 8. With a great stock, you should buy more as it's going down and sell off when it goes up past your lowest average cost. Unfortunately, most investors do just the opposite; they sell off a good stock as it's going down in price and buy as it's going up.

Dividend growth hunters

Investors seeking *dividend growth* aren't interested in the current yield on a stock. They're more interested in finding companies whose dividends increase on a regular basis during a long period of time. Rising dividends often are the signs of a successful company because

- ✔ You need excess cash to distribute dividends.

- ✔ A regularly rising dividend may indicate a friendly and somewhat stable business environment — a very positive indicator.

Of course, you don't want to focus on growing dividends in a vacuum. You also want to look at a company's P/E (price/earnings) ratio to make sure that it's in line with other companies in the industry. The *P/E ratio* is the ratio of the price of one share of stock to the earnings per share of the company (see the section "Stock quotes"). It's a multiple, such as 5 or 10. If a company you're considering for investment purposes has a multiple of 5 times earnings per share, while similar companies in the industry have multiples of 10 times earnings per share, you may want to do some further investigation to find out why such a discrepancy exists.

Investing in companies you like

The strategy of investing in companies you like is one followed by some very successful investors, such as Warren Buffett, Charlie Munger, and Peter Lynch. The strategy is to invest in companies that have products and services you use and believe in. The interesting thing about such companies is that they often also meet the criteria we discuss in the value investing section, so combining value investing with this strategy makes sense. Here's how to make this strategy work for you:

- ✔ Think about a product or service you currently use. Investigate the company that makes it and determine whether the manufacturer is a public company.

- ✔ Determine whether other people have also discovered this company. To find out, compare its price/earnings (PE) ratio with its current growth rate or projected growth rate. Typically, you want a stock with a P/E ratio lower than its earnings growth rate.

✔ Call the company to ask about projected profits and anything else that may help you to make a sound investment decision. Most public companies have designated shareholder liaisons who will answer your questions and see to it that you receive any materials you want to study.

Joining Forces: Mutual Funds

A *mutual fund* is a portfolio of stocks that's managed by a professional company. Investing in a mutual fund is a way to avoid the risk of picking individual stocks. The fund manager's strategy for selecting stocks depends on the goal of the mutual fund (growth, annuity, and so forth), but, in general, the manager wants to spread the risk over a fairly large number of stocks so that a loss on any one stock does not significantly damage the return on the entire fund. Mutual funds are also probably the safest and least costly way to invest in lucrative foreign stocks, which have different fee structures and reporting requirements.

Mutual funds are very popular investment vehicles for several other reasons:

✔ Finding the best mutual funds is now easier because many publications in print or on the Internet are evaluating various funds and giving advice to consumers.

✔ You can rely on the expertise of a professional money manager hired by the mutual fund.

✔ You can achieve a diversified portfolio (one with a variety of different types of stocks and bonds, in other words) with relatively little money.

✔ Although you may not beat the averages in the short term, you'll do well over the long term.

One substantial disadvantage of mutual funds has to do with the associated tax implications. When you invest in mutual funds, you receive an annual statement of investment gains in the form of income and capital-gains distributions, as well as a report on any dividend distributions, which are taxed as ordinary income. Whether or not you reinvest these gains, you have to pay taxes on them, and it's difficult to know in advance how much you'll be liable for. If you invest in individual stocks, on the other hand, you can decide when to take profits and pay taxes on them.

So many mutual funds, how can you possibly choose? Here's a simple guide to follow:

✔ **Decide which types of funds you want to own.** Among the many choices are

- A single, broad-based fund that buys a variety of different types of stocks and bonds

- Specialized funds (for example, high-growth funds)

- Foreign-stock funds

- An emerging-markets fund that focuses on new markets and newer companies

  The choice of fund will depend on your financial goals, how old you are, and how much you have to invest.

✔ **Identify the costs associated with the fund.** Recognize that foreign-stock funds generally have higher costs, for instance. Don't choose funds that have costs higher than industry averages. Look at what other funds of the same type are charging.

We also suggest you look seriously at no-load funds. These funds charge no sales fees and don't use brokers to deal with the public. All your money is invested in the fund.

✔ **Consider the risks associated with the fund.** With a more diversified stock fund, you can better manage your risk. You can even choose funds that invest exclusively in more conservative stocks.

If you're looking for conservative stocks, stay away from those classified as "growth," "aggressive growth," or "capital appreciation." Also, look at how the fund performed in key years of market turmoil, such as 1987, 1990, 1994, 2000, and 2001. If it performed badly, don't invest. You can find performance figures and risk ratings by looking in such publications as the *Morningstar Mutual Funds* and *The Value Line Mutual Fund Survey*.

✔ **Look at the fund's track record.** Be sure to compare apples to apples — foreign stock funds with foreign stock funds, for instance. Also make sure that the overall performance figure of the fund isn't based on one or two years; a good fund has consistently performed well over a protracted period of time.

✔ **Find out who's managing the fund.** Every fund has one person who's a key stock picker. Make sure that this person has a successful track record and plans to be around for a while.

Mutual funds aren't perfect financial vehicles for investment. They often underperform the market while demonstrating fairly erratic performance behavior in general. Nevertheless, if held over a long period of time — say, 20 years or more — with regular investment, they'll typically outperform most professional investors. The key is holding them for a long time. (For more about mutual funds, check out *Mutual Funds For Dummies,* 5th Edition, by Eric Tyson [Wiley].)

Bonds: When Debt Makes Sense

Bonds are debt securities where the issuer of the bond promises to repay the holder of the bond — you — the principal (what was borrowed) and interest at some future date. Unlike stock, the bond holder doesn't have equity or an ownership stake in the company or governmental agency that issues the bond. Basically, three types of entities issue bonds: the U.S. government, corporations, and municipalities.

U.S. government bonds

The U.S. government is the largest debtor in the world — about $9 trillion as of press time. And you thought you had a lot of debt! The government borrows more money than anyone through two types of debt instruments: Treasury debt and federal agency debt.

Treasury debt

We assume many of you have purchased Treasury bills (*T bills*), notes, and savings bonds. They're all debt instruments, but they differ in their maturity date. Take a look at Table 13-1 to see a comparison.

Table 13-1	Treasury Bill Maturity	
Treasury Debt Type	*Minimum Investment*	*Maturity Date*
Treasury bills (T-bills)	$1,000	Less than or equal to one year
Treasury notes (T-notes)	$1,000	2, 5, and 10 years
Savings bonds (Series EE and I)	$25/$50	Earns interest for 30 years

If you look at the returns on bills and bonds over a long period of time, you find that Treasury bill investors have never lost any money, because the government typically pays these on time. On the other hand, those who have invested in Treasury bonds *have* experienced a loss in a given year, even though the government actually paid the bonds when due. What this means is that in a year with a loss, the decrease in the bond price was greater than the interest income the investor received.

You can find out what the various Treasure instruments are paying by looking in the financial section of a major newspaper (such as *The Wall Street Journal* or the *Los Angeles Times*) or by going online. Treasuries are sold through more than 150 competitive auctions throughout the year. You can find the schedule for these auctions at `www.treas.gov/offices/domestic-finance/debt-management/auctions`.

Federal agency debt

Many federal agencies (called *government-sponsored enterprises,* or GSEs) issue debt. Some include the Government National Mortgage Association (GNMA, pronounced "Ginnie Mae"), federal home loan banks, federal farm credit system banks, and the U.S. Postal Service. Experts estimate that there's $2.3 trillion in current outstanding agency debt, which is equivalent to the economies of several countries!

Corporate bonds

Corporate bonds are the smallest sector of the bond markets. This type of debt is issued by large corporations that promise to make payments to the bond-holder over a period of time. In this type of investment, it's important that you check on the corporation's ability to repay. You can do this by looking at the Standard & Poor's or Moody's bond ratings. The rating should give you an idea of how much risk you're facing. For help, look at the section "How bonds are rated" later in this chapter.

Municipal bonds

Municipal bonds are issued by governments and governmental or quasi-governmental agencies that aren't at the federal level. The important thing to know about municipal bonds is that they're exempt from federal income taxation, which makes them very different from other types of bonds. Because they aren't taxed, municipal bonds are most valuable to investors who want to enjoy that extra benefit from a bond investment. To give you an example of the benefit, it's possible to achieve the same after-tax return from a low-yield municipal bond that you do from a high-yield taxable bond.

When you compare bonds that have the same interest rate and maturity, you should choose the one that has the highest after-tax return. Take the following example: Suppose that you're in the 30 percent marginal tax bracket. You'd be as satisfied choosing a taxable yield bond returning 12 percent as you would purchasing a tax-exempt bond yielding 8.4 percent, because the return is the same. On the other hand, you're better off choosing a taxable bond at 12 percent over a tax-exempt bond yielding 7.0 percent, because even after taxes, the yield would be 8.4 percent — 1.4 percent greater than the tax-exempt bond.

Another thing to remember about municipal bonds is that they're not very liquid because investors tend to hold onto them to maturity.

How bonds are valued

Bonds generally come in two flavors: pure discount bonds, also known as zero coupon bonds, and coupon bonds. The difference is simple:

> ✔ **Zero coupon bonds** make no payments to the holders between the dates they're issued and the maturity dates. In other words, you get nothing until the end.
>
> ✔ **Coupon bonds** make a series of equal payments throughout the life of the bonds. So, if you're looking for an annuity, this is the way to go.

As soon as a bond is trading in the bond market, its future payouts are decided, and the only thing that changes is the asking price. Your yield to maturity will go up if you can buy the bond at a lower price because bond prices and yields move in opposite directions.

The amount that a bond pays at maturity is called its *par value* or *face value*. The discount amounts to the difference between the selling price of the bond and its par value. Whenever you're dealing with financial assets such as bonds, you need to understand that the price of a bond is equal to the present value of any future cash flows generated by the bond.

A zero coupon bond has only one cash flow — the payment made at maturity — so the price of the bond is the present value of its face value. Here's an example to make this explanation clear: Suppose that you're considering a zero coupon bond that matures in five years and has a face value of $2,000. Now suppose that the interest rate is 10 percent. To calculate its present value, use the formula shown in Figure 13-2 (or your nifty financial calculator that already has the formula in it).

Figure 13-2: Calculating the value of a zero coupon bond.

$$P = \frac{F}{(1 + r)^n} \quad \text{so, Price is equal to} \quad \frac{\text{Face Value}}{(1 + \text{interest rate}) \text{ to the number of years to maturity}}$$

Or. . .

$$P = \frac{\$2,000}{(1 + 10\%)^5} = \$1,242.24$$

So, the price you'd pay for this bond today is $1,242.24.

Coupon bonds typically pay out semiannually in addition to paying the face value at maturity, so the value of this financial asset is based on the sum of the present value of all payments until maturity. For example, suppose you have a bond that's selling for $850 with a coupon rate of 8 percent, a maturity date of five years, and a par value of $1,000. The coupon payment will be $80, which is 8 percent of $1,000. You can find the yield to maturity through the following formula, where r = 8 percent:

$$80(1 + r)^{-1} + 80(1 + r)^{-2} + 80(1 + r)^{-3} + 80(1 + r)^{-4} + 1{,}000(1 + r)^{-4} = \$850 \text{ (bond selling price)}$$

Or, if you want to save time and frustration, you can enter the numbers into your trusty financial calculator. Either way, you'll get a current yield of 9.412 percent ($80 ÷ $850) and a yield to maturity of 12.180 percent. Not bad!

How bonds are rated

Bonds are rated from AAA to D depending on the rating agency. In general, a bond that's rated A is the most secure, given whatever fluctuations may occur in the economy. If your bond is rated in any of the B categories, there's a chance that your issuer may default on the interest payments. Bonds rated below BBB are called *junk bonds* and are pretty precarious investments for the average person.

The two major rating agencies are Moody's and Standard & Poor's. Table 13-2 shows a breakdown of their rating scales and what they mean.

Table 13-2	Bond Ratings from the Major Agencies	
Moody's	*Standard & Poor's*	*What the Rating Means*
Aaa	AAA	Prime/maximum safety
Aa1	AA+	High grade
A1	A+	Upper-medium grade
Baa1	BBB+	Lower-medium grade
Ba1	BB+	Noninvestment grade
Ba2	BB	Speculative
B1	B+	Highly speculative
Caa1	CCC+	Substantial risk
Caa2	CCC	In poor standing
	D	In default

Why bonds may be good for you . . .

Many investors like bonds because they provide more immediate income than stocks. In terms of performance, they tend to be less volatile than stocks, and they often climb while stock prices are falling. In addition, tax-free municipal bonds are one of a dying breed of tax shelters.

. . . And why bonds may not be good for you

Every investment has a downside, and bonds are no exception. Here are the four major negatives related to bonds:

- ✔ **Companies and governments sometimes default on their interest payments.** What that means to you is that you get hit twice. You lose your income stream, and the price of your bond may drop as well. To avoid this problem, be sure to select highly rated bonds. Bonds that are rated AAA are about as safe as those issued by the U.S. Treasury.

- ✔ **Interest rates rise.** Bond prices are inversely correlated with interest rates; that is, when interest rates rise, bond prices fall, and the earlier that happens, the greater the loss to you.

- ✔ **Investment costs are high.** Not only do you have to invest in larger dollar amounts with bonds, but there are also fees associated with bond purchases.

- ✔ **Bonds are sometimes called or paid off before they mature.** Sometimes bond issuers choose to pay off the debt before the maturity date on the bond. For the bondholder or investor, this situation can cause a problem, particularly if interest rates have dropped. When you go to replace the bond with another, you may not be able to find an equivalent interest rate.

Should I Get Investment Help?

When you consider the tens of thousands of equity securities listed on the global and domestic stock exchanges, it's no wonder that people look for help in making their way through the jungle. In this section, we look at the world of stock brokerage to see how you can use a stockbroker or financial advisor to help you make wise investments. We also look at how you can go it alone, if you choose to.

Hiring a broker

Many people don't have the time or inclination to go it alone when it comes to investing on one of the many stock exchanges. During the worst *bear market* (a down market) since the Great Depression — remember the dot-com implosion in 2000 — even savvy stockbrokers took a bath. Whether you want someone to blame when your investments go south or you just don't want to deal with all the research you'll have to do to invest wisely, stockbrokers can provide many valuable services to investors. The following list outlines the services:

- ✔ They handle the buying and selling of your stocks, bonds, and other investments.
- ✔ They can help you develop an investment plan that works for you.
- ✔ They can help you develop successful investing habits and make you think about the process more.
- ✔ They can encourage you to take risks that you wouldn't do on your own.
- ✔ They can stop you from selling your investments out of panic.

But, in order for you to have a successful relationship with a broker, you need to keep the broker fully informed, which includes your financial status, what you're looking for, and what your goals are. You also need to get educated about what you're doing so that you can speak intelligently to the broker. If you want to be a value investor, you shouldn't leave all the work in the hands of your broker. If you don't do your homework, you run the risk that your broker will make investments that don't meet your objectives. Or you may find yourself with an inexperienced broker who can do you more harm than good. Worse yet, you may be vulnerable to the strong-arm tactics of an unscrupulous broker (yes, they do exist).

If a broker/advisor claims to use technical analysis or market timing or claims average annual returns of more than 10 percent, run the other direction!

Brokers work on commission, so they make money every time you do a transaction, whether you buy or sell. And they don't make money when you don't buy or sell. Hence, they have a built-in incentive to get you to turn over or *churn* your investments quickly. Today, some brokers have differentiated themselves by taking fees based on how much your portfolio grew during the year. They don't charge transaction fees. Of course, in this scenario, the incentive is to pick stocks that have long-term growth potential, an approach that's generally much more beneficial to you.

Here are some things to do before selecting a broker:

- ✔ Talk to friends and business associates to get their recommendations for brokers with whom they have trusted relationships.

✔ Contact your state securities department and ask to find the broker's listing in the Central Registration Depository. Here, you can find out all about brokers, including any history of legal problems. You also can Google your broker's name and firm to see if any complaints pop up. Look for words such as *fine, lawsuit,* and *disciplinary action,* which are definitely red flags.

If a potential broker is also a certified financial planner, he or she must be registered with the U.S. Securities and Exchange Commission or regulators in the state where he or she practices. Check out Form ADV — particularly the Disclosure Reporting pages — where the advisor must disclose any disciplinary action taken against him or her.

✔ Conduct an interview with the potential broker. Is the broker interested in your goals? Does he or she want to help you develop an investment plan? Or is he or she primarily interested in getting you to buy a few "glamour" stocks? Be sure to assess whether the broker/advisor has the required education, skills, and experience to help you.

Going it alone (if you absolutely, positively must)

You don't have to use a broker to invest in stocks and bonds, and that attitude is becoming increasingly more common as investors have direct access to the buying and selling of stocks over the Internet without an intermediary.

One of the biggest reasons that investors decide to do it themselves is to avoid the high transaction costs of investing via a broker. However, even with the do-it-yourself online brokers, little fees can add up. You can also in many cases buy stock directly from the issuing company. Check a company's Web site to see if it participates in direct selling.

According to Jason Zweig, an avid follower of Benjamin Graham's principles, if you can't answer "yes" to the following questions, don't even consider going it alone:

✔ Are you prepared to keep accurate records of all your stock transactions for tax purposes?

✔ Are you willing to diversify your portfolio and reduce your risk by owning 10 to 30 stocks in several industries?

✔ Are you able to put your portfolio on autopilot — that is, do fewer than two trades a year?

Stocks and bonds are great investments for people who take the time to understand the financial markets and seek help.

The Internet has made it easy for potential investors to find all sorts of information on companies in which they're considering investing. *The Wall Street Journal* Online (www.wsj.com), Yahoo! Finance (finance.yahoo.com), MSN Money (money.msn.com), and other sites offer a wealth of information that can, with some study, turn you into an expert on the stock market.

For those who don't, *caveat emptor* — let the buyer beware!

Chapter 14

It Takes Money to Make Money

In This Chapter

▶ Creating a funding plan for your company's financial needs

▶ Obtaining first-stage or start-up capital

▶ Searching and planning for second-stage or expansion capital

▶ Employing other fundraising methods

*M*oney does indeed make the world go 'round. Today, money is available for every type of business. In fact, there's so much money floating around that the money managers are having a hard time; it seems there's more money available than great deals to invest in! So, if you're looking for money to fund a new venture, to support your current business's growth, or to develop new products, the problem isn't finding money; it's coming up with a compelling reason for why the money managers should invest in your company. In other words, how do you tap into that money so your company can start growing?

The market for deals involving *private equity* (an investment in a company in exchange for an ownership interest) is quite simply overheated and highly competitive. In fact, the whole picture has flipped upside-down — at one time, entrepreneurs fought to stand out from the crowd of eager companies seeking funding; now the private-equity firms are battling to get ahead of the pack so they can secure deals to keep their investors happy. Who knows how long this will last, but for entrepreneurs seeking capital at any stage, this is a happy time (for more, on entrepreneurship, refer to Chapter 3).

The bottom line: You can't find money for any idea. Investors aren't stupid. A company that presents a great investment opportunity will get courted by the biggest of the big. If your company doesn't have the potential to scale and tap a very large market; if you don't have a "secret sauce" to keep competitors at bay; and if you don't have a management team that knows how to grow a company, you're out of luck. You need to go back to the drawing board and build something compelling that will get investors excited enough to invest. Not to worry though. This chapter helps you determine your company's financial needs and explains how you can get your hands on some of the money available in the marketplace.

How Much Money Do You Really Need? Setting Up Your Funding Plan

The term "plan" rears its ugly head when you start to figure out your financial needs. To successfully raise money for your business, you need to have a plan — as well as a backup plan and probably even a backup-backup plan in today's business environment, because your chances of getting it right the first time (or two) are very slim. The goal is a funding plan that will guide your search and help you make wise financial decisions.

A funding plan is really quite simple. It has four steps:

1. **Carefully determine exactly what your company needs to reach your goals.**

   You have to plan for several stages of growth and financing. Initially, you want to have enough cash to launch the business and survive until the company is generating enough revenues to cover expenses. Beyond that, you'll establish some milestones such as multiple customer segments, multiple products, and so forth.

2. **Target your potential sources for each stage of financing.**

   Based on the needs you calculate for each stage, you can decide what kind of money you need and who could potentially be the supplier.

   Recognize that some first-round money sources will want to be paid back or cashed out (get their investments back, in other words) before the next round of financing, so make sure that you plan for it.

3. **With the multi-stage plan defined, look at the various tasks you have to undertake to achieve your financing goals and get started *before* you need the money.**

   Raising money takes time, so you shouldn't wait until you need it, when it will be too late. For example, if you need private investors (called *angels*) for your second-round financing, you must start networking now. Angels don't just drop from the heavens when you need them. It takes time to build a business relationship so that you feel comfortable approaching the person about your financing needs and the person feels comfortable listening.

4. **Keep tabs on your progress against the timeline you set.**

   If you're significantly off from your projections, you may need to re-evaluate your plan. Perhaps you were a bit too aggressive in your expectations. Keep in mind that you're in a hurry; investors aren't, so allow for some slack in your overall plan.

As you can see from the funding plan, the kind of money you need to raise and the sources you need to consider depend on where you are in the life cycle of your company. Every business goes through several stages, each with different financial requirements (see Figure 14-1).

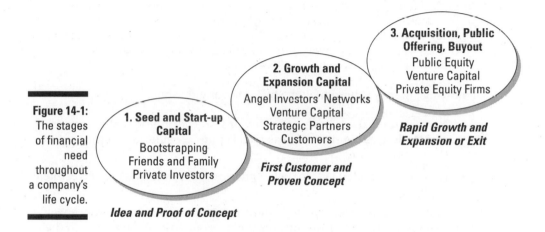

Figure 14-1:
The stages of financial need throughout a company's life cycle.

1. Seed and Start-up Capital
Bootstrapping
Friends and Family
Private Investors

Idea and Proof of Concept

2. Growth and Expansion Capital
Angel Investors' Networks
Venture Capital
Strategic Partners
Customers

First Customer and Proven Concept

3. Acquisition, Public Offering, Buyout
Public Equity
Venture Capital
Private Equity Firms

Rapid Growth and Expansion or Exit

The following list explains the three stages of financial need:

- ✔ **The first stage:** This stage covers the period of time from the conception of the product/service through early start-up. This is where the business concept is tested to make sure that customers want what you're offering.

- ✔ **The second stage:** This stage takes over when the concept is proven and your company is ready to grow to the next level — by entering a new market, introducing new products, or developing multiple locations.

- ✔ **The third stage:** You reach the third stage when your company is looking for a liquidity event so investors can cash out, or you want to acquire another company or be acquired by another company.

Each of these stages has different requirements and accomplishes different goals, which we cover in the following sections of this chapter.

You should know that high-technology and Internet companies often compress these three stages into very short time frames — sometimes months, and possibly even skipping the first stage altogether. What this illustrates is that to assess your financial needs, you need to understand the nature of the industry in which you're operating, the type of business you have, and your attractiveness as a company to the capital markets.

Acquiring First-Stage Money

You know that you're in the first stage of starting your business when the easiest and most likely source of money comes from your own savings and "friends, family, and fools" — in other words, people who believe in you and your business plan. Entrepreneurs aren't bootstrappers because they want to be; they do it because they have to. *Bootstrapping* means finding money and resources (anything and everything they need) by any means possible, including begging, borrowing, and bartering.

First-stage money is hard to come by for several reasons:

- New ventures don't have a track record, so everything that investors and lenders see in the business plan is pure speculation on the part of the entrepreneur.

- New ventures often fail, so they represent perhaps the riskiest investment of all.

- Most new ventures have no intellectual property rights — proprietary assets or secrets that would give them a competitive advantage in the marketplace.

- The founders of the venture themselves often don't have a track record of successful business endeavors.

- Most start-ups are merely "me-too" ventures; in other words, they haven't identified a significant unfair advantage that makes them valuable to customers and investors.

For these reasons and more, entrepreneurs have to bootstrap — rely on their own resources and the kindness of friends and family, or anybody else who will listen to their stories.

Bootstrapping for a new venture has three key principles:

- **Hire as few employees as possible.** Employees are the single biggest expense of most businesses.

- **Lease, share, and barter everything that you can.** When you lease facilities and equipment, you avoid tying up precious capital that you could use to produce your product or service. Bartering also has become a popular way to acquire needed resources. In a barter arrangement, you exchange a product or service that your company offers for something you need from another company.

- **Use other people's money.** You can ethically use other people's money in many ways. Getting customers to pay quickly is one way; convincing suppliers to give you more time to pay is another.

The next sections give you an idea of what to think about when you're considering debt financing for your business or giving an investor an ownership interest in exchange for equity capital. Both are valuable financial resources, but you have to know when and how to use them. These sections help you do just that.

Debt

Debt is a financing source that is, unfortunately, near and dear to many an entrepreneur's heart. You know all those credit-card offers that you get in the mail? Many small businesses don't throw them away; instead, they've started using credit cards as their credit line for quick cash. It's an expensive route, but in a banking environment that isn't always generous to small businesses, going into debt sometimes is the only route that owners can take. In this section, we look at some of the principal sources of debt capital for start-up and expansion. (You can find other types of debt financing to solve issues such as business cycles, cash-flow problems, and so forth. We deal with those topics in Chapter 12.)

Commercial banks

Banks aren't very favorable sources of first-stage money for new companies, which isn't surprising when you consider that a banker's first concern is how a borrower will pay back the loan or credit line. If a start-up company has little or no track record of sales (and most new companies don't!), and it's offering the bank only projected sales (in other words, blue sky), a banker won't have much confidence that repayment is possible.

Bankers operate under very strict guidelines, termed the "five Cs":

Character, capacity, capital, collateral, and conditions

With no track record and only an estimate of expected sales, a new company has already violated at least two of the five Cs: capital and capacity.

But what if you can show a track record from a previous business or from your personal financial status that's strong enough to warrant a loan? Depending on how you negotiate the deal, you'll receive either a secured or an unsecured note. We're betting that the note will be *secured,* meaning that getting the loan will require some form of collateral. *Collateral* is an asset of equivalent value that you pledge against the note, such as your house or a savings account. If you don't repay the loan, the bank has the right to repossess or foreclose on the asset.

But even if that happens, your financial obligations don't stop. Just because you've lost your collateral for defaulting on the loan doesn't mean that you aren't still liable for the loan amount.

Most bankers will ask you to personally guarantee any loan you take out, which means that in addition to any business assets, you're also pledging your personal assets against the loan should you default. Try to avoid this situation if at all possible. Of course, savvy bankers want to cover themselves any way possible, and they're holding all the cards when you really need the dough.

Take the following quiz before making a trip to the commercial bank to see whether you and your business are ready to apply for a business loan:

1. Does your management team have the skills and experience to execute your business strategy?

2. Does your company's financial picture look healthy (positive cash flow, reasonable profit, some assets)?

3. Does your personal financial statement look positive?

4. Can you identify your first source for repayment of the loan?

5. Do you have a second source for repayment?

6. Do you have additional security that you can use to collateralize the loan?

7. Do you clearly understand how your business and your industry work?

8. Can you demonstrate your character and trustworthiness?

Make sure that you can answer yes to all these questions before you approach your banker. Set yourself up for success!

Government sources

You can turn to governmental agencies to help fund your start-up business, which is a good thing because it enables you to borrow back some of your tax dollars that went into government programs to support small businesses.

Be forewarned, however, that any time you borrow from the government, you'll be dealing with a lot of paperwork and time-consuming procedures. (Remember, it takes money to make money.) Furthermore, the government moves at glacial speed to respond to requests. Still, many a business owner has been saved from near death by an SBA loan.

The Small Business Administration (SBA) is an agency that guarantees loans from commercial lenders for up to 90 percent of the loan amount. So, if you default on a $100,000 guaranteed loan, the government will reimburse the lender for $90,000, and the bank will come after you for the rest. Using this program gives commercial lenders the incentive they need to take risks on small businesses. However, just as with any banker, the SBA wants to know that you'll repay your loan, so it will only lend to a business that has a bit of a track record and is a healthy business (see the previous section). So, for start-ups, this may not be a reasonable solution.

We recommend that you check state agencies and sources for financing as well. Many states — Wisconsin and South Dakota, for example — have set up and funded agencies that help new and growing businesses with financing.

Equity

When you seek *equity* sources of capital, you're asking people to invest in your company in exchange for ownership interests, which means that you're willing to share ownership of your business. If you're wondering why you would do this, ask yourself the following: Which would you rather have — total ownership of a company that struggles to get off the ground, or majority ownership in a company that's really going places? We hope you answered the latter. Remember, it takes money to make money. When you give people equity stakes in your company, you give them the right to attend shareholder meetings and voice their opinions, so you must choose your equity stakeholders wisely.

Equity provides the investor/owner with four basic rights:

- ✔ **The right to control the business:** The person who has the majority of the stock controls what happens to the business. That's certainly true in a privately held company, in which the founder controls who gets stock and how much. In a publicly held company, by contrast, shares are bought and sold on a stock exchange, so a group of people joining together can hold the majority shares and control the company. That group may or may not include the founder.

- ✔ **The right to dividends:** Depending on how you set up your stockholder agreements, most shareholders in an equity situation are entitled to dividends if and when the company declares them. *Dividends* are a distribution of earnings to the shareholders. This is a critical point, because most early-stage companies don't distribute dividends. Instead, they retain earnings to grow the company, which is a very prudent decision.

  Entrepreneurs shouldn't seek money from investors who want dividends before the company is well-established.

- ✔ **The right to vote:** Assuming your investors received common stock, they're entitled to vote at the annual shareholders' meeting on such issues as the election of directors and officers and the direction of the company. In most cases, venture capitalists (professional investors) demand preferred stock, which gives them preference in a liquidation over the common shareholders. Normally, preferred stock is nonvoting, but in some instances the investor may demand voting rights with preferred stock — hey, whoever supplies the money wins!

- ✔ **The right to company assets:** Depending on how you write up the shareholder agreements, some shareholders could have claims on company assets in the event of dissolution of the company.

Choosing between debt and equity

Many factors come into play when you're deciding what kind of money you need for your venture. The following sections take a look at some key factors to consider when contemplating the choice between debt and equity.

The purpose of the funds

Why do you need the money? That question sounds simple enough, but few business owners really know why they're seeking capital beyond the very basics: to start the business, to grow the business, and so on. Certain types of capital work in some situations and not in others. For example, if you're seeking capital to finish research and development (R&D) on a new product (called *seed capital*), you can forget getting a loan from banks, most venture capital firms, and, frankly, most every other kind of investor outside of friends and family. That's because R&D is a big sinkhole. It requires a lot of money without producing any return for a long time, if ever.

On the other hand, if you have a successful business and are looking to grow into new markets, you probably have several funding choices. And, in today's global business environment, if you have a sexy Internet business with a great business model or a high-tech venture in the energy industry, the world of capital is yours for the asking. Well, maybe not quite that easily, but you're certainly in a better position than 99 percent of other business owners.

Your preferences and goals for your business

As a business owner, you no doubt want to control your destiny and certainly that of your business. Some business owners aren't comfortable with debt (they're obviously not Baby Boomers), so loans and credit lines aren't options. Others don't want to share ownership with anyone — they want it all, so equity isn't an option.

If you fall into both categories, you have a real problem. You now have to rely on your own resources and the internal cash flows of the company. That may mean that you start and grow much more slowly than you would've otherwise. Nothing is wrong with that approach — unless you're in a fast-moving industry. In that case, if you grow too slowly, you'll probably miss the window of opportunity and give a competitor a chance to bypass you in the market. The important thing is that you choose the financing option that meets your personal needs and the goals of your business.

Your investors' preferences and goals

Although your personal preferences and goals certainly are important, they're by no means the only ones you have to consider. Your investors, if you choose that route, have their own goals, which may be in conflict with yours. Unless you find that rare investor who has a philanthropic interest in seeing your business succeed, you'll deal with an investor who's in the deal for what it will return. An investor is looking at three types of returns in about three to five years:

- ✔ **Cash-flow returns:** A working investor/owner sometimes receives the perks of ownership, such as an expense account, a company car, a salary, and dividends.

- ✔ **Stock appreciation:** At some point agreeable to everyone, an investor can sell off a portion or all of his or her interest in the company and harvest the capital appreciation that the business has achieved. This is a tax-free event, up to the cost basis of the original investment. Also, if investors have held the stock the required length of time, they'll qualify for capital-gains treatment on the gain, which means their tax rate will be much lower.

- ✔ **Tax benefits:** In some forms of business — for example, a Subchapter S corporation or a limited-liability company (LLC) — losses (and profits) are passed through to the owners in proportion to their investment. So an investor can receive pass-through losses (typical in the early years of a business) and pay taxes on profits at the investor's personal income tax rate, which often is lower than the corporate rate.

Finding Second-Stage (or Expansion) Financing

Second-stage, or *second-round,* financing generally is used to expand a business into new markets or new products. To grow rapidly to the next level, most businesses seek some form of expansion capital to cover the cost of building up inventories, hiring more salespeople, carrying out marketing campaigns, ramping up manufacturing, and so on, to name a few options. In this section, we look at several ways you can raise expansion capital.

Getting an angel on your side

Yes, we want to talk about angels, but the kind of angels we're talking about don't have wings and halos, although they sometimes grant wishes. In the capital acquisition arena, an *angel* is a private investor and part of what's known as the *informal risk capital market,* which is the largest pool of investor money in the United States. Because the market is quite large, finding an angel doesn't seem like it would be a problem for an entrepreneur looking for funding. But it isn't that easy.

You see, angel investors aren't listed in the phone book; frankly, they usually prefer to keep a low profile, looking only at deals referred to them by people they trust. So, the key to finding an angel investor is to get to know people who know them. Professional adviser types such as attorneys, lawyers, bankers, and accountants are possible sources. Other entrepreneurs are also good sources because most angel investors have been entrepreneurs themselves; that's why they like helping other entrepreneurs by investing in their companies.

Today many angel investors band together in groups so that they can invest in larger deals and benefit from a shared experience. They generally have rules about how much their members must invest annually and they tend to fill the gap between friends and family money and venture capitalists (VCs; see the next section). One thing angels typically do that distinguishes them from VCs is to spend a lot of time mentoring the start-ups so that they're ready for money. They also link companies to VCs when the time is right.

Although we can't give you one complete description of what angels look like, we can say from our research that they have some common characteristics:

- ✔ They're usually educated males in their 40s and 50s.

- ✔ They typically have a net worth of more than $1 million.

- ✔ They like to invest in companies near their homes so they can enjoy watching the companies grow.

- ✔ They seem to prefer certain types of businesses — particularly manufacturing, energy and resources, and service businesses. Of course, they also compete with VCs for high-technology businesses.

- ✔ They tend to make decisions more quickly than VCs and usually stay with ventures for longer periods of time.

You now have an image of an angel to go by, but don't make the mistake of thinking that all angels are alike. In fact, today you may run into angels who have actually come looking for you, trying to entice you to accept their money. A dream come true? Hardly; it's a symptom of a long *bull market* (rising stock market) with plenty of newly rich entrepreneurs who like the idea of investing in up-and-coming young companies. These investors are looking less and less like angels and more like VCs, however, because they require more due diligence, seek a quicker return on investment time, and set tougher screening criteria. Angels have a much larger market now that VCs are scouting bigger deals. However, many angels still find most of their deals through referrals, so it all comes back to the importance of networking and becoming known within the venture community.

Taking the fast track with venture capitalists (at your own risk)

Perhaps you've heard all the "vulture capital" jokes. In the minds of many people, venture capitalists are placed in the same category with used car salesmen and real estate developers. Why is that? Probably because although entrepreneurs want to build great companies, venture capitalists are in business solely to make money and get out as quickly as possible. They also want the following:

- ✔ A huge equity interest to compensate for the risk they're taking
- ✔ An enormous return on investment
- ✔ A seat on your board of directors

Doesn't sound very attractive, does it? To be fair, venture capital serves an important purpose: It provides the funding that fast-growth companies need to expand.

Although plenty of venture capital is out there for the taking, fewer than 1 percent of all businesses meet the very strict requirements of venture capitalists.

For high-growth ventures, however, VC money is an important source of funding, but it should be considered a second-stage source and pursued only if no private money is available. Some businesses, particularly high-tech businesses and those with heavy asset requirements such as plant and equipment, find it difficult to grow organically using internal cash flows. Growth is expensive and to do it effectively, you need to move quickly. There are additional people to hire, systems and controls to put in place to manage growth, and inventories to build up in anticipation of demand by customers. All these things require large amounts of capital that most business owners don't want to divert from their current budgets.

That's where VCs come in. This type of business is more attractive than a start-up because it has achieved a certain level of success, some of the risk has been reduced, and the business is positioned to grow. The following sections help you understand what VCs are looking for so you don't spend time (and money) trying to get them interested in funding your business if it's not the type of business they look for.

What do VCs look for?

Knowing what VCs generally look for puts you in a better negotiating position. You'll know what's important to them and be able to address those issues in a way that makes sense to them.

Most VCs are interested in three aspects in the following order:

- ✔ **A great market:** Market size in the hundreds of millions of dollars is the minimum — billions of dollars is much better (surprise!). From a fast-growing, large market, a company can achieve high valuations that will give the investor the greatest possible return on investment.

- ✔ **A great management team:** Of course, to take advantage of big markets you need a management team that can execute the business plan. An old adage says that VCs would rather invest in an A team with a B product than in a B team with an A product. What that means is that people make the difference in a company. VCs want to invest in a team that has a successful track record.

  VCs also want to see a team that's fully committed to the company, because a fast-growing company requires an extraordinary amount of time and effort.

- ✔ **A great technology that you can protect:** Traditionally, VCs have looked for the next great technology product — computer hardware, software, communications, electronics, medical devices, biotech, and pharmaceuticals, for instance. They would prefer that you have patents to protect it, so your Grandmother's brownie recipe probably won't qualify (even if Fairytale Brownies is a thriving Arizona-based business).

  Having said that, VCs are now starting to do more of something they rarely did in the past: They're investing in nontechnology companies with great, protectable business models and huge growth potential. So, you may not get money for your new brownies, but you may be able to create the next Wal-Mart. The reason VCs are doing this is because of the lack of great technology deals in the market.

Where do you find VCs?

To work with venture capital firms, you need to be able to locate them. The best way to do so is through a referral. Although many venture capital firms are listed in the phone book, the worst thing you can do when searching for capital is to start calling and sending out your business plan. VCs see hundreds of business plans every month, so the best chance you have of getting some attention is through a referral from someone who knows a VC and knows you, too.

To get a referral, you need to have spent a lot of time networking in your community so that, eventually, you can meet the people who can help you. Attorneys, bankers, and accountants are good places to start! This type of contact won't happen overnight, however. You have to keep working at it.

After you find a VC whose requirements mesh with your venture's capabilities, deal with that investor alone. Don't shop your business plan to several VCs at once. It's a small world, and VCs don't want to feel as though they're in a bidding war for your investment opportunity. You'll discover very quickly whether a VC firm is interested or not; VCs aren't shy about telling entrepreneurs what they think of their "great" ideas.

What happens after you find a VC?

The first thing VCs may ask to look at is the executive summary for your business plan. If they don't find the business concept sufficiently compelling and in-line with their criteria, they won't waste their time reading the rest of the business plan.

If they *are* interested, they may call for a meeting to check out your management team to see whether you are what you say you are. You may be asked to do a formal presentation at that time, and you may be asked some very pointed questions to determine how you stand up under pressure. The first meeting is really a getting-to-know-you meeting. Others will follow as the VCs begin to do their very thorough due diligence — background checks on your team and company.

If the VCs are sold on the investment, you'll move into a period of going over legal documents and negotiating what they want and what you want (typically what they want wins). The nature and terms of the investment will then appear in a term sheet. When the deal is set, however, it doesn't mean that the check is in the mail. VCs usually manage pools of investor money, so they have to do their own prospectus and legal documents for their investors. All this work can take several months. So, the moral of the story is, don't begin the search for VC funding too late. Completing funding will take some time.

And what about private equity firms?

Today private equity firms are receiving a lot of press. What exactly are they, and how are they different from venture capital firms? *Private equity firms* are simply investment funds that traditionally have focused only on very mature, low-risk companies seeking expansion capital. Their popularity is being driven by the number of companies looking to go private to avoid the stringent requirements of Sarbanes-Oxley (see Chapter 10). By contrast, venture capital firms take on riskier ventures at earlier stages and exert more onerous requirements on them. However, in recent times, the line between venture capital firms and private equity firms has blurred a bit, mostly due to the highly competitive state of the investor market. VC firms are now investing in more mature ventures, and private equity firms are taking more risk by investing earlier.

Considering a public offering

If your company is in need of second-stage cash, another way you can raise capital is to do a public offering. A *public offering* is a complex version of a private offering that's regulated by the Securities and Exchange Commission (SEC). Your company agrees to sell a portion of its issued stock to the public via a stock exchange. The first time your company does this, it's termed an *initial public offering (IPO)*.

Why an IPO may be a smart move: The pros

For a growing business, nothing is more exciting or glamorous than a public offering. It can be prestigious and very lucrative, among many other benefits:

- The public offering provides a way for founders and investors to reap the rewards of their efforts by selling off a portion of their stock.

- It gives your business instant clout with lenders and others who may not have given you a second look before.

- It's a way to raise large amounts of interest-free equity capital that you probably couldn't raise by any other means.

- You can use stock in the company as an incentive to attract top people to your organization.

- Because of the prestige of being a public company, it's easier to negotiate deals with suppliers, customers, and creditors and to form strategic partnerships with other companies.

With public offerings, market timing is everything. IPOs are subject to seasonality, which means that sometimes markets are favorable to them and sometimes they're not. Timing for the business is important, too. One rule says to consider an IPO when your company's need for growth capital exceeds its debt capacity. In any case, your company should require at least $50 to $100 million to make it worthwhile and preferable to going with venture capital money (see the previous section).

Some companies that have found the U.S. IPO market hard to break into have done their IPOs in Europe or Asia, where the rules are less onerous. For example, Japanese investors seem to prefer small valuations of $10 to $60 million, because they like to get into an investment at an early stage to increase the potential of reaping greater returns.

Why an IPO isn't always a good idea: The cons

Before you decide to jump on the bandwagon and join the throngs of businesses queuing up to do an IPO, take a serious look at some of the disadvantages of being a public company; then decide if you still want to do it:

✔ Statistics make the picture very clear: In the 1980s, 3,186 firms went public. Today, only 58 percent of them are still listed on one of the three major stock exchanges. To add insult to injury, only about a third of the firms have stock selling above the issuing price.

✔ The year 2001 saw an unprecedented 3.8 percent of all publicly traded stocks dropped from the major stock exchanges. So much for prestige!

✔ Going public is a very expensive process — often costing more than $300,000. That figure doesn't include the commission to the underwriter, either — the investment bank that sells the securities. This commission can run from 7 to 10 percent.

✔ Going public is a time-consuming process that can take from six months to a year to complete. Just learning about the process and what's required of you takes a lot of time.

And you need to prepare far in advance of the actual IPO process, because it will take time to get your business in shape financially. For one thing, you need to put a team together that will help the company through the process. You also need at least three years of audited financial statements — hence the importance of knowing that you eventually want to do an IPO long before you actually do it.

✔ When your company becomes a public company, everything you do becomes public knowledge, including all your financials. Consequently, you're subject to scrutiny by the government and the public in general.

✔ A public company is responsible first to its shareholders and second to its customers, employees, and any other stakeholders. The board of directors and the shareholders now control your destiny.

A public company, therefore, faces intense pressure to perform quickly. Shareholders tend to focus on short-term goals that produce high earnings and higher stock prices, even if those goals threaten long-term performance.

✔ The reporting requirements to the SEC necessitate the hiring of a full-time person to manage everything, which is costly and time consuming. Public companies are subject to Sarbanes-Oxley (see Chapter 10).

What happens during an IPO

Making decision to hold an IPO is just the first step. Here's what happens during an IPO:

1. **After you definitely decide to go for an IPO, you must locate an underwriter or investment banker to sell your securities and manage the IPO process.**

   This step isn't as easy as you may think. The more prestigious firms are very picky about whom they represent, so you probably need to get to them via referrals.

Always check out any underwriter that you're considering using. Make sure that the underwriter has a good track record of successfully completing an IPO. Not all IPOs succeed. If the night before the offering the underwriter can't get the estimated "going out" price or close to it, or you're not *oversubscribed* (oversubscribed is having more buyers than you need), you may decide to cancel the IPO. You'll still have to pay the bills, however. If you do go forward, find a good investment bank that can guide you through the process and afterward offer you financial advice, assist you in buying and selling stock, and help you maintain the interest of the public in purchasing its stock.

2. **When you find a qualified underwriter, he or she will draw up a letter of intent.**

   The letter specifies a price range for the stock and the terms and conditions of the arrangement between your company and the investment bank.

3. **You file a registration statement with the SEC.**

   This statement is known in the business as a *red herring,* which is actually just another term for a prospectus. The prospectus is given to anyone interested in investing in the IPO — typically institutional-type investors such as pension funds and insurance companies.

4. **After you file the registration statement, you publish the advertisement for the IPO in the financial press.**

   This advertisement is called a *tombstone,* and no, it isn't meant to be a bad omen.

5. **You determine on which stock exchange your company belongs.**

   The most difficult exchange to qualify for is the New York Stock Exchange (NYSE), so most small companies go to the American Stock Exchange (AMEX) or the National Association of Securities Dealers Automated Quotation (NASDAQ). You can also choose to go public on one of the many foreign exchanges.

6. **You and your team take a tour of all the major institutional investors.**

   This road show is the best part of the IPO process (next to the party to celebrate a successful IPO). The goal is to get all the investors on board so that when all the SEC requirements have been met, the offering can virtually be sold in a day.

Don't head to the bank yet, though, because the stock value achieved at the IPO may not be sustainable. This situation sometimes happens because you find that there's no real market for the stock; you know this because no one is buying and selling your stock after the opening day. Consequently, the value of the shares could decline to zero (it has happened). This decline means that if, for example, your shares in the company were valued at $300,000 on opening day, a week later they may be worth nothing. This example is a very real possibility.

So, don't let all the news reports of skyrocketing valuations lead you to believe that your company will perform in the same way. Recall what happened to Vonage, the voiceover-IP company, which debuted on the New York Stock Exchange on May 24, 2006. Within the first seven days after its IPO, the stock lost about 30 percent of its value. Needless to say, shareholders weren't happy and filed a class-action lawsuit against the company.

One other important point: Just because you have stock listed on an exchange doesn't mean that you have a liquid asset. The SEC has some very stringent rules about when and how much stock officers, directors, and insiders can sell. Don't plan on an immediate personal cash gain.

We're not trying to warn you away from a public offering. For some companies, an IPO is the best way to raise large amounts of capital and compete on an equal footing in their industries. Just make sure that you consider carefully all the ramifications of going public before making the decision to do it.

Forming a Strategic Partnership to Access Growth Capital

You can use methods other than debt and equity to raise capital or find the resources necessary to grow your business. Very simply put, a *strategic alliance* is a partnership between two or more businesses, as well as an excellent way to share core competencies and reduce the costs of research and development, marketing, manufacturing, and distribution. Strategic partners invest time, money, and expertise in your company; they're really more like stakeholders. Strategic partnerships have helped many companies grow without having to raise costly outside capital and without giving up any equity. Strategic partnerships are particularly important to companies that do business in the global market (see Chapter 4). Often, you can't even do business in a country without having a partner in that country that knows how to handle business there.

Alliances also are critical to small companies looking to compete in a big market. ScanEagle, for instance, is an unmanned robotic surveillance plane developed by an entrepreneurial company, the Insitu Group, based in Bingen, Washington. After about 60 meetings with aerospace giant Boeing, the company finally signed a partnership agreement that made ScanEagle a vital player in the Iraq war — something it could've never achieved on its own.

To be successful, a strategic alliance should be a win-win situation for both companies. To make sure that you create an effective partnership, heed the following advice:

✔ Find a partner that's financially healthy with or without your company.

✔ Find a partner whose business practices are compatible with yours, and whose customers and value chain members are satisfied with their relationships with the company.

✔ Find a partner that has experience in strategic alliances. Just as with a sophisticated investor, an experienced partner understands the risks and knows how to make the partnership work.

✔ If possible, find a company that has excess capacity so that it doesn't have to expend extra capital in plant and equipment to partner with you.

Part IV
Marketing in the New World

The 5th Wave   By Rich Tennant

"How about this–'It's not just CRAP, it's Mel's CRAP'? Shoot! That's no good. I hate writing copy for this client."

In this part . . .

Customers are the focus of every successful business, so it's imperative that you find new ways to grab their attention and build long-term relationships for your mutual benefit. In this part, we explain how you can come to understand your customers' needs and how you can provide world-class customer service. We discuss the best approaches to developing a marketing plan, and we take an in-depth look at advertising and promotion — particularly the world of new media brought about by the Internet and tools that now let users become marketers.

Chapter 15

You Are Nothing without a Customer

*B*usinesspeople often become so focused on brainstorming and producing the best products, setting up employee incentive programs, paying bills, and finding new ways to market their businesses that they forget about the very reason they run a business in the first place: the customer. The customer is the beginning, middle, and end of a business. Yet, too many CEOs *assume* that they know what customers want, how they want it, and when they want it. They never even bother to ask! They think that they're providing customer service, but what is customer service if you don't know what the customer wants?

Here's a quiz to start this chapter. Answer the following questions as honestly as you can without spending any time on them:

✔ Who's the most important person in your business?

✔ Who pays your employees?

✔ Who designs your products and services?

✔ Who determines when it's time to grow your company to the next level?

If you haven't guessed by now, the answer to each question should be the customer. In this chapter, you find out why this is so. We cover everything from target markets to market research to customer needs. You also discover some new trends that are turning the marketing world on its head, and you find out how to prepare an effective marketing plan that will create awareness for your products and services and build long-term relationships with your customers.

Identifying Your Customers and Their Needs

You can't sell a product or deliver a service if you don't know who your customer is. Simply put, your customer is the individual or business who pays you, but it's more than that. Your customer is the segment of a market that needs your product or service most because it solves a real problem he or she is having. Makes sense because if a customer needs what you have, the sale will be easy. There is no secret to understanding your customers' needs. All you have to do is ask. What a concept! Yet, interacting with customers is something many businesses do very badly, if they do it at all. Why is that? We can point to two fundamental reasons:

- Owners assume that because they started the business, they must know what their customers want. Wrong!

- They assume that if they're getting their products or services out on time and with good quality, they've done all they need to do to satisfy customers. Wrong again!

Today, just keeping your customers satisfied isn't enough. You have to build long-term relationships with them. Why? Because the world has changed. Today's customers are jaded; they're bombarded with an endless variety of products and services — so many, in fact, that they end up frustrated and ultimately choose based on the best price. Couple that with the power that Internet search engines have given to customers by enabling them to compare products online and find the best price anywhere in the world, and you have a challenging situation for businesses trying to stand out from the crowd. Even if you do manage to stand out with your product, a competitor that can sell your product more cheaply may win the customer.

Competing on price alone, however, is a no-win situation for everyone. Your best bet is to show your customers that your company offers intangible benefits that make it a better choice than the competitors. To do so, you need to understand who your customer is and what his or her needs are. This section can help you get started.

The customer is the person who pays you

You can't meet a customer's needs if you don't know who the customer is. If you agree that the customer is the person (or business) who pays you — the one who controls the purchasing decision — defining who your customer is will be easier. Suppose that you own a restaurant. Your customers, naturally, are the people who come to your restaurant because you're delivering your food products directly to them and they're paying you. That's a simple example. Now try this one: You manufacture bicycles geared toward racers and sell them through retail outlets. Who's your customer? Your first guess may be that the customer is the retail outlet, because it buys the bicycles from you to sell to its customers, the racers. And in some instances, you'd be right if you, the manufacturer, sold direct to the retailer. The more likely scenario, however, is that you sell to a distributor, which then locates retail outlets for the bicycles. In that case, your customer is the distributor, because the distributor pays you and the retailer pays the distributor. What about the consumer who uses the bike? Where does he or she fit in? The actual user of the bike is the customer of — you guessed it — the retailer.

Now, consider a less obvious example. Suppose, like Charles A. Cocotas, you own a hotel for dogs called Best Friends Pet Resorts and Salons, headquartered in Norwalk, Connecticut. Who is your customer? The last time we checked, dogs hadn't yet learned how to deal with money, so we know the dog doesn't pay you. Chances are, the dog's owner pays the bill. So, although the dogs benefit from Cocotas's services, the owners pay for the services, so the owners are the customers. What does that make the dog? The dog is what we refer to as the *end user*. In the previous example, the bicycle racer is the end user for the manufacturer and the customer of the retailer.

Why is it so important to distinguish between the two? You can't meet a customer's needs if you don't know who the customer is.

Customers want benefits, not products

We're amazed at how many companies take the "Field of Dreams" approach to the products and services they offer: They figure that if they build it, the customers will come. Nothing could be further from the truth. Customers are very smart people. They know exactly what they want, when they want it, and how they want it. And the main things they want are benefits. For instance, Bev and Chris Sanders, founders of Avalanche Snowboards, Inc — a manufacturer of snowboards and related equipment in Lake Tahoe, California — are constantly on the alert for new benefits that they can provide their customers. As they ride the chairlifts, they write down unusual jumps and tricks they see that may inspire new designs. In other words, their designs come directly from what their customers do, so the benefit to the customers is the freedom to try new things.

Assuming that customers buy based on the features of your product or service — the bells and whistles — is a mistake. Customers are more interested in what the product or service can do for them — they want to know "what's in it for me?" Consider this example: Suppose that you have an Internet-based travel company that offers adventure tours to exotic places. Some of the many features of your product/service may include the following:

- Your company puts the whole trip together so that all the customer has to do is show up.
- Your company provides a wealth of information about the exotic location.
- Your company supplies an on-location tour guide.

These features are all well and good, but they don't address the needs of the customer in the form of benefits that let customers know why they should do business with you. Before presenting your travel product/service to the public, try taking each of the features in the preceding list and turning them into benefits for your customers:

- Customers save time and money by going to one place for all their travel needs.
- Customers save time when looking up location information and have access to more information about their destinations.
- Customers experience a sense of security, knowing that a representative of your company will be onsite to take care of any last-minute needs.

As you can see, you're now looking at the features from the customer's perspective. The customer must be aware of these benefits before making a purchasing decision. Think as a customer and your chances of making a sale go up substantially.

Eyeing Key Trends in Marketing

Just as with nearly every aspect of business, marketing has felt the significant impact of the Internet. In fact, traditional media boundaries are eroding as Internet marketing becomes more and more popular. Even seasoned marketers may be surprised that Internet advertising is predicted to be a $26 billion market by 2009. With the Internet passing the one-billion user mark (15 percent being U.S. users), online information sources have leapfrogged offline information sources, and today, approximately 37 percent of marketers' budgets is devoted to Internet marketing.

Today, information and advertising spring from a variety of different sources, and customers are becoming overwhelmed by all the available choices. In this section, we look at three important trends that are redefining marketing.

Grabbing the long tail

Not that long ago, marketing experts were talking about the importance of moving away from mass marketing toward the concept of mass customization, which was based on one-to-one relationship marketing — providing a customized product or service to each customer, in other words. Well, guess what? The experts are back to touting mass marketing, only this time it's new-media-style mass marketing (for more on new media, head to Chapter 2). Because companies can now reach millions of potential customers very inexpensively over the Internet, you can see the emerging phenomenon that has been called *the long tail* by Chris Anderson in his best-selling book by the same name.

Long tail refers to a probabilistic statistical function — in simple terms, the likelihood that an event will happen. What Anderson says is that today companies can serve many very small niche markets by using the Internet; these niches, when aggregated, represent a significant portion of total sales for some types of items (see Figure 15-1 for a representation).

In Figure 15-1, the graph might represent CD sales, book sales, or pretty much any product that's normally sold through brick-and-mortar retail outlets. In the graph, you see the number of unit sales on the vertical axis (Y-axis) and the ranking of those sales from most popular item (ranked #1) to least popular item on the horizontal axis (X-axis). Stores typically stock only the top-selling titles or brands of products because these items move fast, so the stores make more money (makes sense!). However, in the online world, retail shelf space doesn't matter, because there are no shelves to worry about!

So, a company such as Amazon.com or Best Buy can potentially carry millions of titles and cater to each customer's most narrow interests, because such a company can access anything it needs to sell from an endless variety of sources worldwide. For example, if you want to buy a 1935 novel that your grandmother recommended, you can probably find it online.

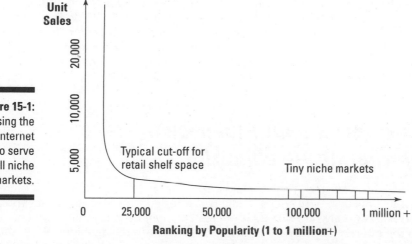

Figure 15-1:
Using the Internet to serve small niche markets.

What's the impact of the long-tail phenomenon? Consumers are spending more time online across a greater number of sites — called *user fragmentation*. Their attention span on any one site is lower, so the bar is raised very high to grab their attention. Relevance has become the mantra of online marketers. Amazon.com has found that one quarter of its entire book sales come from books that don't crack the top 100,000 titles, and that proportion is growing by leaps and bounds. This is niche marketing on steroids, and it's the future of marketing.

Understanding media convergence

One of the key trends that explains why marketing is undergoing a revolution is *media convergence*. Today, most companies and consumers have access to video and content production technology at affordable prices, so what used to be barriers to content creation are now open doors. Anyone with a computer, a video camera, and the right software can produce a broadcast-quality commercial or magazine-quality advertisement and distribute the content over the Internet to a target audience. In this very flat world, Google, for example, sells advertising space, Starbucks sells music, and AT&T is developing television programs. What this means to you is that opportunities that never existed before are now available for the taking.

A company should understand that media convergence is both an opportunity and a challenge. If everyone has access to the same information and technologies and, therefore, can reach the same target markets easily, creating a competitive advantage becomes very difficult. And customers, frankly, are tired of being parsed into little pieces based on who they are and how they behave. So, you need to think creatively about how to take advantage of the new marketing environment while also coordinating, connecting, and reinforcing what you do inside the company with what you do in the marketplace. In other words, take advantage of this media convergence, but make sure that it doesn't distract you from your core business capabilities, which include serving your customers. Some companies have chosen to hire firms that have developed an expertise in new media to do the work for them.

Customers doing their own marketing — oh my!

Nearly everyone today (well, almost everyone) seems to be seeking their 15 minutes of fame. With social-media Web sites such as MySpace, Facebook, and YouTube, anyone with a bit of creativity can become an instant celebrity on the Internet or push a product or business into the limelight. What this means to business owners is that in many cases they may not need to hire expensive marketing firms to handle their marketing to customers if those customers frequent these social networking sites.

Social media tools you see on media sites have taken the concept of viral marketing to a new level. *Viral marketing* is a marketing technique that takes advantage of referrals through social networks to spread a marketing message much as a viral disease spreads from person to person. Some examples of social networking tools that facilitate viral marketing include

- ✔ Blogs
- ✔ Podcasts
- ✔ Vodcasts (video podcasts)
- ✔ RSS Readers (pushes what others are saying about you in the news, blogs, or podcasts to you — this can be good and bad!)
- ✔ Wikis (Web sites that let users create and edit content on any topic)

For example, an enterprising college student decided that the world needed to understand physics, so he posted a video on YouTube called "Physics Guy Rap," where he cleverly delivered a lecture about physics to a class while rapping to a hip-hop beat. The video quickly racked up more than 120,000 views the first day it played, through viral networking. After one networking site got wind of the video, the news spread like a virus all over the Internet, eventually spreading into more traditional media outlets.

Your company can take advantage of many ways to do viral marketing with new media. Here are three tips:

- ✔ **Give something away free.** "Free" is the most powerful word in any language. Advertising free products is a great way to get "eyeballs" on your site.
- ✔ **Make it very easy for people to pass on a message you want seen.** For example, you can enable users to simply click a button to forward the message by e-mail.
- ✔ **Use existing social networking sites such as MySpace, YouTube, and Facebook to reach people who are used to sharing information with their personal networks.** This advertising will dramatically accelerate the circulation of your message.

Creating a Marketing Plan

A marketing plan is really just one part of your overall business plan. A *marketing plan* is a living guide to your goals for starting and building a loyal and sustainable customer base. It contains your marketing goals and the strategies and tactics you'll use to achieve them. But don't think that you can write one marketing plan that will be good for the life of your business (or even for a year for that matter). Rather, an effective marketing plan should evolve with your business, your customers, and the market. This section helps you create the right marketing plan for your company.

Prepare to do the plan

Before you sit down to outline your marketing plan, do some preparation to make your job easier. First of all, it's very important that you include all the members of your management team, as well as key front-line employees, in the planning process — people from marketing, finance, manufacturing, and distribution. The more input you get from all the functional areas of your business, the more successful your plan will be. And don't forget to include the customer in your planning! Ask some of your best customers to give you feedback by inviting them to participate in the planning process. Let them know that what they have to say is important.

A kick-off meeting is probably a good place to start. At the meeting, you can share ideas and assign duties that individuals or teams can undertake on their own. But be sure to regularly meet as a large group to make sure that everyone is on target. Here are some tips for getting started:

- ✔ **Brainstorm a list of possible marketing strategies and tactics.** This list can help you see all the possibilities before you narrow down the choices. You need to have a good understanding of which previous strategies have been successful and which ones have not. You can gain that understanding by looking at other companies in the industry. Find this information in popular business magazines such as *Inc.* and *Fast Company.* Hit some of the major business-resource sites on the Internet.

  Your goal is to collect as many strategies and tactics as you can. At this point, don't worry about whether they're feasible for your company; you really want to make sure you haven't missed a great strategy or tactic. You can judge feasibility after your list is complete.

- ✔ **Try to think like a customer.** Look at your company, its products and services, and its employees from the customer's perspective. In other words, step outside of yourself for a bit and look objectively at your business and what it offers.

- ✔ **Know your competition as well as you know your own company.** Look at what your competitors are doing right and what they're not doing that maybe *you* should be doing. Can you think of ways to improve on what your competitors are doing?

- ✔ **Begin analyzing your options and ranking them.** Start by eliminating quickly those options that aren't possible for your company at this time. Perhaps they cost more than you have in your budget, or maybe they just aren't appropriate for your customers. For example, if your customers aren't regular television watchers, you probably don't want to waste money advertising on that medium.

After you've followed these tips, you can begin to write your marketing plan.

Create a plan in one paragraph

Your marketing plan can be as elaborate as a complete 50-page business plan or as spartan as a one-paragraph plan. In fact, starting with one paragraph that says it all isn't a bad idea. Many very experienced marketers suggest using this approach because it forces you to keep your plan focused and to identify the key components. A good one-paragraph marketing plan has the following seven components:

- **Purpose:** What's the marketing plan supposed to accomplish?
- **Benefits:** How will your products and services satisfy the needs of your customers?
- **Customer:** Who is your primary customer and what's your strategy for building long-term relationships with that customer?
- **Company:** How will the customer see your company? Remember, customers are some of the many people who will contribute to positioning your company in the marketplace.
- **Niche:** What's the niche in the market that your company has defined and will serve?
- **Tactics:** What specific marketing tools will you use to reach customers?
- **Budget:** How much of your budget will you allocate to marketing efforts?

Here's an example of how all this information goes into a paragraph that gives readers the essential points of a marketing plan:

> *The purpose of the marketing plan is to create awareness for ABC Strategies LLC, which will provide state-of-the-art management consulting services to technology companies through direct contact with the customer and via the Internet. The niche that ABC will serve is the small, growing technology company. The customer will see ABC Strategies as a high-quality management consulting firm that provides the latest proven strategies and tactics for managing in a time of rapid change. Initial marketing tactics will include half-day workshops and advertisements in technology publications. Ten percent of sales will be applied to the marketing strategy.*

Defining Your Target Market

You've probably heard the term "target market" before. *Target market* represents the segment of the marketplace whose needs your product or service will satisfy. To put it another way, the target market consists of the customers who are most likely to purchase your product or use your service.

It's important to target a specific market rather than try to hit the whole market at once. Why is this? The answer is simple. Marketing to customers is a very costly undertaking for any business, so you want to be sure that you reach the customers who will actually buy from you. And who are those first customers? The ones in the most pain, because they have the problem that you're solving. They're the ones who will have their credit cards out when your product or service hits the market. This section helps you identify and serve your target market.

Hopefully you have more than one customer: Target the first customer!

In your search for your target or customers, you'll encounter many types of potential customers, so it won't always be obvious which group you should target first. One quick and easy way to help segment all your potential customers is to create a customer matrix. A *customer matrix* is a table that compares all the categories of customers you identify across several characteristics or variables. The typical characteristics used to compare customers are

- The benefits that a particular customer seeks from your products and services.
- The distribution channel you can use to deliver those benefits.
- The marketing strategy that's appropriate for that customer.

Of course, you can add any other type of comparison category you want. These three categories, however, will get you started. Table 15-1 depicts an example of a customer matrix.

Table 15-1	Customer Matrix for ABC Strategies Corp.		
Broad Customer Description	**Benefit**	**Distribution**	**Marketing Strategy**
Rapidly growing technology companies	On-call guidance through rapid growth phase	Direct, onsite to the customer	Referrals, trade journal promotion, seminars

Broad Customer Description	Benefit	Distribution	Marketing Strategy
Start-up technology companies	Low-cost consulting as needed	Online via the Internet — e-mail and online chat	Direct mail, workshops, university programs, links with other business Web sites
Established technology companies	Use of ABC expertise for specific projects	Direct to the customer	Referrals

Notice that each customer requires different benefits from the company. What this really tells you is that you define customer categories by the benefits to the customer. So, for example, the needs of a rapidly growing company are greater and more frequent in terms of management strategies than the needs of either the start-up venture or the established company. Chances are, you won't reach all your customers through the same distribution channels either. In Table 15-1, start-up ventures with limited resources are most easily served via the Internet. Likewise, it follows that if you're reaching different customers through different distribution channels, you'll probably also use different marketing strategies and tactics to create awareness and motivate them to buy.

After you pinpoint your potential target customer, it's time to create a customer profile — an in-depth description of the customer. Market research can help you find out more about that customer and the size of the market for that customer. The next section gives you some suggestions for how to research your target customer.

Do some research on the target customer

Before you do your market research to learn about your target customer, and possibly reinvent the wheel, it's a good idea to find out what others have said about your customer. Companies such as Mediamark Research, Inc. (www.mediamark.com) and the Simmons Market Research Bureau (www.symmetrical.com) study demographic and psychographic (personality, tendencies, buying habits) characteristics of different market segments. They conduct random samples of the population in an effort to provide companies similar to yours the data they need to make informed decisions. You can access the results of their research for a fee, but the best information on potential customers comes from the research you do with the customer.

There are four broad ways to segment a market, which we outline in the following list. These methods are guides for you; don't forget that the best way to understand and define your customers is to get out there and talk to them:

- ✔ **Demographics:** Demographics are the most common type of segmentation. Good market research firms can tell you, down to the precise neighborhood, what people buy, when they buy, how much they buy, and how much they earn. These firms also can give you information on standard characteristics such as sex, age, disposable income, ethnicity, and so forth.

- ✔ **The benefits of the product/service:** Market research can tell you which types of customers are seeking convenience, wanting to save time, or looking for superior quality and are willing to pay a premium for it. If such a benefit is what you're selling with your products and services, you want to know about these customers because they're your most likely purchasers.

- ✔ **Location of your customers:** Customers in various parts of the world have different purchasing habits and different needs. Naturally, then, the location of customers will affect your distribution and marketing strategies, and probably even the design of your product.

- ✔ **Psychographics:** When you look at the personality traits, lifestyles, and behavioral patterns of customers, you're looking at *psychographics*. Psychographics are very important in deciding which types of marketing tactics will catch your customers' attention.

If you describe your customer by using the four segmenting variables we discuss in this section, you'll have a better picture of whom you're dealing with.

Market Research Made Easy and Fun

Market research is about gathering information about potential customers and market segments that can help you understand your customers and their needs. Market research is a lot like doing your taxes. You dread doing them, put them off to the last minute, and then revel in what you learn about your finances as a result of doing them. If you can discipline yourself to do market research, it can reward you with customer intelligence that will get that revenue stream flowing.

In the early stages of market research, your target market description will be quite broad and based on samples of the population done by others. But as you get out in the market and talk to your potential customers, your definition of the target market may actually change, and you may find that your potential customer is really someone quite different from what you originally thought.

Another important reason to do some of your own market research is that you know best what types of information you need for your business. In fact, defining the kind of information you require is actually the first step in doing effective market research. This section explains what information you need to gather and how to find it.

What information do you need?

Smart market researchers always identify the information they need before they go out to talk to customers. Think of how frustrating it would be to have finished a bunch of customer interviews only to discover that you forgot to ask a very important question.

Here's a list of the kinds of information that most businesses need. Of course, you should modify it to suit your specific needs:

- ✔ What do your potential customers typically buy?
- ✔ How do they hear about products and services?
- ✔ How do they like to buy your particular type of product or service?
- ✔ How often do they buy?
- ✔ How can your company best meet their needs?

Also, make sure that you collect data that gives you a sense of trends in the market and the level of demand for the product or service you're offering.

How do you find that information?

Primary data is all the information you personally (or as a team) collect about your potential customers. Basically, you get primary data by observing or talking to customers, suppliers, distributors, and anyone else who can help you better understand your customer and the market. There are a number ways to collect this data and here we look at some of the most common. The method you choose depends on the type of business you have.

You can gather this primary data in many ways, some more effective than others and some more expensive than others. We cover some of the more common data-collection methods in the sections that follow.

Interviews

You can conduct interviews by phone (sounds like a phone survey to us, however) or in person. We favor in-person interviews because you get not only verbal feedback, but also nonverbal feedback. The way a person physically responds to your questions can tell you a lot about whether he is being honest.

Interviews are more costly and time-consuming than mail, online, or phone surveys, but they have the highest response rate (nearly 100 percent, if conducted effectively) and provide the best chance of getting accurate responses. In an interview situation, you have the ability to clarify responses, carry on a discussion so that the respondent can elaborate when necessary, and ask open-ended questions. This is a huge benefit, because open-ended questions provide far more information than yes-no or categorical questions, which ask people to choose from several items. You can use a designed questionnaire for interviews to ensure that you consistently ask the same questions of every interviewee, if that is important to you.

Getting people to participate in interviews is a matter of effectively cold-calling potential participants. It's likely that you contact people who have been recommended to you as potential customers. This is fine as long as these interviewees are truly representative of your target customer. Where you find interview candidates depends on the type of business you have and the type of customer you're targeting. For example, if consumers of music are your target, you can find potential interviewees at shopping malls and outside music stores such as Guitar Center.

Focus groups

Focus groups are like group therapy — you can reach several customers at once to gain insight into their needs or to test an idea on them. Focus groups are great ways to introduce new products and services and to find out the characteristics of the actual customers who will buy. You gather groups of six to ten customers and often enlist the aid of a group facilitator trained to conduct focus groups. You may even want to videotape the sessions so that you can review them more carefully later.

Suppose, for example, that you're introducing a new type of herbal tea to the market. You may choose to do a blind test in which you serve the participants several unmarked drinks, one of which is your new herbal tea. You then ask the participants to rate the drinks and discuss what they liked and didn't like about the products.

Mail and online questionnaires/surveys

If you've bought a new vehicle recently, you've probably received at least one questionnaire from a manufacturer and/or dealer asking you how you bought the vehicle and what you like or don't like about it. The good thing about these mail (and online) surveys is that a company can reach a lot of people relatively easily and quickly. This technique, however, does have a couple problems:

- ✔ The response rate from a targeted audience, even with follow-ups, is small — maybe 15 percent at best.

- ✔ You don't have any interaction with the respondent, so the information you get is pretty basic and not nearly as helpful as methods that enable you to see nonverbal communication and clarify responses.

In terms of valuable information gained, we rank mail surveys toward the bottom of the list of tools for customer data-gathering. Because people receive so much junk in the mail, your survey likely will get lost in the clutter.

Mail surveys are quickly being replaced by online surveys, facilitated by companies such as Survey Monkey (www.surveymonkey.com) and Zoomerang (info.zoomerang.com). The advantage of putting a survey on the Internet is that it's easy and quick for potential customers to respond, but — and this is important — you'll reach only the customers who are comfortable using the Internet. If your target customer is senior citizens or companies, the Internet method may not be the most effective route. Online surveys have an average response rate of around 26 percent, but you should expect a return of somewhere between 10 and 15 percent — similar to questionnaires sent by snail mail.

For any type of survey, though, you need to develop a questionnaire. Many people mistakenly believe that developing a questionnaire is a pretty simple task, but they couldn't be more wrong — the process is actually both an art and a science. Nevertheless, if you use proven methods for questionnaire design, you enhance the chances that you'll get more accurate responses and lessen the likelihood of biasing the outcomes.

Here are a few hints to improve the quality of your questionnaires:

- ✔ Keep the questionnaire as short and as easy as possible, and leave plenty of white space so that it isn't intimidating.

- ✔ Start with the easiest questions and lead up to more complex questions.

- ✔ Ask demographic questions (age, income, and so on) last, when you're about to lose the attention of the respondent.

- ✔ For online questionnaires, follow this advice:
    - • Send a personalized invitation to participate in the survey.
    - • Launch the survey in the morning.
    - • Collect data for at least two weeks.
    - • Send out reminder e-mails.

If you don't want to tackle a questionnaire by yourself, you may want to contact your local college or university to find an expert in constructing successful questionnaires.

Most people tend to increase their income by one category and decrease their age by one category, so take those fibs into account when looking at responses.

Phone surveys

We rate phone surveys below mail surveys in terms of popularity with respondents. Essentially, a phone survey is taking the questionnaire you'd normally mail or put online and asking those same questions over the phone. Think about how you feel when a telemarketer interrupts your dinner (the most popular time of day to call) and wants just a couple minutes of your time. Of course, that estimate always turns into at least 10 or 15 minutes, and by then your dinner is cold and you wouldn't buy from that company if it paid you to!

Clinical studies

Undertaking a clinical study probably is the most expensive route to customer data-gathering. Consequently, they're more popular among very large companies that deal in consumer products. Such a company may, for example, provide a test center similar to a grocery store. Potential customers receive money and are asked to go to the test store and make choices. Usually, a number of new products, including the one being tested, are available. Through observation and feedback from the test customers, the company can discover the potential the new product may have in the market.

Mix and match

No rule says that you can't combine some of the preceding methods in this section to achieve a level of information that satisfies you. Many times, researchers start with a mail or online survey. From the pool of survey respondents, they select those that match the criteria the company has developed and do interviews with them. Researchers may then group the interviewees into focus groups for further study.

How do you figure out how much you'll sell?

The toughest question facing any company introducing a new product or service to the market is, "How do we figure out how much we'll sell?" Unfortunately, there is no totally accurate way to get the answer. You have to triangulate (come at it from three different directions) to get to a number that seems to make sense. Trust us. No one gets it right all the time. The following list presents some tips to help you get as close as possible to the real demand for your product or service:

- ✔ **Look at substitute products.** If your product or service isn't unique or one of a kind (and most aren't), you may be able to find a similar existing product, study its demand patterns, and extrapolate that information to your own situation. Be sure when choosing a substitute product or service that you choose one that uses your distribution channel (see Chapter 18). The number of intermediaries a product goes through to reach the customer affects the final price.

- ✔ **Talk to industry experts.** The people who deal with your type of product or service every day have a good handle on demand, so talk to distributors, retailers, suppliers — anyone that deals with your category of products or services.

> ✔ **Do a test market.** Many companies — particularly those dealing in consumer products — do test markets in cities where the population is generally representative of the United States at large (Denver, for example). Manufacturing a limited production run and employing limited advertising enables you to see whether the product catches on before you incur the huge cost of large-scale production and advertising.

When you add your own experience and understanding of the customer and the market to this list, you've probably done the best you can to predict demand.

You Can't Be an MBA without Knowing the Five Ps

Okay. We know that marketing texts refer to the "four P's of marketing" (product, price, place, and promotion). But it has always seemed a little odd to us that the four Ps never include the most important P of all — people. Namely the customer! If you don't understand the customer, all the rest is just a waste of time. The customer determines the price, how you deliver the product, what the product looks like, and how you promote it. That sounds pretty important to us. Because we spend a good bit of this chapter on the fifth P — people — this section looks at the other four Ps.

Products include features and benefits

Your product or service is really a bundle of features and benefits in the eyes of the customer. Recall that features include such things as quality, service, warranties, options, characteristics, and so forth. Benefits are the intangible aspects — in other words, what's in it for the customer?

If you take our advice and include customer input when designing your product or service, you'll have a big jump on the product side of marketing. The fact that customers design your products and services is, in and of itself, a strong marketing message about your company. The following sections help you position your company, price your product or service, effectively locate your company and product/service, and promote your offering to customers.

Don't forget positioning

You need to position not only your product or service, but also your company. One helpful tactic is to write a positioning statement that explains how customers see your company relative to your competitors. Here's an example of a good positioning statement:

The customer will see ABC Strategies as a high-quality, state-of-the-art management consulting firm providing the latest proven strategies and tactics for managing in a time of change.

After you've written your statement, test it on your customers to make sure that this is really how they view your company. If you find that you're off base, go back and revise your positioning statement and test it on your customers again. You want to make sure that the image you present in all your advertising and promotion reflects what customers expect to see.

Packaging and labeling make a difference

Maybe you never thought of packaging and labeling as part of your marketing strategy, but the way you package your products says a lot about your company — particularly if you're selling consumer products. Packaging should reflect the culture of your company, the nature of the product you're selling, and the channel through which you're selling it.

You've probably seen the unique and whimsical black-and-white, spotted boxes of Gateway computers, inspired by Holstein cows — you can't miss them. This packaging concept is no accident. And you have, no doubt, noticed the similarity between software packaging and books on the shelf. Packaging for consumer products needs to grab the attention of the potential buyer — quickly. In an attractive way, the packaging also should give buyers the information they need to make a purchasing decision. ***Note:*** Of course, industrial products generally are packaged for utility rather than beauty or promotional value. Their boxes simply identify the contents and the manufacturer and are designed to make them easy to transport.

When you market on a global basis, packaging takes on a whole new meaning, because what's acceptable in one country may not be in another (see Chapter 4). For example, in Japan, you won't be able to sell your product unless the packaging is attractive to the Japanese people's discriminating taste for artistic design. Therefore, just like your positioning statement, you need to test the response to your packaging before spending a lot of money on a design that customers won't like.

Pricing requires many considerations

No matter what else you do right, if you don't price your product or service correctly, it won't sell in enough quantity to allow you to make a profit and survive. Pricing is a real challenge for most businesses — especially when you introduce a new product. Customer price tolerance determines where your price should be, but the customer isn't the only arbiter of price. Here are some other things to consider:

Giving your product away — crazy or a great pricing strategy?

What if we told you that you could make money by giving away your product — free! This idea sounds impossible, doesn't it? Well, it's actually a fairly common practice in some industries — particularly on the Internet. Would you pay attention to a recipe for success that could give your company the following?

✔ $200 million in annual revenues

✔ A market cap of almost $3 billion

✔ 25 million customers

✔ 33 percent market share

Well, McAfee achieved those numbers by giving away its core products, virus-protection software. The Santa Clara, California-based company followed the philosophy that getting more users for its software would enable it to uncover more virus samples. The company could then charge for upgrades to its program. This business model has been called the *Gillette method,* named after the razor company that first introduced it. The essence of the model is that you give customers the core product or sell it to them very cheaply, and you plan to make your money on the refills or upgrades. Every company has something that it can give away to provide customers a chance to try a new product or service. So, every company owner should decide what his or her company will give away and what it will sell. The right combination is unbeatable!

✔ You usually can command a higher price if demand for your product or service is greater than you can supply.

✔ If you're distributing a product or service that people will buy no matter what it costs (in economic terms, the price is *inelastic*), you're free to charge more. A simple example of this type of product is milk.

✔ You may have to hold your price down if you have a lot of competition. In this case, if you can show intangible benefits to your customers, they may pay more for your product just to get benefits that they can't get from your competitors.

✔ You usually can charge more for added features, but only if customers perceive them as valuable. They won't pay for bells and whistles they don't need.

✔ If you're introducing new technology, you probably want to charge a higher price initially to recover your development costs and then bring it down as competitors enter the market.

✔ If you successfully position your product among higher-priced items, you may be able to command a higher price.

The strategy you use to price your products may change over time, depending on where they are in the product life cycle. Figure 15-2 and the following list explain the various strategies used at particular points in the cycle:

✔ **Cost-based pricing** is based on adding a profit margin to the cost of producing the product. Of course, you also need to consider how competitors are pricing their products, as well as market demand.

✔ **Sliding on the demand curve** is a strategy in which you introduce a product at a high price and then, as technological improvements let you achieve economies of scale, you reduce the price. This strategy enables you to maintain an advantage over competitors.

✔ **Penetration** is a strategy that's effective in a very competitive market with similar products. Employ it when you need to gain quick acceptance and broad-based distribution. Penetration involves introducing the product at a low price, which produces very minimal profit. Then you gradually raise the price as customers accept the product. This strategy requires huge expenditures for advertising and promotion.

✔ **Demand-based pricing** focuses on finding what customers are willing to pay for the product.

✔ **Loss-leader pricing** calls for you to price your failing or obsolete products below cost to attract customers to other products in your line.

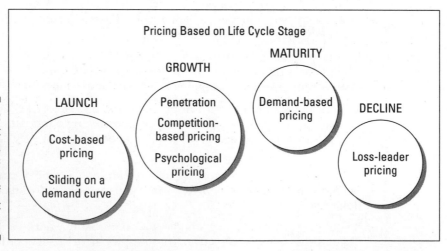

Figure 15-2: Different pricing strategies based on stages of the product life cycle.

Choose a strategy that reflects the type of customer you have, your costs related to the product, and the competitive environment. For more on a really creative way to price, take a look at the nearby sidebar "Giving your product away — crazy or a great pricing strategy?".

Promotion budget: A real guessing game

For your marketing plan, and ultimately for your business plan, you need to consider how much of your budget you should allot to promotion. We can give you no hard and fast rules about how much to spend; it really depends on your industry. In general, however, a new company probably will spend about 20 to 30 percent of its budget on marketing in the first couple years. That figure will go down to between 5 and 10 percent in later years.

Many businesses use the *percentage of sales* technique, which is based on how much, on average, businesses in your industry spend on promotion. That approach probably is more important than trying to spend close to the average for all industries. Still, average percentage of sales in your industry is only a benchmark for your company. For example, if you're trying to differentiate yourself, you may be doing things that your competitors are not, and that additional effort increases your promotional budget. In such a case, the benchmark may not apply. In thinking about the budget, you also must figure out how much you have to spend to achieve your marketing goals. In general, consumer products require a much greater promotional budget than other types of products.

You need to calculate the marketing cost per unit (total marketing expense divided by the number of units sold in the same period) and work to bring that number down as you become more of an expert in marketing tactics. The bottom line is this: How much is a new customer worth to you? Chapter 16 can help you discover some cost-saving, guerrilla tactics.

Place is more than location

In marketing terms, place has to do with where your customers find your products and services. Having a good product or service isn't enough; you need to get it to customers in the manner that's best for them, whether that be a retail outlet, mail order, direct from the manufacturer, or via the Internet. Just because your business is located in a particular place doesn't mean that customers will automatically seek that location when they're looking for your product.

Talking to your customers will tell you where they want to find your product or service. Doing anything other than what the customer expects is a recipe for disaster.

Promote, promote, promote

The purpose of the promotion part of your marketing plan is to firmly establish the identity and vision of your company in the customer's mind. Promotion is, perhaps, the most creative and important aspect of marketing. It includes personal selling, public relations, guerrilla advertising (using limited resources and creative methods), sales promotion, and publicity.

You can't plan an effective promotion strategy if you don't know your customers. Talk to your customers. (We say that a lot, don't we?) Doing so will pay big dividends and save you a lot of time and money. You can find out all about promotion in Chapter 16.

Chapter 16

Getting Noticed with Advertising and Promotion

A merican companies currently spend more than $150 billion a year on advertising. Approximately $65 billion of this total ends up in television ads; about $28 billion in newspaper ads; about $30 billion in magazine advertising; a little more than $11 billion in radio ads; and about $10 billion for advertising on the Web. The rest is divvied up among every kind of advertising you could ever imagine (and, no doubt, some types you couldn't).

Is it any wonder then that everywhere you turn — in most of your business and leisure activities — an advertisement for some product, service, or company is waiting to greet you? Consider the ubiquitous "www.fillintheblank.com" plastered on a towering billboard to promote the latest e-business wonder. What about the flashy advertisements that fill countless newspaper and magazine pages and sound off on the radio and television airwaves. Even a NASCAR racecar — with ads for Home Depot, Sears, Budweiser, or another company plastered all over it — is a form of advertising. Advertising is big — very big.

As the speed of business increases, however, the world of marketing is undergoing a radical transformation. Although the traditional, tried-and-true approaches — such as television advertisements and print ads — are alive and well, the quick rise of e-business and online shopping has turned the traditional world of advertising on its head. Internet advertising is growing by the day, while many of the more traditional sources of advertising — such as newspapers (the annual expenditures for which decreased by 2.4 percent from 2005 to 2006) — are experiencing a slow but steady decline.

This chapter takes a close look at today's wonderful world of *marketing,* which is the process of creating, pricing, promoting, and distributing products and services. This chapter discusses such key marketing techniques as advertising, publicity, promotion, special events, and premiums.

Eyeing the Basics of Advertising

At its heart, advertising is communication with consumers. More specifically, *advertising* is nonpersonal mass communication intended to encourage potential customers to buy a company's products or services. Why advertise? For one thing, companies lose, on average, 25 percent of their customers every year. This loss creates an ongoing need to encourage new customers to buy products or services.

Companies spend billions of dollars each year to advertise their products and services for other reasons as well (in addition to attracting new customers). Here are the key objectives of advertising:

- Improve brand recognition
- Persuade potential customers to buy from you rather than from a competitor
- Generate sales leads
- Promote special events and sales
- Improve the image of the business
- Increase the quantity of items/services purchased
- Increase the amount spent per order

The right advertising viewed by the right people at the right time and place can achieve all the goals in the preceding list. However, you have no guarantee that the right people will see your ad, or that they'll see it at the right time and place. But making this happen is critical to advertising success, and it's central to the focus of advertising agencies and clients alike. This section shows you how to place the right message with the right people where they are most likely to notice it.

Running a successful ad campaign

Companies spend billions of dollars and powerful advertising agencies work thousands of hours to fine-tune ad campaigns for consumers. Advertising has evolved into a fine art of creating a response from people who are a company's potential customers (see Chapter 15 for targeting consumers).

Advertising usually is an expensive proposition, and if it isn't done properly, it can be an incredibly easy way to waste money. Just like owning a boat, an advertising budget can become a big hole in which you dump all your money. Don't let your company's money go to waste and your customers slip through your fingers and into the competition's hands. Plan your advertising efforts and target your best audiences. Be sure to follow these steps:

1. **Set goals for your advertisement.**

   Are you trying to create a good feeling about your company among people who view your advertisement? Are you trying to get people to buy more of your products/services? Are you trying to convince readers that you put quality at the very top of your list of priorities? You should develop your advertisement after you understand why you're advertising, not before.

2. **Develop a budget.**

   Before you advertise, decide how much money you can devote to the effort and create a budget based on this estimate. After you decide on a budget, stick to it. Avoid the temptation to load your campaign full of unnecessary extras at the last minute.

3. **Choose a target market.**

   Who are your most likely customers or clients? Stay-at-home moms and dads who watch soap operas on television? Golfers who love to spend loads of money on vacations to exotic destinations? Techophiles who absolutely must have the latest-and-greatest gadget, whatever it may be? People in your target market should be your number-one priority when it comes to advertising.

4. **Pick a medium.**

   No, not a fortune teller — we're talking about picking which of the various kinds of media you'll use for your advertisement. Your decision will be based in large part on your target market. If you're selling sugar-coated cereal, then you know that you'll find some of your best customers watching Saturday-morning cartoons on television. If you're advertising some hot, new MP3 player, then you'll want to be online where your best customers will find you. For more information about where to place your ad, see the next section.

5. **Create your advertisement.**

   Although you can design your own advertisements, you'll likely be well served by bringing in a professional advertising firm to take on this important task. The best firms can work closely with you to ensure your input into the creative process and your ultimate satisfaction with the final result. This is a case where getting a referral from a colleague or other trusted source is a very good idea.

6. **Place your advertisement.**

Although designing an effective advertisement isn't necessarily an easy task, placing the ad generally is quite easy. Members of the media place a very high priority on advertising sales, and they'll be quite happy to take your money. As a result, most media outlets have made placing ads simple; they'll provide ample salespeople and customer service to help you through the process.

7. **Track your response.**

   Closely track the results of your advertising campaign to find out whether it has the desired effect. In most cases, getting results means people buying your product or service. Is there an uptick in sales after your advertisement runs for a week on a local radio station? Are you getting lots of click-throughs on your Web-based ad — and are these people actually purchasing your products? These kinds of results tell you almost immediately whether you've taken the right approach. They also reveal whether you should continue with a particular ad or whether you should dump it and move on to something else.

8. **Adjust and repeat as necessary.**

   After you have the results of your advertisement, you can adjust your ad — including the ad's design and where and how often it runs — and then repeat Steps 1–7. Ads that run more frequently — for example, on television once every hour, or once a month in a monthly magazine — get a better response from consumers (read: sell more product) than ads that run less frequently. However, this effect is offset by your budget and how much you can afford. When you assess your campaign, a positive change tells you that you're on the right track; a negative response tells you that you've got your work cut out for you.

Running a successful advertising campaign isn't an accident. If you take the time to create a plan to organize your own efforts, your advertising dollars will go further, and your money will hold out longer.

Locating the best place to advertise

The answer to the question, "Where's the best place to advertise?" is simple: Advertise where your potential customers are. If your target customers are buyers of cutting-edge computer equipment, chances are you'll find them surfing the Web or reading a variety of computer magazines that cater to their particular tastes and interests. If you spend your advertising dollars in places where you have no potential customers, you're wasting your money!

Surely one of these places will work for your company's advertisements, based on where your potential customers are:

✔ **Internet:** Web sites are currently the hottest, but also the most uncertain, places for companies to advertise. And, despite early indications, banner ads — those pesky advertisements at the top, side, and bottom of many Web sites — are only marginally effective, with click-through rates of no more than 0.5 percent. The Internet can be the least expensive place to go for advertising. With programs such as Google AdWords (see Chapter 17), you pay a small amount of money — often much less than a dollar — each time a potential buyer clicks on your ad. Expect advertising on the Internet to continue its dramatic growth into the future, but be aware that this form of advertising may be most appropriate for brand building, that is, when you're trying to increase customer awareness of your brand.

✔ **Newspapers:** Although newspapers traditionally have been the first stop for many company advertising campaigns, their popularity is declining as a media outlet, which means they're also becoming less popular as an advertising medium. More people than ever are getting their news directly — in near-real time — from the Web or from 24-hour cable news networks (such as CNN and MSNBC). Many newspapers have established a strong online presence to retain old readers while attracting new ones and tapping into new sources of advertising dollars.

✔ **Magazines:** Magazines are terrific places to advertise because they're typically targeted to specific audiences. You can choose from among car magazines, sewing magazines, news magazines, stereo equipment magazines, sailing magazines, and many more. Each publication has its own unique demographic of readers just waiting to read your advertisement! And don't forget that many magazines are also online, and you may be able to leverage your advertising dollars into both venues at a nominal additional cost.

✔ **Direct mail:** With direct mail, you get to choose who receives your marketing piece, and you get to decide exactly what message to send and how often to send it. Although not particularly effective by itself — the response rates for successful direct-mail campaigns are measured in the low single digits — direct mail can play an important role as part of an overall marketing campaign. E-mail direct marketing has much higher response rates (up to 15 percent), so many companies are choosing this less-expensive route to reach potential customers.

✔ **Radio:** When you have a good idea of who your prospective customers are, you can target them through the selective use of radio ads. Different radio stations have different kinds of listeners. A station that plays classical music all day long, for instance, has a much different listener profile than a station that plays alternative rock all day long.

✔ **Television:** Television advertising can easily be shown at specific times and days of the week, depending on your audience's demographics. A company that advertises on a mid-day television game show may never advertise on a late-night comedy show, and vice versa.

Keep in mind that television advertising is the most expensive form of advertising, so try the other forms first if you can.

✔ **Outdoor signs:** Billboards, the sides of buildings and buses, baseball stadium outfield walls — all are examples of outdoor advertising at its best. If you can put an ad on it, you can bet that someone already has somewhere. In fact, Google plans to create an advertisement on the surface of the moon that will be visible to viewers on Earth. That should get to ALL their target customers!

Keeping your ads honest

We know that you wouldn't intentionally create an advertisement that's deceptive or misleading; however, we must discuss the topic, because the history of marketing in the United States is replete with examples of advertising that's not only misleading, but also outright fraudulent.

Sellers are ultimately responsible for claims they make about their products and services. In most cases, third parties — such as advertising agencies, Web-site designers, or catalog marketers — also may be held liable for deceptive advertising if they participate in the preparation or distribution or are aware of the deceptive claims. (Check out the nearby sidebar "The FTC: The Big Brother of advertising" for more technical info about the laws.)

How can you protect your organization from being hung out to dry when a manufacturer misrepresents a product to you, and you in turn rely on that information in the ads you place? Be sure to ask for hard evidence that backs up a manufacturer's claims instead of simply repeating what the company says about its product. And what should you do if a manufacturer isn't able to provide you with the proof you seek?

✔ **Be especially careful about the claims you make for the product in your advertising.** Avoid making outrageous performance claims, health or weight-loss promises, or specific earnings guarantees, for instance.

✔ **Reconsider your decision to carry the product in question.** If you don't believe in a product you carry, after all, why should you sell it?

Here are some more tips from the Federal Trade Commission (FTC) to ensure that your advertising meets fair practices standards:

✔ Disclaimers and disclosures must be clear and conspicuous. That is, consumers must be able to notice, read or hear, and understand the information you present. A disclaimer or disclosure alone usually isn't enough to remedy a false or deceptive claim.

✔ Demonstrations must show how a product will perform under normal use.

✔ Refunds must be made to dissatisfied consumers — if you promise to make them.

> ✔ Sellers should take special care not to misrepresent a product or its performance when advertising to children. Advertising directed to children raises special issues. Children may have greater difficulty evaluating advertising claims and understanding the nature of the information you provide.

The FTC has published specific guidelines that you may find helpful in avoiding problems in your advertising initiatives. Be sure to check them out at www.ftc.gov/bcp/conline/pubs/buspubs/ruleroad.shtm.

Publicizing and Promoting Your Products and Services

You don't have to spend all your money on advertising to get your prospective customers' attention. In fact, for many companies, advertising is a small part of the marketing mix. For these companies, publicity and promotion are the most effective ways to spread the word about their products and services. This section focuses on how a company uses publicity and promotions to inform customers about their products and services, and how to use guerilla marketing techniques to gain an edge.

Publicity: Getting noticed

Publicity is a message communicated through the media about your company or your products/services because of perceived news value. Publicity is all about attracting the attention of your potential customers by first attracting the attention of the media — newspapers, magazines, radio talk shows, television news shows, Web sites, and similar media outlets.

Good publicity is worth its weight in gold, because when a potential customer sees, hears, or reads a media story about your organization, the perceived credibility of the message is higher than an advertisement offers. Why? Because potential customers tend to believe that the media is unbiased and therefore is more apt to tell the truth. For example, if potential customers encounter gushingly positive reviews of your studio's latest film in the local newspaper, a national magazine, and on radio talk shows, that publicity probably will have a much greater impact on increasing attendance figures than an advertising campaign could. On the other hand, if the reviews you receive are negative, no amount of advertising can save your film. Advertising is a powerful tool, but the right publicity at the right time and place can have much more power.

Besides, publicity is free to you. And that's definitely a benefit!

The FTC: The Big Brother of advertising

In the United States, the Federal Trade Commission (FTC) is charged with monitoring advertising and taking legal action against companies that break the law — something that happens quite regularly, unfortunately.

According to the FTC Web site (www.ftc.gov), the Federal Trade Commission Act empowers the FTC to act in the interest of all consumers to prevent deceptive and unfair acts or practices. Here are two things your organization should absolutely not do, unless you want to run afoul of Section 5 of the Act and have your advertising be considered deceptive:

✔ Engage in a representation, omission, or practice that misleads consumers

✔ Engage in a representation, omission, or practice that affects consumers' behavior or decisions about the product or service

In addition, the FTC considers an act or practice unfair when the injury it causes, or is likely to cause, is substantial, not outweighed by other benefits, and not reasonably avoidable.

The FTC Act is clear: Unfair or deceptive advertising is strictly prohibited in any medium. Advertising must tell the truth and not mislead consumers. Advertising claims may be considered misleading if relevant information is left out, or if the claims imply something that's simply not true. And it isn't enough to make a claim of performance in your advertising; claims must be substantiated — especially when the claims involve health, safety, or performance. The type of evidence required for proper substantiation depends on the product or service itself, the nature of the claim being made, and what experts in the field believe is required. For example, if your advertisement offers specific figures supporting a claim — "tests show that nine out of ten consumers are happier when using our products," for instance — you must have evidence that clearly shows that nine out of ten consumers really are happier when using your products.

As you can probably imagine, all kinds of ways — some traditional and some not-so-traditional — are available to attract attention to your company or product/service. This list presents some of the most common methods of getting business publicity:

✔ **Make a media appearance:** Have you ever watched a television show such as *Ellen* or *The Tonight Show* and wondered how it finds all those interesting people? For the most part, these people found the show themselves — through their publicists. Receiving publicity on a popular, nationally broadcast show can have an incredibly positive impact on a business and on the sales of its products and services. Members of the media are always looking for interesting people to interview; contact your local newspaper reporter, call in to a radio talk show, or try to get your company featured on a local television news show.

✔ **Send out press releases:** A *press release* is a written summary of some newsworthy bit of information about a company, its products, or its services, written in a way to be instantly digestible by the news media, that is, clearly and concisely. Try to keep releases down to a page — two at most. You'll lose your reader if it takes too long to get to your point. Most companies send out press releases all the time — particularly when they introduce new products or services or when they want to announce particular achievements or milestones. If you're not using news releases already, start doing it today. Create a list of media — both local and national — and start sending away. All it takes is one good story to get your company the attention it deserves.

✓ **Hold a press conference:** Want to get your message out to a lot of people at one time? Call a press conference. If your story is sufficiently newsworthy (perhaps your researchers just invented a better mousetrap), you'll have newspaper, radio, and television reporters falling all over themselves to cover your story. Send out a press release to make an event out of your announcement. If you have any friends in the media, invite them to attend. Generate some buzz!

✓ **Write a feature story:** Many magazines and newsletters — particularly those produced by professional associations and local lifestyle publishers — solicit stories from experts in various fields. If you're an author (or represent one) who just wrote a book on dieting and you want to get some good publicity, try writing an article on holiday weight-loss tips for a lifestyle magazine, for instance. In the process, you can plug your book and your Web site. Find the publications most appropriate for what your company does or produces and offer your services. You'll make a busy editor very happy when you do!

✓ **Submit an op-ed article/Letter to the editor:** Most newspapers invite readers and guest columnists to submit articles and letters that address current events or react to the editorial positions of the newspapers. For example, suppose that you're offended by your local newspaper's support of legislation that encourages city government purchases of imported vehicles. As the owner of a Ford vehicle dealership, you could write an op-ed piece (or a letter to the editor) decrying the outsourcing of American manufacturing capacity to foreign countries. Voice your support of legislation that requires the city government to exclusively "buy American." Coincidentally, this article likely will generate (mostly) favorable publicity for your dealership within the paper's distribution area, thereby increasing your sales and popularity.

✓ **Start (or publicize) a Web site:** Web sites themselves have become newsworthy. If a woman decides to sell her kidney on e-Bay, that's news. If a fan starts a Web site devoted to the intricacies of the *Star Wars* mythology, that's news. Most people and things (including companies and their products/services) are finding their 15 minutes of fame through the Internet. You can, too. If your organization doesn't have a Web site, get one. If you have a Web site, make sure that people find it. And how can you do that? Check out *Starting an Online Business For Dummies,* by Greg Holden (Wiley), for plenty of ideas.

Promotion: Conveying information

Whether you focus on advertising campaigns or not, the bulk of your company's marketing efforts and cash probably go into creating and distributing promotional materials. *Promotion* is the conveying of information about your company and its products and services. Although most promotional materials are written or printed for inexpensive and easy distribution, they can also take the form of e-mail messages and Web sites.

Chances are you've already used one or more of the following promotional items in your business:

✔ **Sales letter:** A *sales letter* is a written appeal to a customer to consider buying a company's products or services. A sales letter may contain information about the products or services, as well as special offers for buying sooner rather than later. A sales letter often is accompanied by brochures, product sheets, or other promotional materials.

✔ **Brochures:** Brochures generally present detailed information about a company, product, or service. They can take the form of a simple piece of paper, folded in half or in thirds, or they can be slick, full-color, multi-page marketing pieces or reports.

✔ **Product sheets:** Got a product? If so, you should have a product sheet to go along with it! A *product sheet* is a one-page (often front-only but sometimes front and back) description of a product along with a photo and key specifications. A product sheet should be complete enough to answer your customers' initial questions without overwhelming them.

✔ **Publicity photos:** Publicity photos give your customers (and the media) a good idea of what you and your products/services look like. Generally, publicity photos are accompanied by other promotional literature — perhaps brochures or press releases.

✔ **Audio/video:** Although brochures, product sheets, and publicity photos, for instance, are static, audiotapes and videotapes are dynamic, which means they can convey much more information than a simple piece of paper can. Today, audio or video promotional materials usually take the form of CDs or DVDs. However, with the rise of high-quality streaming video on the Web, the use of online promotional materials is surging.

To see some samples, check out the PR Newswire's MultiVu Web site at www.multivu.com and click on some of the What's Hot video news stories.

✔ **Promotional kit:** A *promotional kit* is a folder that contains some or all of the preceding items in this list. A kit for your company's latest disposable camera, for example, may contain a sales letter, a brochure, a product sheet, a publicity photo, a video, and a working sample of the camera. The purpose is to give potential customers an in-depth look at your product, which hopefully will generate interest and sales.

✔ **Web sites:** Many companies are transferring their promotional materials to their Web sites for a couple reasons. First, doing so costs little or nothing, because you've already invested the money to create the promotional materials. Second, a Web site is on 24 hours a day, 7 days a week — it doesn't sleep, and it doesn't take breaks (well, unless the server goes down!). However, because Web sites depend on people making an effort to discover and visit them, you need to find ways to help consumers along. Plaster your URL everywhere possible: on your products, in your advertising, on blogs where your prospective customers hang out, on the side of the Goodyear blimp — wherever people might see it and be compelled to take the time to visit your site.

As with all marketing materials, you should tailor the use of your promotional material specifically for your intended recipients. Figure out what kinds of materials your target customers will most likely respond to, and then provide them with these materials.

Guerrilla marketing

Organizations in today's marketplace have become faster and more flexible, and companies increasingly are aiming their products/services at specific niches of customers. As a result, the traditional ways of marketing are becoming less and less effective. In their place, advertisers are adopting techniques that are unconventional by traditional marketing standards. *Guerrilla marketing* is the label applied to this particular brand of marketing.

According to Jay Conrad Levinson, the guru of guerilla marketing and author of *Guerrilla Marketing, 4th Edition: Easy and Inexpensive Strategies for Making Big Profits from Your Small Business* (Houghton Mifflin), this new approach can be summed up as

> *Achieving conventional goals, such as profits and joy, with unconventional methods, such as investing energy instead of money.*

Levinson, being the guru that he is, has developed five rules that reflect the guerrilla marketer's view of the world:

✔ **The 10/30/60 rule:** According to Levinson, you should invest 10 percent of your marketing budget to talking to everyone in your marketing universe — whether or not they match your customer profile. Use another 30 percent of the budget to convince people who match your customer profile — your prospects — that they should become your customers. Devote the last 60 percent to marketing to your current customers — producing the most profits at a lower cost per sale.

✔ **The 1/10/100 rule:** This rule says that $1 spent communicating with your staff is equivalent to $10 spent communicating with the trade, which is equivalent to $100 spent communicating with your customers.

In other words, communicating to your employees can be the most cost-effective way to transmit your marketing message to your prospects and current customers. Train all your employees to be familiar with your products and services, so they can accurately tell others about them.

✔ **The rule of thirds:** According to Levinson, one-third of your online marketing budget should go to designing and posting your company's Web site; one-third should go to marketing the site offline; and the final third should go to improving and maintaining your Web site, keeping it entertaining and fresh.

✔ **The rule of twice:** This rule says that remaining truly competitive online will cost you twice as much as you think it will cost.

✔ **The rule of the ruler:** This rule states that although you can delegate the marketing function to others in your organization, you can't delegate the passion and the vision that you feel for it. To ensure marketing success, take command of your company's marketing process and keep a close eye on it, regardless of who's in charge.

Are you ready to supercharge your marketing efforts? Give guerrilla marketing a try — it could make a difference for you. For more information about guerrilla marketing, check out Levinson's Guerrilla Marketing Online Web site at www.gmarketing.com.

Grabbing Consumers' Attention with Special Events and Premiums

If you really want to attract attention to your company, special events and premiums have the potential to do just that. For example, when the automotive company BMW really wants to attract the attention of its potential customers, it invites them to attend the Ultimate Driving Experience, where customers can drive the company's new model cars, accompanied by skilled driving instructors. As BMW says, after you spend a day driving its cars, "your biggest challenge will be saying good-bye." If you want to see how special events and premiums can help you reach your potential and current customers, check out this section for more info.

Giving customers a hands-on experience: Special events

Special events provide a unique forum for potential customers to view, touch, and actually try a company's products before they buy them. In some cases (such as sponsorships), a company's involvement may be a bit more subtle, with no mention of products or services that the company provides. In any case, the goal of a special event is to raise the awareness of companies and their products/services in the eyes of potential customers.

The following list presents several different kinds of special events for different kinds of situations:

- ✓ **Trade shows:** Every industry — from automotive, to online media, to poultry, to publishing — has trade shows. These shows attract a lot of attention from potential buyers. (Actually, they mostly attract attention from competitors that want to scope the competition!) Trade shows allow companies to exhibit their wares to potential customers and the media alongside the products of competitors. Many companies rely on trade shows to generate sales and new business.

- ✓ **Demonstrations:** If you've ever been to a grocery store where a jolly person was cooking and handing out food samples, you've experienced a marketing demonstration. Demonstrations enable consumers to experience (and sometimes even try) products and to make informed decisions about buying them.

- ✓ **Sponsorships:** Many companies sponsor public events to improve their public images while also attracting potential customers. Car races, beauty pageants, charity walks — all are events that need sponsors to help further their causes. And these sponsorships can help companies reach their desired audiences.

Giving away useful items with a message: Premiums

Have you ever been to a baseball game where the home team gave away ball caps? Have local real-estate agents left you calendars with their photos and phone numbers on them? Have you ever received a pencil or pen with the name of a local plumber, or a T-shirt emblazoned with the Web site of the world's largest bookstore? These are all examples of _marketing premiums_.

Premiums serve the dual purpose of getting an item that customers will regularly use in their hands, and sending them a marketing message on that item by emblazoning it with the company or product name. Each time a customer uses the item, he or she receives a small dose of advertising.

Here are some of the more popular premiums that companies put out:

- ✓ Pens and pencils
- ✓ Coffee mugs
- ✓ T-shirts

- ✔ Pocket knives
- ✔ Mouse pads
- ✔ Baseball caps
- ✔ Calculators
- ✔ Tote bags

If you decide to distribute premiums, set a budget in advance and be sure that you're getting as much bang for the buck as possible. If your budget is $25,000, for example, you should get 5,000 premiums for $5 apiece — enough for all your current customers and an extra 4,000 prospects — instead of getting only 2,500 premiums at a cost of $10 each. It all depends on your plan for distributing the premiums and which audience you're targeting.

Don't buy cheap, inexpensive-looking premiums, however! Premiums are a reflection of your company. If the premiums that you hand out are cheap and shoddy, you'll send a cheap and shoddy message to your customers and prospects. Get the best-quality items that your budget can support.

Chapter 17

Navigating the New World of Selling

*I*n years past, salespeople often focused on maximizing the amount of product that they sold, to the detriment of building long-term relationships with their customers. Today, however, salespeople and the companies they work for realize that building relationships with customers offers tremendous advantages. In a trusting relationship, customers are happier, salespeople sell more, and the company's bottom line improves. It's truly a win-win situation.

In this chapter, we explore the shift from the old style of selling to the new style of selling. We explain person-to-person selling and outline the good and the bad of telemarketing. We take a look at selling on the Internet and to other businesses. Finally, we help you consider how to manage your customer relationships and present ways you can keep only your best customers. By the time you're done reading, you'll understand why companies that build relationships rather than just sales goals are sure to prosper in the coming years.

Build Relationships: Forget the Hard Sell

Used-car dealer. Slowly say those words to yourself. What picture comes to mind? You probably can't find a better example of the old style of selling than a used-car salesperson. He is aggressive, pushy, and focused only on making a sale — any sale — now! What will happen two months, two weeks, or even two days from now isn't important. A used-car salesperson absolutely won't let you walk out of the dealership without putting the hard sell on you.

This old-style approach to selling is called *transaction marketing* because it focuses on individual sales, or *transactions*. In transaction marketing, buyers and sellers usually have no ongoing relationship with one another, and communications are limited. The primary goal is short-term: Sell something and sell it now. What? You don't like that pink Cadillac? How about if we repaint it for you? What do we need to do to get you to buy this car right now?

Many salespeople and the companies that employ them (including car dealerships) are now trying a new approach because people are becoming less responsive to the old one. This new approach is based on relationships, not transactions. Indeed, more and more companies are discovering that creating ongoing, long-term relationships with clients and customers can pay off — in increased sales and in decreased marketing costs — over the long run. And these results mean a much healthier bottom line.

With this new approach, called *relationship-based selling,* the focus is on

- ✔ Building a long-term relationship with the customer
- ✔ Selling the benefits of your product or service
- ✔ Providing fanatical customer service
- ✔ Being totally committed to the customer
- ✔ Talking to the customer continuously

Why the change in emphasis from transactions to relationships? It's really quite simple: People prefer to buy from companies with which they have relationships. They want to do business with companies that show they care about their customers. You can show that you care through your commitment to your customers, your superior customer service, and the importance you place on maintaining a relationship rather than simply selling a product.

So, suppose that you want to change your company's sales approach from transaction-based to relationship-based. Exactly how do you do that? Here are the four keys to building relationships with your clients and customers; put these to work in your organization right away:

- ✔ **Build trust.** The first step in developing long-term relationships with your clients and customers is to build trust by doing what you say you're going to do. Trust is the glue that holds business relationships together and makes them stronger and deeper over time.
- ✔ **Create bonds.** Long-term business relationships depend on the creation of bonds between organizations and customers (or between two organizations). Bonds are formed when organizations and people find that they

have mutual goals and interests, and they decide to work together to take advantage of them. As relationships grow, these bonds get stronger.

✔ **Be empathetic.** Being empathetic means that you see a situation through the eyes of another party. If you're empathetic as a salesperson, you'll develop an understanding of a customer that goes much deeper than a relationship focused only on a transaction. Empathy is an emotional link that builds trust between parties.

✔ **Encourage reciprocity.** Sometimes, you have to give a little to get a lot. *Reciprocity* is giving up something that you want to get something that you need. When reciprocity is present in the business selling process — from customer to supplier and vice versa — the result is a stronger business relationship that's built to last.

Telemarketing: Dialing for Dollars

If you've ever had your dinner or slumber interrupted by a telephone sales call, you may think that telemarketing is a bad thing. Certainly, few people relish calls from fast-talking insurance salespeople, vinyl home-siding contractors, real estate brokers, and, more recently, pesky automated calling systems that never sleep and can complete thousands of calls a day. But for companies that use these contacts to sell products and services, telemarketing is a good thing — often a very good thing.

Keep in mind that, there may be better ways of selling for your particular business than telemarketing. In the United States, recent Federal Communications Commission (FCC) rulings on telemarketing, along with the Federal Trade Commission's (FTC) National Do Not Call Registry, have made life much more difficult for telemarketers. Consider all your selling options carefully before you commit significant resources to a telemarketing campaign.

Inbound telemarketing

If you've ever called a company on a toll-free number to place an order for a product or service, you've participated in *inbound* (or *passive*) *telemarketing*. Inbound telemarketing is a particularly effective and fruitful sales technique, because people generally call only when they're ready to place orders to purchase your product or service. These customers often call as a result of print ads, catalogs, radio or television advertising, a Web site, or other forms of advertising that your company uses (see Chapter 16).

Here are some ways you can use inbound telemarketing to your benefit:

- Order taking
- Help-desk solutions
- Ticket sales
- Web site call processing
- Surveys and questionnaires
- Dealer location
- Seminar registration
- Reservations

Although many companies run their own inbound telemarketing operations, other enterprising organizations outsource these operations to call centers — both offshore and onshore — that are specifically geared to handle the task of inbound telemarketing. Call centers are often less expensive than hiring and training in-house staff, buying telecommunications equipment, and leasing phone lines. Another benefit is that the individuals working at call centers generally are specially trained for the task. And many call centers can offer your customers 24-hour, seven-day-a-week service.

Outbound telemarketing

Outbound telemarketing is the active kind of telemarketing that most people associate with the use of the term. In *outbound telemarketing,* salespeople place phone calls to prospects, make quick sales pitches, and then try to sell them products or services. If they can't make a sale right away, telemarketers try to gauge the customers' interest; if they sense some hope, they can turn over the prospects to full-time salespersons who can make more sophisticated sales pitches.

Here are some ways you can put outbound telemarketing to work for your company:

- Sales lead generation
- Customer service
- Appointment setting
- Customer surveys
- Sales campaigns
- Database updates
- Customer care and retention
- Follow-up calls

Just as some companies specialize in inbound telemarketing for other businesses, some companies specialize in outbound telemarketing. You can find plenty by turning to the "Telemarketing Services" listings in the Yellow Pages or by doing an Internet search; just type in the keyword "telemarketing." If you decide to outsource your outbound telemarketing, be sure that the company you hire has a good reputation in the industry. Also, confirm that the company has experience selling the kinds of products or services that you offer. Ask for references and check them.

Selling on the Web

Many companies today are working hard to bring back a level of personalization that many consumers haven't experienced in a long time — and they're doing it through their Web sites. One such company is Amazon.com, one of the nation's top online retailers. It has designed a hugely successful computer database around its Web site, which sells everything from books and music to groceries and home-improvement supplies.

As a returning customer to Amazon.com, you'll be greeted with a list of recommended purchases — all by title and all based on your tastes as reflected by your previous orders. The more you order, the more Amazon.com knows about your personal preferences, and the better the database gets at guessing the items you may want to purchase. What Amazon.com has done with its database is nothing short of astounding, and it offers a hint of the promise of online selling's future.

As time goes on, shopping on the Internet is destined to become a more personalized experience. And as online retailers get to know consumers better, the people reward the retailers with long-term business relationships. The smart e-commerce companies are already well on their way to making shopping on the Internet a rewarding experience for everyone. In the following sections, we consider some specifics of selling on the Web, including business-to-business ("b2b") transactions and online advertising.

Online retailing and wholesaling for business-to-business transactions

The early focus of commerce on the Internet has been on retail sales to individual consumers. This focus is beginning to change as software and security evolve to a point where businesses can collaborate with each other safely and securely. Today, *online retailing* (selling directly to consumers) and *wholesaling* (selling to businesses, which then sell to other businesses or directly to consumers) are more and more popular. For example, Global eXchange Services (which manages one of the world's largest electronic communities, with more than 100,000 trading partners and more than 1 billion transactions a year), IBM, Microsoft, and other software developers are working hard to make business-to-business selling over the Internet speedy, safe, and secure.

For instance, although most companies have chosen to develop closed, private computer networks for their customers to place orders in the past, others are now pushing the envelope by driving sales applications onto the Internet. Executives at clothing manufacturer Fruit of the Loom, Inc., decided against a private network and went with an Internet-based system, initially made available to its 50 key wholesalers. These wholesalers received a dedicated "Activewear Online" computer system, specifically programmed to display Fruit of the Loom catalogs, process electronic purchase orders, and manage product inventories. The Internet makes all these transactions and more possible. (For more on business to business selling, see the later section "Doing Business with Other Businesses.")

Online advertising: Replacing click-throughs with search-engine marketing

In the old days of the Web, most advertising took the form of banner ads — boxes (usually containing just text in the earliest days, with graphics and photographs entering the picture as time went on) pitching some product or service that led to special Web pages or other Web sites when you clicked on them (also called *click-throughs*). Also, as soon as you visited some Web sites in the old days, ad after ad would pop up, grabbing control of your computer and whisking you away into a wonderful state of product bliss. Or so the advertisers would have you think! However, as the Web has become more heavily traveled, advertising has become more sophisticated — and trickier.

Today, you still see banner ads (many of which are animated — all the better to attract your attention) and pop-ups, which even the latest Internet browsers can never seem to completely defeat. However, the big news in online advertising today is *search engine marketing (SEM)*. The three largest SEM vendors are Google AdWords, Yahoo! Search Marketing, and Microsoft adCenter. In general, SEM is growing faster than traditional forms of advertising.

Businesses have voted with their wallets, and the vote is in: Search engine marketing really works. In its fiscal year ending 2006, Google brought in about $10.5 billion from its online advertising services. But how does SEM work? The following list shows how the most popular SEM service — Google AdWords — works so you can see how it may help your organization:

1. **Register your company/product/service on the Google AdWords Web site (adwords.google.com).**

   As part of your registry, you'll decide which level of service to sign up for (starter edition or standard edition), pick out keywords that the search engine will use to link your ad to search results, and write your advertisement. AdWord advertisements are short — just a one-line title and two text lines. As part of its services, Google provides tips and instructions for completing the steps.

2. **Decide how much you want to spend.**

   As an AdWord user, you set both an overall budget limit and a maximum price you're willing to pay when someone clicks through your ad. For example, you may decide on an overall limit of $500 and a maximum price per click of $1. You don't pay for your ad unless someone clicks on it, so in this example, you won't exhaust your total budget until consumers click on your ad 500 times.

3. **Target your advertising to selected customers or areas.**

   You can decide if you want your ad to show up whenever anyone in the world clicks through or just when people in your city or state click through. For example, if you have a dog-sitting business in Phoenix, Arizona, it won't do you much good if a customer in Moscow or Beijing sees your ad and clicks on it.

4. **Monitor your results.**

   Google provides extensive statistics on your ads that you can use to check your success — or lack thereof. With this information, you can determine if you need to make adjustments in your approach.

5. **Make adjustments until you find the ad setup that works for your product/service and goals.**

   AdWords give advertisers who set a higher price per click priority over those who set a lower price per click. Continuing our earlier example, if you set a price of $1 per click and a competitor sets a price of $2 per click, Google will place your competitor's ad higher on the list of ads than yours. If you find that your ad is getting little traffic because it hardly ever shows up, you have to increase the price per click as well as your overall budget to accommodate increased traffic. You may also try different keywords to increase your visibility.

The world of online advertising is in a state of constant flux. With each passing year, new technologies lead to new ways to get ads in front of potential customers. If you decide that online advertising is for you (and most companies today utilize at least some form of online advertising), consider your options carefully and always measure your results. If a particular approach isn't working for you, don't hesitate to try something else.

Doing Business with Other Businesses

The nature of selling to other businesses has changed dramatically over the past decade. The change isn't so much a shift from transaction selling to relationship selling, because businesses have long depended on developing strong relationships with business customers to promote sales. The change is mostly due to the mass computerization of the ordering process and the widespread use of the Web for e-commerce applications. In the following sections, we examine some details of doing business with other business, including electronic data interchange and vendor-managed inventory.

The need for speed (and accuracy): Electronic data interchange

Electronic data interchange (EDI) is a set of standards for the exchange of orders and other business documents from computer to computer in a machine-readable format. In simple terms, EDI is a conversation between two businesses or within a business that's expressed in an electronic format. EDI is the most commonly used electronic commerce format in business because it allows businesses to reduce their costs and improve their efficiency and competitiveness.

Specifically, electronic data interchange offers these benefits:

- **Speed:** Information traveling between computers moves very rapidly with little or no human intervention to slow it down. Sending electronic data (such as purchasing information) across the country takes only seconds.

- **Accuracy:** Computer-to-computer data interchange totally eliminates the errors that can occur when a supplier receives regular manual orders and then rekeys them into its ordering system. EDI leaves virtually no room for mistakes, assuming that the order was correct to begin with.

- **Economy:** The price is right! It costs very little or nothing to send ordering information electronically from buyer to seller. You also see additional savings because of the elimination of several tasks, including the rekeying of data, human handling, routing, and delivery. All in all, EDI results in a substantial reduction in the cost of a transaction.

Before the advent of EDI, most business-to-business sales were handled via paper purchase orders. A buyer received a purchase request from someone in her organization. The buyer reviewed catalogs or discussed the requirement with salespeople to get price quotes or other information about the items to be purchased. After the buyer settled on the items to purchase and where to purchase them, she generated a purchase order to be typed up and mailed out to a vendor. Upon receiving the purchase order, the vendor manually entered the items into its shipping system, pulled the items to be shipped, generated an invoice, and shipped the items and the invoice to the customer. All this back and forth took a lot of time — at least a week or more — and the various data-entry points along the way often introduced mistakes.

EDI short-circuits this entire process by transmitting an electronic purchase order from the buyer to the vendor instantly and then triggering the processing of an order immediately. In many cases, companies ship the items on the same day that the purchase orders are sent out. In addition, EDI systems send accurate receiving documents to the customers when the items are shipped and send invoices directly to the customers' accounts payable departments for payment.

Choosing your partners: Vendor-managed inventory

Some companies — such as manufacturers of aircraft engines or hospitals, which require large quantities of consumable items — use a lot of inventory. For these businesses, the process of ordering, receiving, and stocking inventory can be a very time-intensive process — especially if the company is using old-fashioned, manual systems. What if you could forget about managing your inventory altogether? What if your inventory was always kept up-to-date automatically, with no need for human intervention (ordering, receiving, stocking, tracking) within your organization? *Vendor-managed inventory (VMI)* does just that — and more.

In the uniquely collaborative partnerships formed by VMI, companies farm out their inventory management processes to one or more vendors. These vendors keep their clients properly stocked at exactly the right amounts of inventory at all times. VMI contractors manage this process; they receive regular inventory sales or usage data via their computers — often through the use of electronic data interchange (EDI) and the Internet (see the previous section).

A typical vendor-managed inventory system consists of the following modules:

- ✔ **Inventory-level monitoring:** Indicates past and present inventory levels for all items being monitored. Includes such data as item names, item quantities and reorder points, current inventory levels, and past inventory levels.

- ✔ **Replenishment status:** Indicates vendor replenishment orders. Includes such data as order number, order amount, order date, ship date, and planned delivery date.

- ✔ **Logistics status:** Indicates the logistics status of past and present replenishment orders. Includes such data as order number, ship date, carrier name, truck ID number, and planned delivery date.

- ✔ **Consumption status:** Used for determining planned consumption by the vendor. Includes such data as item location, planned consumption, and planned special events (such as overtime, holiday closings, and so on).

Vendor-managed inventory requires tremendous trust on the part of the customer — the kind of trust that results in long-term business relationships. After the VMI system is up and running and the purchasing company is starting to realize the benefits, the VMI contractor can expect to have a very long and prosperous selling relationship with the customer.

CRM: Getting a Handle on Your Contacts

Customer relationship management (CRM) is the latest-and-greatest way to manage your business's relationships with your customers. In essence, a CRM is simply a computerized database that tracks information about customers. In the old days, customer information — names, addresses, phone numbers, and so on — was filed away on index (or Rolodex) cards or on sheets of paper stapled into file folders. Today, digitized CRM systems are light years ahead of those old approaches to doing business, and a number of computer systems on the market specialize in capturing, storing, and analyzing customer information.

Here's a list of the functions you'll find in a typical CRM system:

- ✔ Company and contact management
- ✔ Lead management
- ✔ Activity management
- ✔ Opportunity management
- ✔ Charting
- ✔ Reporting
- ✔ E-mail marketing and mailing lists management
- ✔ Sales forecasting
- ✔ Microsoft Outlook e-mail integration
- ✔ Notes
- ✔ Business Intelligence management

Computerized CRM systems offer the following benefits to the businesses that use them:

✔ **Enables companies to provide better customer service by centralizing customer information and making it more readily to those who need it.**

✔ **Makes it easy to share customer information throughout an organization — just down the hall or around the world.** You can quickly share info because of its ready availability on most any company computer or even data-enabled phones such as Treo and Blackberry.

✔ **Helps companies give customers exactly what they want, when and where they want it.** As customer ordering information is compiled over a long period of time, salespeople can better anticipate future customer needs.

✔ **Makes the entire selling process more efficient.** It saves both time and money that used to be wasted in trying to coordinate a variety of customer information systems — often paper based — in scattered offices.

✔ **Helps companies retain their current customers by keeping them satisfied while they search to find new ones.**

Is there a CRM system in your company's future? If your business has anything to do with sales, there probably already is! Although you can use CRM software for all sorts of sales-related tasks, the systems generally fall within one of two categories:

✔ **Sales force automation (SFA),** which facilitates the sales process. The system keeps track of current customers, sales leads for new customers, and forecasts and reports on the company's sales pipeline.

✔ **Customer service/support (CSS),** which helps track customer complaints, service requests, repair scheduling, and other customer service-related tasks.

Because choosing the right CRM is a critical decision for your business, take your time when scouting out the right product for you. The right system for you is the one that works and will allow for future growth. Ask your colleagues or industry contacts what they use, and ask the CRM salesperson for references who you can call or e-mail to discuss their satisfaction. And when you select a system and implement it, monitor the rollout closely — checking in often with your salespeople — to make sure it is doing what it is supposed to do.

Keeping Your Best Customers

Many companies make two major mistakes that keep them from increasing their sales and improving their profits (something that doesn't always occur simultaneously, by the way):

✔ They trap themselves in a continual cycle of scrambling to find new customers.

✔ They spend enormous amounts of time and money trying to keep *all* their customers.

Both strategies tend to backfire.

Experts often say that 80 percent of a company's sales and profit come from just 20 percent of its customers. If this is indeed the case, it makes sense to do whatever you can to retain your very best customers and to quit wasting time on your very worst customers — the ones who spend the least money but cause you the most headaches. The following sections discuss how you can build relationships to hang on to your best customers, as well as identify your bad customers so you can get rid of them.

Identifying your best customers

Who are your best customers? Very simply, they're the customers who account for the greatest percentage of your sales — the loyal, repeat customers who cost you the least to maintain and send more dollars to your bottom line. You like these customers! If you adopt a good customer relationship management (CRM) system (see the previous section), finding the best customers — and the worst ones — will be easy!

You can devise your own measures for determining who's a valuable customer, but one way to do it involves statistics. This suggestion is for people who like to crunch numbers. For the rest of you, look at the total revenue generated by the customer and the frequency of its purchases. Compare those figures against other customers. You may decide to take the top 25 percent of your customers and see what they contribute to your total revenues.

Okay, back to statistics. For a moment, look at each of your customers as a series of transactions over time. Now follow these steps:

1. **Calculate the present value of future purchases based on the customer's buying patterns to date.**

2. **To that number, add the projected value of referrals from that customer.**

3. **Subtract the cost of maintaining the customer (costs from advertising, promotions, and so on).**

The figure you calculate is the customer's *lifetime value* to your company. (If you've forgotten how to calculate present value, or never knew how to do it, look in Chapter 12 for a quick refresher course.) Although you shouldn't use lifetime value as the only determinant as to whether you should keep a particular customer, it is a key consideration.

Identifying your best customers is just the first step. You need to find ways to encourage them to *remain* your best customers. More on that in the next section.

Rewarding and keeping your best customers

Customers love to feel as though they're important to the companies that they hand money to. They want you to respect what they're contributing to your success. When you get a chance, therefore, reward your best customers so they *stay* your best customers. The following sections discuss a couple more strategies for making sure that you keep your best customers.

Frequency awards

Airline frequent-flier programs have spawned many frequency reward clones for other industries. The basic principle of *frequency programs* is that the more your customers buy from you, the more benefits they get, and those benefits increase with use. Here are some examples of effective frequency programs:

- Some drugstores have customers sign up for cosmetic cards, photo development cards, and vitamin cards. Every time a customer buys a product in one of those lines, the store stamps the card. When the customer has filled the card, he or she gets, say, a $5 discount on the next purchase.

- Selling season passes to theme parks, water parks, miniature golf courses, and the like is a way of providing discounts to the customers who use those facilities most.

- VIP programs reward a company's most frequent customers. These customers may get special days to shop at discounted rates or receive invitations to events designed exclusively for them. Companies such as Macy's department store have these programs.

Complaint marketing

No company likes to hear complaints, but they're a fact of life in business so you may as well learn to deal with them positively. Look at it this way: Complaints are merely a way to find out how you can improve your company. Continuous improvement is one of the core principles of running a successful business. Plus, when you give customers a forum to complain, you show that you have nothing to hide and really value their opinions.

A win-win strategy for great long-term customer relationships

After you identify your best customers and do what you can to reward/keep them in the short term, you should consider how to keep them happy for life. The strategy we recommend is based on the characteristics of this new business world we live in. If you apply this win-win strategy in your business, you'll sell to satisfied customers who keep coming back for more. Specifically, the strategy is centered on four principles of the new marketplace, which we describe in the following sections.

Owning your market

To be successful in business today, you have to create your own niche in the market and be the leader. When you're the market leader, people look at you differently. You have an automatic edge over your potential competitors. You set the standards in the market and can encourage others to develop products and services that are complementary to yours. That was Microsoft's strategy when it carved out a niche in computer operating systems with its Windows product.

If you find that competitors aren't meeting certain customer needs in your industry, you've found a niche that your business can serve.

Positioning your company

Products come and go, but if you run your business correctly, your company will last for a long time. Therefore, it makes sense to spend as much or even more time positioning your company in the market than your products and services. *Positioning* is attempting to control the way customers perceive your company and its products/services. Taking a proactive approach to positioning your company is important, because if you don't position it, your customers, distributors, suppliers, and competitors certainly will. And they may not position your company the way you want.

With positioning, perception is reality. Whether what's perceived is true or not, the customer makes decisions based on his perception. So, it's important that the perception of your company and its products/services is a positive one. Customers can perceive two identical products differently depending on how they're marketed. For example, you've probably seen a brand-name product in a store located right next to a generic brand that has the same ingredients. Many consumers purchase the name brand for more money just because they perceive a difference, even though one doesn't exist.

Mass customizing (no, this isn't an oxymoron)

One great benefit of technology is that it allows businesses to customize their products and services to meet the specific needs of customers. *Mass customization* is giving your customers what they want, when they want it, and in the specific way they want it. Anything that can be digitized can be customized; manufacturers that use computer-aided manufacturing techniques, for instance, can program in customer changes by pushing a few buttons. Here's another example: Companies that produce written documents can easily customize wording to speak directly to specific customers.

The fundamental requirement for mass customization is a good relationship with your customers. When they trust you, they can guide you in your efforts to give them exactly what they want.

Focusing on things you can't touch or see

Businesses often become so product/service-focused that they can't see or they ignore what's really significant. The most important things about your company and its products/services are the things you can't see or touch — the intangibles, in other words:

- ✔ Quality
- ✔ Customer focus
- ✔ Reliability

When your competitors start competing based on price alone, the only way you can gain an advantage is by adding value with intangibles. Customers tend to buy from businesses with which they have ongoing relationships and where they perceive value because they've invested time and effort.

Getting rid of bad customers

It may sound harsh to encourage you to get rid of your bad customers, but the reality is that they're holding your business back. They're the ones who have a bad debt history with your company. They buy infrequently and in so little volume that if you ran the numbers, you'd find that keeping them actually is costing you money. The most valuable customers, on the other hand, are making you money.

Every company has good customers and bad customers. Your goal is to keep the good customers and get rid of the bad ones. There are two key ways to get rid of your bad customers:

- ✔ **Convert your bad customers into good ones.** Ideally, it would be great if you could simply convert your bad customers into good ones. In some cases, you may want to give it a try. How? Sometimes, you just need to give a bad customer a wake-up call to let them know that the party is about to end. For example, you can say, "If you don't order at least $10,000 worth of coffee beans within the next month, we'll have to ask you to take your business elsewhere." Or you can try giving your bad customers special incentives to buy more of your products/services — such as a one-time discount for signing onto a long-term buying program.

✔ **"Fire" your bad customers by refusing to do business with them.** Unfortunately, some bad customers aren't worth saving. These customers will be bad forever, no matter what steps you take. Do what you can to identify these customers as soon as you can and then simply refuse to do business with them. You don't need to be nasty about it; just tell them that they need to find other companies to do business with. The breakup may sting for a little bit, but short-term hurt is well worth the long-term gain to your business.

Part V
Other Important Stuff

The 5th Wave   By Rich Tennant

"Get ready, I think they're starting to drift."

In this part . . .

We couldn't fit a variety of other important MBA topics in the previous parts of this book, so we created a new part altogether (how's that for problem solving?). In this part, we discuss manufacturing, distribution, and quality — and how the latest technology has had a major impact on each. We explore the most important concepts of risk management. We reveal the secrets of successful negotiation — and how to find win-win solutions. Finally, we review the basics of everyone's favorite business topic: economics.

Chapter 18

Manufacturing and Distribution: It's a Brave New World

. . . .

In This Chapter

▶ Understanding the manufacturing evolution

▶ Purchasing the right amount at the right time and in the right quantities

▶ Getting a grip on materials management and scheduling

▶ Producing a quality product/service

▶ Maintaining your product and manufacturing processes

▶ Looking at distribution as a competitive advantage

. . . .

*O*ver the past decade, manufacturing productivity has increased substantially due to technological advances and globalization, which enable manufacturers to automate routine tasks, track production, coordinate the supply chain, and access low-cost labor. This productivity means that businesses often have excess capacity that they can use to partner with smaller businesses that have compatible products. Excess capacity and the desire to partner with other businesses to take advantage of individual core competencies have helped smaller businesses find a home for manufacturing in the United States.

We've also now seen a return to the idea of giving customers exactly what they want, when they want it. In this chapter, you find out how the manufacturing process has changed and what you can do to maximize profit without sacrificing quality and customer satisfaction. A typical manufacturing plant has five broad functional areas:

✔ Purchasing

✔ Materials management and production scheduling

✔ Production

✔ Quality control

✔ Maintenance

Each area must be designed, and metrics for the process defined, so that the manufacturer can maintain effectiveness at all points of the production process. Along the way in this chapter, we cover these processes and look at how they can be employed most effectively.

Manufacturing Today Is a New Game

Manufacturing traditionally has been a cost center for businesses, with the purpose of making products in batches — large batches. So, the goal of the production manager has been to control costs — at all costs. The idea that manufacturing could be a strategic part of a business didn't cross anyone's mind until fairly recently. Manufacturing is now seen as a strategic part of the larger supply chain for the business, and process innovation has become a significant competitive advantage for businesses that practice it.

Too many manufacturers devote the majority of their budgets to new product development and don't think about how important new process development is. In today's markets, the way you manufacture a product often is the most critical element — perhaps even more so than the product itself. Your innovative process that competitors don't have will give you a competitive advantage in the market and enable you to satisfy your customers' need for speed.

To successfully innovate in both products and processes, strategic manufacturing relies on four critical principles:

- **Real-time data collection:** With the rapid pace of production today and the need to reduce operating costs, manufacturers require information in real time. Bar codes and radio frequency identification (RFID) tags and readers enable manufacturers to electronically tag parts and boxes of the finished product. Then, using a remote reading device they can locate any item and immediately see all the pertinent information about that item, such as part number, date, supplier, and so forth.

- **Flexible and intelligent production processes:** Highly competitive markets require that manufacturers be adaptable to change and quick to respond to customer needs. CNC machines (computer numerical control) can receive input from computer designs and fabricate a component to exact specifications. And you can modify your designs and produce that modified product quickly and easily, saving time and money.

- **Global supply-chain management:** When your product moves through different plants for manufacturing, packaging, and distribution, you can track and manage the process in real time to ensure quality and timeliness. For example, C.R. Bard, a medical device company, adopted an enterprise resource planning (ERP) system that performs this task. The ERP system can track and manage a medical device from the company's manufacturing facility in South Carolina, to its packaging facility in

Mexico, to its sterilization facility in Covington, Georgia, and finally to its distribution facility in another location in Covington. The company can monitor the progress of any product in real time. These systems are often used in combination with RFID tracking devices.

✔ **Just-in-time sequencing in the supply chain:** Many manufacturers have adopted the just-in-time process for managing raw materials and inventory to avoid overstocking, which is costly. For example, Delphi, a supplier to the automobile industry, synchronized its manufacturing activities with those of the assembly line of its customer. It delivers parts when the customer needs them, in the same sequence as the product being assembled.

The next sections discuss how you can use technology to make your processes more efficient and how to outsource those capabilities that you don't have.

Using technology to make things fly

Technology has made a world of difference in the realms of supply-chain management, manufacturing, assembly, and logistics (moving goods from one place to another). Robotics and other forms of intelligent machinery enable a manufacturer to gain productivity, maintain flexibility, and achieve superior levels of quality. The effect is magnified when technology is applied to repetitive tasks and quick setups. Here are three examples of how manufacturers use automation technology in different situations:

✔ **Inventory tracking:** Bar coding and RFID technology (see the explanation in the previous list) have lightened the load for businesses that track inventories. A handheld bar coder enables workers to capture production information without having to enter it into a computer. This technology saves a tremendous amount of time and decreases the chances of errors that often occur with manual data-entry methods.

✔ **Instruction, fabrication, and assembly:** Computer-generated manufacturing has made it possible to program a machine to produce exactly the part you want much more quickly and accurately than a human ever could. Manufacturers that have invested in these state-of-the-art machines now have computer screens on the factory floor where workers can access designs, instructions, and manuals and then make decisions about modifications — all with a few keystrokes. They also can enter order-status information, which can be accessed by marketing, finance, and any other departments within the organization.

✔ **Data mobilization:** Electronic data interchange, better known as EDI, lets you move highly graphical data between remote sites virtually in real time. This technology is important for companies that outsource some capabilities (see the following section). If your designers are in

New York and your manufacturing plant is in Texas, you can easily transfer designs and modify them in seconds with EDI technology. EDI also enables manufacturers to link up with distributors and retailers so that reorders are triggered electronically. For example, if you're a manufacturer that produces items for Wal-Mart to sell, you need to be linked to Wal-Mart's EDI system so that you can be notified of reorder status.

Outsourcing: The "make versus buy" decision

When you partner with another company that will handle certain aspects of your business, it's called *outsourcing*. Would it surprise you to discover that outsourcing has been around about as long as corporations have been? The difference today is that outsourcing is taking place on a global scale.

When you look at the up-front cost of investing in a plant, office, and equipment to run a manufacturing operation, you quickly understand why so many companies look to outsourcing as a way to survive and compete. But outsourcing isn't only about saving money (see Chapter 4).

Not all products are suited for offshore manufacturing. If production of your product requires highly technical equipment and technical people to supervise the production (many biotech products), or the product is very heavy (a road grading machine, for example) with a large footprint, you may not save enough money to make up for the problems you'll encounter when you go offshore. These problems include communication, quality control, transportation issues, cultural issues, and tariffs, to name just a few (you can find more details in Chapter 4).

To have a chance to achieve outsourcing success with the right product, consider these tips:

- ✔ **Start small (a small market or one product) and learn before trying to do too much overseas.** Developing an overseas technical workforce that really understands your business and industry takes time, so start small and grow carefully.

- ✔ **Place someone from your company "in-country" to supervise your operations until you find a local partner you can trust.** You need someone who's familiar with local culture and business methods.

- ✔ **Create a culture that enables employee development.** Be prepared for high turnover in the workforce you hire. Overseas workers are looking to move up and learn new things, so you need programs that enable them to grow so they won't leave your company to find what they need somewhere else.

✔ **Only outsource activities that have a high probability of success and that will run smoothly in the overseas environment.** Generally, these are straightforward production and assembly activities where what needs to happen is very clear. Activities that are associated with many problems or are complex — require special technical skills, in other words — should be kept at home.

However, in some industries, it's still possible to manufacture within the United States, as long as the company has developed efficient processes and taken advantage of manufacturing and operations technology. For example, the Sanmina-SCI facility in Rapid City, South Dakota, competes favorably on a cost basis with plants in China in the fabrication of circuit boards and integrated systems. It does so by providing end-to-end manufacturing capability for companies such as Motorola.

Purchasing: When, Where, and How Much

When you're talking about purchasing raw materials or goods for resale, you need to consider three very important factors:

✔ **Quality:** We define quality materials as those that meet the company's specific requirements, which means that level of quality will be different for every company. Quality normally depends on customer needs, so your market research with the customer will be important to the decisions you make about product quality.

✔ **Quantity:** Quantity purchased always depends on demand by the customer and your ability to manufacture to meet that demand — based on your plant, equipment, labor and so forth. Most manufacturers today take a just-in-time approach to quantity purchased so that they don't have to maintain costly inventories of raw materials.

✔ **Timing:** Timing is about making sure that your plant, equipment, and labor are being used to their full capacity, and that space, like a warehouse, is used only when necessary.

Successful management of quality, quantity, and timing are critical to an effective manufacturing process. This means that you need to find vendors who are willing to work with you to meet your production needs. Choosing a vendor, therefore, is an important decision that will take some time and effort on your part.

One of the first few questions to answer about vendors is whether to use one vendor or multiple vendors for each of the components or materials you require. Getting your materials from more than one source offers an important advantage. If, for instance, something happens to your supplier, you have a backup. But you also have a couple good reasons to use a single vendor for materials:

✔ You'll probably get better service and attention.

✔ The vendor may combine your order with those of other companies so that you can benefit from a volume purchase.

Here's a simple rule to follow: Use one supplier for about 70 to 80 percent of your materials needs, and use one or more vendors to supply the rest. That way you get the best of both worlds. When the time comes to select among a list of vendors, here are some questions to ask the candidates:

✔ Can the vendor deliver what you need, when you need it?

✔ If you use this vendor, what will your freight costs be?

✔ What kinds of services does the vendor offer?

✔ How well does the vendor know the product line it's selling you? Can a representative answer all your questions to your satisfaction?

✔ What kinds of guarantees will the vendor supply, and what are the vendor's maintenance and return policies?

We encourage you to check out vendors carefully. Compare prices, because we've seen prices on simple things, such as a bolt, range from a few cents to more than a dollar. If you stay on top of various vendors' pricing (the Internet makes it easy to do that), you'll put yourself in a stronger position to negotiate a new deal with your vendor when the time comes to do so.

Managing Materials and Scheduling Production

Materials management and scheduling are very important parts of manufacturing. The goal today is to have the raw materials you need when you need them — not before, not after, but right when you need them — hence the term just-in-time. The benefits of just-in-time are many:

✔ You can improve your cycle and delivery times.

✔ You use material only when it's needed.

✔ You can reduce inventory, thereby reducing space needs.

✔ You can increase labor productivity.

✔ You can improve quality.

If you're considering implementing JIT for your manufacturing process, make sure you have the primary components in place:

- ✔ **You know your customers.** Know what their requirements are, because they determine the time to delivery and the actual production process (see Chapter 15).

- ✔ **You have a well-timed production process.** Set up your production so that at each point along the line you're completing a task and that each task takes about the same length of time, which eliminates waiting.

- ✔ **You involve your supplier.** Make your supplier a central part of the process so that you don't need to warehouse materials — your supplier can do the warehousing and get materials to you exactly when you need them.

- ✔ **You have access to tracking technology.** Use the latest in tracking technology so you know where all your raw materials are and where your products are in the process.

Even with just-in-time purchasing and materials management, you will no doubt have some inventory of goods on hand that are used for manufacturing your product or used for sale as finished products. In this section, you find out how to manage inventory to keep costs down.

Grasping the importance of inventory

Inventory consists of materials and goods that you hold for manufacture or resale. Every business has inventory of one type or another, because you need to be able to meet customer demand in a timely fashion. Still, inventory is a costly thing to maintain, so you have to create a balance — between raw materials, work in progress, and finished goods — so as not to have inventory that you have to hold (resulting in a negative Impact on cash flow). The following sections look at some of the costs of inventory and how you track inventory to save time and money.

The hidden costs of inventory

Many business owners don't realize that the hidden costs of inventory can amount to as much as 25 percent of the base cost of the inventory. That's a substantial amount. What are some of these hidden costs?

- ✔ **Financing cost:** The interest paid on money borrowed to purchase the inventory. Most businesses can't afford to pay cash for inventory, so they finance it. This is an expensive way to do business, but it's a fact of life.

- ✔ **Insurance costs:** The cost of protecting the inventory from fire, damage, or theft.

✔ **Obsolescence:** The cost of an inventory that's no longer marketable or usable — in other words, nobody wants to buy it.

✔ **Opportunity cost:** The loss of use of the money that's tied up in inventory.

Do everything possible to reduce these hidden costs. In the section "Purchasing: When, What, and How Much" we talk about just-in-time purchasing, which will help reduce inventory costs. But another way you can manage inventory is by tracking it.

Tracking inventory

Companies can save a lot of money by carefully tracking inventory and maintaining the smallest inventory possible to meet demand. Keeping track of inventory has really been helped by technology — specifically bar-coding and RFID technology. When your company is new, tracking inventory isn't a big problem, because all you do is count it manually. But after your business grows, a manual system becomes cumbersome, lengthy, and prone to error. For these reasons, you need to consider the following three methods of tracking inventory:

✔ **Perpetual inventory system:** These systems are based on keeping a running count of items used or sold via an electronic point-of-sale device (which you've probably seen in your local grocery store). As materials are purchased, workers scan their bar codes or RFID tag info into the system, and the materials are deducted from the inventory. With this system, you have immediate access to the status of your inventory.

✔ **Physical count system:** You probably won't physically count your inventory after you grow a sizeable business. But most businesses still do some physical counting to check for errors in their electronic systems. Of course, to make the physical counting manageable, you need to get your inventory down as low as possible (which is where JIT comes in).

✔ **A combined inventory system:** Some companies use a combined system of perpetual and physical count. They do physical counts on less popular items that they carry in small quantities, and they use a perpetual system for the majority of their items.

To purchase and manage inventory effectively, you need to have a good handle on your manufacturing process. For that, scheduling is a critical function, and we discuss it next.

Making wise management decisions with a Gantt chart

Scheduling is the process of identifying and ordering all the production tasks in a manufacturing process. In Figure 18-1, you see a simple *Gantt chart,* which is one method you can use to lay out the scheduling of production tasks and the timing for each task. It's very easy to create, using the following tools:

Order #	Order Quantity	March				April				May			
		6–9	12–16	19–23	26–30	3–7	10–14	17–21	24–28	1–5	7–11	14–18	21–25
2,753	1,000												
2,754	1,500												
2,755	500												

Scheduled time: – – – – – – – – – – – – – – – – – – –
Actual time: ▬▬▬▬▬▬▬▬▬▬▬

Figure 18-1: Scheduling production tasks with a Gantt chart.

✔ List each task in the vertical column.

✔ Note the time required to complete each task in the horizontal row.

✔ Input a solid line to denote the planned task completion time.

✔ Input a dashed line to indicate the actual progress of the task.

Your best bet is to use Gantt charts for simple projects, where the tasks involved are independent of each other. In this figure, the manufacturer is producing three different orders going to three different customers. Graphing the actual status of the order against the forecasted schedule makes it easy to see how these orders are progressing.

Scheduling with a PERT chart

PERT charts (Program Evaluation and Review Technique charts) are more complex scheduling tools that a company should use when the production tasks involved are *interdependent*. What this means is that they operate parallel to one another or in sequence in such a way that you can't start or end one task until another is completed. Figure 18-2 provides a simple example of a PERT diagram.

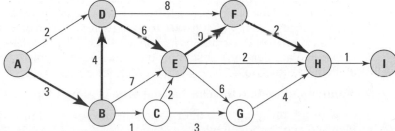

Figure 18-2: Scheduling with a PERT diagram.

The two questions that you want to answer by doing a PERT diagram are

- ✔ What's the shortest time to project completion?
- ✔ Which activities do you have to complete on time to be able to finish in the shortest time possible (the *critical path*)?

In the diagram in Figure 18-2, you see the critical path highlighted. The numbers indicate the number of days it takes to complete a particular task. This company indicates a critical path of 25 days, which is the latest completion time if all the dependent activities are completed on time. Any delay in activities along the critical path will delay the completion of the project.

Here are the steps to execute PERT planning:

1. **Identify the activities you must accomplish to complete the project (such things as brainstorming, design, prototyping, and so forth).**

2. **Figure the time it will take to complete each activity.**

3. **Figure out which activities depend on which other activities.**

   For example, before you can build a prototype of a product, you need to have a design specifying how to build the prototype. So the prototype activity is dependent on a completed design.

4. **For each activity that depends on another activity, (A depends on B, for example) determine if**

   - A can get started before B is complete.

   - A can start at the same time B starts.

   - A must wait until B is finished to start.

5. **Lay out your activities and their dependencies in a network diagram (you can do this with a paper and pencil or use your computer).**

   You won't get it perfect the first time. That's why a computer is handy — it's easy to move things around and make changes to your diagram.

6. **Identify the critical path.**

   It is based on identifying the earliest and latest start and end times for each activity. This is a complex formula that we can't get into here, but you can access plenty of software to assist you with the calculations, such as Microsoft Project, Merlin, and activeCollab (an open-source web-based application). Just enter the data on your project and it will do all the work for you!

7. **Monitor and update the chart as the project moves forward.**

   As with any planning, new information means you need to revisit your plan and make adjustments.

Production: Building the Product

Production is a vital part of a manufacturing business. The quickest and most cost-effective way to increase your bottom line if you're a manufacturer is to reduce your costs of production by becoming more efficient. Manufacturers today plan the production process around what's called *single-unit build,* which is building one unit at a time serially in manufacturing cells. This process means that a product goes through a series of tasks and operations in a continuous flow while remaining inside the manufacturing cell.

Successfully setting up an effective continuous-flow manufacturing process requires several steps:

1. **Work with your suppliers to set up a just-in-time (JIT) system (see the earlier section "Managing Materials and Scheduling Production").**

   This system makes sure that your supplies arrive when you're ready to use them so that you don't have to store raw materials, which is costly.

2. **Cross-train your employees in a variety of tasks.**

   You want employees with more flexibility who can move to different tasks as needed.

3. **Reduce the setup time from hours to minutes.**

   This is the time it takes to get the right equipment ready for a particular product.

4. **Design your manufacturing plant at the same time you're doing product development.**

   This ensures that the plant flow from one task to another is smooth.

Quality: It Isn't Right Until It's Right

When it comes to products, *quality* doesn't mean "best;" it means best as defined by the customer's requirements for features, benefits, and price (see Chapter 15).

To make sure your products reflect the quality level that customers expect, you must align your management, business, and support processes:

✔ Management processes shape the direction of the company, so they consist of vision, values, goals, strategy, and tactics. (Refer to Chapter 5 if you need a review of these topics.)

✔ Business processes, or *operational processes,* are all the mission-critical activities of the organization — such as new product development, manufacturing, distribution, and so on.

✔ Support processes are the activities that sustain the company, such as payroll, human resources, and accounting.

This section helps you make decisions about how to manage quality as you carry out your business processes.

Build quality into your processes

Different manufacturers have different points of view on how to monitor quality during the production process. One point of view — the traditional way — believes that you should inspect the product at the end of the process. However, with this method, you have to go back through all the stages post-defect to find any issues, which can really slow down the process. More and more companies monitor and inspect at several stages (or every stage) throughout the process. This way, you can catch the defect early, before your product is finished.

So, how do you choose which quality method is right for you? We make it easy for you. Do what modern manufacturing plants are doing: Build inspection into your processes. Don't wait until the end!

In cases where inspection will destroy the product — for example, a food product — it's better to inspect by taking a random sample. Makes sense — you don't want to eat all your products, especially if the food products you produce are meant for dogs and cats!

ISO 9000: Passing the ultimate test

For today's global business world (see Chapter 4), the International Organization for Standardization, in Geneva, Switzerland, has developed some international quality standards. These standards — in the form called *ISO 9000* — make it easier for a product to be sold in the international marketplace. They do so through a series of quality standards and a certification process. The standards are now accepted by more than 157 countries. But to even begin to meet ISO requirements, you need to develop a quality-management system. To read more about the details of ISO 9000, check out the Web site www.iso9000conference.com/index.htm. You also can look at *Quality Control For Dummies,* by Larry Webber and Michael Wallace (Wiley).

Other quality measurements

As with almost every other topic in business, quality has its own buzzwords and trendy ways of measuring and controlling for quality. Some of them have been around a long time — they've just been given a facelift and a new title.

We don't have space to go into all of these methods, but we list a few of the most common and give you a reference for where to find more info:

- **Six Sigma:** Motorola originally developed and trademarked this set of practices for eliminating defects below 3.4 defects per million opportunities. Today Six Sigma incorporates many quality improvement methods from years of practice including Total Quality Management (TQM), quality control, and zero defects. (Check out *Six Sigma For Dummies* by Craig Gygi, Neil DeCarlo, Bruce Williams, and Stephen R. Covey [Wiley].)

- **Kaizen or Lean Manufacturing:** This is a Japanese word for "improvement." In the quality world, this approach is about continuous improvement in the workplace and has been associated with Toyota's production system and the work of quality guru W. Edwards Deming. The goal of this approach is to eliminate waste or activities that don't add value to the process. (Check out *LEAN For Dummies* by Natalie J. Sayer and Bruce Williams [Wiley].)

- **Seven Tools of Quality:** Quality engineers have figured out that you can solve most quality problems with just seven quantitative tools. Check the American Society for Quality at www.asq.org/learn-about-quality/seven-basic-quality-tools/overview/overview.html for more on these seven tools.

- **Balanced Scorecard:** This is a management tool that simply guides you through the process of developing metrics to set performance targets and measure four areas of your business: financial, customer, business processes, and learning and growth. (Check out *Balanced Scorecard For Dummies* by Charles Hannabarger, Frederick Buchman, and Peter Economy [Wiley].)

Process/Equipment Maintenance: Keeping the System Running Smoothly

In manufacturing, *maintenance* refers to the care and feeding of the processes and equipment used to produce a product and also to after-sales service with the customer. The following sections give you some ideas for how to take care of the investment you've made in your production processes.

Maintaining processes and equipment

No matter how careful you are, every machine will break down eventually, which means not only costly repairs, but also a potential loss of sales from the downtime. So, what can you do to handle plant and equipment maintenance? You basically have four choices:

- **Undertake a program of preventive maintenance.** We highly recommend this program, in which you regularly check and fix machines before they break down. With this method, you can control when your downtime happens and schedule it for a slow season.

- **Have backup machines waiting.** Modern manufacturing facilities typically organize their equipment so that if one machine goes down, they can shift the work to another. If production is the life blood of your business, the cost of maintaining backup equipment, or equipment that isn't used full time, is simply a cost of doing business.

- **Build up inventories at every stage of the production process.** That way at least part of the process can continue if something breaks down. However, this method doesn't work well if you're using a JIT system. It's probably a good choice, though, for a small manufacturer that doesn't have the strong supply chain relationships required for a JIT system.

- **Maintain equipment during downtime.** You may have noticed that most Internet companies now schedule downtime to maintain their servers, and they warn their customers about that downtime in advance. They usually choose a time in the middle of the night or during the lowest access time in the day to avoid frustrating their customers and potentially losing business.

Designing an after-sale service and warranty program

Most companies provide some form of warranty with the products and services they sell. They provide this after-sale service to protect themselves from liability and, more importantly, to demonstrate that they stand behind what they produce.

Warranties come in all shapes and sizes and depend on your business and industry, but here are a few guidelines you can follow when designing your warranty program:

- Check standard warranties in your industry to determine the appropriate length.

- Determine which components of the product, or which aspects of the service, you want to cover.

- If you have components made by other manufacturers, secure pass-through warranties from them to ensure that you don't invalidate their warranties inadvertently. A *pass-through warranty* means that the original manufacturer takes care of any problems or service required.

✔ Plan to have customers conveniently return the product to you or your distributors if necessary rather than to the maker of a particular component.

✔ Plan for how you'll educate your customers about your warranty policies and services. Whatever you do, make the policy easy for the customer to understand and the services clear about what the customer should do in case of a warranty problem.

Today's product laws state that any product is covered by warranty from the minute it hits the customer's hands, whether or not the customer returns a postcard stating when and where the product was purchased.

Distribution and Logistics: A Great Way to Compete

Distribution comprises all the ways that you move your product to your customers — distributors, retailers, and the Internet, to name a few options. *Logistics,* by contrast, is the management of goods, information, and services from the point of origin to the market — for example, transporting the manufactured product to the customer via some mode of transportation, such as a truck. Logistics includes transportation, inventory, warehousing, materials handling, and packaging. The rise of the Internet and global supply chains has led to new distribution and logistics strategies that are more compatible with the fast-changing marketplace. This section looks at some of the major changes in strategy today.

Eyeing some new distribution strategies

Technology once again has provided new solutions to old problems, opening the door to great opportunities to innovate in distribution, but technology isn't the only source of innovation in distribution. Companies are finding all sorts of ways to deliver benefits to customers.

The following list presents four changes taking place right now in distribution:

✔ **Companies are moving along the value chain.** The value chain is really the distribution channel, but you should recognize that at all points along the channel, value is added to the product. Today, companies are taking over activities in their value chains, either upstream from them or downstream.

✔ **Companies are shifting to bundled solutions rather than individual products.** A manufacturer may now bundle distribution, support, and information with its product for a package price.

✔ **New classes of customers are appearing.** Traditionally, only big companies could access production tools for developing things such as commercials. No more. Today, production tool producers are marketing to small companies and individuals at prices they can afford. Look at all the people developing their own commercials and posting them on YouTube. Do these YouTube "customers" have product and service needs? You betcha!

✔ **Everything old is new again.** Many years ago, who would have thought that a company would come along and give coffee a whole new life and a new distribution channel? Starbucks did so by making the process of drinking coffee an experience. That new value, added to a very simple, existing product, enabled the company to seek out new customers and charge higher-than-normal prices for its coffee.

So, how do you choose a distribution strategy for your company? You consider what will make your customers happy — it's as simple as that! Here are some things to think about when choosing the most effective channel to deliver your benefits to the customer:

✔ **Cost:** Cost includes everything that relates to marketing and distributing the product to your customer.

✔ **Market coverage:** With some products, such as the Apple iPhone or a new beverage, it's important to reach as many customers as possible as fast as possible. Trying to accomplish this yourself may be an impossible task, so you need to use intermediaries (wholesalers, distributors, retailers, and so on). Selling to just three distributors can give you the potential to access hundreds of retailers.

✔ **How much control you need:** If you have a product that requires a lot of education or unusual marketing tactics to get sales, such as a new medical device, you don't want to choose an intermediary that carries competing products. You may need to use a direct channel, such as the Internet, to control the information flow to the customer.

✔ **Speed and reliability:** Today's customers expect products right *now!* If your customers are like that, you need to find a distribution channel that puts the customers in control of the speed with which they receive the product.

Nailing down logistics: Head 'em up and move 'em out

When you just need to move product and you don't know the best way to do it, you need to contact a logistics firm. Logistics is about controlling the flow of goods and resources from the source of production to the marketplace. When you contact a logistics firm, you'll find out that it can do a whole lot more than just find you the right truck, train, ship, or plane to ship your cargo, as well as negotiate the best prices. It can also package, warehouse, and manage inventory. In fact, many firms today are choosing to outsource these specialized tasks to professionals.

For example, large companies such as Wal-Mart are requiring even small suppliers to meet their rigorous standards for packing, shipping, and tagging for RFID tracking (see the first section in this chapter). Because many small companies don't have the resources to meet these requirements, they outsource to third-party logistics companies (such as UPS Supply Chain Solutions).

We suggest you focus on what you do best and leave the rest to someone who can do it better. Check with others in your industry to get recommendations for the best logistics firms.

Chapter 19

The Ins and Outs of Risk Management

Most people are optimists. Sure, plenty of businesses fail every year, but few entrepreneurs honestly think that their businesses will be among the scores of also-rans. Natural disasters — earthquakes, hurricanes, tornadoes, floods — happen, but they certainly won't happen to my business! And even if they do, the company will be just fine, thank you. Robbery, Internet attacks on computers, arson, embezzlement, fraud — these crimes are happening all over the world, but that doesn't mean my business is at risk. Somehow, most business people like to think that they'll be untouched by business disaster year after year, with their customers, businesses, and investments intact.

Unfortunately, the world is a risky place, and bad things really do happen to even the most well-prepared, good-hearted, and competent businesspeople. This is a post-9/11 world, where the very real threat of terrorism has added an additional layer of risk to all the ones people have traditionally experienced. The question isn't, "Will something bad happen to my business?" Instead, the question is, "Will I be prepared *when* something bad happens to my business?"

This chapter is all about business risk and how to manage it. You find out how to develop and implement a winning risk management process, as well as how to identify and act on potential vulnerabilities. You discover the many kinds of insurance available to businesses today, and you see how to train your employees to avoid or even eliminate risk altogether. Finally, you get some advice on how to monitor the latest high-tech computer risks — the Internet- and e-mail-imposed risks that can cost you your business in the blink of an eye.

The 4-1-1 on Risk Management

The key to dealing with risk — whether in the form of natural disaster, theft, property damage, personal injury, and so on — is to anticipate it and have a plan in place for dealing with it. *Risk management* is the process of understanding and anticipating risks and then taking steps to minimize its impact on a business and the people within it.

Here are the four basic steps for managing risk:

1. **Identify potential risks.**

   The possibilities for loss are almost endless. What types of risk is your business exposed to?

2. **Assess and prioritize potential risks.**

   If your business is located in Miami or New Orleans, chances are you won't have to worry about earthquakes. You should, however, prioritize the purchase of insurance in the event of a hurricane or flood.

3. **Select the right risk management tools to deal with each potential risk.**

   Develop a risk management process (your overall approach to managing risk) and plan (a document that spells out a set course of action to mitigate or respond to specific risks) that features specific strategies for dealing with risk in your business. In some cases, prevention is the right course of action. In other cases, employee training may do the trick. Sometimes, you can simply buy insurance to cover your risk. We explore some of the different risk management tools available to you later in this chapter, in the section "Purchasing Insurance to Shift the Risk."

4. **Evaluate the results of your risk management strategies and revise or renew them as appropriate.**

   Periodically revisit your risk management process, strategies, and plans to ensure that they're providing the desired protection to your business. If they are, terrific — keep on doing what you're doing. If they aren't, however, don't hesitate to adjust your strategies or plans where necessary.

If you follow these four steps for managing risk in your business, you'll be way ahead of the game if the "unthinkable" occurs. And, unfortunately, tragedies happen to businesses just like yours more often than you can possibly imagine.

Managing Risk (Before It Manages You)

You can — and should — manage risk to protect your company. In fact, many insurers make the development of a risk management process or plan a condition of granting insurance coverage. No risk management process can prevent every possible setback from occurring, but a good risk management process can minimize the financial loss your business will suffer, as well as help prevent injuries and death.

You can take precautions in case something bad does happen, and this section gives you some pointers — including how to create a risk management process, how to determine what risks you're vulnerable to, and how to take action.

Developing a risk management process

A formal risk management process greatly reduces your company's exposure to risks and undoubtedly saves your organization time, money, and loss of employee productivity. Creating a risk management process requires the concerted effort of one or more employees during an extended period of time. These employees include top management as well as individuals tasked with leading the risk management process. Here are seven steps for developing a risk management process that really works:

1. **Get the commitment of top management.**

   To create a risk management program that will work over the long haul, you must have the support of top management. An explanation of the potential risks to the company of ignoring this vital process — supported with hard facts and figures — will generally be enough to gain the support of even the most reluctant manager.

2. **Assign one person to lead your company's risk management efforts.**

   One person should have ultimate responsibility for your organization's risk management process. Such a policy ensures accountability and prevents finger pointing if something goes wrong and the business isn't prepared for such an event. This individual will be in charge of leading and implementing the steps that follow.

3. **Establish a risk control committee.**

   Employees can participate in the risk management process by helping to identify risks and by taking actions to minimize their potential impact on your organization. The committee should also track risk and employee injury trends and take action to reduce risks and injuries. Make sure that the committee includes a broad cross-section of employees from all levels and all parts of the organization.

4. **Create an emergency action plan.**

If the unthinkable — a fire, an explosion, a natural disaster, a terrorist attack — happens, will all your employees know exactly what to do and where to go to protect themselves and your organization's property from damage or destruction? An emergency action plan ensures that they will.

5. **Establish a formal self-inspection program.**

Is your workplace safe? Are you sure? A self-inspection program should identify potential safety hazards and take action to make repairs or corrections. Conduct a vulnerability analysis (see the next section for details), and use members of your risk control committee to conduct inspections throughout your organization.

6. **Establish an accident and safety incident-investigation program.**

The most well-protected organizations learn from accidents and incidents, and they use this information to help prevent future accidents and incidents. Appoint someone in your organization to investigate every accident and safety incident to determine what lessons you can learn from the mishaps.

7. **Develop a training and education program.**

Train and educate your employees to identify hazards, prevent injuries — to themselves and to others — and respond appropriately in case of emergency or disaster.

The previous steps are the basics of establishing a strong foundation of risk management in your organization. You may wish to do even more. You may want to tap into the expertise of consultants who specialize in risk management as you go through the process. Whatever you decide to do, don't forget that sufficient foresight and planning can help prevent losses and reduce risks.

Conducting a vulnerability analysis

Before you can effectively manage the risks that your organization is or will be exposed to, you need to understand the specific risks you're up against. The goal of *vulnerability analysis* is to assess the probability and potential impact of the different risks that you identify.

Use the Vulnerability Analysis Chart (Figure 19-1) to score your organization — the lower your score, the better. If you identify risks with a high score, give them a high priority in your organization and address those risks immediately — if you haven't already taken care of them. Make the following steps, adapted from processes developed by the Federal Emergency Management Administration (FEMA), a part of your vulnerability analysis.

Vulnerability Analysis Chart

TYPE OF EMERGENCY	Probability	Human Impact	Property Impact	Business Impact	Internal Resources	External Resources	Total
	High Low 5 ←→ 1	High Impact 5 ←————→ 1		Low Impact	Weak Resources 5 ←→ 1	Strong Resources	

The lower the score, the better

Figure 19-1: A Vulnerability Analysis Chart to assess your company's exposure to risk.

Step 1: List potential risks

In the first column of the chart, list all the potential risks that could affect your facility and the people in it. Be sure to consider risks that could occur in your facility or within your community. Bring your risk control committee into the process to help ensure all possible risks are brought to light.

As you consider the different risks that could possibly occur, think in terms of the following potential areas of risk:

✔ **Human error:** What potential employee error-driven risks are your business exposed to? Are your employees trained to work safely? Do they know what to do in an emergency? Consider potential risks as a result of

- Poor training
- Poor maintenance
- Carelessness
- Misconduct
- Substance abuse
- Fatigue

✔ **Business:** What kinds of risks does your organization face that are uniquely business risks? The risks that a business faces can be quite different from the risks that an individual faces. Consider potential risks as a result of

- Malpractice
- Embezzlement
- Product liability
- Fraud
- Loss of key person
- Errors and omissions
- Construction defects
- Worker injury and death
- Nonperformance

✔ **Historical:** What types of risks have your community, your facility, and other business facilities in your area faced in the past? Consider potential risks as a result of

- Fires
- Severe weather
- Hazardous material spills
- Transportation accidents
- Earthquakes
- Hurricanes
- Tornadoes
- Terrorism
- Utility outages

✔ **Geographic:** What can happen as a result of your facility's geographic location? Consider potential risks as a result of

- Your proximity to flood plains, seismic faults, and dams
- Your proximity to companies that produce, store, use, or transport hazardous materials
- Your proximity to major transportation routes and airports
- Your proximity to nuclear power plants

✔ **Technological:** What could happen if you experience a process or system failure? Consider potential risks as a result of

- Fire, explosion, or hazardous materials incident
- Safety system failure

- Telecommunications failure

- Computer system failure

- Power failure

- Heating or cooling system failure

- Emergency notification system failure

✔ **Physical:** What types of risks does the design or construction of the facility pose? Does the physical facility enhance safety or detract from it? Consider potential risks as a result of

- The physical construction of the facility

- Hazardous processes or byproducts

- Facilities for storing combustibles

- Layout of equipment

- Lighting

- Evacuation routes and exits

- Proximity of shelter areas

Step 2: Estimate the probability of the risks

In the Probability column of the chart, rate the likelihood of each risk's occurrence by using a simple scale of 1 to 5 — with 1 as the lowest probability and 5 as the highest. You need to rely on your own experience — and the experience of others in your company or industry — to develop reasonably accurate numbers. If your business is located in Kansas, for example, you know that the risk of a tornado probably rates a 4 or 5.

Step 3: Assess the potential human impact

Analyze the potential human impact of each potential risk — the possibility of death or injury, in other words. Assign a rating in the Human Impact column of the chart by using a 1 to 5 scale — with 1 as the lowest impact and 5 as the highest. Again, draw on your experience, or on the experience of others in your company or industry to develop reasonably accurate numbers.

Step 4: Assess the potential property impact

In the Property Impact column of the chart, consider the potential for property losses and damage. Assign a rating by using a 1 to 5 scale — with 1 being the lowest impact and 5 being the highest. Consider potential risks in terms of

✔ Cost to replace

✔ Cost to set up temporary replacement

✔ Cost to repair

For example, although a utility outage will likely have a low probability of property loss or damage — perhaps a 1 or 2 — a terrorist attack resulting in physical damage would score higher, perhaps a 4 or 5.

Step 5: Assess the potential business impact

Consider the potential loss of market share due to the potential risks you identify. Assign a rating in the Business Impact column by using a 1 to 5 scale — with 1 being the lowest impact and 5 being the highest. Consider potential risks in terms of

- ✔ Business interruption
- ✔ Employees who can't report to work
- ✔ Customers who can't reach your facility
- ✔ Company in violation of contractual agreements
- ✔ Imposition of fines and penalties or legal costs
- ✔ Interruption of receipt of critical supplies
- ✔ Interruption of product distribution

For example, an earthquake could potentially result in your offices being made off-limits by authorities for days, weeks, or even months, creating a major and potentially long-lasting business interruption.

Step 6: Assess internal and external resources

Assess your company's resources and your ability to respond to situations. Assign a score to your Internal Resources and External Resources by using a 1 to 5 scale — with 1 representing a lack of resources to respond and 5 representing more than sufficient resources to respond.

To perform this evaluation, consider each potential risk from beginning to end and evaluate each resource that you need to respond. For each risk, ask these questions:

- ✔ Do we have the needed resources and capabilities to respond?
- ✔ Will our external resources be able to respond to us in adverse times as quickly as we may need them, or will they have other priority areas to serve?

If the answers are yes, you can move on to the next assessment. If the answers are no, identify what you can do to correct the problem. For example, you may need to

- ✔ Develop additional risk management procedures
- ✔ Conduct additional training

✔ Acquire additional equipment

✔ Establish mutual aid agreements

✔ Establish agreements with specialized contractors

Step 7: Add the columns

Total the scores you've rated for each potential risk. The lower your score, the better. Risks with a high score should be given a high priority in your organization and addressed immediately. Although this is a subjective rating exercise, the comparisons help determine your risk planning and resource priorities.

Taking action

After you've assessed your potential risks and prioritized them by their urgency and potential impact, you need to take action to reduce them or eliminate them entirely. Consider four basic strategies when selecting your risk management tools; keep them in mind as you decide what strategies you'll pursue to reach your risk management goals:

✔ **Shift the risk.** One way of dealing with the risk of loss is to shift the risk to someone else. When you buy an insurance policy, you shift the risk to the insurance company. When you draft contracts with subcontractors that require them to carry liability insurance, you shift the risk to your subcontractors and their insurance companies. (For more information, turn to the section "Purchasing Insurance to Shift the Risk" later in this chapter.)

✔ **Avoid the risk.** By identifying and correcting hazardous situations — say, for example, by repairing the brakes on a company delivery truck — you can avoid potential risks altogether.

✔ **Reduce the risk.** Although you can't entirely avoid some risks, you can reduce them. For instance, training your employees in the proper techniques for lifting heavy objects substantially reduces the incidence of back injuries, which result in lost productivity. (For more on employee training, see the later section "Training Employees to Minimize Risk.")

✔ **Assume the risk.** In some cases, an organization may decide to bear the financial burden of a risk. By self-insuring for workers' compensation claims, for example, or by paying higher deductibles on insurance policies, an organization assumes all or part of a risk of loss. This course of action should be taken only after a very careful assessment of the risk, along with a detailed cost/benefit study.

Whatever you do to address risks, do something! After you've determined that a potential risk of injury or loss exists, you have to take action by shifting, avoiding, reducing, or assuming the risk. Don't waste time hoping that the risk will go away if you just ignore it. It won't.

Purchasing Insurance to Shift the Risk

When you buy insurance for your business, you shift the risk of loss to a third party — in this case an insurance company. The insurance company essentially is betting that you won't suffer a loss due to the risk. It hedges its bet by collecting a sufficiently high premium — at rates based on the statistical predictions of *actuaries*, people who specialize in the mathematics of risk — to make money off your business even if you do suffer a loss at some point down the road.

Here are the most important and common kinds of insurance to consider buying (and maintaining) for your business:

- ✔ **Liability:** If someone is injured or has property damaged or destroyed while on your premises or while using your product or service, your organization may be sued for millions of dollars in damages. *Liability insurance* protects your organization from these kinds of financial losses. If you lease your office or manufacturing space, your landlord probably requires you to carry a certain amount of liability insurance for protection.

- ✔ **Property:** Natural disasters such as earthquakes, floods, and tornadoes wreak billions of dollars worth of property damage every year. But an estimated 70 percent of all business-property losses happen not as a result of natural disasters, but because of employee negligence, errors, or lack of planning. Property insurance generally covers the risk of property loss due to fire, smoke, wind, and other sources of damage or destruction.

- ✔ **Business interruption:** If property damage or another situation forces your business to close until you can repair or rebuild your facility, business interruption insurance covers you for the risk of lost sales.

- ✔ **Technology risk:** Most businesses today have information technology exposure to their business operations. Companies are at risk from invasion by electronic intruders, whether the damage occurs on an external Web site or an internal *Intranet,* a company network. *Cyberinsurance* describes a group of insurance policies that protect a company against losses from hacked computers, virus attacks, copyright infringement, Web content liability, and other technology-related risks.

✔ **Environmental:** If your business has anything to do with construction, landfills, underground storage tanks, chemical production, recycling facilities, maintenance facilities, or anything else that may have or come into contact with a negative environmental impact, environmental insurance — designed to protect your company if it's found responsible for damaging the environment — is right up your alley.

✔ **Malpractice:** Also known as *errors and omissions (E&O)* or *professional liability* insurance, business malpractice insurance covers professionals who give advice during the normal course of business. Doctors, lawyers, consultants, accountants, and stockbrokers are among those who need malpractice insurance in case their clients are injured — physically, financially, or emotionally — as a result of their work. Errors and omissions insurance have received much greater attention as a result of the financial misdeeds of Enron, Tyco, and other companies similar to them.

✔ **Fidelity bond:** This is a specialized, but widely used form of insurance that protects employers from theft, larceny, or embezzlement committed by covered employees.

✔ **Ocean marine:** The oldest form of insurance in existence, ocean marine insurance covers four key areas pertaining to transporting goods via ship: the vessel or hull, the cargo, earnings (such as freight, passage money, commissions, or profit), and liability (also known as protection and indemnity).

✔ **Key person:** Smaller businesses that depend on one person — perhaps the founder or chief executive — to lead the organizations and bring in business usually carry *key person* insurance. In the event of this person's death or incapacitation, key person coverage pays a fixed amount to the business — much as a life-insurance policy pays a fixed amount of money to a surviving spouse or other beneficiary.

Other, more-specialized forms of insurance — including terrorism insurance (which, by the way, is very difficult to obtain) — may be appropriate for your situation. If you're not an expert in the insurance industry, hire someone who is or find a qualified insurance broker who can explain and recommend different kinds of insurance for your business to purchase, as well as how much coverage to buy. A reputable broker should be able to search the insurance market for you to get the best coverage at the best prices — definitely a win-win situation. For more information on insurance and risk, be sure to visit the ISO Web site at www.iso.com. Also, be sure to take a look at *Insurance For Dummies* by Jack Hungelmann (Wiley).

Training Employees to Minimize Risk

Employees are some of the most powerful tools in the toolbox of any company that's looking to reduce its risk of loss. Employees can not only proactively identify and cure potential risks (refer to the section "Conducting a vulnerability analysis"), but also can train others to do the same. The result is a much safer workplace with improved employee morale and productivity.

Safety training can cover any potential risk in the workplace. Because each company and industry is different, you should tailor your employee training to the exact needs of your organization. Typical topics include

- Bloodborne pathogens
- Correct lifting techniques
- Ergonomics (adapting working conditions to better suit employees)
- Respirator safety
- Forklift safety
- Electrical safety
- Office security
- First aid and CPR
- Evacuation plan

Employee safety is important — not only to companies that rely on their employees to work productively and efficiently, but also to the federal government, which established the Occupational Safety and Health Administration (OSHA) to save lives, prevent injuries, and protect the health of America's workers. The key to employee safety is the behavior of the employees themselves. Human error is reported to be the single largest cause of workplace emergencies. Incentives can play a role in rewarding safe employee behavior, thereby decreasing the amount of incidents that take place.

Here are some guidelines for using incentives to encourage safe behavior at work:

- **Customize the incentives for your organization.** What works for one company may not work for yours. Each organizational culture has its own unique needs and motivators. If you pick the right incentives (things that the employees themselves value), your safety program will be much stronger than a program that uses no incentives or the wrong incentives.

✔ **Distribute the incentives fairly.** For an incentive program to work, incentives must be distributed fairly. Avoid contests that reward only a few people or that reinforce the view that safety is a matter of chance or luck. Heartland Foods and W.R. Grace instituted lottery-style programs that have the potential to make everyone a winner. Employees of these companies who meet safety goals can receive scratch-off tickets called "safety bucks." An employee can redeem a buck immediately if it contains matching symbols. If not, the employee can still accumulate bucks and redeem them later for gifts or other awards.

✔ **Make your incentives meaningful and timely.** Incentives are meaningful when they're well proportioned to specific behaviors or results. In other words, employees who exhibit safe behavior during the course of an entire year should receive a more significant reward than employees who exhibit safe behavior for only a month (although you should still reward and encourage these employees for their safe behavior). Also, give rewards — whether they're material gifts or verbal acknowledgments — in a timely manner, soon after employees reach their goals. Doing so boosts the impact of the incentive.

New Technology, New Risks: Internet and E-mail Threats

The rise of the Internet and new computer and telecommunications technologies has revolutionized the business world. Now an employee can work (and virtually be) most anyplace around the globe, with a complete suite of office tools available 24/7. Although these technologies have revolutionized business in so many ways, they've also revolutionized the world of risk — and not always in positive ways.

Truth be told, cyberspace is still a fairly new place for most people, and it's still pretty wild and wooly around the edges. Hackers, cyber spoofs, viruses, worms, digital defamation, cyber extortion, intellectual-property (IP) infringement, and so on are just the tip of the iceberg when it comes to the risks that businesses today must contend with. To ignore these technology risks is to put the long-term survival of your business in peril. To help you get a better idea of the technology risks you and your business may encounter and how to protect your IT interests, this section takes a closer look at some of these threats.

Although you don't personally have to be an expert in computer security (unless that's your job — in which case you'd better be an expert!), you must at least understand that the threat to your company's computers, networks, e-mail systems, and more, is very real. Just because your systems haven't been attacked yet doesn't mean they'll be safe tomorrow. You need to make sure you have good security in place to protect your company's information technology and intellectual property — often a company's most valuable asset — and talented experts to install the security and monitor the threats on an ongoing basis.

Viruses, Trojan horses, worms, and other strange beings of risk

When you become familiar with the world of information technology, it may seem as though there are people who sit around all day thinking up new ways to get into your computer, take it over, and tend to their own nefarious purposes. Actually, there are many people — *hackers* — who do exactly that. Why? Some do it for the challenge, and some do it for the fun of watching their work create mayhem within an organization, but others do it for the money. Someone, after all, is paying for all those fake Rolex and Viagra ads that bombard computers around the world each and every day.

Hackers have a variety of tools at their disposal — the vast majority of which are software-based. The term for intentionally destructive software is *malware*, which is a shortened version of the term "malicious software" — software that infiltrates a computer system without the owner's consent for the purpose of damaging it. Within this overall category of tools is an alphabet soup of potential threats, including the following:

- ✔ **Virus:** A self-replicating software program that can infect other connected computers independently of human action. Most viruses are designed to stay hidden deep within a computer until the time comes to do its duty, which could be anything from sending out spam (messages in bulk) to other computers to crashing your hard drive. Although many viruses are destructive, some aren't; however, all are designed to infect as many other computers as possible before being detected.

- ✔ **Worm:** Malware that can replicate itself across network connections but without modifying or attaching itself to a host program. Similar to a virus, worms can be used by hackers to do all sorts of malicious things.

- ✔ **Trojan horse:** A software program that says it's one thing — something that appears to be harmless on the surface — but turns out to be something destructive. An odd e-mail message you get that says something along the lines of, "Here's the file you requested," may actually contain

Trojans. When you click on the file to open it, your computer becomes infected with malware programs that can do things such as record your keystrokes or copy passwords and send them to the hacker.

✔ **Denial of service attack:** Using thousands of computers under their control, hackers can target a specific computer network with an overwhelming amount of incoming traffic — far more than normal — causing the network to slow down or crash due to the strain to its systems.

✔ **Mail bomb:** A denial of service attack on an e-mail server, causing your e-mail system to slow down or crash.

✔ **Hoaxes:** Although they're not actual pieces of malware, hoaxes can spread hysteria among employees over nothing. However, over time, hoaxes cause employees to become less vigilant to real threats.

Computer security experts estimate that the annual monetary losses suffered by businesses globally due to the work of hackers numbers in the billions of dollars. Although this number is huge in itself, be aware that personal computers and computer networks aren't the only things at risk of attack. Hackers can compromise any device that has a computer chip and communicates with the outside world. This increasingly means cellphones, PDAs (personal digital assistants), and wireless networks are also at risk.

Dealing with threats to your information technology

So, if you've read the previous sections, you understand that the threat to your information technology is real and that hackers are working 24/7 to find new ways to get into your computers and access all your juicy data. Now what? The good news is that you can do a number of things to reduce the risk to your business. The following list outlines some of the most important steps you can take to increase the security of your information technology *right now:*

✔ **Dedicate an employee or consultant to protect your computer systems.** If your company is large enough, consider putting one person — either an employee or a consultant — in charge of watching over your information technology security, scanning for new threats, and constantly monitoring your systems for signs of unwanted entry.

✔ **Install anti-virus software (and keep it up to date!).** You can find many sources for good, reliable anti-virus software — and some basic versions can be obtained at little or no cost.

However, keep in mind that many hackers specifically target anti-virus software, hoping to get into your computer before your software vendor realizes that a new threat is on the horizon. This means that you need to keep your anti-virus software up to date and scan your system regularly for viruses.

✓ **Install firewalls.** Every communication portal to the outside world needs to be locked down with a firewall through which hackers can't pass. *Firewalls* can take the form of software programs or hardware devices, such as network routers. And don't forget to lock down your wireless networks, too. These are particularly common entry points for hackers today.

✓ **Install redundant systems.** Instead of just relying on one anti-virus software package or type of firewall, you should incorporate many different forms of security into your computers and computer networks. The idea is that, if one of the systems becomes vulnerable to attack, the other systems will be ready to step in and block the attacks.

✓ **Install e-mail filtering.** Using an e-mail filter is a simple and inexpensive way to block the most common entry point for malware — your employees' e-mail messages. You can configure your filters to block the following:

- Executable files (which most viruses and other malware are)

- Resource-hogging (and, potentially, copyright-violating) video and audio files

- Graphics files and photographs

- E-mail from specific Internet-service providers such as Gmail, Yahoo!, Hotmail, and so on

✓ **Back up your systems regularly.** You should regularly back up your computers — at least once a day — so that if a hacker manages to crash your hard drives, your systems can recover and carry on as if nothing ever happened.

✓ **Train your employees.** You should assume that your employees need to be educated about the technology risks your organization faces. Take the time — and spend the money — to train your employees. Tell them what they can do to avoid compromising your information technology, and enlist their active help in fighting the threats.

The bottom line: Avoiding technology threats — and avoiding potentially massive damage to your data and your business — requires constant vigilance. Are you prepared to meet the challenge?

Chapter 20

In Business, Everything Is Negotiation

*Y*ou're looking for a new location for your business, but you have rather limited cash flow — you can't afford more than $3,000 a month to lease office space. You call a real estate broker who finds the perfect location for $3,500 a month — $500 more than you can manage. Will the subsequent negotiation be easy or difficult?

Remember, the broker works on commission, so he must sell or lease properties to make money. The broker certainly knows that you're interested, but what do you know about him? How has his past month gone? Did he lease a lot of properties, or has the month been dry? Is this a hot commercial property, or has it been on the market a long time? Are many other properties available, or is it a renter's market?

Or perhaps you're fine in your present office, but you have a new product idea that you want to launch. It will require some outside sources of capital, because your company doesn't have the resources to spend on a risky innovation. What you need is risk capital. Do you know what investors are looking for in these types of investments? Can your company survive a deep investigation, which is part of the due diligence that investors conduct? Do you have a compelling story that will sell investors on your product idea?

These are just two examples among the hundreds of situations in which business owners and managers must negotiate for items or services they need or want. In this chapter, we explore the nature of business negotiation and give you some tools that enable you to do an effective job of negotiating in any business situation. Anyone can learn to negotiate successfully by following the guidelines provided in this chapter. It just takes planning, practice, and patience.

Ready to Rumble: Negotiation 101

As a businessperson, understanding the basics of negotiation is essential so you can effectively negotiate even the smallest, most insignificant debates within all your business relationships. Hiring an attorney or professional negotiator to handle your every negotiation isn't financially feasible (although we strongly suggest that you hire a good attorney for major negotiations, such as selling your business).

Consider the following scenarios: It's Monday morning. Before leaving for work, you and your spouse must agree on who will take the kids to their doctor appointment after school. You probably have to negotiate to decide who's in the best position to take on that task. Maybe you each have an errand to run after work. Whose task is more important? Who can change what he or she had planned?

You arrive at your office, and your business partner wants to discuss fitting two new projects into your already overburdened schedule. Will that discussion require some negotiating skills? Are you predisposed to take on more than you can handle? After this first encounter, another employee asks for a raise that's far beyond what your budget allows. How can you satisfy your employee's needs and the company's needs at the same time? Is that a negotiation? Because you're now running late, you must call a customer to reschedule a lunch appointment for 1 p.m. If the customer can't easily change her schedule, you find yourself in a negotiation over what to do.

By noon, you've already had four different negotiations!

This section takes a closer look at negotiations and helps you identify what type of negotiation you're dealing with and what you need to do to prepare to enter that negotiation from a position of strength.

Matching your strategy with the type of negotiation: Is winning everything?

No two negotiations are alike, but there are some broad categories of negotiation types that can help you define the context in which you'll be negotiating. In their book, *Everything's Negotiable . . . When You Know How to Play the Game* (American Management Association), Eric Skopec and Laree Kiely give some important criteria for figuring out the type of negotiation you're facing so that you can design the most appropriate strategy to achieve the objective you've set. Here are the four broad categories of negotiations and under what circumstances they're typically used:

✔ **Win-win (we both come out on top):**

- The issue is important to you.

- You value your relationship with the other party.

- You have enough time to search for an approach and solution that satisfies everyone.

✔ **Win-lose (I win, you lose):**

- The issue is important to you.

- Preserving your relationship with the other party doesn't matter.

- You have the time to beat the other party into submission.

- You can't use a win-win strategy because the other party will take advantage of you.

✔ **Lose-win (I'll let you win this one):**

- The issue isn't important to you.

- You value your relationship with the other party.

- You're under time constraints and want to finish the negotiation quickly, so you're willing to lose to accomplish that.

✔ **Lose-lose (we should just get this done):**

- The issue is relatively unimportant to both parties.

- You may build a relationship based on mutual suffering. Time and/or transaction costs are primary considerations.

- You're willing to compromise to resolve the situation.

Although it would be nice if both parties could win in every negotiation, win-win situations often aren't possible. In fact, sometimes you may even choose to lose a negotiation. Why would you go into a negotiation planning to lose?

✔ You may choose not to play the game. Recall the many times a day you face negotiations, most of which probably are B- or C-level issues. Because the rewards for these issues aren't great, working to come up with a win-lose or a win-win negotiation isn't worth your time, resources, and effort. For example, you may decide that you don't want to take consulting projects with difficult clients. Although the monetary reward is enticing, the excessive costs in terms of stress, time spent learning to deal with the persons, and general frustration make the prize less valuable.

✔ You should consider taking a loss when you have an absolute deadline that you won't meet if you go for a winning solution.

✔ You may choose to lose because you want to put your company's efforts into more important issues. The classic example is dealing with a disgruntled customer. You know the saying, "The customer is always right." If you subscribe to that maxim, you'll lose when the customer demands satisfaction — even when the customer is wrong. We know of several retailers that accept returns from customers even when the customers obviously didn't purchase their items at their stores. Why would these retailers maintain such a policy? Because they want satisfied customers to tell others about their positive experiences. If a retailer loses one customer just to win a negotiation, the loss of that disgruntled customer can translate into a loss of nine additional customers — the number of people to whom the disgruntled customer tells his or her tale of woe.

Of course, if the same customer pulls this trick on a regular basis, you'll eventually have to get rid of the customer by making him or her lose the negotiation. This is called *playing hardball;* businesspeople use this tactic when they don't expect to ever deal with the customers again, because the cost of retaining them as customers is greater than the loss of their business.

Preparing for a negotiation: What you need to ask yourself

A business negotiation requires some thought and preparation if you want to be effective and achieve your desired outcome. MindTools (www.mindtools .com), a great career site that we often recommend, suggests that you answer some critical questions as you prepare for a negotiation:

- ✔ **What do you want to walk away with after this negotiation? What does your opponent want?** You need to know what you're trying to achieve by negotiating — what outcome do you want? You also need to figure out what your opponent's objective is. Try putting yourself in your opponent's shoes and figure out how you'd approach the negotiation from her perspective.

- ✔ **Do you and your opponent have anything to trade or offer to make a deal work?** You should always go into a negotiation prepared to give something away, typically something that doesn't matter a great deal to you, but is considered valuable by your opponent.

- ✔ **What are the alternatives to a negotiated agreement?** This often is referred to as your *BATNA* (best alternative to a negotiated agreement). In other words, what's your Plan B? What happens if you can't come to an agreement?

- ✔ **What are the interests of the various parties to the negotiation?** Not all the parties who influence the negotiation may be present at the bargaining table. The real parties are those who can say "yes" or "no," in other words, the decision makers. It's always best to negotiate with someone who can make a decision. Failing that, you need to attempt to get that information from the person with whom you're negotiating.

✔ **What are the consequences of winning or losing the negotiation?**
Calculating the upsides and downsides of your negotiations is a wise
thing to do because they can affect your strategy. If the upside is high —
you gain a lot from winning — you'll likely employ a win-win strategy if
your relationship with your opponent is important to you. On the other
hand, if that relationship isn't important, you may be more willing to go
for a win-lose strategy if win-win isn't working. Remember, however, that
your opponent is looking at the negotiation in the same manner, so if nei-
ther of you cares about the relationship, coming to a win-win agreement
is going to be tough.

✔ **What may prevent a successful agreement?** Can you identify ways to
overcome these challenges? Is there a *zone of possible agreement*
(ZOPA)? The best way to end up with a resolution that everyone is satisfied with is to find issues on which you can both agree. Start with those
first to set a positive tone and send a signal that you're trying to achieve
a win-win agreement.

✔ **Who has the power in this negotiation?** Who stands to lose the most if
you can't agree? Whoever has the most to lose will probably be the
toughest negotiator. At the same time, whoever has the most to lose will
also be more likely to try to find areas of agreement and attempt to
arrive at a win-win solution.

✔ **Are there any possible compromises?** Compromise usually is the last
resort, because compromising is essentially a lose-lose situation unless
the issues about which you're compromising aren't significant.

Understanding the ethical side of negotiation

Eventually, every negotiation comes down to this question: What is the right
thing to do? Assuming that you're the negotiator, the answer depends on
your value system and how you believe the other party will respond. The
answer also stems from a series of questions that you should ask yourself.
There are no right or wrong answers to these questions; you simply need to
decide if the answer you choose is compatible with your ethics and value
system. The following list presents a few of these questions:

✔ **How much candor is required for a successful negotiation?** For example,
we advise you not to reveal your walk-away price or your BATNA (see the
section "Ready to Rumble: Negotiating 101") because doing so will put you
in a weaker position to negotiate. One could say that you're failing to
disclose material information, but one could also argue that disclosing
too much information may make a win-win solution impossible.

✔ **Are you required to ensure that the ultimate outcome is fair?** If the outcome is win-win, you can assume fairness, but how do you judge a

win-lose outcome as fair? You probably don't consider it fair. That's why win-lose should only be undertaken when win-win isn't a possibility.

✔ **Is the use of economic pressure unethical?** Most people are inconsistent in their views of this answer. People may resent the store owner who increases the price of generators and lumber just before hurricane season, but they're okay with the airlines charging more for the same seat a week before the flight than they charged two months before.

Only you can decide how you would respond to these questions. You also need to recognize that your opponent may have a different value system. For example, your opponent may believe that a win-lose negotiation is fair and a good resolution. Figuring out your opponent's value system isn't easy, but you can get a clue from her tactics after you've spent some time in negotiation with that person.

Sizing Up Any Deal's Critical Elements

To understand what really goes on in a negotiation, you need to consider the three critical elements of any deal: power, time, and information. You'll be successful in your negotiating efforts to the extent that you can control these three factors. Consider one of our examples at the start of this chapter: You want to lease some office space for your business, but the monthly price is too high for your budget. If office space is in short supply, then the broker has power because he can easily find another lessee. On the other hand, if there is an abundance of office space, you, the business owner, have the power because you can choose from many possibilities. If you must be out of your present location within two weeks, then time is an issue for you. Finally, information plays a role when the broker knows more about your needs and timing than you know about his. The next few sections look at each of these negotiating factors in more detail.

Power is a good thing

The first thing you need to know about power in negotiations is that to have power, you must believe that you have power, and you must present an aura of power. Remember the Wizard of Oz? He cloaked himself in an aura of power; he spoke with an authoritative voice and never let anyone see who he really was.

Former President Jimmy Carter's federal budget director, Bert Lance, was famous for creating a perception of power. He acted as though he didn't need money — as if he had options— so he managed to acquire 381 loans from 41 banks. Of course, the minute the bankers found out that he needed these loans to pay back other loans (robbing Peter to pay Paul), his sources dried up completely. The moral of the story? Use your power wisely!

Several types of power (or lack thereof) come into play in negotiating situations:

- **Sometimes you have legitimate power:** Your position determines your *legitimate power.* As CEO of a company, you have legitimate power to make decisions in negotiations, so you need to let people see you as capable of carrying out that role. If the other party involved in a negotiation is the CEO of a company, you must be sure that you see that person as a peer, an equal. Don't give your opposition more power than he or she is entitled to because you'll weaken your position in the negotiation.

- **You have the power to reward . . . :** *Reward power* is the ability to offer rewards to the other party for agreeing to something you want in a negotiation. This power is similar to an incentive system you may use with your employees to get them to be more productive (see Chapter 7). Be sure that you reward only those solutions that you're looking for. If you reward every point of agreement you come to, the reward loses its value to influence.

- **. . . And the power to punish:** We don't encourage you to use *coercive power* in a negotiation setting, because doing so probably won't lead to a win-win conclusion. People don't like to agree because they must. A far better power tactic is to get the other party to do something because he or she wants to; in that situation, your opponent will see the rationale and the benefit of the solution.

- **You may be an expert in some area . . . :** As an *expert,* you have a particular skill or knowledge that the other party doesn't have. That additional knowledge or skill gives you a certain amount of power and enables you to deal in a less emotional way. In any negotiation, you should define what expertise you have that may give you power in the process.

- **. . . Or you may just be charismatic:** Perhaps you've witnessed instances where a lawyer's reputation and expertise have enabled her to win over a jury, even when the evidence pointed in the opposite direction. Of course, part of that persuasion is due to the next type of power: charisma. Yes, *charisma* — that certain something that some people have that attracts others to them — can play an important role in a negotiation. Charisma can intimidate and distract the other party. One party may be in such awe of the person sitting across the table that he immediately loses any power he may have possessed. If you're negotiating with a charismatic person, remind yourself that she needs something from you, too.

Time is on your side

Because of the information technology revolution, people today believe that transactions, tasks, and meetings should happen instantaneously. They lose patience when others don't seem to have any sense of time or appreciation for their deadlines. Frankly, no nation focuses on the clock more than the United States. Americans often plan their days down to the minute — especially in the business world.

A "get it done now" attitude, however, doesn't work well when you're sitting at the negotiating table. During a negotiation, the person who isn't operating by the clock definitely has the edge.

Eastern cultures are masters at the game of patience and relationship building. They tend to take the long view of the outcome of a negotiation, whereas Americans look for the quick win. One classic example of the effect of time on a negotiation took place during the Vietnam War, when the United States was trying to persuade the North Vietnamese to come to the bargaining table. The attempt took months, and the United States grew very impatient. What the U.S. negotiators didn't take into account was that the Vietnamese had been fighting a succession of different parties — including the Chinese, Mongols, French, and Americans — for 627 years! Consequently, the 32-year-old Vietnamese war was peanuts compared to that. When the Vietnamese finally agreed to meet in Paris to negotiate a peace, the U.S. delegation rented a hotel room on a week-to-week basis. The Vietnamese delegation rented a villa outside of Paris with a two-and-a-half-year lease!

Now, which party had the power of patience on its side? In reality, the Vietnamese also were working under a deadline, but their negotiators didn't want the Americans to perceive that they were. The Vietnamese wanted to retain the power of time on their side. And they did. A resolution to their mutual problems occurred in the final moments before the U.S. deadline.

When you go to the bargaining table, remember these tips about time:

- ✔ Be patient and try not to reveal your deadline.

- ✔ Understand that each party has a deadline, no matter what picture the other party paints for you.

- ✔ Recognize that you probably won't achieve a negotiated agreement until the last possible moment.

Information is the key

Fundamentally, negotiation is about gathering information so that you can reach a decision and achieve a resolution. Each party strives to give only the information that's absolutely necessary, and each party attempts to gather loads of information from the other side to gain an advantage in negotiating a resolution. Information is particularly important if you want to achieve a win-win solution, because you must understand each party's interests to find a way to satisfy those interests.

To gain information you need from the other party, you may try to appear a bit confused about what the other party says. Although this advice may seem quite the opposite of what we say in previous sections about gaining power, rest assured that we're not asking you to roll over and appear stupid. Asking for clarification on something simply forces the other party to restate a demand in another way. Maybe that new statement will provide a piece of information that you didn't have before.

Of course, you should recognize that the other party is trying to do the same thing with you! Here are three more tips that should help you control the flow of information:

- ✔ **Control the information you give out and carefully word what you say.** Give only as much as you have to and then stop talking.

- ✔ **Practice active listening.** Take notes and attempt to find patterns in the other party's arguments that will lead you to an understanding of what he or she really wants and why.

- ✔ **Watch the other party's nonverbal cues carefully.** More than 70 percent of communication is nonverbal. For example, if you note that while you're speaking, the other party sits with her arms folded in a closed position, you can assume that she isn't receptive to what you're saying. On the other hand, if she leans forward when you speak, you know that you're saying something that interests her.

Let's Make a Deal: How to Play the Game

Playing the negotiation game is much easier if you know the rules and you think about how you're going to play before the negotiation starts. Seasoned negotiators recognize the natural sequence of activities that take place during a negotiation. (A sequence that assumes you've done the necessary preparation.) The reason the sequence is "natural" is that it makes sense and the order is logical. When you don't follow the sequence, things can get crazy, and negotiating becomes more difficult. The following sections cover the sequence of negotiation and the importance of setting goals for the encounter. We also give some tips for making sure that you come out of a negotiation with a good deal.

Following the natural sequence

The simple sequence of negotiation has four parts:

1. **Set the stage and chat with the players.**

   Creating an environment conducive to good negotiation is important. Often, this environment is a neutral playing field so that one side doesn't have the home-court advantage over the other. You also want to spend some time on pre-negotiation chatter to put everyone at ease and to establish procedures for the negotiation process.

2. **Separate interests from positions.**

   Most negotiations start with the parties stating their positions, such as "I must get $45/unit." However, position statements reflect a win-lose attitude and don't leave the door open for other potentially more effective negotiating strategies. You must get beyond position statements to discover what the other party really wants — their interests in the negotiation. Separate the people from the problem. Perhaps the other party's real goal is to cover his costs. If that's the case, you may be able to satisfy this interest in many ways. As a result, you have the potential for a mutually beneficial outcome.

3. **Create alternatives that can offer a win-win solution.**

   After you understand each other's interests, you can begin to develop proposals that can meet them all. Don't worry about making a proposal complex and legally correct at this point. You merely want to establish agreement on the fundamental points of the negotiation. It's important, however, that you consider all possible solutions that fall into the win-win category.

4. **Construct a winning agreement.**

   The final stage of the negotiation is where all the fun happens. If the negotiation is typical, you'll be running up against a deadline — yours or the other party's. Now it takes some trading, bargaining, swapping, and perhaps even compromising to mold the agreement into a form that's acceptable to both sides. If you can find some objective criteria for making decisions that suit your situation, you'll be more likely to reach a fair agreement.

Each time you reach final agreement on a point, have both parties initial that point of agreement so you feel like you've accomplished something and can move forward.

Knowing what you want before you play the game

One of the biggest problems people have in negotiations is that they don't know what they want to have achieved by the time the negotiation is over. How do you successfully negotiate when your target keeps moving? If you can't define a goal for a negotiation, don't negotiate.

You can become a more effective negotiator if you consider the following tips:

- **Go in with a plan.** Negotiating for something important isn't the time to "wing it." Set some objectives that you want to achieve, and decide what you're willing to give up to make things work.

- **Put yourself in the other person's shoes.** Try to figure out the other party's interests and needs. Ask questions and try to see things from the other person's point of view.

- **Be a super listener.** You always learn more by listening than by speaking. In fact, talking too much in a negotiation can hurt you, because you give away too much information. Always let the other party begin and do most of the talking.

- **Never threaten or intimidate.** Explaining your point of view is necessary, but don't issue subtle threats about what will happen if the other party doesn't accept your proposal. This only serves to alienate the other party. In addition, you're less likely to achieve an amicable solution.

- **Be patient.** "Patience is a virtue" is certainly true in a negotiation. The Japanese, for instance, use their incredible patience as a negotiating tool, and it works. Most people have deadlines and are in a rush to make things happen. If a Japanese negotiator discovers your deadline, he or she won't even begin the actual negotiation until just before your deadline so that you'll agree to almost anything to close the deal and meet your deadline.

- **Define an acceptable backup strategy.** What if you can't come to a win-win agreement? This is a very important question, because you need to know whether you can afford the luxury of walking away from a negotiation. If you've defined an acceptable backup strategy, you put yourself in a better position to walk away from a bad situation.

Making sure you end up with a good deal

How many times have you heard people boasting about great wins at the negotiating table? Usually, they attribute their wins to some great tactical skill on their part. For example,

> *I always use the silence tactic. It works every time. My opponent gives me her final offer, and I remain silent. My silence throws her so off guard that she starts backing down even further and gives two concessions to get me to respond. During the entire negotiation, I only made one insignificant concession. Boy, was I the master of that negotiation.*

Was he the master of that negotiation? Maybe not. Just because his opponent made some concessions doesn't mean that they were valuable. They may have been her giveaways. What if she had planned to make seven concessions and only gave up two? Now would you say he was a *master negotiator?*

Here's the point: A negotiation is successful to the extent that it achieves the goals set by the parties involved. In other words, both parties in the negotiation must define what success means to them.

The following list looks at some signs of a good outcome:

- ✔ **A good outcome beats your other choices.** Working on an agreement with the other party must be more valuable than your best alternative to the negotiation, or negotiating doesn't make sense. Your backup option — your BATNA or second choice — should be a good one, but the outcome from a negotiated deal should have much greater value because you put more effort into it.

- ✔ **A good outcome makes everyone happy.** To get the other party to accept your deal, you must satisfy his or her interests, at least in part. The classic story of two siblings fighting over an orange illustrates this idea. Each sibling wants the entire piece of fruit, but each is willing to accept something less rather than get nothing at all. So they divide the orange in half. The first sibling proceeds to throw away the fruit and use the peel to bake half a pie. The second sibling throws away the peel and eats the fruit. Of course, if they had understood each other's interests, they could have found a better way to satisfy them both.

- ✔ **A good outcome is the best solution among many.** Generating more than one solution to a situation and then choosing the best of the alternatives is an important step in negotiating. With this method, you're more likely to choose the most optimal solution. In the case of the siblings with the orange, a much better solution would have been to give one sibling the whole fruit and the other the whole peel. That additional option would have satisfied both their interests and provided a win-win outcome.

✓ **A good outcome occurs when no one is taken to the cleaners.** Everyone should come away from the negotiation feeling that, given the circumstances, the achieved outcome is the best possible end. If both parties don't clearly understand the rationale for the outcome, you haven't achieved an optimal outcome.

✓ **A good outcome tells everyone what to do and how.** After you've reached an agreement, ensuring that both parties understand what to do — and when — is important. Coming up with some action steps is a good way to make sure that both parties carry out the agreement in the way that everyone expects.

Some do's and don'ts of negotiations

You can find many great books about negotiating in business situations, but allow us to save you a bit of trouble by consolidating some important information. All the how-to books contain some very basic rules that are true in every negotiation. The following lists present these basics that you can use as a checklist before you begin your negotiations. First up, the don'ts of business negotiations:

✓ **Don't say yes to a proposal the first time you hear it.** Even if the proposal is too good to be true — especially if it seems too good to be true — wait and hear it again before making your final decision. The other party may be testing the waters to gauge how desperate you are for this deal.

✓ **Don't be the first to name a price.** Always try to get the other party to initiate the talk so that you gain important information that will help you negotiate more effectively.

✓ **Don't negotiate with yourself.** Some people, faced with silence after an offer, feel the need to fill the space with chatter. Often, they end up raising their price or inadvertently justifying the other party's point of view. At that point, they may as well end the negotiations, because they've lost any power they may have had.

✓ **Don't be afraid to say no.** Remember that the opposite of no is yes. In a negotiation, there's really nothing in the middle between yes and no. So, if you're not happy with something you hear, just say no. Doing so forces the other side to possibly reconsider and present the idea in a different way that may be more acceptable to you.

✓ **Don't be intimidated.** Everything in business is negotiable, even if you're dealing with writing in contract form. Don't be intimidated by professional-looking documents with "iron-clad" terms.

✓ **Don't trust the other party's actions.** If the other party arrives late to the negotiation or appears disinterested, don't assume that this action reflects a lack of interest. The other party just wants you to think that.

> ✔ **Don't talk about the deal or the negotiation in seemingly empty offices, hallways, restrooms, or elevators, and definitely not on airplanes.** You just never know who's listening.

Now that you know what not to do, here are a few things to do in every negotiation:

> ✔ **Do try to hold the negotiation at your site or at a neutral site.** Going to the other party's office puts you at a disadvantage, because your opponent will be more comfortable and will also have the power to control your level of comfort in the room to his or her advantage.
>
> ✔ **Do deal only with the person who can make the decision.** When you buy a car, the salesperson may claim that she must talk with her manager first. That move only gives the two of them a chance to renegotiate the deal. Control the negotiation by making a deal only with the person who can say yes or no.
>
> ✔ **Do control your temper and emotions.** If you can't control yourself, let someone else do the negotiating for you. Yelling and screaming never results in a good deal.

Think of negotiation as a game — a game you can win if you prepare for it, practice, and define some specific, achievable outcomes that will offer all parties to the negotiation a win-win solution.

Chapter 21

Econ 101: The Basics of Economics

- -

In This Chapter

▶ Looking back through history at conflicting economic theories

▶ Examining fundamental economic questions

▶ Considering the effect of key economic concepts

▶ Adding knowledge to the value creation equation

- -

O kay, we admit it. Economics isn't a topic that gets everyone excited; in fact, we'd love to know how many people actually skipped this chapter, thinking that they'd never use its contents. That's too bad, because economics is about choices — choices we make every day.

When you go to the local deli to grab a quick lunch, you encounter many issues related to economics: the price that you pay for your sandwich, the way the food products that you eat are produced, and whether the restaurant can afford to hire enough staff, among others. How you choose to spend the money you have left after taxes is an economic decision — namely, a decision about resources. Resources are typically limited, thus forcing you to determine how to allocate them. The resource decisions you make every day are exactly like the resource decisions that nations around the world make. The difference is that your decisions are on a much smaller scale (unless you're Bill Gates or J.K. Rowling, who each make more resource decisions than many individual countries!).

In this chapter, we talk about these and other economic principles that affect you and your business. You also discover that economists don't often agree on things — particularly when looking at the impact of the entrepreneur on the economy. This chapter explores some basic economics related to business that help round out your MBA experience.

Why Adam Smith Knew What He Was Talking About

Who is Adam Smith, anyway? In 1776, Smith wrote *The Wealth of Nations,* a book that both marked the beginning of modern economics and made Smith a household name (mostly, anyway) more than 200 years later. In it, he wrestled with a paradox:

> *"How is it that water, which is so very useful that life is impossible without it, has such a low price — while diamonds, which are quite unnecessary, have such a high price?"*

Isn't it interesting that we continue to grapple with this issue today — for instance, as we struggle to understand the valuations of Internet companies that own unique ideas rather than valuable property or manufacturing processes? A company producing a product that everyone uses may have a very low valuation, while a company producing something that only a small percentage of the country uses has a stratospheric valuation. How can we explain that?

The answer to the paradox is something that any economics student today can answer. Water isn't really a scarce item relative to diamonds, so it costs more to get more diamonds than it does to get more water. Smith didn't have economic tools about supply and demand to arrive at that conclusion, but he did recognize that "value in use" isn't the same as "value in exchange." Basically, you usually can't price an item higher simply because it's more useful. In fact, quite the opposite is true.

A product's highest price is determined by its *marginal utility,* which is the value of its last usable unit. So, if you apply Adam Smith's paradox, water has a relatively low price because it's everywhere and is so useful. Diamonds, on the other hand, have a relatively high price because they're scarce by comparison and not a necessity — they have marginal utility, in other words.

You can take two rules away from this discussion:

- ✔ **If your company produces very useful products, the products will become commodities and the price will come down.** As a result, you must sell in large volumes to make a profit. For example, Intel's microprocessor chips came down in price very quickly after they first hit the market as the latest technology. Within a few months, they became the standard and Intel now sells them in large volumes at a very low cost.

- ✔ **If your company produces products that are limited in their use and availability, the price will go up.** That means you'll probably sell fewer products, but you'll make more money on each product. Mercedes, for instance, intentionally produced its CLK car in short supply at introduction to keep its value up. In some locations, customers paid as much as $5,000 more than the manufacturer's suggested retail price (MSRP).

Before we go any further, let's be clear about the two flavors of economics: macro and micro economics. *Macroeconomics* is the study of the economy as a whole and all the factors that affect the economy, such as inflation, investment, international trade, and unemployment. *Microeconomics,* by contrast, studies households, individuals, and companies and how their decisions affect such things as supply and demand, prices, and so on. In the next section, you get a glimpse into the ongoing battle among classical economists such as Adam Smith, the neoclassic economists (literally "new classic"— these were the mavericks of their time), and Austrian economists such as Schumpeter, and what it all means to you.

Classic versus neoclassic: Almost as good as pro wrestling

Today, experts and businesspeople understand that entrepreneurs play a critical role in the economy, but economists didn't always believe that. Adam Smith was really the first person to define "capitalist" as an owner-manager who brought together land, labor, and capital to form a successful enterprise and make profits. During the next 100 years, people began to argue furiously about Smith's theories and add to and subtract from them with their own.

In the late 1800s, economists such as Leon Walras and Alfred Marshall developed models by using the tools provided by mathematician Sir Isaac Newton. These models ignored the entrepreneur and focused on perfectly competitive markets with plenty of buyers and sellers who made sure that supply equaled demand and created that nirvana called equilibrium. *Equilibrium,* in economic terms, simply means that the supply of goods produced equals the demand by customers. Today, the only place where this type of near-perfection exists is in commodity markets, such as the Chicago Board of Trade, where buyers and sellers actually meet on the trading floor to buy and sell.

For market equilibrium to exist, several things need to be in place:

- Every buyer and seller must have information about all the transactions that happen.
- No one buyer or seller can influence the market.
- The market determines prices.
- Products and services need to be fundamentally alike so that the only difference among them is price.

This type of market — essentially a commodity market — is predictable, distributes income fairly equally, and has been the primary model of economic theory in the United States (the neoclassic theory). The *neoclassic theory* is compatible with large corporations and economies of scale, which means that as the size of a company increases, it can produce its products more cheaply because it can buy raw materials in larger quantities and can use its plant and equipment more efficiently. But this neoclassic theory has had its legions of critics because it doesn't account for entrepreneurship, which disrupts market equilibrium by causing new demand that didn't exist previously.

And in this corner, we have the Austrian point of view

At the end of the 19th century, the classical economists — primarily from the Austrian school — got tired of the fact that the neoclassic economists were ignoring entrepreneurs. Joseph Schumpeter — often called the father of entrepreneurship as we know it today — preached that there's no such thing as equilibrium between supply and demand and that markets are actually chaotic (the stock market is a great example of chaos). He referred to entrepreneurship as "creative destruction," because the innovations of entrepreneurs destroy old markets and build new wealth. A modern example is Apple Computer's user-friendly microcomputers, which ended the dominance of the minicomputers from such companies as Digital Equipment Company (DEC). And Dell Computer helped end the dominance of retail computer outlets by selling directly to customers via the Internet and direct mail.

The important fact to glean from this information is that it's actually difficult to find good examples of companies that are very profitable because they're very big. In fact, when you're producing at high levels, you're probably producing commodity products with low profit levels, so the only way to make more profit is to reduce your costs of production. On the other hand, if you're a smaller company producing a non-commodity product, you can charge higher prices and have higher production costs and still make more money. In addition, because you're smaller, you can change more rapidly in response to market changes. So, size is important, and in this case, smaller often is better.

And the winner is . . .

One of the more important moments in economic theory occurred in 1979, when economist David Birch published the results of his research on all U.S. firms from 1969 through 1976. His findings were astounding. What he found was this:

> Small firms (100 or fewer employees) created 81 percent of net new jobs in the United States.

This discovery meant that the small businesses, not big corporations, were driving the U.S. economy. Shocked by the finding, mainstream economists were quick to say that it was bunk. But when economists replicated Birch's study, they found that his conclusions were correct!

This finding means that understanding economics today is about understanding entrepreneurship and how entrepreneurs affect and drive the economy.

Poring Over Fundamental Economic Questions

Economics deals with three fundamental problem areas for any society:

- ✔ What should we produce and how much?
- ✔ How should we produce these goods and with what resources?
- ✔ For whom should we produce these goods?

Although the questions of what, how, and for whom are the same for a communist country or a free enterprise system, the way economic organizations deal with the questions differs. Every business deals with these questions. They form the basis on which you start a business, and the answers are guided by some fundamental principles, which we look at in the next sections. The following reviews the fundamental principles by briefly looking at the major economic systems.

The lowdown on economic systems

An *economic system* is simply a set of laws, institutions, and activities that guide decision making. Every economic system seeks to answer the questions about how to allocate scarce resources. We summarize the different systems for you here:

- ✔ **Traditional economic system:** Economies that are based on farming and use simple barter trade have traditional economic systems. This system remains only in remote areas, such as some parts of tribal Africa.

- ✔ **Pure market system:** This system is based on supply and demand with little or no government control. The e-Bay reverse auction system is a form of a pure market system.

- ✔ **Command economy:** This system is run by a strong centralized government and focuses on industrial goods instead of consumer goods. The former Soviet Union had a command economy.

✔ **Free enterprise system:** Most democratic nations have this economic form where individuals can make economic choices. This system is also called *capitalism* or *market economy*. It's characterized by competition and a profit motive (entrepreneurs love this). Competition comes in four flavors:

- **Perfect competition:** You have a lot of buyers and sellers and no one giant company can affect price.

- **Monopolistic competition:** Many sellers produce differentiated product and their goal is to dominate a niche in the market.

- **Monopoly:** A particular commodity has only one seller who controls supply and prices. Free market economies don't like monopolies.

- **Oligopoly:** There are a few competitors that dominate an industry. The automobile industry is a great example of an oligopoly.

The United States and the European Union don't have pure free enterprise systems. They have mixed economies, which means that they combine the principles of market and command economies. They have a centralized government for things such as national security and regulations for the common good, but in business, they generally display a free enterprise system.

The law of supply and demand: You can't build it and expect them to come

In a free enterprise system, or mixed economy, the marketplace determines the price of a product. Supply and demand interact to produce a price that customers are willing to pay for the number of products that manufacturers are willing to make. In a nutshell, supply and demand affects pricing in the following ways:

✔ If a product is in great demand, but is in short supply, the price will rise.

✔ If there is a large supply for a product and little demand for it, the price will go down.

✔ Prices stabilize when demand equals supply.

The law of scarcity: You can't have it all

When you consider the three economic questions, the economic principle in play is the *law of scarcity*. That's because economic organizations wouldn't have to answer the questions if they had unlimited resources. Because organizations don't have unlimited resources, they have to allocate their scarce resources between necessities and luxuries.

Your business certainly is an economic organization that must make decisions about scarce resources. Which products or services to produce, how to produce them, and for whom — these will become key questions that you have to answer before you can successfully negotiate the marketplace.

How do you answer those questions? You answer all three by answering this one: *Who is your customer?* Your customers (target or current) tell you what to produce, when to produce it, and how to get it to them (see Chapter 15). In addition, your suppliers and other entities in your industry can help you choose the most cost-effective means to produce the product.

Bottom line: To answer the questions, pound the pavement and talk to people in your industry.

The law of diminishing returns: That last bite of apple pie

The *law of diminishing returns* describes how much extra return you get on your output as you add extra units of input. Suppose that you have a factory that produces widgets. As you add labor to the production process, your ability to produce more goods increases to some point and then begins to diminish; this means that each person you add produces less than the previous person. Maybe you can think of it this way: The first taste of ice cream is always better than the last — that's the law of diminishing returns.

In business you need to figure out the point at which you're the most productive. That point determines when you achieve the biggest gains for your efforts.

The knowledge economy: It defies the scarcity principle

The *knowledge economy* is a modern concept that suggests that today much of the economic focus is on the production and management of knowledge assets. Knowledge assets are intangible assets, not physical assets such as products, land, and labor. They come about when individuals and companies turn information into proprietary knowledge (know-how or intelligence). Today, the creation of value and economic performance is dependent on the effective production, exploitation, and management of knowledge assets. Indeed, the modern business environment has experienced an explosion of knowledge assets in organizations — facilitated by modern information technology such as computers, software, networks, and telecommunications.

For example, if your company develops a new product, it has created a physical asset that is subject to basic economic principles such as scarcity and diminishing returns. In the production of that product, however, you often also develop a proprietary process for producing the product (a trade secret) and know-how from your experience producing the product that your competitors don't have. That intangible asset is knowledge and it gives you an advantage in the market because you and you alone own it.

You can also replicate knowledge assets without further cost to your company. Like software where the initial development costs are high, but replication costs approach zero, knowledge assets produce high margins and add value to the more traditional physical assets. The service economy, for example, relies on knowledge assets.

Although capital, labor, and land often are constrained (remember the concept of scarce resources), the good news about knowledge assets is they don't follow the traditional economic principle of scarce resources or diminishing returns.

What Some Key Economic Concepts Mean to You

What's unique about the U.S. economy is that individuals own and control the factors of production. The factors of production are land, labor, capital, and entrepreneurship. For example, if you own a restaurant, you may decide to open another in a nearby city, hire 15 people, and pay them $12 an hour to prepare and deliver your food products to your customers. You control your business decisions as an owner or executive — as long as the decisions are within the law. For example, where you can open a new restaurant depends on the zoning restrictions for commercial development.

But ownership and control of the factors of production aren't the only economic concepts that come into play in business. The following sections take a look at some key economic concepts that affect every business.

Riding the rollercoaster of economic cycles

The economy isn't really in equilibrium for very long. It's subject to many changes in the form of business cycles. If the economy is in a period of prosperity and inflation of prices and incomes, it will eventually taper off and a contraction will take place, during which activity slows down. If the contraction lasts long enough, the economy will slide into a recession or collapse into a trough, called a *depression*. The slow recovery from a trough is called *expansion*. The following sections look at these different business cycles and how you can prepare for changes.

Inflation: Blow a big bubble

Inflation is simply a period when prices rise sharply. During times of inflation, your dollar purchases less in terms of goods and services. Not all prices rise, but on average they do. So, if you get a 3 percent raise and the price of the goods and services you buy goes up 7 percent, for instance, you won't be able to buy as much with the same dollars.

Two different scenarios cause inflation:

✔ When there's too much demand and too little supply, prices rise. This is known as *demand-pull inflation*. It often happens when the government cuts taxes or when consumers save less.

✔ When production costs skyrocket, *cost-push inflation* occurs. Manufacturers usually push the costs along to the customer in the form of higher prices. Of course, then workers demand higher wages so that they can pay for these higher prices. As a result, unemployment typically is high during this time because the higher costs aren't driven by demand, so companies aren't hiring.

Recession/depression: When the bubble bursts

When the economy doesn't grow for a period of at least six months, it's said to be in a *recession*. Both the 1980s and the 1990s started with recessions. During a recession, people typically cut their spending — a behavior that, in turn, causes the recession to get worse, because it slows down the economy even more.

A very bad recession can turn into a *depression,* which is when many businesses fail, prices drop, and supply exceeds demand. October of 1929 was the start of what's known as the Great Depression, when business activity dropped by 40 percent and the unemployment rate was the highest it has ever been.

Preparing for changes in the economy

How can your business prepare for change in the economy? Here are some tips:

✔ **Stay aware of what's going on by reading newspapers and surfing the Web.** The following Web sites are good places to start (see the following section for more on following the economy):

- *The New York Times* (www.nytimes.com)

- *The Wall Street Journal* (www.wsj.com)

- Bloomberg (www.bloomberg.com)

- The Department of Commerce (www.doc.gov)

- CNNMoney (money.cnn.com)

✔ **Watch for leading indicators.** For example, the leading index — which consists of such things as the Producer Price Index, the Consumer Confidence Index, and the Manufacturers' Orders for Durable Goods Index — declines for about nine months prior to the onset of a recession. The Consumer Price Index, interest rates, and unemployment typically decline for 13 months prior to the onset of a recession. You'll also hear these indices referred to regularly on national news programs, so watch for them.

✔ **Stay as liquid as possible.** You want to be able to have cash on hand to expand in good times and a cushion to help you survive the bad times.

Measuring the health of the economy

Economists regularly measure the health of the economy during the year. What they find determines everything from whether the government raises interest rates to whether you get a raise (important stuff!). The sections that follow look at some of the more common indicators of economic health.

Gross Domestic Product

The *Gross Domestic Product,* also known as the GDP, is the total dollar value of all goods and services produced in the United States. It's essentially a record of how much workers produced for consumers to purchase — the cost of living. GDP looks at only new goods — for example, new cars.

Consumer Price Index

The *Consumer Price Index,* also known as the CPI or the cost of living index, represents the change in price of a specific group of goods and services over time. This group of goods and services is called a *market basket,* and it includes about 400 items in such categories as food, housing, transportation, clothing, entertainment, medical care, and personal care. As a business owner, you need to be aware of the CPI because it affects the rent you pay on your facility or the wages you pay your employees.

The CPI actually is a measure of inflation. When you read that inflation has gone up a certain percentage, more often than not a change in the price of things people typically buy has taken place.

Income

Income is a way of measuring how much money is available to be spent by individuals and businesses. National income includes such things as wages and salaries, self-employed income, rental income, corporate profits, and interest on savings and investments.

Economists are most interested in disposable and personal income. *Personal income* is all income received before taxes are paid, and *disposable income* is what's left over after taxes.

Unemployment

The United States seems to take the issue of unemployment very seriously, and why not? It represents the percentage of the labor force that's actively looking for jobs. If the number is low, most everyone is happy, but if the number is high, people start to get nervous about their own jobs.

From an economist's point of view, the United States is at full employment when the unemployment rate is less than 6.5 percent.

Balance of trade

In the current global economy, you hear a lot about things such as balance of trade because nearly every business is affected by global conditions. The difference between the value of the United States' exports to other countries and its imports from other countries is termed the *balance of trade*. In an ideal situation, a country wants to bring in more money from exports than it spends on imports. This situation is considered a *positive balance of trade,* or a *trade surplus.* If, on the other hand, a country spends more for imports than it takes in from exports, it has a *negative balance of trade,* or a *trade deficit.* Unfortunately, the United States has been operating at a trade deficit since the early 1970s.

If you have a product that's suitable for exporting to other parts of the world, the Department of Commerce is ready and willing to help you — actually far more ready and willing than if you were wanting to import products. Go to the DOC Web site at www.doc.gov to find out what's available to you.

National debt

The United States as a whole hasn't done much better than its individual people about staying out of debt. For years, the United States has been running a national debt in the trillions of dollars, which means that the government is spending *much* more than it's taking in.

The U.S. government gets money to spend not by earning it the way you and I do, but by selling various types of bonds. Perhaps you've even invested in some of these savings bonds and treasury bonds. Each time the government issues new bonds, it adds to the national debt. When you purchase a bond, you're actually lending the government your money, and the government agrees to pay you interest on that money over a specified period of time so you'll get back more money than you put in.

Part VI
The Part of Tens

The 5th Wave   By Rich Tennant

In this part . . .

Every *For Dummies* book ends with top-ten lists, and this one is no exception. Here, in a concise and lively set of condensed chapters, you'll find tips that will help you to become an effective participant in any organization. We show you how to avoid the most common mistakes that managers make, we present the best ways to market your products and services, and we let you know how you can improve your company's cash flow — right now!

Chapter 22

Ten Biggest Mistakes Managers Make

In This Chapter

▶ Keeping employees and customers satisfied

▶ Involving employees in all levels of the business

▶ Focusing on recognition, communication, and fun

*E*veryone makes mistakes — and managers are no different than anyone else (despite what some of them would like you to believe!). Although an MBA or other business training can teach you proper and successful business practices, you'll have to deal with times when things go wrong — sometimes very wrong. It's okay to make mistakes — that's how people learn. However, if you make the same mistake over and over again, you have a problem. The real trick to becoming an effective manager is to learn from your mistakes, avoid them in the future, and help others in your organization to avoid them, too.

This chapter gives you a chance to review the ten biggest mistakes managers make without actually having to make them yourself! The chapters of Part II dive into management duties in deeper detail.

Taking Employees for Granted

A long-standing debate still rages on in the business world about who's more important: customers or the employees who serve them and produce the products that they buy. You can say that without your customers, you have no business (and many managers are quick to recite this mantra as they ask their employees to work 60-hour weeks), but it's just as true that without employees, you have no business. Without recreating the debate here, we can safely say that managers sometimes mistakenly take their employees for granted.

Every employee wants to do a good job and be noticed and recognized by a manager for his or her good work. When employees don't get recognition from their managers, they start to assume that the bosses don't care, and morale is sure to plummet. And when employee morale plummets, their performance suffers and they start looking for new employers.

Don't get so caught up in your managerial work and responsibilities that you forget to tell your employees "thank you" for jobs well done. Let them know that you care and are paying attention — early and often. They'll respond to your interest by being more productive and being happier employees. And happy and productive employees produce happier customers and clients, not to mention a healthier bottom line.

Taking Customers for Granted

Isolation from the customer — the person or company that buys your products or services — can create real problems in your organization, especially when it stems from managers and employees forgetting that their job is to serve the customer, not the other way around.

A manager may assume that because a person or company is a customer today, he/she/it will be around tomorrow, too. This is a very dangerous assumption to make. Today, more than ever before, consumers have options for where they spend their money. You have to earn your customers' business every day of the week; you can't afford to leave it to chance.

Managers often have long lists of people or entities that they serve. At the top of those lists should be customers and employees. Customers are at the top because they pay the bills, and employees are at the top because they directly serve the customers. Keeping both happy is a sure recipe for success. (Chapter 15 will help you tap into the power that is the customer.)

Failing to Lead

People want not only firm and decisive leaders, but also a voice in the decisions that they make. The best leaders seek input and information from everyone in their organizations, and they take that input and info into account when they make the decisions they've been hired to make. As the poster above the desk of Dr. J. Robert Beyster — founder of the $8 billion science and engineering firm Science Applications International Corporation (SAIC) — said during every one of the 36 years he led his company and its employees: "None of us is as smart as all of us."

Leaders aren't just born; they can be made. You can take some steps to improve your leadership skills. For instance,

- ✔ Read books on the topic of leadership.
- ✔ Seek honest and candid feedback from your employees and peers.
- ✔ Practice your leadership skills at every opportunity. The more you exercise your leadership muscles, the stronger they'll get.

For more on the challenges of leadership, head to Chapter 6. Chapter 7 gives you the lowdown on employee motivation.

Not Setting Clear Goals with Employees

Goals are nothing more than the steps employees take to achieve the organization's vision. Also, goals act as tangible, measurable milestones for employees to gauge their progress on the road to achieving the organization's vision. Goals give employees something to strive for — making their jobs more interesting and fulfilling. Managers who fail to set clear goals to achieve the organization's vision end up with employees who are confused about their priorities and what's important. The employees may do things that seem important to them, but they may not be doing the things the organization needs them to do. Chances are, employees won't be happy with this ambiguity, and you can bet that managers won't be happy because the employees won't be heading in the right direction.

Managers work with their employees to set clear and measurable goals — and then hold their employees accountable for achieving them. As people achieve goals, the organization moves closer and closer to the vision of its leaders.

Forgetting What It's Like to Be a Worker

One of the most common complaints about managers is that, somewhere along the way, they forget what it's like to be a regular employee. They forget how hard it is to deal with unruly customers; how tough it is to get a job done with a computer that's two generations out of date; or how tough it is to cancel family vacation plans because of another "crisis" at work.

Employees aren't a manager's slaves, servants, or children. The next time you plan to do something that will put an employee in a bind or in an extreme inconvenience, first put yourself in his or her shoes and then consider just how important what you have in mind is to the organization. An employee should understand if you ask him or her to work an occasional weekend here or there, or if you need to squeeze just one more year out of that old computer due to the budget. But if these inconveniences become habitual, something is wrong; you need to step back and figure out what it is and how to fix it.

And don't forget to look in the mirror — the problem may not be with your employees, *your* manager, or your clients or customers, but with that person looking back at you.

Stealing the Spotlight

A manager can wreck an organization by hogging the credit and stealing the spotlight from his or her employees. People don't want a boss who takes all the credit for his or her employees' accomplishments and who wants the spotlight at all times. That is a time-tested recipe for creating employee dissatisfaction and — ultimately — disengagement.

Don't refuse to shine the spotlight on those hard-working men and women who get things done in your organization. Share credit as often as you can and you'll find that your employees will step up and become more enthusiastic than ever.

Sidestepping Opportunities to Delegate

One of the biggest mistakes a manager can make is to fail to delegate in one or both of the following ways:

- **The responsibility for getting a task done.** "Gee, I can get this job done a lot faster and more accurately if I just do it myself."

- **The authority to get a task done.** "Susan, check with me before you commit to that purchase."

Managers who fail to delegate bog themselves down with work, become dreaded micromanagers, and miss out on terrific opportunities to develop their employees' skills.

Focus on doing the tasks that you're uniquely responsible for (hiring, firing, creating and executing budgets, and so forth) and allow employees to do the jobs they're uniquely responsible for. And be sure to delegate not only the responsibility to get tasks done, but also the authority employees need to do their jobs effectively and efficiently. They shouldn't have to run to you to get permission every time a decision needs to be made.

Communicating Too Little, Too Late

Communication is the lifeblood of any organization. And as the speed of business continues to increase (and it will — you haven't seen anything yet!), it's imperative that you dismantle and discard the barriers to communication within your organization and create and reward a culture of communication. Information is power, and far too many managers hoard information and give it out to their employees only when it suits their purposes, if at all.

Organizations can no longer afford this behavior, if they ever could. In a time when most companies have equal access to markets, capital, technology, and personnel, the ability of your organization to identify the latest, most relevant information, process it, and distribute it efficiently to all affected workers is a definite competitive advantage. Make information available to the people who need it — in real time and as completely as possible. If you aren't getting vital information to your employees, you can bet your competitors are getting it to *their* employees.

Hiring Too Fast (And Firing Too Slow)

Hiring too fast is a common mistake managers make. Have you ever been in a rush — a *big* rush — to fill a vacancy on your staff? For whatever reason, you felt the need to streamline the hiring process — perhaps throwing it out the window altogether — to get a warm body in an empty seat. But the flip side of this problem — firing too slow — can be almost as bad. If you let an under-performing employee linger on your staff, your other employees will begin to wonder why you're putting up with an underachiever — and your over-achievers will begin to think about becoming underachievers, too.

When it comes time to hire a new employee, take the time to recruit and inter-view a variety of candidates. Check their credentials and ask for references — and then call them. Have the prospects come back for multiple interviews so they can speak with other people in your organization with whom they'll be working. And when it comes time to fire an employee, don't hesitate. Your actions speak louder than words. What are your actions saying to your employees? (For more on hiring and firing, see Chapter 8.)

Forgetting to Have Fun

Having fun is one of the easiest ways to boost morale in an organization. Work is serious stuff, so you have to make your workplace a fun place to be. Think about it for a moment: If you spend just eight hours at the office each workday (and many people spend much more, including lunch time, after-hours social activities, off-site conferences and training, work brought home, and the time spent commuting to and from work), you live almost a third of your life at work or partaking in work-related activities.

Do what you can to give employees a chance to exercise their creativity while they break up the monotony of their jobs, delighting and entertaining your customers in the process. The good news? Having fun doesn't have to be expensive. In fact, the best ways to have fun often are the least expensive — and they make work a blast for both employees and customers. For example, management at Southwest Airlines looks for and encourages humor on the job. If you fly Southwest, don't be surprised if a flight attendant with a tray full of cups "accidentally" trips in the aisle and sends the cups flying into your lap. The cups are empty, of course, but the practical joke is always good for a laugh — for passengers and for employees.

Chapter 23

Ten Effective Ways to Market Your Products and Services

In This Chapter

▶ Connecting to your customers through your marketing

▶ Establishing trust and long-lasting relationships

▶ Reaching your target customers over the Net

*I*n today's marketplace, customers are so used to advertising — whether in the form of a television commercial or Web banner — that they don't even notice it anymore. In fact, unless you have the latest cure for obesity, wrinkles, or a rotten love life, you can forget about a connection. Customers just will not pay attention to your marketing efforts; that is, if you rely on traditional means of advertising to mass markets.

In a Web 2.0 world — where anyone with a Web site and a video camera can produce a commercial spot seen by millions — marketing is about giving customers what they want, when they want it, and in the way they want it. You can't push products and services down customers' throats anymore. This chapter fills you in on some hot, innovative, and effective ways to get your customers' attention. (For more on marketing, you can soak up the information in the chapters of Part IV.)

Build Trust with Your Customers

Certain customers may buy a product or service from you on impulse, without knowing much about your company, but will they come back? To attract the best customers to your business — those who generate referrals and buy regularly from you — you have to build trust.

How do you build trust with your customers? Customers trust your business when

- ✔ They sense that you know what you're talking about.
- ✔ You give them a suggestion that actually works.
- ✔ You understand what they want and give it to them.
- ✔ You do what you say you're going to do.

Trust is something your business has to earn, but the effort is worth it because trust pays back big time in the form of loyal customers who tell their friends.

Tell an Interesting Story

To market your product or service effectively, you need to tell catchy stories that make the news and capture people's attention. For example, how did Ben and Jerry's crack the tough premium ice cream market? It wasn't just because the company has great ice cream. It was because it had a great story to tell. Ben and Jerry's is a Vermont company owned by people from Vermont who put their hearts and souls into their ice cream. And they gave their ice cream personality with creative names such as Cherry Garcia, Phish Food, and Chunky Monkey.

Here's another example: Southwest Airlines' flamboyant attitude toward its customers is legendary in the airline industry, and it's one of the primary reasons that Southwest has become such a successful company in a very tough industry. Imagine being served drinks by Bermuda-shorts-clad Herb Kelleher, the founder of the company, or having the traditionally boring flight security lectures rapped by an energetic flight attendant.

Become Effective at Web Content

The primary reason customers come to your company's Web site is for information — they want to find out something, and find it quickly. To provide effective information for your customers, you need to know who your customers are. Your Web site's tone should reflect what your customers feel comfortable with. Unfortunately, this is precisely where most business Web sites fail their customers, because they don't know how to give customers what they want as quickly and concisely as possible. Chapter 15 deals with getting to know your customers.

Unless you want your Web site to come across dull as dishwater, you need to develop a style and tone that matches your target customers. For example, a Web site selling primarily to the New Millennial crowd (ages 16 to 24) should have a completely different tone and look than one catering to business professionals or retirees (see Chapter 2). And when it comes to text on a Web site, less is more. The faster you can get your company's message out, the sooner your customers will click on the shopping-cart button and make their purchases. Try to keep information on your site to fewer than about 500 words.

Utilize Affiliate Marketing

One of the best ways to creatively market your company and its products/services is to market on the Internet. That in and of itself isn't creative, but if you find interesting ways to link to other companies' sites that are compatible with yours — called *affiliate marketing* — that is creative. For example, suppose your company is in the travel business; you target large corporations to get their retreat and conference business. You should approach the top retreat and conference companies and convince them to put a link on their sites to your travel site, and vice versa. That way, when an event planner at a large corporation is perusing conference sites, he or she can easily come to your site to get the details and make travel arrangements.

Be careful about trying to be everything to everyone. You don't want to put links on Web sites that don't show your company in a positive light. Likewise, you don't want ads for unrelated products and services on your site. If, for example, your Web site is about do-it-yourself shelving, you don't want to confuse your customers with ads for videos or domain names.

Consider Mobile Marketing

Is it time for you to take your company's marketing efforts to customers' mobile devices? Actually, most of the research done so far has found that half of customers are in favor of mobile marketing and half are against it. The half who appreciate mobile marketing are the teens and 20-something groups, but only when the information is relevant to their needs and interests and presented in a compelling way.

The Mobile Marketing Association (www.mmaglobal.com) believes that this form of marketing reaches people when they have nothing better to do than to look at their cell phones or PDAs (personal digital assistants). The question is, how do you know if your target customers are happy to hear from you? You ask them! Holding some group interviews should give you the answers you need.

The only thing known for sure is that the 18- to 34-year-old age group has their mobile devices with them all the time. They like music and video games. So, if your marketing campaign is targeting this group and you can incorporate music and/or video games and send them to their mobile devices, you may have a winner.

Give Your Product Away

So, you want to make a lot of money and you have a great product or service to offer. Why not give it away to customers? No, we haven't lost our minds; we're serious. That's how Netscape started. Microsoft as well. This strategy isn't new; for example, Gillette, the razor company, followed this strategy years ago. It gave away its razor knowing that its customers would continue to come back to purchase the blades — the consumable part of the product.

You need to decide what you must sell and what you can give away. Every company has something it can give away, even if only for a 90-day free trial. Free sampling is the quickest way to get customers to try out your products and services. Certainly the big consumer-products companies such as Procter and Gamble know this because they spend millions each year to sample new products and services to customers.

Just make sure that the product you give away has a consumable aspect to it so that your customers need to come back to purchase new products — such as new blades, new ink cartridges, or new coffee capsules.

Make Customers Your Marketing Stars

Your best customers are true testimonials to your company's success, so why not put them in the public spotlight and let them shine! For instance, if you sell to other businesses, you can feature their companies and how they use your products or services on your Web site, in your newsletters, and in your television commercials.

Many successful companies, such as Microsoft, IBM, and Kinko's, use this marketing tactic. What better way to show everyone that your customers are important to you? Let them benefit from your advertising along with your company.

Build Relationships, Not Sales

To be successful in business today, you need to build long-term relationships with your customers and interact with them in ways that will make the relationships better for both parties. The nature of marketing has changed radically as a result of mass customization and technology, which have made it possible to reach individual customers and give them exactly what they want, when they want it (see Chapter 17 for more).

Building long-term relationships doesn't mean sending customers questionnaires on a regular basis. You want to give customers easy and interesting ways to converse with your business so you can really understand their needs. For example, Lexus invites its best customers to a special black-tie reception when its new models come out; Porsche, on the other hand, invites its best customers to try out new models on the racetrack! During these events, the companies can get feedback in a relaxed environment and make sure that customers and salespeople interact as people. When it comes time to purchase a new vehicle, the customers will want to deal with people they know. In your business, look for ways to build long-term relationships, and the sales will follow.

Get Your Customers Emotionally Involved

To get your customers to pay attention to what you're selling, try using advertisements that tell a quick but memorable story — a story that gets your customers emotionally involved. If you're fortunate enough to be selling a product that gets people excited while it just sits on the shelf (how about that iPod you just bought), this advice isn't for you. However, most businesses sell products that don't generate a lot of enthusiasm without some effort on their part.

For example, Home Depot came up with a marketing plan to try to sell power tools to husbands who want to convince their wives that they need them. In a commercial, a husband points to a power drill and proclaims, "This is your new kitchen!" The ad definitely makes a strong case for the purchase of a pretty boring item. You can make any product or service interesting and connect emotionally with your customers if you look at the product or service in a new way.

Go Local in a Global World

Finding products and services anywhere in the world is fairly easy in this age of connectivity. Just go online to a search engine, type in a product that you want, and up it pops. So, business owners who want their products and services to rank high in the search engines optimize their Web sites by using keywords so that what they offer comes up high on the search engines' lists when customers search for those keywords. That's great if you don't care if your customers are in Boston or Borneo. But, what if you want to serve a local region or a specific country?

In this case, you don't want to have to deal with people in other parts of the world. One thing you can do is to make sure that you recognize who you're serving. Every region has its own linguistic differences, so the keywords that customers use to search for products or services may be different. For example, in the United States, a customer may search for "labor-saving device," while in the United Kingdom, a customer would type in "labour-saving device." That small difference in spelling can make it easier for your U.K. customer to find you, and it demonstrates that you're thinking locally while dealing with customers globally.

Chapter 24

Ten (Or So) Steps to Improve Your Cash Flow

In This Chapter

▶ Exploring immediate or advance payment

▶ Holding onto your money as long as you can

▶ Checking your paperwork and tightening your processes

*C**ash flow* is nothing more than the net result of the money that comes into your organization less the money that goes out. The less money that goes out, the better your cash flow. Each of the suggestions in this chapter helps you better manage your cash flow.

Manage Your Accounts Receivable

If you aren't keeping a close eye on your accounts receivable, you're missing a terrific opportunity to improve your cash flow and the health of your business. No matter how much you love your customers (and businesses do love their customers!), some of them invariably don't understand how important it is to you that they pay their bills on time. A day or two late usually isn't a big deal. A month or two late always is a big deal. As soon as your customers get in the habit of paying late, getting them to pay on time can be almost impossible. You have to identify your late payers as soon as you can and then take steps to get them to pay promptly.

Require Instant (Or Advance) Payment

If you don't already do so, requiring payment on delivery or even in advance will definitely be worth your while. Make this one of your company's standard policies, and don't apologize to your customers for requiring payment before you start work. We can think of another situation that's even better: getting paid in advance. Many businesses require deposits, retainers, and other forms of advance payment as a normal part of doing business. If you've had an addition built onto your house or new windows or a roof installed, you know that building contractors often require deposits before they start to work.

Accept and Encourage Credit Card Use

Have you noticed that most online stores require customers to provide payment at the time of transaction, and that they generally ask consumers to pay with credit/debit cards? This isn't an accident. You'll not only get more sales if you accept credit cards (don't forget, credit cards aren't real money, right?!), but you'll also get your money more quickly than if you simply send out invoices. (*Note:* Extensive research by the credit-card industry shows that companies that accept credit cards enjoy up to 40 percent more sales than those that don't.)

You'll have to pay your credit card company or bank a fee for the privilege (fees vary widely from provider to provider — be sure to shop around before you sign up for a plan), but most companies have found that the additional sales generated and the enhanced cash flow more than make up for the fees.

A number of online payment services are available that can accept credit cards from customers on your behalf and then deposit the funds for your products/services directly into your bank account. Perhaps the best known of these services is PayPal (www.paypal.com). PayPal and similar providers charge fees of their own, but the charges tend to be lower than what you'd pay through a bank or other credit-card-processing service.

Hold Onto Your Money

Every invoice has a due date. Whereas some businesses may require payment 30 days after delivering an invoice, others may require payment in only 15 days or less. Why do they do this? Because they want to make sure *they* have healthy cash flows! Of course, the idea is to make sure that you take care of your company's cash flow first and worry about someone else's later.

How do you do this? By holding onto your money as long as you can. By waiting to pay until payment is due, you'll have the benefit of your cash longer, and you'll positively impact your cash flow. Now, don't get us wrong: You should always pay your bills on time. If you want happy vendors — and if you want to avoid pesky calls from bill collectors — don't make a habit of paying invoices after they're due. But we also advise that you don't get in the habit of paying your bills sooner than you have to.

Make Sure Your Invoices Are Correct

Before you send out your invoices, make sure that they're absolutely correct. Check to see that the items provided and the quantities are correct. And while you're at it, make sure you have them addressed to the right place and the right person. When invoices go to the wrong places or people, they tend to sit around unpaid or, worse, quickly find their way into the trash. If you want to get paid sooner rather than later (and we're sure you do), double-check all your invoices before they hit the mailbox.

Many companies simply reject invoices that have mistakes in them. Believe it or not, they won't call you first to ask why you made the mistake, and they probably won't send you an e-mail asking for clarification. They'll simply reject the invoice. And if an invoice is rejected, it won't be paid, and it may not even be returned to you. After all, the company you invoiced also is taking advantage of a preceding tip (don't pay sooner than you have to). And by sending an incorrect invoice, you're giving the business an easy way to extend the payment time without breaking the rules.

Give Prompt-Payment Discounts

You give a *prompt-payment discount* when you allow a customer to decrease a payment by some set percentage — say, 1 percent — for paying an invoice within a specific period of time (usually 10 or 20 days). Offering a prompt-payment discount to your customers can be a powerful incentive for them to accelerate their payments, thus improving your cash flow. In many cases, this positive impact on their cash flows exceeds the small amount of money the companies lose in extending the discounts.

Prompt-payment discounts can allow you to experiment and have fun. First, start with the standard net/30 payment terms (all the money must be paid within 30 days) and analyze the average time your clients take to pay. Next, offer a minimal prompt-payment discount to your clients — perhaps 0.5 percent/20 days — and see what happens. Be sure to publicize the discount prominently on the invoices so the right people notice. Does the average time your clients take to pay change? As soon as you hit on the right combination of discount and time, stick with it, and watch your cash flow improve!

Follow Up on Late Payments

If you decide that you've waited long enough for payment, don't be shy about following up on it. You can follow up in a few different ways, each one down the list a bit more serious:

- ✔ **By note:** If the amount owed isn't very much and the invoice isn't long overdue, a friendly note on a copy of the invoice may be sufficient to motivate payment.

- ✔ **By e-mail or snail mail:** If the payment is dragging on and you want to get more serious than a simple note on an invoice, you should send an e-mail message or a letter to your customer specifically requesting payment.

- ✔ **By phone:** When your patience has run out — and you want to head off a potential payment crisis — the most effective way to encourage prompt payment is to personally pick up the phone and call your customer directly.

Be respectful but be firm. The sooner you follow up on late payments, the better your customers will understand that you make prompt payment a priority, and the more likely they'll be to pay on time in the future.

Keep Track of Your Expenses

One way to reduce the amount of money that flows out of your organization — which improves your cash flow — is to manage your expenses. Only spend money if you absolutely have to. Think you need a new computer? Why not try to get another year out of your old one? Or maybe you can upgrade the motherboard for a small amount of money. Perhaps you can find an inexpensive used — but more up-to-date — computer online, at a site such as Craigslist (www.craigslist.com), for instance.

Here's one more component of managing your expenses: projecting your cash inflows and trying to match them with your cash outflows. This money management can really pay off. For example, if you expect a big payment from a reliable customer two months from now, you should defer all possible expenses until you have that cash in hand. That way, you'll avoid the dreaded cash crunch that can occur when you spend more money than you have available.

Index

• *I* •

• P •

• Q •

• R •